The GREEK ISLANDS

GUIDE TO THE BYZANTINE AND MEDIEVAL BUILDINGS AND THEIR ART

The GREEK ISLANDS

GUIDE TO THE BYZANTINE AND MEDIEVAL BUILDINGS AND THEIR ART

Paul Hetherington

Quiller Press

BY THE SAME AUTHOR:

Mosaics
The 'Painter's Manual' of Dionysius of Fourna
(Translation and commentary)
Byzantium
Byzantine and Medieval Greece: Churches, Castles and Art

Note: While the information given here is as accurate as could be established during the research period, in a time of rapid development the chance of errors in the text due to subsequent change cannot be eliminated; the author and publisher would be grateful for corrections, but cannot be held responsible for inconvenience or loss sustained by anyone using this book.

ISBN 1 899163 68 9

Text and photographs copyright © 2001 Paul Hetherington

Published 2001 by Quiller Press Ltd,
46 Lillie Road, London SW6 1TN.

The moral right of the author has been asserted.

Front cover: Astypalaia, Khora with view of the kastro.
Designed by Jo Ekin
Printed in China through Colorcraft Ltd., Hong Kong

CONTENTS

A NOTE ON THE SPELLING AND TRANSLITERATION OF GREEK NAMES

Complete consistency is never possible in this problematic field. Where accepted English forms exist, such as 'Chios', 'Corfu' 'Crete', and 'Rhodes', they have been retained, but where some form of transliteration was needed the following equivalents have usually been used:

ß is given mostly as b, but sometimes as the phonetic v,

γ as g (rather than the phonetic y),

η as i (rather than long e),

κ as k (rather than c),

υ as y when next to a consonant (to distinguish it from i), and v when linked to a vowel,

φ as f (rather than ph), and

χ as kh (rather than the phonetic h).

This means, for example, that the Cretan capital appears here as 'Irakleio', rather than Iraklion, Erakleio, Eraklion, Herakleon, Heracleion, Hirakleion, etc., all of which can be found.

The basis for the spelling of island names is that used in the modern Michelin map of Greece. The form for place names, of which a surprising variety can be found, has been taken from the nearest sign-post, as being the point at which the traveller's quest has to be at its most local; the individual island maps to which the traveller usually resorts quite often give different spellings from those on road signs. As every Greek traveller will confirm, no 'Ordnance Survey Map' of an island has yet been made, and the small sketch map of each island included here is only intended to serve as a general indication of relative location.

ABBREVIATIONS

To avoid repetition of frequently-used words, particularly the longer ones, these few abbreviations will be found in the text:

cap, caps for capital, capitals

C for century

CP for Constantinople

EC for Early Christian

N, S, E, and W for the points of the compass.

RC for Roman Catholic

STAR RATING

This has been used to indicate the relative interest of a location for the traveller, and may help in planning priorities or a choice of objectives:

*** of outstanding interest

** of considerable interest

* well worth making a detour.

ACKNOWLEDGEMENTS

The author of a book of this kind inevitably accrues many debts. The literary sources of all kinds that I have used are so numerous that acknowledging them individually would upset the balance of the text in a way that would not be appropriate for a guide book, and so I would just like to assure the many scholars whose works I have drawn on that no-one is more aware of this debt than myself. In addition to the innumerable and anonymous debts to the local populace that any curious traveller in the Greek Islands accumulates, I would also like to record specific thanks to Maria Vassilaki, Alix McSweeny and David Rawlins who have shared their local knowledge with me, and to Eufrosyne Doxiadis for her characteristically generous help at various stages; I would also like to record my thanks for financial support from the Central Research Fund of Wimbledon School of Art and from the Society of Authors. But my greatest debt must as always be due to my wife, Rachael, whose presence, when she was able to accompany me on my Aegean travels, was always an encouragement and a delight and when she could not, bore my absences there without complaint.

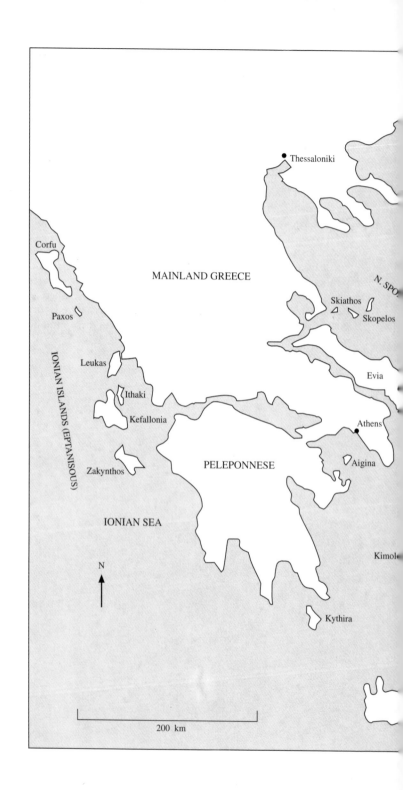

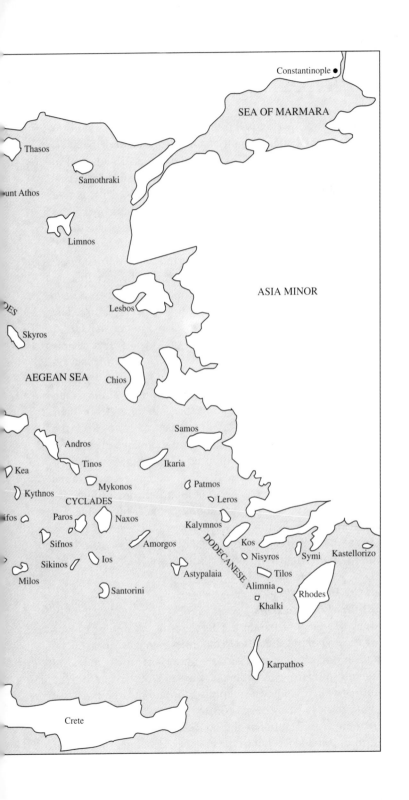

INTRODUCTION

This book has been written with three main objectives: one is to gather the principal Early Christian, Byzantine and medieval buildings and art that still survive in the Greek Islands and to present them in a way that makes them accessible to the interested viewer; the second is to make them more easy for the traveller to locate than other travel guides achieve; and the third is, where appropriate, to set them in the context of their period, and so convey something of the background against which they were created.

The emphasis on the classical period that has tended to dominate the common perception of Greek culture may lie behind the fact that no such attempt has hitherto been made, and it is hoped that this traveller's *vade mecum* will go some way to creating a more balanced picture. The entries and maps describe how a modern voyager among the Greek islands can locate a monument or locality of this period, and then be able to establish its principal areas of interest. As the starting-point is always taken to be the building or object before the reader, it should not be used as a comprehensive architectural or historical study, but as an explanatory record of what the islands still have to offer from their varied, and often turbulent, past. The user may wish to read the introduction to an island before it is explored, and then have the book in hand as sites are located. In some cases the modern appearance or function of a building has been amplified by reference to accounts written by travellers in earlier centuries, although their allusions are often tantalisingly oblique. While the book makes no claims to completeness, all the most significant locations on forty-seven islands are covered here, and all have been visited by the author; the local information given about them was correct at that time.

The scope of the book:
- *The geographical boundaries*
It could be claimed that to separate the fortunes of the Greek islands from those of the mainland and the Peloponnese creates an artificial division that did not always exist in the minds of their medieval inhabitants. Yet the modern perception of the land of Greece is very different from that which would have applied throughout the medieval period. Its boundaries have been constantly changing for many centuries; for example, not only has the mainland frontier with Turkey changed four times since 1881, but in the case of the islands (to cite just

one case), the most important of the group forming the Dodecanese had last been under the control of Hellene compatriots only during the thirteenth century; successively the Genoese, an international order of knights, the Turks and then the Italians, who only ceded the islands to Greek rule in 1948, had all exercised effective political and occupational control, and even then a determined attempt at post-war annexation by the Soviet Union had to be resisted before the Dodecanese returned, after seven centuries, to Greek possession.

With the Byzantine devotion to the concept of *taxis*, or "order", if those living on the islands of the Aegean had a sense of being subject to any identifiable higher authority it would not have been to any city now in modern Greece, but to the temporal and spiritual leaders in Constantinople, the seat of the Greek emperor (or "the Emperor of the Romans", as he would have been known) and of the Orthodox patriarchate. The city on the Bosforos inaugurated by Constantine in 330 had retained the hegemony of all aspects of life in the Aegean throughout the medieval period, and it was to be invasion by external forces that brought about significant change. The distinction between the islands and what we may now think of as 'mainland Greece' is not one that would have troubled a medieval Hellene. In any case, of the sixty or so inhabited islands that form the bulk of what is now held as Greek territory, almost all have their own medieval history which in many cases is different from those in neighbouring groups, and sometimes even from islands within the same group.

It is this variety that has made the formation of the broad parameters of this book hard to establish. Geographical limits were the easiest to define as being based directly on current political status, and so included in this study are the Ionian Islands (the 'Eptanisous'), and all the main Aegean groups (Northern and Southern Sporades, the Cyclades and the Dodecanese), with the other islands, large and small, which tend to defy easy grouping such as Crete, Thasos, Samothraki, Limnos, Lesbos, Chios and Kythera. However, even this simple formula has entailed omitting Cyprus, as governed separately, and the North Aegean islands of Tenedos and Imbros, as now under Turkish rule; also omitted are the islands of Levkas and Evia (Euboea), now linked to the mainland and so covered in our previous study (see *Further Reading*, p. 350) although all of these played a significant part in later medieval Aegean history.

- Chronological limits

Forming a chronological framework was more problematic. While the Peace of the Church and the foundation of Constantinople in the early 4th century offers a logical starting-point (the earliest site covered here is the catacomb on Milos, which must at least in part be a 4th century monument), arriving at a closing point was much more problematic. The end of the Byzantine period is traditionally equated with the capture of Constantinople by the Ottoman Turks in 1453; the Turkish subjugation of the mainland was effectively complete (except for the Venetian coastal holdings) by 1466, but no such general limit applies to the islands. The ejection of the Knights Hospitaller from Rhodes in 1523 (with the Turkish presence then continuing until 1912) offered itself as one definitive point, and was adopted for that island. This date could not logically be used for many other of the islands, however, as it would have been perverse to ignore the continued flourishing of a free Christian presence and culture after that date in islands not then occupied or subjugated. Already by 1460 Limnos was in Turkish hands, with Lesbos following two years later; in 1537 a group of the Cyclades was annexed, and from 1566 more islands of the Archipelago joined those already under the Turkish crescent. In 1617 another group of the Cyclades saw Ottoman occupation, Crete being defended by the combined Venetian and Cretan forces until 1669, while to take the most extreme case of all, it was not until 1715 that the Venetians finally yielded Tinos to the Turks, followed only in 1718 by the Saronic island of Aigina. All this makes it difficult to sustain the moment of eventual complete Muslim subjugation as a general limitation.

So while the point adopted as an appropriate one to close the history of an island's medieval sites has in most cases been the final Muslim occupation, in a few others the chosen point has been the result of an individual decision, dictated by particular conditions. Although in some of the fortified sites the Turks continued to improve the defences to take account of developments in artillery, they do not seem to have regarded most of the islands as of any great importance; the boundaries of the Ottoman empire were continually expanding, and the Greek islands, particularly after the departure of the Hospitallers, did not offer any great threat to such a far-flung frontier. It has been said that the Turko-Venetian Treaty of Karlovitz of 1699 marked the end of the post-Byzantine period in Greece, and the beginning of the modern age, and while not all would agree with this (the start of the War of Independence in 1821 could well be cited as opening the modern period) by the late 17th century a different phase had certainly begun.

- Criteria of selection

A word should also be said here on the criteria that governed the choice of sites that have been included. A book which had as its aim the listing of every occurrence of Early Christian, Byzantine or medieval survivals throughout the Aegean and Ionian islands would simply not be a realistic or attainable project, and the result, even if it could be achieved, would be of encyclopaedic dimensions; an element of choice as to inclusion or exclusion of individual sites sometimes had to be made. This could change from island to island, due to the greatly varying quality, quantity, density and interest of what has survived. The island with easily the largest medieval inheritance is Crete, where there are still over 600 churches dating from before the Turkokratia in a condition that allows them to be studied (besides a number of secular survivals), while the entries on the monuments of another of the larger islands, Corfu, do not reach double figures. In both cases the accidents of history have taken their toll, but the varying conditions that governed their medieval development have produced a widely differing legacy. So it was evidently essential that varying criteria should be applied to the entries for the forty-seven islands covered by this book; the result, while certainly dealing with all the major monuments surviving from the medieval centuries, in some cases has inevitably led to the inclusion of monuments on one island which on another would not been thought sufficiently prominent to be included. If a reader's familiar favourite has been omitted, we can only invoke forbearance with these criteria.

Decisions sometimes also had to be made that concerned a building's condition: at what point was a surviving monument so dilapidated, altered, overpainted or disfigured that its interest to the user of a guide book was insufficient to warrant inclusion? Again, choices of this kind had to be reached on individual bases, and sometimes took into account other monuments that were in the vicinity; a site that might otherwise have been omitted is included if it is found not far from a more major location about which no such doubts existed. This problem was particularly prominent when it came to the question of the ground plans and mosaic floors of Early Christian churches. In some cases mosaics have been left open to the elements, and so are at least visible, even if suffering from the hazards of wind-blown earth or sand in which weeds can take root, but in others the Greek Archaeological Services have taken the step of covering mosaics with a layer of gravel over nylon netting; this fulfils the intention of providing them with some protection, but inevitably renders them invisible. When the latter was found to be the case it has been noted, but it led to some sites being omitted as what otherwise remained to be seen was so minimal. Specialists will know where to look for more complete information on any published remains.

The historical context: some general features

Until the 6th century the organisation and government of the huge empire centred on Constantinople was administered on the basis of relatively small 'provinces', but from that century a different and larger unit of administration was adopted called a 'theme'. The military and civil commander of a theme was appointed from 'the City' (i.e. Constantinople), and while in time themes became smaller and more loosely organised, we know that in the 10th century the seventeen eastern themes included an Aegean theme as well as one based on Samos, and that the former is known to have covered the Cyclades, Sporades, Chios, Lesbos and Limnos, although its extent varied considerably over later centuries. The twelve western themes included one based on Kefallonia, which in effect comprised all the Ionian islands.

Ecclesiastical allegiance would have been channelled through local clergy and the local suffragan bishop to the metropolitan and ultimately to the patriarch, again located in 'the City'. The variations in ecclesiastical administration are often evidence of the shifting economic and political fortunes of a locality. In just the same way it was from 'the City' that the civil administration of the tax collectors would make their usually bi-annual descent, measuring land, counting dwellings and levying dues.

But apart from considerations such as this, every island mentioned in this book would, at least for some periods, and in one or more ways, have been an exception to any perceived norm. It is the widely differing fate of individual islands (or groups of islands) that makes the writing of a brief history of those now under Greek government so difficult to simplify. In many cases it was nothing more nor less than the fact of its geographical location that shaped an island's history throughout the medieval period. Just as the fate of the whole Dodecanese was transformed by the arrival of the Hospitallers on Rhodes, with the inhabitants of these islands then finding themselves at the forefront of the permanent conflict with the infidel a short distance across the sea in Asia Minor, so was that of Aigina, so close to the shores of Attica, acutely affected by the arrival of the Catalan regime in Athens, and becoming subject to a succession of Catalan 'Lords'. In each case it was the accident of geography that dictated the course of a substantial period of an island's development. The other crucial factor which must have determined the direction of an island's history (and so of its inhabitants) would have been its size. Of the many scores – even hundreds – of islands in the Aegean area (and no attempt is made here to decide when a rocky outcrop emerging from the sea should be called an island) it was often the factor of its size, combined with at least one good harbour to encourage trade and commerce, which determined whether or not an island retained its population and so could play a part, however modest, in the history of medieval Greece. Factors such as these are briefly summarised at the start of each island's entry.

The main phases of medieval Aegean history from the 4th century to the Turkokratia:

Given here is a brief historical outline of the period covered by this book; the entry on each island then opens with its own individual introduction which relates it to this broader picture.

- *The early centuries*

All through the 4th and 5th centuries and well into the 6th the Aegean must, in spite of its fragmented geography, have been an area of substantial security; the Eastern Empire, although suffering Slavic invasions on the Greek mainland, and, despite many problems of economic and social stability, did not suffer from significant disturbance within the Aegean area. If evidence was wanted for this, it can be seen in the striking phenomenon of the numerous basilicas – often very large – built close to the sea both on the mainland and in so many of the islands; Kos, Kalymnos, Karpathos, Chios, Crete, Samos, Samothraki, with many others, can all show impressive church building from the period up to the later 6th century erected within a few metres of the shoreline. These prestige buildings, which when they were built must have represented a major, if not the principal, investment for their local economy, are often so close to the sea that spray from the waves reaches their excavated mosaic floors which archaeologists have now uncovered. These buildings speak now of a well-organised ecclesiastical structure with strong central government; this was the period of the first six Oecumenical Councils, running from the 1st in 325 in Nicaea to the 6th in 680 in Constantinople, and could be said to represent the first phase of the establishment and consolidation of the universal Church.

- *The Arab expansion*

It was to be the expansion of Islam, following the death of Mahomet in 632 and the decisive Arab victory at Yarmuk in 636, that was to provide the first danger of invasion from the sea. There had been temporary Arab invasions of Cyprus in 649 and Rhodes in 654, but a decisive point was reached in 827 when, after a succession of attacks on Crete, Spanish Arabs eventually achieved full occupation of the island and its subjection to Muslim rule. The entire Mediterranean area had felt the surge of Arab expansion, and from the 8th century no Greek coastal site on either the islands or the mainland was safe from Arab raids, and there were many inland incursions. Even islands in the northern Aegean were attacked, and the island of Limnos was severely sacked in 902. The danger from this new power discouraged extensive building so accessible to the sea, and for centuries it became normal for islands to create fortified settlements inland from the coast, and often concealed as well as possible from the seaborn marauders.

- The middle Byzantine period

The success of the Arab expansion was just one factor in the Mediterranean world of this age. The Arabs were finally ejected from Crete in 961 in what, with hindsight, can be seen as the last major Byzantine military success, and their presence was never again as decisive. In many ways the 10th to the 12th centuries were the period of the greatest Byzantine accomplishments, but this was achieved against a background of the gradual weakening of central control from the capital on the Bosforos. While Byzantine rule in Asia Minor and much of what is now the Greek mainland was largely maintained, in the Aegean area, where government had taken a variety of forms, even from the 10th century it is clear that the capacity to control, defend and tax such a large number of scattered islands started to become increasingly problematic. The system of 'themes' had been the operative organisational and governmental mechanism from the 6th century; in the 10th century there were seventeen eastern Themes covering the Aegean and Asia Minor, but as central control diminished this system began to be inadequate and a simpler and larger administrative unit gradually took over; two of these provinces covered the Aegean: one known as Kolpos, which included Lesbos, Samos and some of the Cyclades, and that of the Aegean sea, which included Limnos, and other northern islands. But this was already not fully operating by the early 12th century and had become largely irrelevant by 1200. It is only in some isolated cases, such as Chios and Patmos, that we can find evidence of imperial interest in the form of substantial foundations; even when inscriptions of this period indicate aristocratic interest in a building (as on Andros and some Cretan churches) their scale is not impressive.

- The Fourth Crusade

One effect of the crusading movement, which had begun in western Europe in the 11th century, had been to reveal to large numbers of the European aristocracy the riches of the Eastern Empire. It was this experience which, combined with the loosening grip of any overall authority in the Aegean, was ultimately to allow the occurrence of the single most pivotal event of the medieval period in the whole Mediterranean area. This was the enterprise known as the Fourth Crusade, which took place in 1204, and which has always ranked as one of the most disgraceful of the many shameful episodes of European history.

It was to lead to the sacking of Constantinople by the Western crusading forces, the election and setting up of a Latin emperor on the Greek throne and the occupation of mainland and island Greece by various Western powers and family dynasties. The Fourth Crusade was one of the pivotal events of medieval Europe: nothing thereafter was the same, and the face of Byzantine Greece was changed forever. Our chief concern here is with the islands, and it was to be Venetians, with their overwhelming interest in maritime trade, who emerged as the most persistent and successful colonisers of both the Aegean and Ionian island groupings. From the early 13th century the entire orientation and disposition of the Aegean world was permanently changed, and the dominant and most persistent presence was to be that of the colonial power of Venice. Only the Genoese were to present any consistent, and often locally successful, opposition to the might of the Serene Republic.

Many features of the inception and operation of the Latin Empire of Constantinople remain uncertain, but one that is based on surviving documentary evidence is of seminal importance for the understanding of developments in the Aegean in the centuries after 1204; this is the *Partitio Terrarum*, or *Partitio Romaniae* – the Deed of Partition under which the Byzantine empire (still then known as Romanía) was shared out among the Western powers.

Probably published in the autumn of 1204, it was the outcome of the deliberations of a committee that consisted of twelve non-Venetians and twelve Venetians, which was charged with producing an agreed 'partition of the lands' of the empire that they had conquered. The lists of geographical entities (towns, islands, districts, etc.) were based largely on current Byzantine taxation documents, and the transliteration of their names into Latin has caused some confusion; however, the general distribution has now been largely established, and a basic division allowed for the new Latin emperor (who had then been elected as Baldwin I) to own a quarter of the empire, the Venetians to have three-eighths and all the other crusaders to share the remaining three-eighths. All the Greek islands that were named in the Partition are given here: allocated to the Latin emperor were Limnos, Mytilini (i.e. Lesbos), Chios, Skyros, Samos, Samothraki, Tinos and Kos. The share of the Venetians was listed as consisting of Aigina and Andros, and then the Ionian islands of Corfu, Leukas, Kefallonia and Zakynthos. (No islands were allocated to the other crusaders.)

While Venice clearly intended openly, and understandably, to assert her possession of the Ionian islands, what must count as a glaring absence here are the names of at least thirty of those in the Aegean; while Crete was dealt with separately, even the largest and richest islands, such as Rhodes and Naxos, as well as smaller ones such as Milos, Thasos and Ikaria, are not mentioned. There has been much discussion of some ambiguous wording in the Deed that might have been construed as referring to the Cyclades, but this meaning is not now held; in the same way, the mention of a Dodekanisos is now thought to refer to an island in a lake in Macedonia named after the twelve apostles, and not to the group with its capital at Rhodes.

One suggested explanation for this has been that the absent names did not figure on the current taxation lists because by 1203 (the last year for which Byzantine tax accounts were available) it had become impossible to collect taxes from those islands, and they were in effect by then outside imperial control. This is certainly persuasive, but (although there are many other place-names that did not appear) the question should be asked: who benefited from these 'errors of omission' in the case of the islands? What maritime trading power knew every good harbour in every island of the Aegean, but did not introduce those names into the Deed of Partition? The answer has to be that it was Venice and the Venetians; certainly, it was they who were to become the *de facto* beneficiaries of this basis of allocation. What was not mentioned in the Deed of Partition remained unallocated, and so could be regarded as available to anyone.

- Venice and the island duchies

Who then, was the first to take advantage of the Aegean being opened up to private acquisition and ownership? Enrico Dandolo, the shrewd old doge of Venice, blind, forceful and immensely tenacious and who had been present in or around Constantinople from 1203, had an ambitious and energetic nephew, Marco Sanudo. It would have been entirely characteristic of Dandolo, before he died in 1205 (being buried in Agia Sofia), to have encouraged his nephew to carve out for himself his own island dukedom in the Aegean. Whether abetted by his uncle or not, this he did. He seized the island of Naxos (the most desireable and the richest of the Cyclades), ejecting the Genoese force that had already occupied part of the island, added ten surrounding islands to his holdings, and became the Duke of Naxos, a title that he held from the newly elected Latin emperor in Constantinople. It was this dukedom which was to give the word 'archipelago' to the world; first called the

Duchy of Naxos, Venetian documents begin to refer to the Dukes of the *Egeopelagos*, or *Aigaion Pelagos* 'Aegean Sea', so arriving at the 'Duchy of the Archipelago'.

Marco Sanudo could not have known that this dukedom would be the most durable of all the similar principalities that would spring up in the Aegean, but he set a pattern that was to be repeated a number of times, and most of those who took advantage of these opportunities were Venetian. Thereafter, the Ghisi in Tinos and Mykonos, and later in Serifos and Skiathos, the Castelli in Kythnos, the Michieli in Kea, the Querini in Amorgos and Astyplaia, the Venieri in Kythera, the Gozzadini in Sifnos and Kythnos, as well as the Genoese Gattilusi in Lesbos and Limnos and the Bolognese Barozzi in Santorini – all found that it was possible to establish themselves more or less securely in an island base. They regarded the Aegean as their oyster, from which they could extract and retain any such pearls as they were able to find.

Not all of the families settling themselves in the Aegean were Venetian; the Genoese remained their permanent rivals, and individual families such as the Barozzi, just mentioned, and the da Corogna, probably from Spain, all retained some island holdings, while the Catalans in occupation of Attica took over Aigina between 1317 and 1451. But the lion's share always went to Venice, although what had begun as an enterprise that favoured the Republic quite soon incurred the displeasure of the Senators on the Lagoon. Marco Sanudo only held the Duchy of Naxos as a suzerain of the Latin emperor, not of Venice, and Venetian control only arrived for short periods quite late in the life of the Duchy; in the same way in a number of the islands Venice had to wait until the local dynasty foundered before eventually moving in and establishing control, usually through a system of governors who served two-year terms.

- The Byzantine Empire based on Nicaea

Although the Byzantine emperor had been ousted from his capital by the Latin invaders, a government in exile was established by the imperial court after 1204 in the city of Nicaea (the modern Iznik) in western Asia Minor. Here many of the traditional functions and dignities of the Byzantine court were maintained, and (more importantly) the new imperial dynasty that rose there began to recover some of its lost island territory. From c.1225 this government in exile had regained control of the off-shore islands of Lesbos, Chios, Kos, Samos and Ikaria, and in 1261 succeeded in recovering Constantinople and ejecting the Latin usurpers.

- The final centuries of the Byzantine empire.

For almost two centuries after the return of the Byzantine emperor to Constantinople there was a spectacular cultural flowering within the city and in what remained of the empire. The Greek islands, however, saw very little of this. A few islands were recovered for the Byzantines by a successful campaign in the 1270's, but the Venetians were never dislodged from the central Duchy of Naxos, and the Genoese not only held on tenaciously to the rich islands such as Chios but consolidated their own fortified enclave in Pera, across the Golden Horn from Constantinople. The economy of the empire never recovered from the devastating effects of the period of Latin rule and the subsequent civil war within the ruling Palaiologue dynasty.

The result was that the islands were to remain for the most part under the control of the various Latin family dynasties which had founded them for between one and two centuries after the fall of Constantinople in 1453.

The Knights of the Order of the Hospital of St John of Jerusalem; the 'Knights of Rhodes'

The former is the full name of the international military religious order that had grown up in Jerusalem, but had been driven from the Holy Land in 1291. The role of the Knights in Palestine had been to protect pilgrims to the holy places and to administer the 'Hospital of Saint John' in Jerusalem, where they cared for the sick. The Knights (often called 'Hospitallers'), after a few years in Cyprus, became established in Rhodes in the years 1306-10, and, while continuing their work in caring for the sick, also took as a further raison d'être a war against any force representing Islam. The 'Knights of Rhodes', as they then came to be called, had soon spread their activities to most of the Dodecanese, but in January 1523 were forced by the Turks to leave Rhodes, and in 1530 established their base in Malta. Their influence in Rhodes and the Dodecanese was profound, but relatively self-contained and did not greatly affect the rest of the Aegean, and their activities will be referred to in the appropriate places later in the book.

Pirates, corsairs and 'privateers'

Although the Arab threat was reduced when the emperor Nikiforos Focas finally recovered Crete in 961, their role as predators was taken over by groups of pirates who could roam the Aegean in bands that encountered little or no significant or organised hindrance. This phenomenon has always resisted any clear analysis or even definition, but it is mentioned ceaselessly from the 11th century onwards as one of the few constant features of medieval island life in the Aegean. It came to be accepted as a fact of existence by the major powers in various treaties, and individual pirates were known by name, their position sometimes being almost protected by an institutional approach to their way of life. The ruling dynasty on Limnos in the late 13th century, the Navigaiosi, for example, supported nine pirate galleys, and in 1341 a pirate (for it is hard to find another word) called Ligorio Assanti from Ischia actually held a share of the island of Nisyros in fief from the Knights of Rhodes. In 1357 a huge ransom was paid for the return of the Byzantine emperor's son-in-law, Halil, who had been captured by Genoese pirates. In 1410 the Duke of Naxos was rebuked by the Venetian Senate for allowing his island to be used as a base of operations for Basque and Catalan pirates, attacking the sultan's shipping; why, he felt, should local Latin lords risk their lives attacking the Turks when pirates would do it for them as a return for favours? The English traveller Bernard Randolph who was in the Aegean in the 1680's tells of a "Corsican privateer of good family" who was posthumously made a Knight of St Mark by the Venetians in gratitude for the havoc he had wrought on the Turks, and a Provençal called Hugues Creveliers roamed the Aegean at this time with a fleet of twenty ships, demanding protection money from all coastal settlements; he was eventually blown up on board his ship by a servant whom he had offended, and later became the model for Byron's poem 'The Corsair'. A Roman Catholic priest was supplied to Ios in the 17th century specifically to administer to the spiritual needs of pirates who had settled down there, no doubt with families, and as late as 1714, when the Turks finally declared war on Venice, the continued harassment by Venetian pirates was given as a *casus belli*. Even Theodore Bent travelling in the Cyclades in the 1880's was told of pirate attacks within living memory.

Whatever the precise nature of this phenomenon, the insecurity that it produced must have had a devastating effect on all aspects of island life; even the Turks at the height of their power feared the damage that could be done in a brief raid by a small but utterly ruthless and self-serving band. The ease with which hostile forces of any national or religious origin could arrive and decimate the coastal settlements of the Aegean had a decisive effect on the urban development of the entire area. As mentioned above, the confidence that allowed the development of Aegean coastal sites had largely disappeared by the end of the 7th century, and would not reappear for well over a millennium.

The Ionian islands

A range of different factors came to bear on the development of the
Greek islands in the Ionian sea, sometimes knows as the Eptanisous, or
'Seven Islands'. From Corfu in the north of the island chain to
Zakynthos in the south, even before the loss of the Italian provinces
these were among the more remote parts of the empire from
Constantinople, and so harder to govern and to defend; their importance
in the early centuries was largely due to their proximity to Italy and the
remaining parts of the Byzantine empire there. As the empire shrank
and the mainland province of Epiros with its Byzantine despot became
the main focus of government in western Greece, the position of the
Ionian islands became increasingly exposed. Not only had they become
something of a Byzantine outpost, but Italians and Normans from
southern Italy, as well as Venetians from the Adriatic, all saw the value of
their location. As a result the Ionian islands were subject to invasion and
occupation by foreign powers for some time before 1204, when the face
of the Aegean had been transformed by the forces of the Fourth
Crusade. As in the Aegean, different islands developed in quite widely
divergent ways.

First to be invaded by western powers was the largest of the group,
Corfu; although attacked by the Normans in 1081, it was not until 1147
that it was briefly held by a later Norman force. The same fate later
overtook Kefallonia, when William II, the Norman king of Sicily,
succeeded in occupying the island in 1185. Thereafter it was to be
families from southern Italy, the Orsini and the Tocchi, that formed
ruling dynasties in Kefallonia, Ithaki and Zakynthos. But it was natural
that it would be the Venetians with their vigorous trading interests
throughout the Levant, who developed the most persistent territorial
interests here, and they marked this by ensuring that the three largest
islands of Corfu, Kefallonia and Zakynthos were allocated to them in the
Deed of Partition of 1204. Thereafter, whoever ruled any of the Ionian
islands usually did so under some form of Venetian tutelage; although
the Byzantine Despotate of Epiros recovered Corfu during the 13th
century, and both the Angevin and Navarrese powers also intervened, it
was the Venetians who exercised control in the long term; only after
1797 did their grip on the main Ionian islands finally slip.

The Ottoman occupation of the Greek islands

Traditions are still current about the conditions that prevailed during the
period of Turkish occupation of the Greek islands which are inconsistent
with the physical evidence; this historical outline provides an
opportunity to look briefly again at the attitude of the Ottoman power to

the islands as they came under its control.

The establishment of the first Latin duchies and lordships in the Aegean was to be followed in about a century by the early sultans of the Ottoman dynasty coming to power in Asia Minor. While the Seljuk Turks had expanded rapidly over Anatolia after the Battle of Manzikert (1071), it was to be the Ottomans who became the principal Turkish power in the Mediterranean, furnishing the sultans who achieved the great conquests of the 15th and 16th centuries, and whose dynasty came to be feared throughout Europe.

Firstly, it could be said that while the fall of Constantinople in 1453 was clearly a catastrophe for the immediate empire and (within a few years) for the mainland of Greece, life on the islands continued in many cases largely unchanged. This was, of course, because most had not formed part of the Byzantine state for centuries, and were occupied by foreign (mostly Venetian or Genoese) 'lords' or 'dukes' whose interest would have been in maintaining their own domains. Monastic and village life probably continued with relatively little disturbance on many of the islands for a long time after 1453. It was only the Hospitallers, based in Rhodes, with their much greater international support, and whose raison d'être was to wage war against the Muslim power, who constituted a real threat and so brought down Muslim reprisals upon the Dodecanese. The Turkish response here was to mount the sieges of Rhodes in 1480 and 1522, both absorbing huge resources of all kinds; the second was successful, and the Knights were forced to withdraw, but no other island was to receive such attention until the long siege of the Cretan capital of Irakleio in the later 17th century.

The conclusion seems to be clear: the smaller, scattered and relatively poor islands of the Aegean were not felt, in the later 15th and earlier 16th centuries, to be worth the major investment that would have been needed to subjugate and retain them. Only in a few cases of strategic importance, such as Limnos, did the Turks have a real interest in occupation, and there the Genoese presence had been so oppressive that the inhabitants actually petitioned the sultan to come and rule them instead (see page 199). But from the occupation of Lesbos in 1462 it was to be over two centuries before they could lay claim to Crete. The fact is that as the Ottoman empire expanded, the Turks constituted a small and diminishing minority of the population in the territories that they occupied, and it was a matter of simple expediency that they should not oppress the peoples that they had conquered to a degree that would cause widespread revolt. It was usually the case that so long as any agreed payment was received, the Turks seem to have been prepared to leave the great majority of the islands alone; as their empire's frontiers moved outwards, the occupied islands of the Aegean were not apparently regarded as being of great territorial significance. Their final subjection had in many cases been the result of attack by a single highly motivated admiral, such as Barbarossa, rather than a centrally-planned major campaign.

This generally tolerant approach can be confirmed empirically. Any visitor to the Greek islands will receive the impression that, even after the occupation by the conquering Muslim power, the building of small-scale churches flourished to a greater extent after the Turkish occupation than during the Byzantine period; the same can often be seen in the case of larger churches and monasteries. Some islands still offer many scores of churches founded in the 17th and 18th centuries, although the permission to do this varied both in time and from place to place. It was normally sought from the local Turkish pasha, and his agreement was often accompanied by the insistence that the foundation should be a replacement of an existing building. It must be this that accounts for the disappearance of many medieval churches, and may partly explain why the arrival of Ottoman rule did not lead to any new types of church building. Even so, we find that the sultan Murat III in 1580 gave express permission to the inhabitants of Naxos and neighbouring islands to build both churches and monasteries as they wished, and to use bells, although this course may have been adopted here to encourage Greek opposition to a Catholic presence.

The same territorial features seem to have governed Turkish attitudes to the military buildings of the islands that they occupied. In some cases, such as Limnos, Rhodes, Chios and Lesbos the Turks can be seen to have made considerable efforts to modernise and adapt what they took over, with the kastro of Lesbos being still occupied by the military early in this century. But in most cases they must have either decided that a castle offered such a safe refuge for a prospective rebellion that it should be largely dismantled (as may have brought about, for example, the dismantling of Exobourgo on Tinos), or that it was of such little apparent value that it could be ignored (as in the Hospitaller castles on Kos).

In general, therefore, it seems that Muslim rule in the Greek islands after their conquest was in many ways quite tolerant of Christian observance. It was mainly the great cruelty of the child-tax, or 'blood-tax', exacted from lands that they had conquered, that earned the Turkish power its reputation for wilful oppression. This involved the visit every five years, and then more frequently until it became an annual tribute, of an officer of the Janissaries with a local clerk who would be equipped with a list of all the families in the town or village. (The

Janissaries were an elite corps of dedicated soldiers, not allowed to marry, and which was originally composed solely of men who had formerly been Christians.) All the boys aged six or seven in the locality would be assembled, and one in five (and later even more) would be taken away, converted to Islam, and enrolled in the Janissaries. Greek families would in this way lose their strongest youths, and sometimes the only son of a family would be taken. The child-tax no doubt lay behind the repeated later travellers' accounts of island women dying unmarried and childless through lack of husbands.

AIGINA (sometimes AEGINA)   Αίγινα

Med. (Catalan): La Eguena, Eghena, Engia.
Island group: Saronic. (*Nomos*: Attica.)

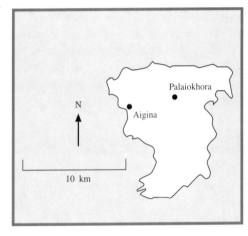

The proximity of this island to Attica tended to give its medieval history a different shape from that of the islands of the Archipelago to the E. Its considerable importance during the EC centuries must have been partly due to this, and c.580, during the Slavic invasions of the Peloponnese, it became a refuge for the inhabitants of Corinth; like many other of the islands it suffered Arab raids in the 9th C. Although the island was one of the two in the Aegean that was awarded unambiguously to Venice in the Partition of 1204, and although it was Venetians who presided over the Duchy of Naxos, it was the Catalans, who had invaded Attica early in the 14th C and established their rule in Athens, who took over Aigina. We find that a succession of the Catalan dynasties lived on the island, styling themselves as Lords of Aigina (or sometimes "Aigina and Salamis"); with Don Pedro Fadrique (c.1350) followed by John Fadrique from c.1355 (under whom the island became a bishopric), Alioto I de Caupena in 1400 and Antonello de Caupena 1440-1451 they formed a continuous succession (see page 347, below). On his death without heirs, the latter bequeathed the island to Venice and from that year a Venetian governor was appointed who was responsible to the Governor of Nauplion. Their rule was still present in July 1499, as we know that the Turks raided Aigina that year.

In October 1537 the much feared admiral of the Turkish sultan Suleiman the Magnificent, Khaireddin Barbarossa (in fact a renegade Greek from Lesbos), attacked Aigina in the course of a savage campaign against the Greeks; after a four day bombardment of the acropolis of Palaiokhora it fell, the male population was slaughtered and 6000 women and children were taken away as slaves, leaving the island completely depopulated. After repopulation by Albanians it was held by the Turks until 1654, when the Venetians re-took it, and it was to remain one of their last island possessions in the Levant, being finally ceded only in 1718.

The importance of the island during the EC centuries caused the building of several basilicas; some have been discovered, a few with remains of floor mosaics, although none can now be seen. More importantly, the Archaeological Museum is currently closed, and this means that the visitor cannot now see a unique 4th C floor mosaic exhibited there, which its inscription reveals to have been that of a synagogue, and even gives its cost; from the 7th C the building had become a church. There are also a few medieval inscriptions collected here from various locations, including Palaiokhora.

Aigina town

1) Markelon tower* (Currently closed.)
On Odos Thomaïdou, some 50 m. SE of the modern church of Agios Nikolaos, you will easily see this unusual and unique survival from the Latin occupation of the island.

It would seem to be externally in a relatively fine state of preservation, and the only alteration (besides the addition of some windows) must be the massive entrance staircase added to the S face; this is manifestly later, and probably replaced another form of removable access. Like much of the medieval building on the island, the tower is built from the local sandstone, with the slight talus at the base ending at a broad projecting string course; the carefully built bartizans on each corner still preserve their angled slits where they project from the vertical walls. This could well be the only direct survival from the Catalan presence in the island, which lasted from the early 14th C to 1451, and the strongest likelihood must be that it originated in the period of the Fadrique dynasty's rule.

Although it cannot be entered, this very unusual (if not unique) survival is well worth seeking out. There are no physical survivals of the many decades of Catalan rule in Athens, and so this may be the sole relic of their long presence in the Aegean.

No trace can now be seen of the EC basilica that was excavated close to this tower, and of which some areas of floor mosaic were found.

2) Omorphoi Ekklesia / Agioi Theodoroi
13th C church with dated fresco cycle** Normally locked; key held at Archaeological Museum kiosk.

The route here is impossible to explain easily; it is 1.4 km. due E from the quayside in an approximately straight line going past the large modern churches of Agios Nikolaos and Agia Paraskevi, and is found some 300 m. down a narrow concrete road among olive and pistachio groves.

This small church known both by its dedication to the two Saints Theodore and by the title of *omorphoi ekklesia* ('beautiful church') is a simple, single-cell hall built of local dressed sandstone, with the only external decoration formed by some simple dog-tooth brick ornament over the W door; its chief attraction is the frescoes which decorate its interior, which an inscription dates to either 1282 or 1284, naming the donor as a Leon Sagoumalas. They form a virtually complete scheme covering the vault and bema, and are in quite good condition and without significant re-painting; it is perhaps the relative isolation of the church which has allowed its decoration to remain undisturbed. The style is quite a primitive one, but the scenes contain some unusual elements; of the 12 scenes in the vault of the nave seven are of the Passion, and include the quite rare subject of the Elkomenos (Christ being led to the crucifixion), while in the Nativity the Virgin is shown nourishing the infant Christ. The Virgin Platytera in the apse is a relatively early example of this type.

These are certainly the earliest and most complete frescoes on the island, and a visit to this small isolated church is a rewarding experience.

Palaiokhora   Παλαιοχώρα

Total of 35 churches, mostly of 14th/16th C★★★ (See Pl. 2).

On the road travelling due E from Aigina to the temple of Afaia it is impossible to miss the colossal agglomeration of modern buildings which is the foundation dedicated to Agios Nektarios (only finally canonised in 1961); Palaiokhora is signed to the left up the same turning as that used by visitors to this vast construction, but you continue past it for another 500 m. The buildings are dispersed over a wide hillside site; all are open and have their dedications displayed.

William Miller wrote of Palaiokhora: "No site in Greece is more lovely, none more mediaeval", and it is one of the most extensive and interesting, but least well known, Byzantine towns in all the islands; if possible, a whole day should be devoted to a visit here.

It was probably as the result of Arab raids in the 9th C that this became the main focus of the island's population, and served as its capital throughout the medieval period, with its bishop elevated to a metropolitan in 900. Besides the attack by Khaireddin Barbarossa in

1537, with the destruction of many of its buildings, it suffered further damage when re-taken by the Venetians in 1654; in spite of this, there is still an enormous amount left, and the extensive fresco remains, although unaccountably neglected, fully repay a careful visit. The two attacks on the hill-top town must have wrought considerable damage, but besides the substantial number of churches still surviving from the 15th C or earlier, there are pictorial records from the last century which even show some of the original fortifications still surviving round the S and E area of the hill, and ruins of a few houses can still be found today. Re-population (much of it by Albanians) must have begun quite soon after Barbarossa's raid, as many of the churches here were built or restored in the 16th and 17th C; surviving inscriptions record works of this kind in 1533, 1610, 1619 and 1674 – all during the Turkokratia. In the 1820's travellers still wrote of there being some 400 houses surviving here, with between 3,000 and 4,000 inhabitants (the whole island now has some 8,500). (One might ask where the materials from these hundreds of houses have gone, and one answer might include the huge modern construction in the valley below.) From 1826 until 1828 it was the capital of the newly liberated Greek nation. The impression as the hill comes into view now is reminiscent of Geraki and, although on a more modest scale, of Mystra, in the Peloponnese.

Of the 35 churches and monasteries that can still be found in and close to Palaiokhora, 25 of the most prominent or interesting are described here. They all share a number of common features: the great majority are built of the local dressed sandstone, they display a carved lintel over the main door, virtually all have masonry iconostases still in place, and of these it is common to find only the central and S of the three openings to have been made, giving an asymmetrical character to the E end. The surviving frescoes do not display any particular homogeneity, and were certainly executed over a considerable period of time, but without exception their roots are in the Byzantine world and owe little or nothing to the W presence on the island. Interestingly, only one church has a dedication to the Virgin, suggesting that the local Greeks wished to give prominence to unequivocally Byzantine saints.

The churches here correspond for the most part to four general building types: most common is a simple, domeless hall with a barrel-vaulted roof, and although a few of these are quite sizeable this type is used for all the smaller buildings; in some cases these have a second chamber built on to the W end, providing one continuous space with just a supporting vault. A second type has an adjacent nave or parekklision, forming a 'double-nave' plan, and it is uncertain precisely why these were built; the presence of Venetian and Catalan rulers in the island has been cited (comparable to e.g. Naxos) but they would have been located more in the area of Aigina harbour. A third type (of which there are five) is of the conventional inscribed-cross, domed design, and in all of these except the leading one (Episkopi) the dome is carried on external bearing walls; most of these have had additions, usually to the W end. It is the fourth type which is both the most striking and seems to be peculiar to Palaiokhora: its form is that of a barrel-vaulted hall with its length oriented N/S, and mostly divided into two conjoined chambers, but with the eccentric feature of an apse, bema and iconostasis installed in the NE corner; this arrangement leaves the greater part of the interior space open and without a natural focus, as if it might have served temporary functions as a place of instruction or for gatherings that might have had a secular purpose.

The first church that you will reach, **Agios Kharalambos**, is beside the road and although slightly outside the main group provides a modest introduction; it began as an example of a 15th/16th C barrel-vaulted hall church, but a parekklision (in effect, a second nave) was either added at an early date, or built simultaneously. There are four other churches of this design in Palaiokhora, and while this one has been described as a double-nave church for twin rites, you may not find this convincing. The interior has no other special interest to offer.

It is at the crest of the hill beyond here that the visit to Palaiokhora starts in earnest; here you will find the church of **Timios Stavros** ('the Venerable Cross'). The building (probably restored in later 16th/17th C) is not exceptional, but inside there are some paintings surviving on the masonry iconostasis and the N wall beside it which are of interest; these are now overpainted, but the image of the Man of Sorrows (or *Akra Tapeinosis* – 'the ultimate humiliation') in the niche of the diakonikon seems untouched and may be of the 14th to 15th C. The subject became more widespread in Byzantine art only from the later 13th C, and indicates that the local Greek population here (you will find other examples of this subject, always in the niche of the prothesis where the eucharistic gifts are prepared) was in touch with this metropolitan development.

Just beyond this church the path across the hillside divides; the suggested route involves taking the left fork here, rising towards Episkopi. After passing two roofless churches with no interior frescoes surviving (the larger of them is a double-nave plan, and the only one with a dedication to the Virgin – the Panagia Giannouli), you will come to the interesting church of **Agios Giorgios Katholikos**; this is the largest example of the third 'Palaiokhoran' type, with its altar enclosed behind a protruding 'box-form' iconostasis in the far NE corner from the SW entrance. A fine Latin inscription over the door names Antonio Barbaro, the (Venetian) Consul of Nauplia, with the date of 1533. This must refer to a restoration, or perhaps to its adoption by Venetian Catholics, as the frescoes here contain two phases of earlier Byzantine painting; with no space close to the altar for their usual position, the figures of four superbly painted bishops occupy the N wall and in the apse an impressive painting of the theme of the Virgin Platytera, in which the youthful Christ blesses the viewer with both hands, fills the conch. The former must be a 14th C work, with the latter somewhat later but still of the 15th C. Again in the niche in the N wall of the bema you will find an image of the Man of Sorrows. Were it not for the presence of other churches of this design this might be regarded as an isolated case of adaptation, but it must be seen as the most prominent example of this highly unusual 'Palaiokhoran' type; one can speculate that in the absence of a communal plateia or place of assembly for the inhabitants, this may have been the closest approximation to a meeting-place that they had.

If this is perhaps the most unusual and interesting of the churches of Palaiokhora, the one that you reach next, known as **Episkopi** but dedicated to **Agios Dionysios**, must have been the most important. (This is incidentally the base of the site guardian.) Both the scale and its domed design signify it as the metropolis, or bishop's church, and to emphasise this the carved lintel displays the imperial eagle. The original building was probably of the later 15th C, but an enlargement took place early in the 17th C. The interior shows the dome carried on four columns, but with the S pair engaged with the wall; the aisle added to the N (or NE – the orientation is in fact SE/NW), was the major feature added later, and a painted inscription states that renovations were completed in 1610, with frescoes "by the hand of Dimitrios the painter, of Athens". Of his work the *Pasa Pnoê* in the vault of the bema is impressive, and on the S wall his fresco of SS. Peter and Paul show them holding a model of the church with a large and prominent dome. Both inside and outside the church there are caps surviving from earlier centuries, presumably from previous churches built on the site.

Just above and beyond this is perched the small cell of **St Dionysios**, an archbishop of Aigina in Samyndo, and close by to the W the small and later church of **Agios Nikolaos** has a particularly finely carved lintel with doves and formalised flowers. Just below Episkopi is **Agia Anna**, the most primitive of all the church buildings here, with no frescoes, and the rock of the hillside forming part of the wall. Lower down the hillside the simple but large church of the **Metamorphosis** offers inside its reconstructed iconostasis a striking sequence of (?)14th

C frescoes: eight feast scenes, the Old Testament Trinity and a huge image of the Virgin filling the conch of the apse. The nave of the church will be later, but the apse paintings were preserved from the previous building.

Further E but on the same level the church of the **Koimisis tis Theotokou** (Dormition), also a simple barrel-vaulted hall, has even more extensive frescoes surviving from the 14th/15th C, albeit in a poorer state; a fine series of scenes down the N side of the barrel vault has been partly obscured by recent whitewashing nearby, but the Second Coming over the W door has escaped this. The nearest church to the E is **Agios Dimitrios** only some 20 m. away, but offers no special interior interest, but has a plaque above the entrance saying that it was restored in 1619 by members of the Spyridon family; further on, though, the 15th C frescoes of the **Agioi Anargyroi** include an impressive image of Abraham in Paradise, and a classical Ionic cap is re-used in the S wall arcade.

Further on down this path a striking series of standing figures faces the visitor on entering another church dedicated to **Agios Nikolaos**; this is a further example of the third 'Palaiokhoran' church type, and the wall facing the entrance has for this reason particular prominence which the artist has exploited in placing the four life-size male martyrs. The sombre colour range emphasises the individuality of this fresco, which (although apparently undergoing restoration in 1572) must be late 14th/early 15th C in date. Continuing eastwards the small church of **Agios Ioannis Theologos** is one of the five built with a cupola; its 14th C frescoes are mainly confined to the apse, and contain a fine figure of St George on horseback, but are in fairly poor condition. An interesting inscription from this church now in the Archaeological Museum requests the reader to pray "for the forgiveness of the sins of your servant Count Pedro" (i.e. Pedro I Fadrique), and so must be c.1340-50; this sheds an intriguing light on the relationship of the occupying Catalans with their subjects. Other smaller churches at the far E end of the foot-track are **Agios Menas, Agios Eleutherios, Agia Makrina** and the monastery of **Agia Kyriake** – the last with a large parekklision or second nave dedicated to the **Zoödokhos Pigi.** The latter contains some of the most extensive frescoes in Palaiokhora, with a substantial cycle of the Akathist Hymn and the Second Coming. These are passed on the way to that at the furthest extent of the upper track, **Agios Mikhail Arkhangelos**; although without any frescoes its simple forms are enlivened by some unusually interesting carved stone panels over the S entrance.

On the summit of the mountain occupied by Palaiokhora was located its kastro or comparable fortified stronghold; there are now only a few outcrops of masonry and the remains of four towers, with glimpses of two cisterns below ground level (one circular and one rectangular) that survive to remind us of the essential function of this citadel. Begun in 1462, these fortifications must have been intended to provide protection for the whole population in times of danger. The large double-nave church here, bearing the dedication of **Agios Giorgios** and **Agios Dimitrios tou Kastrou**, must have a special significance; it is indubitably a double-nave design, and it also probably dates from the 17th C, making it among the latest of the churches to be built here; it has no frescoes or inscription, and must represent an attempt by the Venetians to re-integrate with the Greeks after 1654, when twin rites would have been celebrated here. Earlier this century a tablet inscribed in Greek was found built into the wall of this church recording "the building of the holy church of the Archangel Michael in 1293" by a member of the aristocratic Byzantine family of Bryennios, named Constantine; it is supposed that this tablet was taken from either the church of the **Taxiarchis** to the W, or that of the **Archangel Michael** to the E (see below).

Retracing your steps back NW, you will find another of the few domed churches, the **Taxiarchis**, with some good frescoes in the bema and the iconostasis enclosing a classical marble column. The 14th C frescoes include the rare subject in the apse of the young Christ standing in a chalice between four bishops; if this was the church built by Bryennios in 1293, these must have followed a decade or so later. Further back to the NW a small track leads off to **Agios Ioannes Prodromos**, a large barrel-vaulted church; in an arcade on its S wall are some fine frescoes that may be among the earliest to survive in Palaiokhora. Close by down the same track **Agios Euthymios**, probably 14th C, is of the same type; its frescoes are later (15th/16th C) but are of less usual subject-matter: that of SS. Constantine and Helena holding the Cross is the only such image here, while beside them a saint on horseback (presumably St George) has a small white-clad figure of a bishop riding behind him, rather than the boy of Mytilini.

The last three churches you will find before rejoining the original route all offer features of interest; one, **Agios Giorgios**, formed in the quite common Palaiokhoran way from two chambers joined end-to-end, has one of the most impressive frescoes of an OT figure in an image of the prophet Elijah on its N wall, and another, **Agios Stefanos**, is a further example of the type, unique to Palaiokhora, of the bema confined to the NW corner of its rectangular, barrel-vaulted space. Just to the N of these is the simple but quite large barrel-vaulted church of

Agios Athanasios, formed from two joined chambers; the masonry iconostasis also has two eccentric openings. An inscribed plaque from here in the Archaeological Museum records yet another 17th C restoration, carried out in 1674 at the expense of Giorgios the son of Solomon.

So the abandoned capital town of Palaiokhora has much to reward the careful visitor; more extensive than its 'counterpart' on Kythera, and offering a greater range of building types and fresco decoration than any other such site in the Aegean islands, your day here should not be hurried. Just note that no refreshments are available, and be sure to have strong shoes.

ALIM(N)IA   Αλιμ(ν)ιά

Med: Alymnya, Lemonia, Limonia.
Island group: Dodecanese (*Nomos:* Dodecanese).

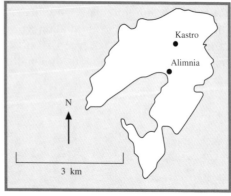

This tiny, rocky island off the W coast of Rhodes only enters historical records in 1366 (see below), with no mention of it being made by medieval historians of the Aegean. Today it remains virtually uninhabited and used only for military training and summer goat grazing; a small abandoned monastery and a church close to the water's edge are all that are left of some pre-war buildings. Any ecclesiastical affiliation must have been with Khalki (40 mins. away to the SW by modern caique), which in turn was dependent on Rhodes. The ruined castle just below the summit of its main mountain ridge is the only evidence of its significance in the medieval period.

Hospitaller castle ruins★★ Unenclosed.
The castle is some 200 m. above sea level, in full view of the landing beach, and can be reached in some 40 minutes scrambling up a steep and trackless slope.

This small castle owes its medieval presence to an agreement reached in 1366, whereby the Hospitaller Grand Master, Raymond de Bérenger, assigned to a *burgensis* of Rhodes named Borrello Assanti of Ischia the two small islands of Khalki and Piskopia off the W coast of Rhodes; in return, Borrello Assanti had to pay 200 gold florins a year and he undertook to build on the even smaller island of 'Limonia' (Alimnia) a strong tower *(turris)* with castellation and a water cistern of stated size. He agreed to provide three men to staff it, and the Hospitallers would provide three more.

As you approach the ruins, ceramic fragments offer ample evidence of pre-Christian presence, and this is confirmed by the masonry of the castle itself; several courses of classical cut masonry indicate that the castle builders were using the remains of Hellenistic fortification as a basis for their construction. The castle (which, although more than just a 'tower', never had a ground area of more than some 10 m. x 8 m. in overall extent) was given the form of a wide U in plan, with a broad terrace on its S side flanked by twin arms joined by a broad central area, originally barrel-vaulted; there are now no signs of the cistern, and no significant space exists for any outer enceinte. The use of pre-existing fortifications was quite a common feature of Hospitaller castles, and can be found on nearby Khalki, as well as on Symi and Tilos. The orientation of the castle here makes it clear that it was intended to face across to the W coast of Rhodes stretching away along the horizon, and the large Hospitaller castle at Kritinia is in full view. It is clear that de Bérenger intended that this small castle should form part of the network of observational posts that the Knights developed during the 14th C; the unusual broad terrace constructed to face across to Rhodes, would have provided an ideal fire signalling point. There is space for up to three fires burning in combination, as was reported to be the practice on Symi. What now appears as a large hole in the S wall overlooking the terrace may once have contained the escutcheon of Raymon de Bérenger (1365-1374), which would have proclaimed him as the originator of this small but spectacularly sited castle.

110 years later, in 1476, there is evidence that the castle here was still in use, as the Hospitallers' records show that what is called the *turris antiqui* on Alimnia needed to be repaired to whatever state was needed *pro custodie insula rhodi*. It is of interest that the castle on Khalki, bearing the arms of the Grand Master Pierre d'Aubusson (1476-1503) which is in full view from Alimnia at sea level, goes out of sight as you climb the hill, and remains hidden from view from the castle here by a slightly higher ridge to the SW. One could guess that Borrello Assanti was tempted to reduce his building costs by making use of fortifications already in existence, and that ideally his construction should have been built higher up and in view of Khalki. While it could be surmised that Alimnia was an early and modest start at creating a signalling post as part of the W coast defences, and that it was in due course superseded by the castle on Khalki, the known history of Alimnia shows that it was restored at the same time that the much larger castle on Khalki was being built; the two must have been functioning simultaneously, although covering an almost identical field of vision from SW to NE, but with each one out of sight of the other.

This beautiful and remote little island deserves a leisurely visit, and while pondering these questions you should have the castle ruins to yourself.

AMORGOS

Αμοργός

Med: Amurgospoli, Amergo, Morgo.
Island group: Cyclades (SE). (*Nomos*: Cyclades).

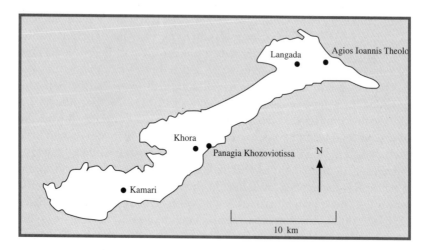

Langada • Agios Ioannis Theolo

Khora • Panagia Khozoviotissa N

• Kamari

10 km

T his long, narrow island lies towards the outer fringe of the Cyclades, angled NE/SW, and was known in the medieval period for being well-watered and quite prosperous, with two ports; these attractions were no doubt part of the reason for the frequency with which it changed hands. Although not mentioned by Byzantine sources, the island is the home of one of the most famous monasteries in all the islands, the Panagia Khozoviotissa, and this must have been a major attraction before the coming of the Latins.

Forming part of the famous Duchy of Naxos from 1206, Amorgos was first held directly by Marco Sanudo; the island was re-taken from the Sanudi by the Nicaean emperor John Vatatzes after 1250 as punishment for Angelo Sanudo's support for the Latin empire in CP, and he gave the island to Geremia Ghisi, a member of another Venetian family. The Ghisi only held the island for about 25 years, as under Licario, the Veronese adventurer who was in the service of the Byzantine emperor Michael VIII Palaiologos, they were expelled (probably in 1276) and the island was returned for a time to Greek rule from CP. This too was not to last long, and in the treaty between Venice and the Greek emperor agreed in 1303, Amorgos (with Serifos and Kea) was assigned to Venice and the Barozzi family; Venetian dominance continued and in the 1419 treaty between Venice and Turkey, Amorgos figures among the

38 places identified by name by the sultan as having Venetian suzerainty. The island became the subject of the strange medieval practice of being bought and sold in notional fractions: early in the 15th C Venice owned half, but later sold a quarter; then in 1446 the Venetian Senate authorised the sale to Giovanni Querini, "Count of Astypalaia", of the quarter of the island of Amorgos that was then still owned by Venice, so that he could then buy the other three-quarters; in that year he duly became the "Count of Astypalia and Lord of Amorgos". Remarkably, and in the usual absence of any map, there never seems to have been any dispute about who owned what. The island succumbed in 1537, like so many of the islands, to the onslaught of Khaireddin Barbarossa and went under permanent Turkish occupation in that year. It was later to suffer more than most islands from pirates, a particularly severe raid of Maniote brigands occurring in 1797.

Little of this turbulent medieval history can now be found reflected in the buildings of Amorgos. The Kastro installed by the Venetians, which might have been expected to be a substantial stronghold, must have been one of the most modest in the Cyclades, and it is left to its famous monastery to dominate the island's post-classical survivals.

Monastery of the Panagia Khozoviotissa***
Usual monastic visiting hours.
The road leading E from Khora divides as you come within sight of the seashore far below; take the left fork and in about 1 km. you will reach the steps leading up to the monastery.

This is the undoubted star attraction on Amorgos. Uniquely impressive in appearance, and defying all architectural conventions, its siting is unforgettable as you come across it hanging against the cliff face some 100 m. above the sea, looking SE across to Astypalaia. Its origins lie in a strong oral tradition, which claims foundation in 1088 by the emperor Alexios I Komninos, although all the supporting documentation is later (see below). Another legend associating its name with a Palestinian monastery of the Virgin of Khoziba, near Jericho, is persuasive, if needing final verification. The legend tells of monks fleeing from Arab attacks in the 9th C, and arriving (via Cyprus) at Amorgos with their icon. In a variant of this, their icon, broken in two in Cyprus, arrived here miraculously where the two parts joined themselves together at the foot of their rock.

If you think that the building that resulted from this extraordinary choice of location perhaps looks to a modern eye to have more in common with Le Corbusier's design for Ronchamp than Byzantium, you would be correct, as the architect has acknowledged his debt, but the 17th C Frenchman Pitton de Tournefort was his usual acerbic self when he described this unique building as resembling more "a Chest of Drawers (*armoire*) fix'd toward the bottom of a hideous Rock... and entered up a ladder... The Caloyers are very slovenly..." and so on. The monastery achieves its form by having the katholikon and the monastic rooms and cells all either built out from the cliff face, or hewn out from inside the rock itself, and so there could never have been any question of a conventional layout, in which the katholikon occupies a central courtyard and is surrounded by the other monastic buildings.

Among the oldest surviving documentation is a sigillion of 1583, signed by the Patriarch Jeremias II in CP and still preserved in the monastery, in which the imperial foundation is attested. A copy also exists, made in Aigina in 1825 of a chrysobull of c.1262 of the emperor Michael VIII Palaiologos, in which numerous properties held by the monastery (metokhia and farms) on other islands are enumerated. If this is genuine (there are apparently doubts) it would indicate an early and influential founder. Another document of May 1263 exists in which the emperor Michael VIII Palaiologos confirms rights and possessions of the monastery, and mentions a metokhion on Ios, but again doubt has been cast on its authenticity.... Travellers in the later 19th C (such as Ludwig Ross and Theodore Bent) were being told that there had been a portrait of the founding emperor in the narthex, but it had been destroyed by a rock falling from above about 15 years before. It is unfortunate that while a sequence of contemporary documents exists confirming the imperial origins of the Nea Moní, Chios, there is no such direct evidence here. Another legend of its foundation (recorded in the 16th C) tells how a sign of the Virgin's approval of the site took the form of a large nail found high on the cliff. A disadvantage of the site is the fact that falling rocks have from time to time demolished parts of the buildings; it does seem inherently improbable that a 12th C imperial foundation would have been initiated in such an extraordinary location. However, the most cogent reason for quite an early medieval date for this amazing building must remain its very exposed position; at no time after the 11th C would one expect to find that a monastery had been founded in such an isolated position in full view of the sea, with the known danger of both Turks and pirates, and even Bent in 1884 described having to enter it by crossing a wooden drawbridge. Oral tradition must here be given full weight.

Once inside the monastery, the visitor is conducted by one of the few remaining monks to the quite small katholikon (now dedicated to St John the Baptist, but previously to the Entry of the Virgin) and can see a few adjoining rooms. Among the fine later icons displayed on the iconostasis in the katholikon are that of the Panagia Khozoviotissa (much darkened), to the left of the doors and covered with its silver revetment, while perhaps the most striking is a large icon of the "Let everything that hath breath" (*pasa pnoe*) located over the entrance door.

If you ask you may also be shown the refectory, library and sacristy, where some cases (donated by the Benaki Museum, Athens) display some of the collection of manuscripts, vestments and silver, but the layout of the rest of the monastery means that it remains *terra incognita*. A recent catalogue of the library lists 98 books, of which 23 are in manuscript on vellum, with several containing illumination, which makes this one of the outstanding island monastic collections after Patmos; some of them are exhibited here. The sacristy also contains a number of pieces of later silver (one inscribed and dated 1674, another of 1682). The heraldic floor slabs with what might have been the arms of the Venetian family of Sanudo, reported last century, did not survive the laying of a new floor in 1896. Otherwise the architecture that you will see seems nowhere earlier than 15th C (the lunette over the entrance doorway, with pierced, slightly Italianate decoration, may be the recognisably earliest piece of detail), and most is later, some perhaps dating from the 16th C, when (by tradition) two monks from Crete and Kalymnos re-founded it after a period of abandonment. There are unfortunately no fragments of earlier sculpture or decoration incorporated, as is the case in another rock-cut church on Nisyros. There has clearly been a constant process of modification, re-building and addition over the centuries as and when the need arose; dates of 1632 and 1668 inscribed on interior arches are an indication of this almost continuous process.

You will be left with the memory of a dazzling and uniquely daring work of combined construction and excavation from the cliff face, with a truly staggering outlook, but which guards its precise origins behind its brilliant and spectacular facade.

Khora: Kastro★   Remains of small fortress.
Locked: the key can be borrowed from the office of the Koinotita Amorgou, on the Plateia just below the Kastro.

What is named as the Kastro is readily visible as you approach Khora from Katapola, occupying the entire summit of a small rocky pinnacle dominating the town from the N edge. It is sufficiently modest for one to imagine that the modern Khora may have absorbed a more extensive kastro that would have been built by the Ghisi, but there are few signs of this, and the road system does not suggest any such medieval presence.

Entry to the Kastro is up a steep flight of steps and through a late chapel of Agios Giorgios on the N side; emerging from this you will find an oval sloping area approximately 30 m. x 10 m. The walls (now very dilapidated and rebuilt) enclose this space, which contains a small cistern, and the remains of a tower occupy the S end. There was clearly never any attempt to install artillery, and it can never have been intended to be much more than a look-out point; from the highest part the sea can be seen to both E and SW of the island, although not the port of Katapola itself, hidden by a fold of the hillside. It most probably dates from the period of the Ghisi family's presence, as the Sanudi would have been based in their much more developed kastro on Naxos.

There are roads (mostly dirt, but some tarmac) running most of the length of the island from Khora. That to the NE reaches the other port of Agiali, with Tholaria and Langada in the hills above; that to the SW links Kamari, Arkesini and Kolofana. While scenically very grand, the attractions in either direction for the medievalist are predictably rural in character and some only fragmentary. In several isolated churches you can find occasional re-used classical or EC sculptural pieces or some damaged Byzantine fresco survivals, but time has mostly taken a heavy toll.

To visit a few of the more substantial survivals, and taking first the SW route, at **Kamari**, to the right of the road, you will find the small triple-nave church of **Agios Nikolaos★**. Some fresco remains here could well be 15th C (key kept in shop nearby); the three elements forming the church were built at different times, perhaps on the site of a small EC basilica, but there are no traces of mosaic flooring or early sculpture. A later parekklision adjoins the N nave. Further on, to the left of the road the even smaller church of **Agia Triada** at **Arkesini** adjoins a pre-Christian tower; the church is 14th/15th C, but is devoid of decoration; (the earliest surviving inscription in any church on the island is of 1683.)

Taking the NE route from Khora towards Langada in the NE, you will pass two remote churches of pre-Conquest date; one, **Agios Ioannis Chrysostomos**, was a monastic dependency of the Khozoviotissa, and the other, under an overhanging cliff, is dedicated to the **Panagia Theoskepasti**. Having reached Langada, a stony mountain track running due NE brings the walker in some 4 km. to the massive and heavily buttressed broad-domed monastic church of **Agios Ioannis Theologos★★** on the slopes of Mount Kroukelos; this was at one time a metokion of the Panagia Khozoviotissa, and is certainly considerably earlier (a 9th C date is claimed, although this is probably too early). It is often shut, but if you can visit it on 8th May or 26th September you will experience a full local festival celebration. You will find various elements of re-used antique sculpture (almost certainly from an ancient local temple), and the conch of the apse contains fragments of what was an impressive fresco of Christ Pantocrator flanked by two half-length saints; these may well be 12th C, and there are further fresco fragments overhead.

ANDROS   Άνδρος

Island group: Cyclades (NW). (*Nomos*: Cyclades).

L ying slightly outside and to the NW of the main body of the Cyclades, the geographical separation of Andros from the main island groups of the archipelago tended to give its history a different emphasis over the medieval centuries. Its ecclesiastical links were initially with Rhodes, from where a suffragan bishop was appointed, but by the time of the 681 Church Council in CP Andros sent its own bishop, and in the 9th C the island was developing closer ecclesiastical links with the mainland and Attica.

It was both larger and more fertile than most of the Cyclades, with one of its principal products being silk; this was even mentioned by an English participant in the First Crusade called Saewulf, who was here in 1102, and silk production remained a staple part of the island's economy into the 17th C.

A surprising fact about Andros gives an indication of the way that up to the 12th C islands could develop in highly individual ways. A good record exists that a place of learning flourished on the island in the 9th century; a learned Byzantine called Leo, later known as both Leo the Mathematician and Leo the Philosopher, and who later became famous both in these fields and in astronomy (as well as becoming an iconoclast bishop of Thessaloniki) had studied rhetoric, philosophy and science here as a young man under a teacher called Michael Psellos. This is a striking indication of the way that centres of learning (or 'academies') could still exist in relatively out-of-the-way parts of the empire, long after Justinian had closed the university of Athens.

C.1125 the Venetian Doge Domenico Michieli ravaged Andros during a campaign which took in attacks on Rhodes, Chios, Samos, Lesbos and Paros. In the Deed of Partition of 1204 the island is the only one of the Cyclades specified unambiguously as being allocated to Venice, but this did not prevent it being taken by Marino Dandolo and it became, with Santorini, a sub-fief of the Duchy of Naxos. At this time, too, it received a Latin bishop who was a suffragan of Athens. By chance, Andros became, after the Greeks had re-taken CP in 1261, the centre of a dispute between the Duchy of Naxos and the Venetian Senate. The widow of Marino Dandolo, the first baron of Andros, called Felisa, had re-married a Jacopo Querini; the title of her son by this marriage, Niccolo Querini, to the island, was not recognised by Marco II, the Duke of Naxos. Querini appealed to the Senate in Venice and Marco II was summoned there to answer the charge against him; his response to the summons makes very clear the way that new dynamics had developed in the Aegean: he refused to come, and said that the Duchy of Naxos, not the Senate of Venice, was the proper court to decide the dispute. He later bestowed the island as a sub-fief on his half-sister, Maria Sanudo. In 1384 Francesco I Crispo, Duke of the Archipelago, gave Andros in fief to Pietro Zeno, who promised to obey their son Giacomo; he remained lord of Andros until 1427.

In the treaty of 1419 between the sultan Mehmet I and Venice, Andros was mentioned as one of the islands that the sultan specifically recognised as subject to Venice, but the relative impotence of the Republic immediately after the fall of CP to the Turks gave the Genoese an opportunity to attack and plunder Andros.

Late in its life as part of the Duchy of Naxos, Andros passed into the hands of the Sommaripa family of Verona; in 1468 Turkish forces attacked the island and the reigning lord, Giovanni Sommaripa, was killed, the khora sacked and many of the islanders carried off, but the family managed to retain a precarious foothold there. From 1537 and the expedition of the sultan's admiral, Barbarossa, the Sommaripa family, with the rest of the Duchy of Naxos, became a tributary of the sultan; however, he was able to remain on the island, and it was not to be until 1566 that the final eviction of the Venetian lords took place under Pilaï Pasha.

Unlike many of the islands, Andros has virtually no classical remains at all; this makes it very much an island for the medievalist, and the surviving buildings reflect quite well the balance of the forces involved in its medieval history.

A logical and convenient sequence of entries has been difficult to achieve, as all visitors will arrive at Gavrion and there is no clear or favoured direction in which to tour the island from there; so it is suggested that the visitor should scan the locations mentioned here as part of the preparations for any touring.

Andros town / Khora

1) Ruins of 'Mesa Kastro'*
Unenclosed, but isolated on a rocky, sea-girt outcrop linked to the harbour mouth by a steeply arched stone bridge.

The most accessible and prominent surviving relics of the long Venetian presence on the island must be the ruins of the kastro here, which occupy a spectacular site at the harbour mouth, and those of Epano Kastro (see below). From the size of its rocky base this can never have been much more than a massive citadel in which the ruling family could live securely, and with little scope for housing any large numbers; the harbour itself must always have been small (having now been long superseded by that of Gavrion) but a fort of this size would have deterred the habitual attentions of pirates. All that is left now is the central tower or keep, and there were probably further defences on the perimeter; 18th C descriptions mention a statue of Mercury fixed over the entrance, which would probably have been a classical piece. Venturing over the bridge will provide you with a closer look, but does not add significantly to the perception of its function. It must date from the arrival of the Venetians in the 13th C, and the Sanudi lords certainly lived here during the 14th C; its purpose must have been to provide security for the ruler where he could have a sea watch kept, and was a first line of defence in the event of a sea-borne attack. The much larger site at Epano Kastro would have been where any substantial numbers were sheltered.

2) Archaeological Museum **
(Open 8.30-15.00, closed Mondays; entry charge).

The collection here consists mainly of classical material found on Andros, but there are two displays in the later rooms of EC and Byzantine sculpture which make it one of the most impressive of such collections outside Athens and Thessaloniki. Besides a 3rd C BC stele in which an 11th C cross and Christian inscription have been carved, there are fragments of sculpture from various churches on the island that you may be visiting. Several EC pieces from Korthi are evidence of buildings that have now vanished, but from the church of Taxiarch Michael, Pitrofos (Melida) there is a 12th C templon fragment, and the most outstanding feature here is a pair of columns from the 12th C templon of Agios Nikolaos, Mesariá, (see below, p. 22) of which the complex design and 'knotted' colonettes cannot be regarded as provincial work. Venetian rule is also commemorated in a further display which includes some fine inscriptions.

It is worth trying to visit this museum early in your stay on Andros, as there has clearly been a policy of assembling here the outstanding sculptural heritage of the island rather than leaving it in its original church locations.

Mesariá   Μεσαριά

1) Church of Taxiarch Mikhael **
Locked and unused; key with Archaeological service in Andros/ Khora. A small metal sign in the village street points S down a passage-way to this church some 70 m. away.

Almost all the interest here is on the exterior, as there is no painting or sculpture on the interior, although an inscription of 1158 gives the important information of the names of the emperor Manuel Komnenos (1143-1188) and the patriarch Luke (1157-1170) as founders. The medium-sized church was originally a centrally-planned domed cross-in-square; perhaps surprisingly (given the founders) there was always only one apse, and a broad narthex was added later. The first decoration that you will see is the delicate carving round the marble door-jambs and lintel of the W door, where animals stand out in relief from formalised vegetable ornament; this must be from the original 12th C foundation, and so was presumably re-installed after the new narthex was completed. It is of unusually fine workmanship and in excellent condition – there are few Greek churches where you will find such accomplished external decoration still in situ; you can also see further fragments of sculpture embedded in the wall above. Going round to the S side the masonry junction of the narthex and the main building is very evident, and there is a later doorway with an inscription dated 1772; this may well be the date of the wooden iconostasis inside, and perhaps of the later narthex as well.

The best preserved part of the building is the exterior of the E end, although you will have to push away the overhanging fig-tree branches to view it; here good cloisonné, masonry forms the wall and apse, where the NE face has a brick star-pattern and some cufic ornament. It is very clear that the window was much larger and triple-light before it was filled in, but the carved marble dividing members are still in place. Brick was also used in the surround of the N doorway (now blocked up), and the eight openings in the drum of the cupola have pierced marble screens which, if not contemporary with the building, could well be.

Mesarià was clearly the focus of an unusually gifted *marmaras* (marble carver), and this church amply repays seeking out as (besides the tranquillity of its rural setting among lemon and fig trees) it is rare to find work of this quality still in place on its original site. (See the next entry).

2) Church of Agios Nikolaos ★
Frequently open. A large church, sited beside the road almost opposite the passage down to Taxiarch Mikhael; this is the main church of the village.

The interior here is now renovated and is devoid of interest, but it is worth pausing to look at the carved marble members surrounding the exterior of the S doorway; this is less inventive than that on the doorway of Taxiarch Mikhael opposite, but is still of the 12th C and of good quality. It is from this church that the templon columns were taken that are now in the Archaeological Museum in Andros town, which are certainly outstanding work, and the remainder of the templon from here must be counted as a major loss.

Pitrofos / Melida   Πιτροφός / Μελίδα

Cemetery church of Taxiarch Mikhael ★
Sited just to the N and above the road that crosses the island from Stavropeda to Andros, it lies between Melida and Pitrofos, but is closer to the latter; it is easily seen from the road, up a concrete track of some 100 m. Ask for key in Pitrofos.

There is no mistaking the impressive, domed profile of this 11th church, with a broad octagonal drum and three faceted apses. The interior, with the cupola supported on two columns and two piers to E, is completely plain (templon fragments from here are now in the Archaeological Museum, Andros town), so the chief interest must be in its exterior. Here the heavy whitewash goes some way to concealing its other attraction and interest, which is the fine cloisonné masonry of its E end; however, the high quality masonry and brick patterns can readily be seen under the whitewash; the main apse retains its original triple opening, although partly reduced. In the E retaining wall of the cemetery has been fixed a beautifully carved marble memorial to a well known Byzantinist, Laskarina Bouras (1941-1989).

Palaiopoli   Παλαιόπολι

Submerged remains of buildings *

The village of Palaiopoli, which now straddles the coast road down the W side of the island, was the Byzantine capital of the island during the medieval centuries. The scattered and fragmentary remains of a few early buildings can be seen at various points between the main road and the shore; the sites of two basilicas have been identified, but in general these are too exiguous to be worth seeking out. The most interesting clear survivals from the medieval period are all underwater; even from the road you can easily see the outline of a small harbour wall, and snorkelling in the bay here reveals traces of several more buildings. The explanation for their presence below the surface must involve a landslip or geological fault that lowered the level of the land at this point, but it is not known when this occurred.

Mesathouri   Μεσαθούρι

Church of Koimisis Theotokou *

Locked; ask for key in kapheneion in the village to W. This small village is reached down a steep, winding concrete road, and the church stands beside the Plateia at its centre.

Although this medium sized church has been modernised and added to more than once, the central area and cupola all seem original 12th C building; the domed, inscribed cross plan can be found in several other locations on the island (such as Pitrofos and Korthi) and the curious double cap on the cupola seems to be an Andriote speciality.

While more for a specialist, the church here certainly repays the short detour from the main road.

Epano Kastro   Έπανο Κάστρο

Ruins of castle ★★
*Unenclosed. From Kokhilos take a narrow concrete road signed to 'The
Panagia'; in 2.5 km. of winding concrete and dirt road you will reach the
steps leading up to this castle.*

The Venetians, probably under Pietro Zeno, would have built this
substantial stronghold in the 14th C as a look-out to the E, and as a
refuge for the local population; its spectacular site covers a long, narrow
area approximately 200 m. x 50 m., and must in its original state have
been an effective piece of defensive building. Its walls could have
sheltered several hundred people for a limited time. Now the chief
remains are a tower or keep still partly standing at the NE end of the
enclosure, with remains of store rooms and cisterns along the N walls.
There is no sign of later adaptation or modernisation by the Turks, and
it must have been obsolete by the 16th C; the only historical reference to
it is from 1421, when Marco, second son of Pietro Zeno, pledged
support from here. The modern chapel (the Panagia) occupies the S
slope, and must replace the medieval church known as the Panagia
Agridia; from here you look down to the bay of Korthi, while the bay of
Melissa lies to the N.

The fact that we know that in the 1420's the local Venetian lord still
chose to live here is interesting, given his countrymen's traditional
dependence on the sea and the existence of Mesa Kastro. The location
and outlook at Epano Kastro is outstanding, and will have changed little,
fully repaying your climb.

Korthi   Κόρθι

Church of Agios Nikolaos ★
*Locked; ask for the key at nearest house to E. A small sign on the main road
to Ormos Korthiou points S up a concrete path to Άνω Κόρθι ; some; 400 m.
up this you will reach the church of Agios Nikolaos.*

This is another of the 12th C churches on Andros which has been
modernised at various periods. It is a medium-sized domed, inscribed-
cross design, with the cupola carried on two columns and two piers, and
having two further piers to the W. The core of the building is certainly
original, although the masonry is nowhere as distinguished as that of
Mesaria or Pitrofos; there is now nothing of decorative interest left
inside, but a section of its carved 12th C templon screen has been used
as the external lintel (at eye level) of a window on the N side, again

showing what was lost when these were replaced.

Before leaving, the visitor might wish also to admire some tall and impressive ruins of Venetian farm buildings immediately to the W, which speak eloquently of the prosperous past for the island.

Monastery of Panakhrantos   Μονί Παναχράντος

14th / 15th C monastery *

Opening times are very flexible. Approaching Mesaria from W, turn right on to the 'by-pass' just before entering the village, and then immediately right again on a road signed to Πέρα Χωριά; after 3.8 km. an insignificant sign points up a winding dirt road on your left to the monastery, which you will reach after 2.4 km. of rough climbing.

There is now no clear sign of the quoted 10th C foundation date for this monastery, but its domed katholikon certainly contains features from the 14th / 15th C. The most interesting parts are the frescoes in the apse and prothesis, which must be of this date (although not in good condition) and the unusual templon screen; the latter is of masonry, with its columns coloured, and some frescoes of the same period still surviving on the upper level. Only the topmost part is of wood, and later, while the lower areas display some superb Iznik tiles. There are a number of quite good, if late icons, but of exceptional interest is an embroidered epitafios hanging in the narthex, which again seems to be of the same period as the frescoes and (due to its only being used once a year) is in excellent condition.

All the other buildings are later, but the considerable climb here is rewarding for the superb view, the interest of the katholikon, and not least for the unusually warm *acceuil* which you may receive from the monks.

Moní Zoödokhou Pigis   Μονή Ζωοδόχου Πήγης

Convent with 14th C frescoes *

Usual hours of access. On the road between Gavrion and Batsi a sign that reads "Tis Agias" points up a dirt road winding inland; after climbing for 3.5 km. you will reach the quite extensive but completely isolated convent buildings.

The only medieval remnants here are confined to the narthex and W wall of the katholikon, where some frescoes, including an impressive figure of St John the Baptist, may well date from the 14th C. The rest of the building, and certainly its decoration, seem later. Note a large 18th

C embroidered image of the Zoödokhos Pigi (the "Life-giving Fountain") on the NW pier; this became a popular subject in later Byzantine art, and two of the miracles performed at the fountain, which was just outside the walls of CP, are shown in the foreground of the scene here. In the courtyard a few fragments suggest that there have been earlier buildings here but the fabric of those that remain seems otherwise to be later.

The buildings here repay the climb, and the height provides a huge panorama, with the sea visible on both sides of the island.

ASTYPALAIA   Αστυπάλαια

Med: Astia, Astinphalea, Stampalia, Stupalea.
Island group: Dodecanese (W) (*Nomos*: Dodecanese).

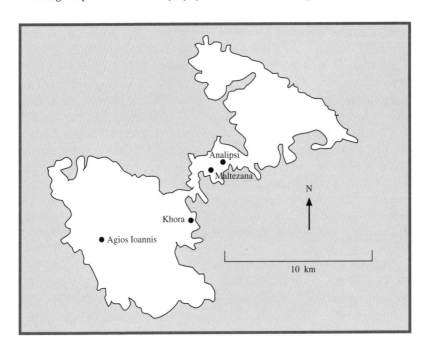

The rather isolated location of Astypalaia between the Cyclades and the Dodecanese affected its medieval history in several ways; an early close link was formed with the Cycladic island of Amorgos, but it later became attached to the Dodecanese, and is now associated with this E grouping. The fact that it was close to the sea routes between Egypt and CP meant that it attracted pirates who wanted a base from which to launch their raids on passing shipping.

The island receives only a few mentions by medieval historians, but it is known that the rich and important monastery of the Panagia Khozoviotissa on Amorgos (traditionally founded in the 11th C) owned considerable amounts of land here. By 1277, in the new dispositions after the return of the Greeks to CP, the Sanudi, who had occupied Astypalaia, had been ousted, and for some 60 years the islanders had apparently maintained an independent, if rather precarious, existence. However, their lack of protection meant that in 1334 the island had been sacked by the Turks under Umur Pasha, and its population removed; when Christoforo Buondelmonti visited Astypalaia c.1418 he reported that it had been deserted, but was then being resurrected by Giovanni (Zanachi) Querini "at the time of the Council of Constance" (1414-1418). The latter had been rector of Tinos and Mykonos from 1411, and must have cast covetous eyes on a potentially attractive and currently uninhabited property which would give him an independent seigneurial existence; he purchased the island in 1412-13, gave himself the title 'Count of Stampalia', having been 'Count of Tinos', and brought families from the islands of Tinos and Mykonos to populate it. (This angered the Venetian Senate, as the operation was carried out in their galleys and caused depreciation of the two Venetian-held islands, and he was fined 200 ducats for every islander so transported.) In 1413, when the first groups were arriving, he had created a punning name for the khora of Astinea ("new town") as opposed to Astypalaia ("old town"). The Turks, in the treaty that they established with Venice in 1419, included Astypalaia among the islands which they recognised as having Venetian suzerainty. After the expedition of Barbarossa in 1537, unlike the rest of the Cyclades, it was under direct and permanent Turkish control.

Buondelmonti c.1418 reported having seen *plurima castellata desolata* on the island, but his accuracy should perhaps be questioned here; he often made his observations from the ship on which he was sailing, and the rocky profile of cliffs and headlands could be mistaken for man-made constructions. There are in any case now no significant fortified remains other than the Kastro recorded below, and even the 'Kastro Agios Ioannis' on the W coast mentioned by Dawkins in 1905 cannot now be detected.

If lovers of Venice detect a similarity between the name of this island and that of a piazza and palazzo in that city, they are not mistaken; the Querini-Stampalia neighbourhood in Venice was proudly so named by the family that colonised Astypalia (Stampalia).

Khora

Kastro**
Substantial ruins with two churches.
Gated, but open. (See front cover).

It was not until 1413 that the island was purchased and taken over by Giovanni Querini, then Count of Tinos. This goes a long way towards explaining the character of what is still universally referred to as the

Kastro here, but which in reality approximates more to a large Renaissance fortified urban palazzo complex than to the kind of 13th/14th C Latin-built kastro found all over the Aegean.

Superbly sited to overlook the harbour mouth, and occupying the site of the ancient acropolis, it is reached by the steep ascent from the port (either steps or winding road) and you enter through quite a massive gateway. At eye level to the left as you enter is part of a heavily whitewashed escutcheon of the Querini, and the vaulted entrance tunnel supports on its E side the church of the Panagia tou Kastrou, rebuilt at a later period. The entrance is the only part of the building with a genuinely fortified aspect, and even here the outer face has received a facade in a more Renaissance style. Once inside the large, open interior space (a pointed oval of some 110 m. x 35 m.) you feel that if it was paved, and the surrounding buildings were not ruined, you could be in a rather irregularly shaped Venetian 15th C piazza.

The only two buildings carefully maintained are churches: one over the gateway and the other, Agios Giorgios, towards the S side of the complex. Both are domed and have undergone later rebuilding, as they would presumably have been originally designed for the RC rite; they are normally locked and the interiors offer nothing of particular interest, but on the steps up to the Panagia tou Kastrou you will see part of a second Querini escutcheon in relief, again largely filled in with whitewash. For the rest the many domestic buildings lining the exterior walls are all in various stages of disrepair, but at no point can one feel that one is in a fortified kastro of the type that can so often be found on other islands; the main preoccupation of the people who lived here must have been far more concerned with the enjoyment of their surroundings than with security and defence. The houses vary considerably in size, but it seems many were built up to three storeys high, and as population became more dense expansion may have had to be upwards rather than horizontally. At no point is there any trace of provision for artillery; on the contrary, large windows overlook the harbour, and the wooden supports of a number of balconies are still projecting out from the walls of harbour-prospect houses where the Venetian (and presumably, after 1537, local Greek or Ottoman occupying) inmates could sit, enjoying the air and view over the coast and sea. The structure of the housing makes it seem improbable that these were later insertions, and certainly no fortress was ever built with these priorities; the inhabitants (who could well have eventually numbered five or six hundred, and quite possibly more, although being reported as only four hundred in 1470) must have felt that there was little need to be too concerned with security. In emergencies the area enclosed could have sheltered over a thousand for a short time; it must be assumed that the pervasive danger from pirates was answered by the massive fortified entrance. Towards the S end of the interior area are some EC caps, column fragments and bases that suggest that this may have originally been the site of an EC basilica; it is certainly the kind of location where this could be expected. The attitude of the Greeks of later centuries to their Venetian lords is, incidentally, well demonstrated by the fate of the three carved Querini arms; two of these reliefs, as already mentioned, are so heavily clogged with whitewash that they are quite difficult to see, while a third can be seen inserted sideways as a prop for the side of a collapsing second-floor window.

Among the kastra of the islands, this compares most closely with those on Sifnos and, to a lesser extent, that on Kimolos, but neither of these offers such a close reminiscence of a semi-fortified Italian palazzo, and its evocation of an agreeable colonial life lived under the Aegean sun; a leisurely visit here is a must while on the island.

Of the scores of EC buildings recorded on Astypalaia, the great majority have only the most minimal remains; there are just six sites where mosaic floors have been found, but most are very fragmentary, and only the three described here offer remains which can still be visited easily.

Khora

EC floor mosaic adjacent to the modern church of Agioi Anargyroi* Unenclosed.
Where the road leaves Khora to loop round Skala to go N towards Marmari and the isthmus, the modern church can be seen on a small terrace some 10 m. above the road; the mosaic can also be glimpsed (but not reached) by looking down from the dirt road passing above it going to Mesariá.

The remaining areas of mosaic (approx. 8 m. x 6 m.) are from the narthex, threshold and part of the nave and S aisle; only four colours appear to have been used, and the designs are all abstract patterns. The original basilica must have been of some size, as what seem to be vestiges of the synthronon can be found just outside the apse of the modern church. The style of the mosaics suggests a 5th / 6th C date.

The site can easily be reached on foot from Khora or Skala, and the peaceful surroundings and outlook make it an attractive objective.

Analipsi

5th(?) C floor mosaics of Talaras baths★★
Unsigned and unenclosed.
Having arrived at the jetty, turn left and walk parallel with the sea; in the second field that you reach you will find the mosaics, partly hidden by reeds.

These are certainly the most unusual mosaics on the island, and although not of high quality their type and subject-matter cannot be matched elsewhere in the Aegean, hence the second ★. They probably formed the floor of the frigidarium of some baths, suggesting a phase of some prosperity here in late antiquity. Their theme relates to the months and seasons of the year. The varied subjects include a central roundel enclosing a beardless figure holding an orb (perhaps the *tykhe* of the island) surrounded with the twelve signs of the Zodiac, geometric shapes enclosing heads representing the twelve months and the four seasons. Although clearly secular, and thought by some to be Roman, we have followed Pelekanides in suggesting a date in the EC era.

This quiet location is quite unannounced, but its interest repays a leisurely visit.

Maltezana

EC floor mosaic of basilica "of Karekla"★ Unenclosed. (See Pl. 17).
Leave the coast road at the first headland on coming out from the village of Maltezana, where the most prominent feature is a memorial recording the loss of a French ship under a Captain Bisson in 1827. Follow a foot track round the headland for about 200 m. beyond this and you will find the mosaic floor immediately beside the sea.

The building was originally a triple-nave basilica some 15 m. long, but there are now only part of the mosaic floor and some wall and column bases surviving; the sea is so close that erosion from the waves has caused part of the S aisle floor to fall away on to the rocks, and this may also have been the fate of a baptistry. Almost all the mosaics are of abstract patterns, and the colours are as usual restricted to some four basic hues, but those in the narthex exhibit more freedom and have a decorative border depicting dolphins. They are dated by style to the 5thC.

This beautiful and isolated site, wetted by the spray from the waves in windy weather, is yet another example of how the sea seems to have exercised a particular fascination for the church builders of the 5th and

6th centuries; with Agios Stefanos on Kos, or Agia Photeine on Karpathos (to name only two) this demonstrates again a tendency which quite disappears after the 7th C.

Agios Ioannis

Small, remote 12th/13th C church*
Unsigned. Normally kept locked.

This remote little church, built on a terrace overlooking the rocky cliffs of the W coast, is reached by a series of dirt roads winding over the bare and beautiful but desolate interior of the W half of the island.

The church, when you arrive at it at the end of a narrow track, is a domed, cruciform plan, with the unusual feature of the N and S arms extended to exceed the length of either the W arm or the apse. It is hard to determine its period, but it seems more probable that it antedates the Venetian presence in the island than that it is a 16th/17th C foundation. The interior is innocent of all decoration. Modern maps indicate a 'Kastro Agios Ioannis' here, and over ninety years ago Dawkins and Wace reported seeing a ruined tower and outworks at this point, but the minimal remains now visible on the summit across the valley from this church do not justify the use of this name; however, the magnificent outlook here amply rewards the traveller.

CHIOS   Χίος

Med: Scio, Scios.
Island region: E Aegean. (*Nomos:* Chios).

In spite of its position close to the coast of Asia Minor, the island did not play any major part in Byzantine history until the later medieval period; it appears to have been administered by the Byzantines in the 9th/ 10th C as just one of many of the islands of the Aegean theme, with only occasional evidence of special military or naval importance. This is surprising as it was one of the most prosperous of all the Aegean islands, strategically located close to the Asia Minor coastline, and there was building activity here in various parts of the island from the EC period to at least the 6th C, and then imperial interest in the building

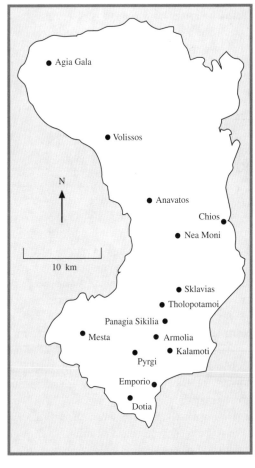

of the Nea Moní in the mid-11th C gave new momentum. Its obvious attractions meant that the Turkish emir Tzachas was, in 1089, one of the first foreign powers to capture the island, but it was later retaken, and in 1125 the Venetians made a retaliatory raid and (according to a strong tradition) removed the valued relic of the body of St Isidore, the patron saint of Chios; the relic was taken back to Venice and eventually installed in a special chapel in San Marco.

After 1204 the island was awarded in the *Partitio Terrarum* to

Baldwin of Flanders, the Latin emperor of CP, but he was unable to retain it and, with other islands that were closer to Nicaea, some time in 1225-26 the Nicene emperor John Vatatzes was able to bring it again under Byzantine control. However, its fortunes from the later medieval period became more closely linked to those of Italian states, particularly Genoa, than to CP and as a result of the Treaty of Nymphaion in 1261 Chios began a long period of Genoese control. This was in the hands first of the Zaccaria family in the persons of the brothers Benedetto and Martino, ruling from 1304 to 1329, who (although nominally vassals of the Byzantine empire) could be said to be the only 'lords of Chios' that the island knew who had comparable status to the dynasties in the Cyclades, but the Byzantines drove them out and a brief period of Greek rule then intervened until 1346; defence from CP was too difficult to sustain, and at this point after a siege of eight days the other Genoese dynasty of the Giustiniani took the entire island and began its occupation that was to last until Chios was captured by the Turks in 1566. The Muslim presence was continuous until 1822 except for a brief period of Venetian dominance in 1694-95.

It was to be a uniquely Genoese concept that dominated the commercial development of Chios throughout the later medieval period. As in other centres such as Cyprus and Corsica they set up a form of trading association called a *maona* (perhaps a contraction of Madonna, under whose care their business was placed), with twenty-nine partners or *maonesi*; it is the name of this entity which reappears again and again in the documents of the period, rather than any individual. (A comparison could be made with the status and function of the British East India Company.) The *maonesi* had some limited political power but their interest was primarily commercial, being chiefly concerned with control of the Chiote crop of mastic. This is a substance produced nowhere else in the world, and still forms part of the island's economy; it is a gum which oozes from the trunk of a low shrub, and which the 17th C traveller Bernard Randolph thought was so named after the Italian *masticare*, to chew. He reported that Chiote women would chew it as it "cleanses and prevents the aking of the teeth and causes a sweet breath", although it was also used in the production of varnish. This was always the chief source of the island's wealth, with the crop selling for huge prices. An indication of the commercial significance of Chios is that by the early 16th C there was a British consul stationed there to look after the interests of his country's traders.

The island played an outstanding part in the Greek struggle for independence, and was notably the subject of savage revenge by the Turks in 1822, when over 70,000 of the island's population were killed or enslaved when the Turkish admiral's flagship was blown up in the harbour by Admiral Kanaris; the massacre became the subject of the famous painting by Delacroix which he exhibited in 1824. It was probably from this point that the town's extensive defensive walls, which appear in many earlier illustrations, were dismantled. The town also houses today the collections of both Adamantios Koraes and Philip Argenti, later scholars identified with the island; the latter has published numerous volumes recording the history of the island, largely expressed through original documents.

The long Western presence here has had the effect of producing a balance in the major artistic survivals on the island from the medieval centuries; while the most artistically outstanding monuments are all Byzantine, the Genoese contribution is also prominent, but in the field of military and defensive building. They not only built up and administered a system of watch-towers and defensive forts, but even initiated the concept of fortified villages, as well as constructing bridges and aqueducts. Fragments of these can still be seen in the countryside, and while the most prominent are noted here they are too numerous to describe individually.

There is no clear itinerary or sequence in which the various sites might be visited, so after covering the island capital, entries will be grouped loosely by area within the island.

Chios Town

1) Kastro★★★
Castle overlooking the harbour of Chios. Ungated and open.

This constitutes easily the most prominent survival of the long Latin presence in the island. The viewpoint that provides the clearest impression of the form of this substantial *Castrum* appears when approaching the port of Chios from the sea; its walls and bastions rise impressively from sea level, and the bulk of the structure can best be seen from this angle. It is sited to the NW of the harbour, and waves still break against the NE extremity of its main seaward wall. With the land rising outside it towards the main Plateia of the town, it is clear that its primary purpose was as a land-based stronghold for an essentially maritime power. This remains, with the castles of Mytilini on Lesbos and Myrina on Lemnos, the largest and most impressive of such buildings in this part of the Aegean.

The original Byzantine citadel was not on this site, but somewhat to the NW of the town on top of a small hill; this was already being called Palaiokastro in the 14th C. It is possible that there is some Byzantine building remaining in the fortifications of the Genoese kastro but successive periods of use and development will have overlaid them, and its current aspect is now that of a Genoese creation, with a few late Venetian additions. It was under Martino Zaccaria that building here began (without the permission of the Byzantine emperor, which should have been sought), in c.1328. Two further building phases that took place under the Giustiniani in 1404 and 1427 gave it its main forms, with some modernisation after a siege in 1433. Thereafter the major addition was made by the Venetians in 1694/95, who built the huge Torrione Zeno, facing NE and displaying its major provision for large cannon. There was a substantial amount of internal building here – the governor's palace, various administrative offices and a number of houses, giving it the character of a small town. During the Turkokratia the richer inhabitants who lived within the Kastro were all said to have a vineyard and tower outside the walls, in the area now occupied by the town and its *plateia*. The layout of the main internal area with houses, workshops and warehouses will have changed little over the centuries, and it still serves the Greek population today. The church of Agios Giorgios was a Byzantine foundation, perhaps as early as the late 10th C, but all the detail is now late.

The Kastro has the form of a rough pentagon, with an irregular curved side facing on to the harbour. Its massive walls were strengthened by up to nine rounded towers, and the easiest way to gain an impression of its scale and arrangement is simply to walk round the enceinte on the top of the walls, most of which are still standing. The main entrance gateway in the SE corner provides an epitome of the history of the Kastro: the Venetians were here long enough in 1694-95 to leave an imposing outer facing with a fine inscription recording the name of Doge Silvestro Valerio; this has now been defaced (presumably by the Turks). It provides the facade for an outer gateway that must be Genoese, and this leads in turn to a brick-lined tunnel 15 m. long through the thickness of the wall that may be part of the earliest phase of building under the Zaccaria. (For the *Giustiniani Museum* on the right just inside this entrance, see below.) Of particular interest is the huge bastion in the middle of the NW sector; this is the "great tower" that is mentioned in documents from 1381. It is still roofed by much of a fine brick semidome, and displays a marble plaque (now invisible from ground level outside due to Turkish extensions) with three shields carved on it. This may have been moved here at a later date, and will have been created after 1413, as at this date the Giustiniani arms of a triple-turetted castle had added to them a 'chief' of a crowned imperial eagle, as seen here. The second large bastion in this sector, to the S, also displays the same triple escutcheon. The original exterior face of the walling in the whole W sector was vertical, but a section of masonry has been applied giving it a pronounced talus; this may be Turkish overlay of an originally Genoese structure. The ditch round all the land walls is now dry, but a 16th C map shows it full of sea-water with what appears to be a fixed bridge providing the only entrance from the land; a 19th C water-colour in the Koraes/Argenti collections shows that it still held water then, and the Frenchman Pitton de Tournefort, visiting here c.1700, mentioned in his usual rather disapproving tone that it had "an indifferent ditch". The moat was filled from the sea for all of the early history of the *castrum*, and if the ensemble is seen as a moated stronghold, originally built before the age of effective cannon, to protect the harbour and (in time of need) the local population as well, its form and function need little further explanation. The same 16th C map mentioned above shows four jetties immediately to the W projecting into the sea and lined prolifically with windmills, readily protectable from the Kastro.

Unlike so many of the castles built in the islands by W powers, this has remained in continuous habitation, and among its quiet, winding streets that were settled in the Turkish period the sense of the Levant seems very close, increased by a small Turkish cemetery still surviving beside the Plateia Frouriou.

2) Church of Agia Myrope and Agios Isidoros★★

Site of the original basilica of St Isidore.

Take the seaside road N out of the town for 3km., then immediately opposite the four newly restored windmills turn left up Odos Agias Myropis, and after 80 m. turn left into Odos Kleme which leads to Plateia Agias Myropis kai Agiou Isidorou.

The small, flat-roofed, modern concrete church fenced off in this open space (keys held at house on N side of the Plateia) occupies what must be the most important EC site on Chios: that of the original basilica of St Isidore, the patron saint of the island. It is probably the sixth church on this site, and remains of several intervening structures can still be seen. It was in the 5th C that the first basilica was built here, and the huge blocks marking the outline of its single apse are still in place and open to the sky, but the eye is first caught by a re-erected column of Proconnesian marble of great refinement, its delicate fluting partly set off by cabling; much further spolia lies around the precincts. Entering the modern church much of the extensive mosaic flooring of this first basilica can still be seen; mostly of simple, abstract "knot" and interlace design, built up in black, white, ochre, grey and terracotta, it carried an evocative dedicatory inscription by one "Arkadeios, son of Phokaios, sailmaker", but this is unfortunately hidden by the wooden floor covering. Against the N wall of the church a short flight of steps winds down to a small crypt which housed the tombs of the patronal saints; the broken top of one is held to be that of St Isidore, whose remains were taken by Venetians in 1125 and removed to Venice.

Four subsequent re-buildings occupied the site to probably the late 14th C, and fragments from these later buildings appear outside the church, particularly to the W, where more mosaics are a metre above the original floor level. At that point a smaller, centrally-planned, domed, inscribed-cross church was built, of which part of the cupola was still standing in 1866, but collapsed in an earthquake in 1881.

The complex building history represented by these survivals is not readily apparent, but the significance of the site for Chiote history makes a visit here well worth while, and has been the reason for its ** grading.

3) Chios – Museums

The Byzantine Museum,★ in a former mosque at 12 Odos Kanari on the SE side of the main Plateia, has an agreeable jumble of architectural fragments in its courtyard and in the vestibule of the former mosque (the building itself is permanently closed). Among the caps, lintels, etc. of Byzantine, Genoese and Turkish origins are a number of fine Genoese inscriptions; earlier this century these were distributed in various parts of the town, but have now been collected here. St George was the patron saint of Genoa, and he figures prominently on several items, and most notably on an impressive carved sarcophagus of Ottobuoni Giustiniani dated 1445, which is the most artistically outstanding piece here. The finely decorated Venetian 17th C cannons were brought here from the kastro earlier this century.

The Giustiniani Museum★ has recently been opened in a restored large house just inside the main entrance gate of the Kastro that is held to have been the palace of the ruling family. It displays a 5th/6th floor mosaic transferred from a site near the town, some fragments of 13th C frescoes taken from the Nea Moní and a small collection of later icons.

The Archaeological Museum houses mainly classical material, but there is a case of electrotypes of medieval coins of Chios, assembled from examples in England, Germany, etc., which (as always) are highly informative of the island's history. Chios was the only Aegean island to mint gold and silver coins during the 14th-15th C, due to the flourishing mastic trade.

The Koraes/Argenti Library displays little of Byzantine or medieval interest, but is a rich source of documentation for the history of the island.

A small and attractive fountain close to Odos Limenos a few metres from the harbour exemplifies the later history of Chios: a bowl at its apex is probably Genoese, and the dolphins and anchor finely carved in marble relief below is certainly Venetian work; each face has a beautifully cut Turkish inscription, and a further 19th C Greek text tells of the donation of the ensemble to the town by the philanthropist Syngrou.

Nea Moní   Νέα Μονί

22 km due W of Chios. A convent still in use: usual monastic hours and conditions of entry. (See Pl. 18).
Ready access by road, with various forms of transport possible.

Although founded as a monastery by two hermits (or perhaps, by tradition, three), early imperial interest and donations means that it was in effect an imperial foundation, and it must take pride of place among all the riches of Byzantine church buildings of the Aegean islands. Superbly sited, its mosaics, although damaged by the earthquake of 1881, form the third surviving example (with Hosios Loukas, Stiris, and the monastery at Dafní, both in mainland Greece) of the middle Byzantine mosaic system; those on Chios, however, have been subject to less radical restoration than these. Given the history of Chios over the last eight centuries we are indeed fortunate that these mosaics still exist at all.

The foundation of the monastery was due to the discovery of a miraculous icon on Mount Provateion, in the centre of the island, during the reign of the emperor Michael IV (1034-1041), and it is now accepted that it was largely built during the reign of Constantine IX Monomakhos (1042-1055), with the mosaics being installed from c.1049; documents from 1045-1051 record a catalogue of imperial donations to the monastery – money, land, fruit trees and so on. In 1749 the traveller Lord Charlemont was shown a painted portrait of the emperor and his wife, the empress Zoe, designated as *ktitors*, but this has long disappeared. The katholikon, although somewhat smaller than the other two mentioned above, is still a highly impressive and elaborate building and must be the work of teams of masons and mosaicists specially sent from CP. Its design is a complex one, and forms three distinct spaces. You enter the katholikon by a door in the large exonarthex, of which the apsidal forms to N and S make it the broadest part of the building. You will then cross quite a narrow and dark transverse inner narthex, which is domed and still has considerable amounts of its mosaic surviving. Finally, you enter the much lighter and more spacious naos, of which the design must represent the most sophisticated architectural thinking of the period. The builders started with a square plan, to which the three apses were added on the E side; then as the walls were raised they developed a regular octagonal form at the level of the cupola drum. This has left the main space completely free of columns or piers, and produced a striking rhythm of eight niches, alternately deep and shallow, narrow and wide.

The sheets of sombrely purplish marble (quarried locally) covering the lower walls give way to the mosaics which fill these niches, emphasising the light and richness of the upper zone. This would have been even more evident when the cupola mosaics were still in place, but the cupola itself collapsed in the 1881 earthquake. The mosaics which survive in the eight niches, although damaged in parts, exemplify both the skill of the Byzantine artists in exploiting the concave forms of the squinches that they had to fill, and the relative freedom that could be applied within the canon of the middle Byzantine decorative scheme. Some points of interest to note are the mosaic of the Deposition, which is not a subject within the Dodecaorton, and had not previously been given such prominence, and the sequence of four evangelists and four seraphs which occupied the eight squinches supporting the drum. Unusually, there must also have been four roundels of saints above the four broader niches, as the titles of St Phillip and St Andrew still survive. The character of the mosaics certainly suggests an innovative and dynamic artistic personality at work.

Returning to the inner narthex, the mosaics here are also highly individualised, filling the two transverse barrel-vaults and all adjacent spaces. The remaining scenes of the Dodecaorton appear here, as do quite an extended sequence of the Passion and many portrait roundels; the cupola with the Virgin in its oculus is the earliest surviving example of this subject shown guarded by military saints and martyrs, and conveys an idea of the lost Pantocrator in the main cupola.

Before leaving this unique site, make a tour of the complex, with its matchless view to the E towards the sea and the Turkish mainland. The main ossuary is normally closed and that to the immediate E of the main entrance is late, but note the impressive defensive tower and do not miss the fine cistern to the SW of the entrance gate, both of the 11th C and contemporary with the main foundation; the decorative brickwork round the cistern's entrance and the imposing series of columns supporting the shallow saucer domes of its roof indicate the importance given to this aspect of monastic provision, and the actual structure no doubt reflects that current in CP itself, where there are known to have been over 100 such cisterns. It was much admired by the Florentine traveller Buondelmonti, who wrote c.1418 of the *cisterna miro artificio fabricata.* The refectory is not normally on view, but if you can penetrate there you can see a table of inlaid marble, probably also dating from the 11th C.

Allow, if you can, a full day for visiting this important and spectacular site and enjoying its matchless surroundings.

Agia Gala   Άγια Γάλα

Chapel built against cliff at cave entrance*
NW extremity of island.

The small chapel dedicated to the Panagia Agiogalousena can be found projecting from the cliff just below the modern village; most of the interior space is provided by the cave against which it is built, but the exterior of the apse and the cupola are much in evidence and could be 14th/15th C. The interior decoration is all later, as are the Iznik and Delft plates on the outside, but the setting is highly picturesque and the unusual ensemble in spectacular country makes a rewarding visit.

Emporio   Εμπορειό

EC baptistry and ruins of basilica*
Unsigned.
Take the road from beside the harbour signed to the Black Beach, and after 50 m. take track off to the right into apparently private land; the baptistry is protected by a new stone-built structure at the far side of the field.

The acropolis area on the headland to the S of the village of Emporio was the site of a fortress surviving from Roman times until its destruction in the 7th C. Quite a large 6th C basilica with mosaic flooring was discovered here, with a substantial baptistry. Little can now be seen of the basilica, with just a sector of the floor mosaic with a simple repeated scallop design remains from the S end of the narthex, but the cruciform font to the SW still survives intact and unburied; it is protected by a modern circular building reproducing the form and size of the original. Although its gate is kept locked, the font can easily be seen, and its design is unusual in that two ends of the cross are rounded and two are flat.

Considerable other remains were excavated here, but have now been covered over; nevertheless the location and ambience make this worth seeking out.

Dotiá   Δοτιά

Substantial fortified Genoese tower, partly ruined*
Some 4km along the road from Emporio to Dotia this cannot be missed, some 200 m.W from the road, easily reached on foot through mastic groves.

Again, it is the Genoese presence which has left the most prominent survival in this area. Until recently it was the most complete example of a number of such buildings, being the central keep of a small fortress, but in the last 25 years a sector of the wall has collapsed. Fragments of the perimeter wall can still be seen, indicating that there were small rounded towers at each corner. The plan of the tower is some 30 by 20 m. and it is about 20 m. high to the castellation; it is built of local stone with ceramic filling in the mortar, and the base of the wall is battered. The interior originally had three storeys, with quite complex barrel-vaulting over two of them; entry can be made through a ground level hole, and once inside the remains of elaborate brick vaulting of the upper two floors can still be seen. An exterior stone stair-case, which would have ended in a wooden section that could be removed, is still visible. In its form and construction it has much in common with the tower beside the sea on Samothraki known as *Pyrgos Fonia*. It must date from the later 14th/15th C, and its function must have been both to act as a defence and refuge for the local workers on the mastic crop, and to form a link in a chain of watch-towers and other forts on the island, giving advance warning of pirate raids to the inhabitants of *Pyrgi* and further inland. Even in the 1680's Bernard Randolph reported how great care was taken to inspect every boat arriving anywhere on the island, and news would at once be passed "making smoke signals in day, and showing lights at night" to the next village or strong point. The interior and part of the external wall has collapsed in the last 25 years.

The towers at *Pyrgi* and *Mesta* were much larger, but can now no longer be seen properly due to dismantlement and later building; a tower at Pityous in the N of the island is in better condition but smaller, so this remains the best surviving example of this building type.

The Panagia Sikilia Παναγία Σικήλια

Byzantine monastic church, 12th/13th C* Remote, but may be open. (See Pl. 24).

Some 4 km. S of Tholopotamoi on the road to Pyrgi a sign points down a dirt road to the S; following this hilly track for some 5 km. will bring you to this remotely sited, attractive monastic church.

It is small and built on a domed, inscribed cross, single apse design with a considerable W extension and remains of a belfry over the W gable. The side walls are arcaded, and an area of sophisticated brick patterning in the gables of the crossing is unusually rich and makes use of the local speciality of *phialostomia*; the exterior has been recently renovated, and virtually nothing remains of any monastic buildings. The interior has no painting or other decoration, but the remote setting and decorative exterior brickwork of this church make it well worth the bumpy journey to reach it.

Armolia/Apolykhnon Άρμολια / Απόλυχνων

Kastro Orias; small Genoese fortress*
Unsigned and unenclosed.

The small kastro here, due N of the village, is easily seen crowning the hill-top to the N. of the village, but the approach to it is only for the well-shod and energetic enthusiast. It can be reached either by walking N. from Armolia through mastic groves and terraces and then up a steep rocky hillside, or from the W, after taking a turning signed to *Bessa* and *Lithi*; after 2 km. a track to the right gives you a slightly better start. Either route is a scramble.

This small but impressive fort – certainly more than just a defensive tower – is comparable with *Volissos* although somewhat less heavily fortified. An inscription records that it was built in 1446 by Geronimo Giustiniani, and it fits into the pattern of defensive buildings constructed by the Genoese to provide safe shelter for local Chiotes, and in this case probably for a small permanent garrison as well. Built on a roughly trapezoidal plan, with a tower in the SE wall and a narrow entrance in the SW angle, a series of chambers was built against the interior wall to provide shelter for the garrison and any islanders taking refuge. No regular approach route seems to have existed.

Pyrgi   Πυργοί

Church of the Holy Apostles★★
Open most of the time; if locked, enquire about the key in nearest café in the Plateia.

This was one of the larger fortified villages, with substantial walls and a very large 3-storey refuge tower, but very little is now left of these. However, down a short arcaded alley just to the E of the main Plateia you will glimpse this small but impressive 12th/13th C Byzantine church. Its exterior has no major additions, and its forms and decoration are all contemporary. Note the quite lavish use of the Chiote speciality of rows of the crimped *phialostomia*, each forming a small cross and inserted to be flush in the wall surface; on this scale they are particularly effective, and may perform a function of ventilating the masonry. On entering the small, domed narthex you will be drawn at once into the much lighter and more spacious naos; here again the dome carried on its broad octagon without the use of columns indicates that this is another manifestation on a smaller scale of the influential design of the Nea Moní. All the decoration is later, with the main areas painted in 1665 by a Cretan artist, Antonios Kinigos; the W influence, which was usual by then, is shown in an interesting misunderstanding of the Anastasis subject, where he has included the awoken soldiers before the open tomb of the Resurrection; the cupola is 18th C. After the Panagia Krina this is the most complete of the architectural progeny of the Nea Moní.

The prominent geometric decoration in grey and white on many of the houses in Pyrgi, of which the local people are very proud, turns out on enquiry to be only quite a recent development; if it has medieval antecedents it is probably in the field of Genoese secular building in the Kampos district, where examples survive of stone-work on which simple geometric patterns can be found, but nothing as complex as the modern forms.

Kalamoti   Καλαμωτή

Monastic church of the Panagia Agrelopou, with 14th C paintings★
The church lies about 1 km. SW of the village down a dirt road, E of Pyrgi and due N of Emporio. None of the surrounding monastic buildings have survived so this modest domed, inscribed cross church stands in isolation. Its rural setting contrasts with both its exterior, where the door-frame is formed from re-used classical Ionic mouldings and with

its interior, where the frescoes are of considerable distinction, although in poor condition. Most of the subjects are quite standard, but particularly impressive are the full-length figures of saints and the three donor figures in the narthex; these are the best preserved and one carried the name of Irene Mentoni. The ensemble is dated by style to the first half of the 14th C, and the island has no more distinguished example of Palaiologue art than these paintings.

Sklavia   Σκλάυια

1) Kamenas Pyrgos. Genoese secular building*

The flat, fertile area S and SW of Chios town, known as Kampos, still retains a number of medieval vernacular buildings with some original features; mostly these are rather fragmentary, and are difficult to locate due to the many high stone walls that divide the land, but the remains of a defensive tower can be seen from the road at this location. Turning NW off the road between Chios and Armolia a smaller road serves the village of Sklavia; here you can see on the right at about 50 m. from the road the greater part of the Kamenos Pyrgos, a tower built under the Giustiniani. Constructed of local stone, some of the arcatures and corbelling survive on the upper courses; this provides an example of the many secular survivals of Genoese presence in the island in the 15th/16th C.

2) The church of the Panagia Krina**

Reached down a further signed turning off this road, at the end of a short dirt track. (See Pl. 19).

After the Nea Moní this is one of the outstanding church buildings of the island, and it is one of the earliest churches to be built in emulation of it. The exterior, in its completely rural setting, immediately catches the eye, with quite elaborate brick patterns and blind niches round the apse, a large main cupola and a smaller one over the narthex. A partial inscription on the templon (now dismantled but present) gives a date of between 992 and 1091, and as the design of the building is so clearly dependent on the Nea Moní, its construction is now dated to 1056-1091. The interior has frescoes from up to six different phases.

You enter the church through an added porch which is now roofless, but contains some classical spolia, including a relief of two garlanded bulls' heads. The exonarthex is also an addition, but earlier, and here there are wall tombs to N and S, with traces of richly clothed lay portraits; fragments of a Last Judgement are on the N wall, and there is a small cupola. An inscription has made it possible to date these to 1287. After crossing a small transverse narthex, you enter the main naos, and it is here that it at once clear that the inspiration for its spacious quality is the Nea Moní; there are no columns, and the octagon below the cupola is carried ultimately on eight niches, alternately wide and narrow. This similarity with the Nea Moní is not continued by the fresco decoration, which is mainly contemporary with the building; the artist here adopted a very personal use of the spaces available to him, with five of the niches holding one major scene above another – as for example in the large S niche where the Baptism of Christ is painted above the Presentation. An earthquake in 1390 may have damaged the cupola; the frescoes in the drum of the cupola of twelve prophets have been overpainted, but were probably originally late 14th century, and their date may be due to this factor. From the post-Byzantine period are some of the frescoes in the bema, but much of the naos was re-painted in 1734 by one Michael Anagnostis, and his work includes the unusual painting on your left on entering the naos: it is an allegorical subject, representing "the World" and "Life".

Even if it were not the main surviving "copy" of the Nea Moní this impressive church in very rural surroundings fully repays an unhurried visit.

Volissos   Βολισσός

Ruins of Genoese castle★ Unenclosed.

The ruined castle that occupies a spectacular site on the hill-top above this small town must (after the *Castrum* in Chios town) be the most prominent single survival of the Genoese presence on Chios, and it does not appear to have been modernised by the Turks. After a scrambling entry up a steep track you will find large parts of the central keep remain.

Originally a rough trapezoid quadrilateral with six rounded corner towers, a keep on a square base was built into the SW corner, and an outer enceinte now merges with older buildings of the village that has grown down the hillside. We know from documents that while the smaller defensive towers of the island had a permanent staff of only two or three, the Genoese maintained a mercenary garrison of nine men here, paid by the *Maonnais*; it is of interest that it was formed mainly from Genoese, rather than local Greeks, as the latter could not always be entrusted with weapons which might be used against the occupying Italians.

It was clearly intended to protect the NW sector of the island, while a much smaller fort – little more than a tower – occupies the hilltop overlooking Kardamyla covering the NE of Chios.

Chiote villages

The countryside of Chios still offers several villages with much surviving medieval character, layout and vernacular buildings. It has become clear that the Genoese rulers initiated a policy of grouping rural communities round a central tower and providing fortified defences against pirate raids; the tower at Dotia near to Emporio was no doubt part of this planned protection policy.

Mestá** (Μεστά) in the SW of the island is the village which has most clearly retained the characteristics of a defended village. You will at once be struck by its unusual character, and it has been shown that it is exceptional in being planned from the start. Its design was governed by the concept of building an entire village so that it could withstand pirate raids; this is in contrast to the usual Greek village development where growth took place piecemeal round a particular centre, and the concept here must have been due to its Genoese originators. Built on a five-sided plan, the houses on the outer walls faced inwards and backed on to the fortifications, and some of these can still be seen today; shortage of space within this fortified area caused building across the streets at first floor level, and the tunnels that this produced, reminiscent of the Old Town of Genoa, still today form much of the character of Mestá. The large 19th C church (inscription of 1861 over W door) was built on the site of the central fortified tower; this was a huge, rectangular structure of which the external walls can still be identified, measuring some 50 x 60 m. The Florentine Buondelmonti, who was here c.1418, was the first to mention the gate and tower of Mestá with the appreciative comment: *"Amistae portum laudamus et turrim"*.

Avgonyma (Αύγωνυμα) in the W part of the island is more specifically Greek in form, but with several houses that still display medieval Genoese features.

Anavatos* (Άναβατος) slightly to the N still offers much of the appearance of a Byzantine village; its unplanned but impressive medley of stone-built houses, some still inhabited, clings to the mountainside, with a steep cliff falling away to the W. It may have been originally intended to house a Genoese garrison to cover the W side of the island from pirates landing here and hoping to raid the town from the W; the two double-nave churches, one of them still roofed, suggest a mixed population of Greeks and Latins. The only major disturbances here over the centuries would have been the decimation of its inhabitants by the Turks in 1822 and the earthquake of 1881.

CORFU (Kerkyra) Κέρκυρα, Κόρκυρα

Med: Korypho.
Island group: Ionian / Eptanisous. (*Nomos*: Kerkyra).

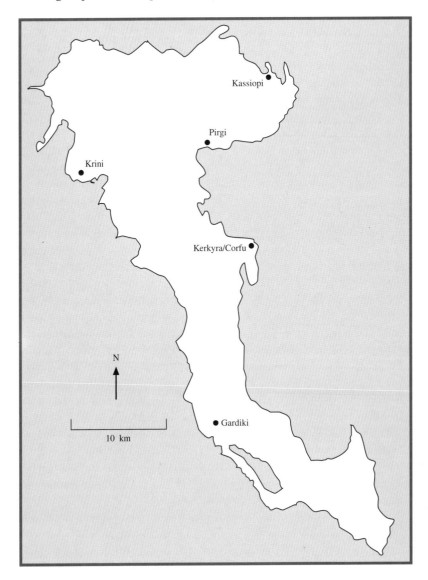

The largest and by general consent the most scenically beautiful of the
Ionian islands, Corfu lies just off the coast of N Greece and Albania, and

retained importance for a variety of reasons right through the medieval period. Although it is always grouped with the other 'Seven Islands' of the Ionian Sea, the history of Corfu developed over the centuries in a way that was different from the other islands at almost every point. Traditionally the island was Christianised in the 1st C by the disciples of St Paul, Jason of Tarsus and Sosipatros of Achaia, and bishops of Corfu certainly attended all the church councils from the 1st in 325 to the 7th in 787.

Being so remote from CP meant that it was both hard to govern and difficult to defend; its political orientation also developed more in relation to the mainland coast such a short distance away, dominated for long periods by the despotate of Epiros, based in Arta. The island must have seemed a vulnerable target for the Saracens, who burnt the main town of Corfu in 1033 and the Normans began a long period of involvement in the island's affairs with attacks in 1081 and 1147, the latter achieving occupation. The Byzantines recovered the island in 1149, but in the Deed of Partition of 1204 the Venetians made sure that it was specified as coming under their control, and from 1207 Corfu only played a peripheral part in Byzantine affairs. Its location meant that it would always be coveted by the Despotate of Epiros, which occupied the island from 1236; in 1259 the despot, Michael II, gave the island to Manfred of Sicily as the dowry of his daughter Helene; this started a further series of W interventions, and by 1267 the island was in the hands of the Angevin rulers of Naples, with Philip of Taranto enjoying a reign of almost 40 years as "Lord of Corfu". In 1382 the island passed to the Navarrese and in 1386 (by request of the Corfiotes) it finally came into Venetian hands. Corfu was then to remain a Venetian dependency for 401 years, and although the island had to withstand Turkish attacks, it is exceptional in that there was never a long-term Muslim presence there.

In spite of the early ecclesiastical importance of Corfu, and its elevation to a metropolitan see in the 11th C, the island had to accept a Latin archbishop from 1229, and was unable to have its own Greek metropolitan after 1367; from then until 1799 the Orthodox population was governed by a protopapas, or 'chief priest'.

Corfu became one of the islands which enjoyed a place in the minds of many Greeks after the fall of CP (and in some cases even shortly before) as the part of Greek territory that could still be thought of as being Greek, but where Venetian interests provided some security from the Turks. Important relics arrived from CP in 1456 when the bodies of a 4th C saint, Spyridon, and of Theodora, the wife of the iconoclast emperor Theofilos (829-842), were brought here, Spyridon being later adopted as the island's patronal saint. Among the living Greeks who came were Caterina, the wife of Thomas Palaiologos and sister-in-law of the last emperor; she died here in 1462, as did the diplomat and historian Giorgios Sphrantzes some 16 years later. The island became for a time in this way a kind of *byzance après byzance*, to which the nostalgic sight of cricket being played by white-clad figures on the immaculate turf of the Plateia beside the Spianada has become a charming 21st C complement.

The surviving buildings of the island reflect its varied history, in that only a few Byzantine churches have survived the turbulence of the centuries, with castles surviving more readily.

Corfu town, Kerkyra

Like so many of the Greek islands the most telling comment on the medieval significance of Corfu is received when you approach it from the sea, where you are at once conscious of the impressive heights of the Old Fortress (Palaio Frourio) rising above the shore-line. Already established in the 6th C, its walls contained the entire town of Corfu until the 13th C, and its aspect at this time might have partly resembled that of Monemvasia in the Peloponnese; the canal that now separates it from the land was only given its current appearance by the Venetians in the 14th/15th C. However, although of Byzantine foundation, the Fortress took on its present form much later; it was built between 1546 and 1588, and was frequently altered, with some parts such as the garrison church of St George and the barracks resulting from the British 19th C presence. So this, as well as the chillingly awe-inspiring mass of the New Fortress to the N of the harbour, which was built between the later 16th and 19th C, fall outside the scope of this study, but it could be mentioned that the 'two peaks' (koryfaí) of the Old Fortress supplied the Greek name of the island, later adapted by the Italians. Again and again it was the Old Fortress which was to save the town and the island from attackers, and it must always have been the emotional focus of the Corfiotes. The later commercial development and prosperity of the town may in part be responsible for the absence of medieval remains, but among the 14 churches destroyed during fighting between the Italian and German armies in 1943 there were certainly some medieval casualties.

So for Corfu town the chief interest now lies in just two buildings that have survived from post-classical times, and one museum; the former are located at the S end of the bay of Garitsas and the latter in the town itself.

1) The Antivouniotissa Museum★★★ (usual museum hours, closed on Mondays, and easily located up two broad flights of steps leading up from Odos Arseniou, overlooking the harbour) is devoted to the display of all the main portable works of Byzantine art on the island. The town authorities were strangely late in acknowledging the intrinsic importance of Byzantine art to the island's cultural history, and until the recent opening of this museum the only Greek icons displayed were in the Museum of Chinese and Japanese Art. However, the church of the Panagia Kyra Antivouniotissa was for several reasons an excellent choice for this new venture; the building itself is probably late 15th C and exemplifies very well the tradition of later Corfiote church design, with its dependence on long Venetian influence. A broad, single, timber-roofed nave is enclosed by a wide 'narthex' that has arms extending round to embrace both sides of the nave, and forming a spacious U-shaped ambulatory with a roof lower than that of the central space. There are many Venetian features in the detail, but the concept represents a local tradition.

The strength of the collection exhibited here lies in some 90 icons, and although the earliest date from just after the fall of CP, the general quality is high and condition is good; the forms of the church with its broad extended narthex/ambulatory have been well exploited to produce a rewarding display. Among the more striking icons is a later 15th C panel of the Macedonian school of the Virgin Hodegetria from Kastellana of outstanding quality (no. 170), an icon of c.1500 depicting St George with the boy from Mytilini, whom he had miraculously saved, riding on the saddle behind him (no. 186), an icon with an interesting series of scenes from the life of the little known monastic saint Theodore (no. 191) and two impressive life-size images of St Cyril of Alexandria and St John Damascene (nos. 171 and 172), the former by Emanuel Tzanes and dated 1654 and the latter of 1682 by Ioannes Tzenos, working closely in Tzanes' style. These particularly demonstrate the importance of artists from Crete in disseminating later Byzantine traditions of painting, which can also be found here in 16th C icons by the renowned icon-painter Michael Damaskinos originally created for the church of the Trimartyros. In the SE end of the 'ambulatory' a 16th C wall-painting over a tomb has just been restored, and there are numerous grave slabs in the floor which give a strong feeling of the continuity of local life. The body of the church has been largely preserved, with its spacious nave cleared to give a completely authentic period character. The rather over-grand marble iconostasis displays a range of icons of which three in the lower tier are notable, all dated 1612 and signed by Michael Abrami who is known to have worked elsewhere on Corfu. This ensemble exemplifies again the way in which Corfu was a meeting-ground for Venetian and Greek artistic trends which produced its own individual style.

At present there are no exhibits from the pre-Conquest period; the museum is nevertheless the current resting-place of two examples of monumental art from the EC and Byzantine periods which are not on display. One is the mosaic floor removed from the narthex of the basilica at Palaiopolis to the S of the town (see below); the other is some 12th C frescoes taken from the church of Agios Nikolaos at Kato Korakiana, some 20 km. NW of Corfu town. It must be hoped that a way will be found of displaying these important items. Even so, this well-appointed museum repays a leisurely visit, and is an example that some other islands could well emulate.

The other focus of interest lies to the S of the broad Bay of Garitsa, on the peninsula N of the lagoon of Khalikiopoulo (comfortable walking distance, following signs to Kanoni). This is the area known as **Palaiopolis** as it was the site of the ancient city of Corcyra, and has retained many interesting features. The area was sacked by the Goths in the 6th C but current excavations are revealing successive Greek, Roman and EC buildings.

2) EC basilica of Agia Kerkyra★★
Substantial excavated ruin. Enclosed, due to continuing excavations, but can easily be viewed from the road.

Dated to before 450 by an inscription of the bishop Jovian (Iobianos), the church itself is still of considerable size and was still in use in the 17th C, when its belfry was built on to the NW corner; its walls, up to 20 m. high, are now roofless. In form it was originally a grandiose five-aisled basilica, but was re-built in the 12th C with just a single nave. Its fabric contains re-used classical spolia from a Doric temple, and the depradations by Saracens in the 11th C and Turks in 16th mean that there must have been successive restorations. A separate building on the N side may have been a baptistry chapel; a fine 5th/6th C mosaic floor by the artist Elpidios, with an inscription, abstract patterns and depictions of birds has been removed from the narthex, and is currently kept in the Antivouniotissa Museum, although it is not on display.

[Just across the road from this site, and opposite excavated Roman baths, are the gates of the 19th C British-built mansion of Mon Repos; the overgrown grounds of the estate, which are now open every day, contain an unexcavated Greek temple and surround the elegant country house where Prince Philip was born in 1921.]

3) Church of Agioi Iason kai Sosipatros**

Open 8.30-14.00 and 18.00-21.30 (in Summer) by attendant in house adjacent to NW corner.
The church is easy to find, some 200 m. N of the Palaiopolis excavations in the suburb of Anemonylos.

This is the one outstanding gem of Byzantine architecture on Corfu. The dedicatory saints, as disciples of St Paul, were traditionally the founders of Christianity on the island (see above), and the church dedicated to them was originally the katholikon of a monastery. In form it is a domed, inscribed-cross design, and with only a few external alterations it represents the mature perfection of middle Byzantine church building, with no significant traces of local practice. In design and construction its appearance suggests that a team of masons from central Greece or even nearer to CP travelled to Corfu to execute it; its date has usually been put in the early 12th C, but now the early 11th C or even late 10th has been suggested (although not entirely convincingly), by comparison with some major churches in central Greece, such as Hosios Loukas in Stiris.

Below the broad, octagonal drum of the cupola, the E exterior is perhaps the most striking, with the central, faceted apse flanked by two smaller, rounded ones, and their high rounded windows outlined in dog-tooth brick patterns; the cloisonné, masonry here is topped by a rich course of Cufic brick patterning. The S wall shows signs of later alteration, possibly during the life of the original monastery. The W facade has had a later belfry added to the N, but otherwise here too we can see a perfect example of middle-Byzantine building with the added interest of two inscribed panels integral to the masonry; these have been published several times since the 17th C and are somewhat worn, but their text is repeated inside in recent copies and name the Proedros Theofanos as the ktitor. The cloisonné masonry is particularly inventive, and incorporates single, double and triple vertical tiles forming groups of II and III.

The interior has lost all its fresco decoration except for a detached 12th C fresco fragment of St Arsenios, archbishop of Corfu, on the N wall. Otherwise two large 17th C icons of the patronal saints (with their inscriptions describing them as 'apostles') provide the main artistic interest; they are of quite high quality and may have originally formed part of an earlier iconostasis, the present one being a rococo Venetian marble creation. The two fine marble columns supporting the cupola to the W (most probably re-used from a classical temple and at that point inscribed with the cross you can still see) give an indication of the richness that the interior would have originally displayed, and form a further contrast with the two 18th C tombs said to be of the patronal saints. (There is now no sign of the tomb of the late Byzantine historian and diplomat Giorgios Sphrantzes, once said to be here.)

Nowhere else in the Ionian islands will you find such a perfect example of middle-Byzantine church architecture, so make sure you allow it all the time that you can.

Agios Markos, near Pirgi

Church of Agios Merkourios and Prophetis Elias★

Near the village of Agios Markos, some 4 km due W of the village of Pirgi on the E coast, you will find the chapel in a small fertile plain about half a km. due S from the village.

The architecture is undistinguished except for the fact that it has a single nave but two apses; this the only church with this feature on the island, and accounts for its dual dedication: the saint Merkourios, and the prophet Elijah. The main interest here, however, is provided by the frescoes and two inscriptions; that in the N apse gives the name of Nicholas, a *droungarios*, who is said (with his brothers) to have built and decorated the church in 1074/5 during the reign of the emperor Michael VII Doukas. A *droungarios* was a military rank and probably explains the dedication to a military saint, Merkourios. The date means that these are the earliest dated wall-paintings on the island, and although showing areas of damage they can still be readily seen. The fresco programme does not suggest great sophistication, but the pairs of standing figures in the apses are impressive; those in the N apse are the prophets Elijah and Elisha, and in the S apse the two saints are Basil and a military saint, probably Merkourios. Among the figures on the N wall Saint Marina can be seen slaying Beelzebub in an episode from her legend.

Although these are not sophisticated paintings, they have a power and directness that make this church a rewarding one to visit.

There are fragmentary remains of Byzantine wall paintings in a few other sites, besides those from the roofless church of Agios Nikolaos, Kato Korakiana, now in the museum. Among these are the churches of Agios Blasios at Kamara, the small single-chamber church of Agios Mikhail sto Vouno at Ano Korakiana and that of Agios Nikolaos stou Tatsourina at Sgourades, S of Omali, but the great majority of churches have either no decoration, or painting of the 17th-19th C. This is the case with the spectacularly sited monastery of Pantokratoros at the summit of the mountain range of that name in the N of the island, but here the visitor finds that the monastery court yard is filled by the base of a huge steel television mast erected there during the dictatorship. However, there are three castles round the coast of the island, all of which repay visiting.

Kassiopi

Extensive castle ruins**
Unenclosed.
Due N of Corfu town and close to the N tip of the island is the resort village of this name; opposite the modern village church a winding footpath leads uphill and soon divides, the right fork leading shortly to the castle gate.

Fortunately ignored by the village visitors are the quite substantial remains of the enceinte of a castle, built to look across the straits towards Albania and Butrinto. The massive gateway, though partially ruined, still has traces of port-cullis grooves in its outer section, with the inner opening lowered at a later period by brick insertions. Once inside the walls the extent of the ensemble becomes evident. The total area enclosed by the circuit of walls (all of local stone) would be substantial – some 200 x 250 m. – and the enceinte is protected by large towers at 15 m. intervals. Some of the towers are currently used as housing for farm animals, but most of them, and the enceinte, are in quite good condition, although for the most part there are no buildings surviving within the large enclosure.

The site itself has no special natural strength apart from the rising ground on which its stands, and the sequence of towers suggests that defence was needed on the whole circumference. The impression is given that it was intended to provide an area of safety for a substantial number of the local population, rather than house a garrison or defend a strategically important installation or road. This confirms that the castle as we now see it was substantially a product of the period of Angevin rule in Corfu, and that it was intended to protect the local population during the later 13th C when Charles of Anjou, now calling himself "King of Corfu", was pursuing a policy of appeasement towards the Corfiote Greeks. (He owed his strength partly to papal support, and so had offended many of the Orthodox believers of the island.) The Venetians, when they finally took over Corfu in 1386, must have been responsible for the dismantling of the entrance gate, and they may also have reduced its effectiveness in other ways in case it fell into the hands of the Genoese.

Take your time exploring this site, as (given the proximity of the beach) it is remarkably undisturbed, and the Albanian coast with the site of Butrinto in view across the straits provides a memorable outlook; the castle at Butrinto was included in Helene's dowry with Corfu, as it was held by the Venetians to be "the key of Corfu". The relatively complete state of the enceinte makes it hard to see how, within 100 years, a legend had grown up that the castle here had been deserted because its inmates had been poisoned by the breath of a fiery dragon.

Krini

Angelokastro. *Med*: Castrum Sancti Angeli.
Substantial castle ruins★★
Unenclosed.
Shortly before the road reaches the resort of Palaiokastritsa on the W coast a right-hand fork leads up towards Krini; after some 4 km. the castle can be seen, but you will have to descend and park transport before climbing the steep track up to the entrance.

There are claims that this medium-sized castle may have been built during the reign of the emperor Manuel Komnenos (1143-1180), and it must in any case have been established by 1272 as it was then taken over by the Italian Giordano di San Felice, the vicar-general and captain of Corfu who was acting on behalf of Charles of Anjou, the ruler of Naples (see above). It may be a Byzantine foundation although it must be said that (for its size) it is not in a typical Byzantine site, as Angelokastro is in the tradition of small but virtually unassailable strongholds that make use of exceptional natural defences; in this case the wall in the W/NW sector drops away vertically by some 250 m. to the sea below, and all other approaches, including that to the entrance gate, are all very steep. Its location overlooking the harbour of Kastritsa and controlling sea traffic from Italy, ensured that this was the second most important castle in the island after Corfu itself. In 1386 it was besieged by the Venetians and in 1403 the Genoese regarded it as sufficiently crucial to besiege it for a year, and even then they were driven off with help from Palaiokastritsa.

The enceinte occupies the entire summit of the rock pinnacle, which is some 50 m. across. There would have been no space for large towers in the enceinte, but a small look-out tower survives at the extreme N point of the walls. The Kastro now has two chapels; one is cut into the rock near the NE enceinte and probably dates from the building of the castle, and the other is a recent one built on the summit, and probably replacing a medieval original; just to the W of it, though, are a number of burial sites have been cut into the rock, suggesting that this may have been a sacred site before it was fortified. There are a number of cisterns and underground chambers, all now largely overgrown, and traces of several other buildings above ground. This makes the absence of a clear indication as to the date of Angelokastro unusually regrettable; its construction from local stone without any use of brick, and its site, suggest that (if it was a Byzantine foundation) it has been largely rebuilt.

Having reached the summit here you will want to absorb the significance of this crag-crowning site, as the strength of its position is still momentously evident today.

Castle of Gardiki

Byzantine castle★★.
Gated but open.
Travelling S from Agios Mathaios, after approx. 5 km. turn right where the road forks, and the castle is beside the road just past the junction; the W coast (here a flat beach) is about 4 km. away at this point.

This is the most interesting and problematic, but the least spectacular, of the castles on Corfu; the choice of its location is hard to explain, and it does not figure in the historical sources which relate to Angelokastro and Kassiopi. Its siting is consistent with Byzantine practice of giving a low priority to the use of natural defences, in that at no point is it endowed with any advantage of height, nor are there are any traces of a moat or ditch surround. It is the only castle on the island which retains unequivocal elements of Byzantine masonry; the regular courses of ceramic tiles in conjunction with dressed blocks of stone are very evident in the tower which is closest to the road, and which is the part of the kastro that you will probably see first.

Entrance is through a substantial and still intact gateway set at right-angles to the wall, and readily visible from the road, but in this and the walls and other towers of the enceinte the tile courses easily seen in the SE tower nearest to the road are not repeated, although brick is used quite freely. Once inside the walls you will find a virtually complete enceinte with seven of the eight original towers still standing. There would seem to be at least two periods of building represented, with part of the entrance possibly making a third. The masonry of the SE tower is not repeated elsewhere, but that found throughout the interior is quite consistent, as though an existing Byzantine edifice (perhaps very modest in size) had been used by a later builder as the basis of the much larger fortress that we see today. The tower to the S may have contained a chapel, and fresco fragments were visible here until recently.

But more enigmatic is the purpose behind building a fortress here at all. The nearby coastline is very shallow, and will certainly have receded over the centuries (there is a small enclosed lagoon beside the sea close by) but it is difficult to believe that there could ever have been a natural harbour in this area. The use of terrain is consistent with Byzantine practice, and the kastro may be the result of the Despotate of Epiros needing to protect some aspect of its interests in or near Corfu. The Norman attacks of the 11th and 12th C would thus seem to be most probable reason for building the castle here, with the mid-12th C being perhaps the most probable point at which Byzantine resources chanelled from the ruler in Arta might have been mobilised for this purpose; however, there would also no doubt have been other times when the turbulent history of the island might have provided the need for a protective fortification of this kind, and an element of uncertainty cannot be avoided. There is a complete lack of inscriptions or documentation, and experts have differed in views of its chronology from the reign of Michael I, Despot of Epiros (1205-1215) to the period 1235-1257, but the different periods of building suggest to us a more complex history.

Be prepared to spend some time here, as the opportunity to examine such a relatively undamaged Byzantine stronghold is rare.

CRETE   Χρήτη

Med: Candia, Candy.
(*Nomoi*: Irakleio, Khania, Lasithi and Rethymnon.)

C rete has always been exceptional among the Greek islands. Not only is it the largest (indeed, it is among the largest islands in the Mediterranean), as well as having been the home of one of the oldest recorded civilisations of the world, but its southern position meant that it was the closest of the Aegean islands to Africa and so furthest from CP.

Unlike Cyprus, its position never made it important as a posting station for pilgrims or crusaders on their way to the Holy Land. It could be this peripherality that was the reason for no Cretan bishop being present at the first church council in Nicaea, although smaller islands such as Kos, Rhodes and Corfu were represented; it may also have been the cause of the island being included in the diocese of Macedonia in the early 4th C ecclesiastical organisation of the empire.

After early attacks by Vandals and Slavs in 457 and 623, the first

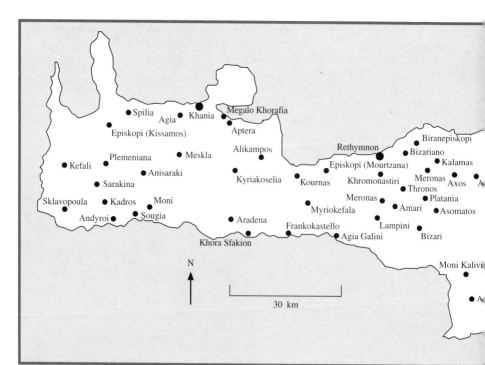

occupation of the island in the medieval period began in 824 when a force of Spanish Arabs landed and, having established a base on the site of the modern Irakleio, by 827 had subjugated the whole island. Opinions as to their treatment of the indigenous Christians varies, with some authorities claiming wholesale destruction of churches; while there were certainly over 40 EC buildings in existence at the time of the Arab conquest, of which little remains today, the metropolitan church at Gortys (that was certainly a century old at the time of the Muslim occupation) must have been allowed to stand and operate throughout the period in which they were present. In general, their attitude was probably more tolerant than otherwise.

The Muslim presence on Crete meant that they had a base from which they were able to attack wide areas of the Aegean, and it was to be one of the last great military exploits of the Byzantines that they succeeded in 961 in mounting a huge expedition that re-conquered Crete. This was carried out under the personal command of the emperor Nikiforos Focas, who brought back immense booty to CP, and his name is now commemorated in the main street of Irakleio.

The Byzantines, anxious not to lose control of the island again, maintained a military organisation there which only came to an end in

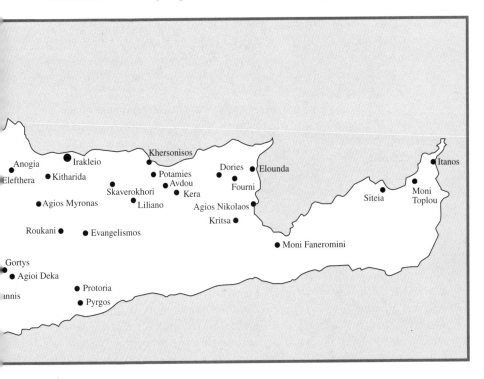

1203 when the emperor Alexios IV Angelos ceded Crete to Boniface of Montferrat, the leader of the main crusading force. In August 1204 Boniface sold it to Venice for the bargain cash price of 1000 silver marks, and this was how, despite initial opposition from Genoa, the long period of Venetian presence on the island was inaugurated. Crete was the first major colony of the Republic, and its administration, with the wealth that flowed from it, must have been a major feature in the Venetian exchequer. Taxes and labour obligations weighed heavily on the Cretan population, who periodically revolted. The island became an important trading base with the whole of the Levant, and agricultural production of such things as olive oil and cheese, and even timber, became cash crops, sold on to the Venetian masters.

While the Venetians were tolerant of the religion of their Orthodox Christian subjects, they were sensitive to the powerful focus for discontent that a strong local church could provide, and they installed a Latin archbishop, also limiting the number of Orthodox clergy allowed in the island to 130. The distant rule of the Senators on the Lagoon created some resentment, and there were several revolts (particularly in 1363 and 1453) in which both Greeks and locally domiciled Venetians took part, although these never succeeded in ousting the rule of the Serene Republic. This was only finally achieved by the Turks in 1669, when, after a siege of Irakleio that had lasted for 21 years, the Muslim power that had been in de facto occupation of the rest of Crete from 1645 finally achieved the surrender of the last major Christian outpost in the Levant; only the much less significant island of Tinos was to survive longer in Venetian hands.

The overall shape of the history of Crete in post-classical times is in fact simpler than that of many much smaller islands to the N, with their incessant changes of rule, and has been conveniently divided into four well-defined periods:

- the EC and first Byzantine period from the 4th C to 827;
- the Arab occupation of 827 to 961;
- the second Byzantine period from 961 to 1204;
- the Venetian period from 1204 to 1669.

The indigenous Byzantine and Venetian culture that developed in Crete from the 13th C was extremely vigorous, and as a result the island has many times more surviving Byzantine monuments than any of the others. This abundance has made it necessary, in order that a balance is maintained within the book, to exercise greater selectivity in assembling the entries for Crete. To indicate what is available it could be said that early this century Guiseppe Gerola published a census of what he called the *Monumenti veneti* which enumerates some 600 buildings of all kinds (fortifications, hydraulic installations, etc., as well as churches) in a state that could be studied, while the surveys of Kalokyris (1973) dealing only with wall paintings, Gallas / Bourboudakis (1983) and the *Reallexikon zur Byzantinischen Kunst* (1990) list approximately 180, 150 and 278 churches respectively with surviving Byzantine paintings. Different criteria can be applied by different authorities, and the entries on 66 sites which follow here (which naturally concern more than just churches with frescoes) will include all the major survivals, and as many of the lesser as seemed appropriate within the context and intentions of this guide.

The wealth of surviving art represented by this medieval heritage has encouraged a considerable literature on the painting styles of Byzantine and Venetian Crete. Space does not allow any extended discussion here, but a few factors could be mentioned. Two examples of aniconic painting have been found in the area of Agios Nikolaos on the bay of Mirambello, which, like the aniconic art in Naxos and other Cycladic islands is now thought to be 10th C or later; otherwise the earliest dated painting is of 1225 at Amari, and so from after the Venetian occupation had begun. From the mass of fresco painting from the 12th to the 13th C, stylistic connections have more readily been established with Asia Minor than with centres in mainland Greece, but from the Palaiologue period there tend to appear more restrained versions of the fantastic painted architectural backgrounds and vigorously distorted figure style that had developed in CP. It is often easiest to speak before the 15th C of Cretan painting in terms of its relation to metropolitan trends, but from the later 15th and 16th C a 'Cretan school' can certainly be said to have existed, although opinions vary as to much of its character. The influence of Venice is unavoidably present, with constant commercial and artistic traffic between the Adriatic and the Venetian colony. During the 13th C we find more artists beginning to sign their work, and the painter John Pagomenos left his name on the frescoes in eight churches between 1313 and 1347, with the names of more than ten others known from their signatures before the mid-15th C. Anyone wishing to make a more detailed study of Cretan art and artists should make use of specialised studies such as that of Konstantin Kalokyris (see p. 350).

All the Cretan sites are given here in a single alphabetical sequence; this avoids the traveller either having to follow a pre-determined route, or knowing in which *nomos* or district a particular village is located.

Agia
Αγία

Close to Agia Episkopi. (*Nomos*: Khania).
Ruined basilica of the Panagia. ★ Unenclosed.
*Completely unsigned; coming from Khania take right turn at sign to
Kurtomados, branching left after some 100m. on to a dirt track and in about
250m. you will see the isolated ruins on the right among fruit trees.*

This is an impressive ruin of a triple-aisle basilica, with all three apses
and both lateral walls still standing to 4-5m.; 5 of the 6 columns down
the nave are still in place, as are parts of the chancel enclosure. A
building of this type and on this scale (some 18m. from threshold to
apse) would have been the seat of a bishop (this is still reflected in the
local name) and as it now stands the church is held to be a re-building
of an EC basilica after the re-conquest of Crete from the Arabs; there
are traces of a narthex to the NW, and the proportion of the nave is very
broad for its length, suggesting that the original basilica would have been
longer. The fabric that you now see, with a careful double course of brick
in the main apse, must date from the late 10th or 11th C, after the
reconquest from the Arabs, but certainly well before 1204.

While not the easiest place to find, persistence will be rewarded and
you will have the site to yourself.

Agia Galini
Αγία Γαλήνη

(*Nomos*: Rethymnon).
Church of the Panagia. ★ Usually open.
*About 1 km. before entering the resort village, the church (now used as a
cemetery chapel) can be seen some 50m. off and below the road on your left.*

This is a broad hall church, of which the distinctive feature is the
provision of four deep flanking recesses. These seem to have been added
at an early date (?14th C), two each to the N and S sides of the nave,
and each with a separate pitched roof. Their original function is now
hard to determine (possibly for use as tomb chambers?) but they now
give the interior an extremely spacious and airy quality. There was also
an earlier W wall of which the remains were noted by Gerola a few
decades ago, but can now no longer be seen. The effect of these changes
is to have made the interior wider than it is long; the building has been
recently renovated and there are no frescoes, but it is included here as it
offers this unusual design and is the only medieval survival in the
neighbourhood of this popular and (in season) populous resort.

Agios Myronas   Άγιος Μύρωνας

(*Nomos*: Irakleio).
Church of Agios Myron. ★ Locked; key with papas.
You cannot miss this building just beside and above the road at the top of a
flight of steps on the W edge of the village.

The large, triple-apse church is built on a domed inscribed cross plan
with the dome supported on piers, and with a substantial domed narthex
added later. Its scale, which is a surprise in this modest village, must be
due to its having originally been the seat of a bishop. The renovated
texture of the exterior at first looks misleadingly modern, but this is an
impressive example of substantial 13th C church building combining
Byzantine design with some of the techniques of the Venetians; the
narthex is later (perhaps 15th C) and Gerola suggested that it had a
second, smaller dome. The high drum of the main cupola is particularly
impressive, with its decorative, recessed arcading and engaged
colonettes; note too the fine lateral arcading on the exterior N and S
walls. The painting of the interior is all quite late, but the exterior is an
impressive and accessible example of this architectural type and well
repays a visit.

Agioi Deka   Άγιοι Δέκα

(*Nomos*: Irakleion).
Church of Agioi Deka. ★ Unlocked.
Easily found some 100 m. to the S of the central area of the main street of this
large village.

This modest 3-aisle basilica is probably a 13th C building, but will
almost certainly have had earlier origins, as the six large granite columns
lining the central nave seem unlikely to be being used here for the first
time. Its proximity to Gortys suggests the columns derived from there,
and supports the claim to an early foundation; the Ten Martyrs of Crete
may well have been honoured with an early shrine here as five of them
came from Gortys; they were martyred in 250 AD on 23rd December,
which is their feast day, and were named Theodoulos, Satorninos,
Euporos, Gelasios, Eunikianos, Zotikos, Pontios, Agathopos, Basilides
and Euarestos.

The interior is mainly interesting for the few surviving paintings
which are restricted to images of the ten standing saints painted in the
soffits of the arches – an unusual location, but they must be
contemporary with the building. Christoforo Buondelmonti visited here

c.1419, making a rather exaggerated comparison with Sta Trinitá in his native Florence, and being struck by the fine blue ground of these frescoes; Gerola mentions other frescoes then just visible in the narthex.

Agios Ioannis   Άγιος Ιωάννης

(*Nomos*: Khania).
Church of Agios Pavlos.* Open.
Just under 1 km. from the Faistos site entrance travelling in the direction of Matala, you will find this striking building beside the road on the left.

Three periods of building can be established in this unique small complex. The oldest part is a small square chamber which now serves as the apse, its four massive piers supporting a low blind cupola; this may be pre-Christian, and if so its absorption into a church is unique in Crete, but it must date at latest from the earliest Christian period. Arched openings to N and S (now filled in) show that originally it must have been little more than an aedicule; fresco fragments here are probably 12th C. To the W of this was added, about a thousand years later, a square chamber with a substantial cupola. More frescoes survive here, with evangelist portraits of Luke and John in the squinches, and a painted inscription round the W half of the interior of the drum provides a date of 1303-4; naming as it does the emperor Andronikos II Palaiologos, it is one of the eleven such inscriptions in Cretan churches with an imperial association. This could well be the date at which this central element was built, although if there had been no inscription aspects of its construction might have suggested a century earlier. Finally, the large narthex with its wide, open arches and Venetian qualities must have been built on in the 15th/16th C.

For a variety of reasons this is a uniquely interesting and rewarding building to visit, and is both accessible and open.

Agios Nikolaos   Άγιος Νικόλαος

Bay of Mirambello (*Nomos*: Lasithi).
Church of Agios Nikolaos.* Usually locked.
This modestly sized church lies in the grounds of the Minos Palace Hotel on St Nicholas Bay, opposite some tennis courts; the whole area occupies a small promontory to the N of the main town. The key is held at the reception desk of the Minos Palace Hotel (passport has to be left as surety).

The church itself has a single nave but with a low cupola carried on broad pilasters, and without any projections to N or S. The main interest here is provided by the fresco decoration in the bema and apse; there are two layers clearly discernible, and the earlier one has the distinction of being aniconic. There is just one other example of this in Crete, and although not extensive is of considerable interest; as on Naxos, where there is more of this form of decoration, a minor tradition must have persisted in the post-iconoclast centuries. The church building and this fresco layer probably date from the later 10th or early 11th C, and the later painting (in the conch of the apse and bema) from the 13th/14thC.

Even without the considerable intrinsic interest of its decoration, this church should be visited as being the only surviving Byzantine building in the vicinity of this resort, and must indeed be the only building worth looking at here.

Alikampos   Αλικάμπος

(Nomos: Khania).

Church of the Koimisis Theotokou.* Locked.

Approaching the village from the N, you will pass the track down to the church on your left at the last bend before reaching the first houses, but continue on into the village to locate the papas who holds the key, and he will come down to open the church for you.

The church is a modestly sized, completely simple barrel-vaulted hall with a small rounded apse and no later additions; the only external relief is provided by eleven ceramic bowls let into the W facade. (The immediate vicinity is being excavated as possibly the site of an earlier church). The principal interest here is the extensive frescoes which are inscribed as being by the hand of the artist Ioannes Pagomenos; they are dated 1315-16, and so quite early in his career, as the last of his eight signed works is dated 1347. They cover all the interior surfaces, and their condition is quite good, with damage being mainly confined to the portraits of the ktitors; in the apse the Virgin Eleousa is particularly effective, as is the Koimisis on the W wall. The subject matter is all quite standard, with only the Mandylion as well as the Keramion on the E wall over the apse being unusual. Pagomenos' rather provincial, almost rustic, style (as in the other seven churches he painted) seems here entirely appropriate to the scale of the church and to its locality.

This is one of the most easily accessible of the churches painted by Pagomenos, and is recommended if you wish to experience a representative early example of his work.

Amari
Άμαρι

(*Nomos*: Rethymnon).
Church of Agia Anna.* Open when visited.
Signed to the S of the road through the village, and on the left in fields some 600m. down a well-surfaced new road.

Now a simple hall church, there must at one time have been a second nave on the S side, as there are both internal and external remains. The N exterior displays an impressive arcade, but the chief interest here is the fact that the remaining frescoes in the apse are the earliest dated painted work in Byzantine Crete, with a donor's inscription that ties them to the year 1225, thus providing a firm starting point for forming a chronology. The ascetic and dematerialised style of the bishop represented in the apse just below the inscription (Andrew, the 7th C hymnographer and archbishop of Crete) is close to that found in parts of mainland Greece in the previous century.

The snowy crests of Mount Ida looking down on this peaceful valley provide an additional reason for recommending a visit to this modest but significant church.

Anisaraki
Ανισαράκι

(*Nomos*: Khania)
1) Church of Agia Anna.* Unlocked. (See Pl. 4).
Coming from Kandanos, the church is signed to the left of the road at the beginning of the village, 30m. down a steep path, among olive trees.

This is a very simple hall-church, but its interior offers the dual interest of a masonry iconostasis and some interesting and accurately dated frescoes. The inscription naming the donors (the priest, John, and Basil, son of Peter) gives a date of 1457-62, and this can be applied to the whole interior. The iconostasis is damaged along the top, but (by comparison with e.g. that of the Moni Kalyviani) very little has been lost, and it would appear to be a good example of a simple version of the transitional type that in due course gave way to the familiar, more extensive, wooden form. The frescoes that you can still see on it are of the standard subjects for this location (the Virgin on the N and Christ on the S). Among other frescoes, although mostly not in a good state of preservation, are an impressive image of the St George on horseback, with the boy of Mitylene riding behind him, and some quite intimate scenes of Joachim and Anna and the infant Virgin. A point of minor interest is provided by the fine portraits of the donors on the S wall, who appear to be holding a model of the church roofed with a dome; it is not possible that the present building was ever domed, but some fragments of large columns outside the W door suggest that it may have been replacing a larger, earlier church to which the donors' model is perhaps related.

2) Church of the Panagia.* Unlocked.

At the opposite end of the village from Agia Anna you will see the Panagia signed from the road, from which it is only about 20 m. distant.

This is a small and simple late 15th C hall-church, with evident Venetian influence in its construction. Its main interest lies in its frescoes, which although not all in good condition do contain colourful and interesting passages. The sea giving up its dead on the N wall is an usual subject and particularly graphic, as is the Massacre of the innocents in the lower vaulting of the S side; scenes of the Virgin's childhood are also effective. This graphic treatment is very much a feature of Cretan art at the end of the 15th C, and although not dated by any inscription, this must be the period of both the building and its decoration.

Anogia   Ανώγια

(*Nomos*: Rethymnon)
Church of Agios Ioannis.* Open when visited.
The church is in the centre of the upper part of this large village, standing in its own plateia.

This is quite a substantial double-nave church, with frescoes in the S nave and narthex. The construction of the two naves is not completely identical, and that to the N may be slightly later. The frescoes remain the point of chief interest here, and (although sooty in parts) the assurance and elegance of their style suggests they are of Palaiologue date and probably of the first half of the 14th C; this is no doubt also the date of the building of the S nave. Besides fairly standard subjects, with the meeting of Joachim and Anna, in the apse, there is an impressive sequence of five standing female saints on the N wall, opposite St George on horseback.

This is the only medieval building to survive the destruction of the village in the last war, and its frescoes make it a rewarding one to visit.

Anydroi   Ανύδροι

(*Nomos:* Khania).
Church of Agios Giorgios Anydriotis.★ (Unlocked.) (See Pl. 15).

A delightful metalled road running E from Palaiokhora and traversing a rocky gorge brings you to Anydroi in 5 km.; the church is visible some 30m. S from the main village street.

Now a double-nave church, that on the N can be dated by the long inscription on the right of the entrance, which names several donors and informs us that the frescoes are of the year 1323 and are the work of the artist Ioannis Pagomenos. The S nave is later, probably by almost a century, and the exterior indicates how the cross vault only covers the nave of the N side. Pagomenos' frescoes appear as a mature and almost severe work of the artist's middle age – his last known work is of 24 years later. They are in quite good condition (although there is the usual mutilation of e.g. Judas in the Betrayal scene), and contain, among many other subjects, an extended cycle of scenes from the life of St George, including various tortures, and a majestic image of the saint on horseback killing the dragon. The frescoes in the S nave are in much worse condition and display a more rustic and less expressive style.

This is in every way a rewarding church to visit, adjacent to village houses but with mountains rising behind and the valley opening down to the Libyan sea to the S.

Aptera   Άπτερα

(*Nomos:* Khania).
Ruined monastery of Agios Ioannis Theologos.★
Fenced, but may be left open.
The classical site is signed to the S off the Khania-Rethymnon road; traverse the village, which you will reach in 2 km., and you will shortly arrive at the site.

Although very little now survives from the medieval period, this visit is recommended for several uniquely impressive features. An important and continuously occupied locality from the 7th C BC, the Christian buildings were destroyed by the Arabs, but later rebuilt. Now, not far from the huge Roman brick-lined cisterns, the main surviving buildings are of the monastery, overlooking Souda Bay. The only church building is a late chapel, but there are massive and extensive outbuildings; the talus on the N and S sides of the main structure must be a Venetian addition.

For a medieval specialist there is little of specific interest here, but Aptera illustrates well the continuous use of a huge classical site right through the late antique and medieval period, and the magnificent outlook that it offers across the mouth of Souda Bay to the Akrotiri peninsula offers many resonances, both mythological and historic.

Aradena   Αράδενα

(Nomos: Khania.)
Church of Mikhael Arkhangelos.*
Normally locked; key in Anapoli. (See Pl. 4).
Some 1.5 km. beyond the scattered village of Anapoli you reach the deep gorge which separates you from the ruinous and deserted hamlet of Aradena. For the energetic there is still the footpath zigzagging down into the deep ravine and up again (until 1986 this was the only access to the village), or you can take the new steel bridge over the gorge.

This must be the most spectacularly sited church in Crete, and with its village it is the survival of a Greco-Roman settlement with fine natural defences. There was originally an EC basilica here, and the church now perched on the lip of the gorge occupies the space of its central nave; it is hard now to imagine that there was land space for the two side aisles, but the synthronon of the original basilica is prominent on the exterior. The present church, with its tall, rather inelegant cupola, is probably 14th C; the frescoes of its interior are of this period, but not in good condition; their style can be seen to derive from that developed by Pagomenos whose frescoes you can see in a number of churches in W Crete.

This is certainly a visit not to be missed if you are anywhere in the area; even if you are unable to gain access to the church interior, the site and the ruined village buildings will still make a memorable impression.

Arkhaia Elevtherna   Αρχαία Ελεύθρνα

(Nomos: Rethymnon).
Church of Sotiros Christos and Agios Ioannis (unlocked) and excavated EC basilica in late classical site** (unfenced).
Close to the Margarites end of this village a concrete track (quaintly signed to 'THE ANCIENTRY') winds down into the valley; it can take a car, but walking is advised.

In 500 m. you reach a modest double-nave church now used as a cemetery chapel; it was originally a domed, inscribed-cross church of

11th or even late 10th C, but a chapel was added by Venetian builders, probably in the 15th C. There may have been an earlier church on the site, but there is very little to confirm this. The only remaining fresco is a rather fragmentary 14th/15th C cupola image of the Pantocrator, and the same period may have seen the installation of a large floor tomb; the latter also seem elsewhere to have been a Venetian import, and it suggests that there was a Venetian settlement here of some prosperity.

This church was probably one of the most recent buildings of the locality, which had been inhabited since at least the 10th C BC, and the outlook here over the quiet valley below the acropolis of Arkhaia Elevtherna cannot have changed for centuries.

Continuing for 700 m. down the track you will come to the excavation of a large 2nd-4th C villa, with several rooms and some floor mosaic fragments still in place. Immediately adjacent to the E of this are the impressive excavated remains of an EC basilica, some 18 m. from threshold to apse. Some fragments of templon screens have been re-erected, there is fine opus sectile in the presbytery floor and remains of an ambo in the N nave. Mosaics in the narthex have been gravelled over, but the bases of three substantial classical herms are witness to a pre-Christian existence in this quiet valley.

The whole site combines the qualities of historical continuity over many centuries, complete isolation, highly interesting survivals, strong atmosphere and being relatively little known. Be sure to allow plenty of time for your visit.

Asomatos   Ασόματος

(near **Epano Arkhanes**). (*Nomos*: Rethymnon.)
Church of Agios Ioannis Theologos.★
(Locked; key in Epano Arkhanes).
Start from Epano Arkhanes (now often just 'Arkhanes') and ask for the key at the kapheneion beside the broad plateia with four bronze busts and a memorial. (The three-aisle basilica here is rather disappointing, but a small museum has been installed in its SW corner with some old service books, late icons, vestments, etc.) From the plateia take the small signed road to Vathypetro, and after 2.1 km. you will see the sign to Asomatos on the left; follow this (mostly concrete) road for 1.5 km., taking an early right turn, and at another right fork you will find the church on your left, just below the road among vineyards and beside two oak trees.

The building is a very simple early 14th C hall church, but the interest is in its interior, which offers an unusually complete fresco scheme dated to 1347 by the inscription of the founder, Michael Patsidiotes. The style of the frescoes shows no great refinement, but their vigorous directness is particularly impressive and the condition quite good. Of interest is the Deesis composition in the sanctuary, where St John Theologos has replaced the more usual image of St John the Baptist, and besides conventional NT feast scenes in the nave there are some from the apocryphal legend of St John.

The interior is quite dark, so a torch will help, but its authenticity repays the trouble of seeking it out.

Avdou   Αβδού

(*Nomos*: Irakleio).
1) Church of Agios Antonios.★ (Open.)
Approaching from the N, turn left on entering the village, and you will find the church occupying a small plateia in about 100 m.

It is a simple, 14th C, barrel-vaulted hall church of modest size, but its frescoes are of particular interest. They are datable by style to the early 14th C, and at first sight may appear to be in poor condition, but much of the painted area is in fact the intonaco, or underpainting, of fresco buon, or true fresco; this means that the upper layer has gone, but we are left with very sharply defined and durable painted images. The artist was clearly conversant with Italian practice in terms of technique, and some of the more emotional qualities of such scenes as the Crucifixion (N side) could also derive from this area, although the elaborately furnished table of the Last Supper (also N vaulting) is a Cretan speciality. The vivid image of the Meeting of Peter and Paul (S side) is not common in Crete, and may also owe something to Italian influence.

2) Church of the Panagia.★ (Locked; key in kapheneion).
Some 200 m. to SE of Agios Antonios, in open space on the edge of the village.

While the chief interest in Agios Antonios lies in its interior, here the main characteristics can be appreciated from the outside. Its design is that of a cupola over a cruciform plan, but with the E and W bays extended equally; the quite tall, broad drum of the cupola is carried on squinches over the angles of the crossing, and has four tall lancet windows. This is probably a later 15th C building, with very clear Venetian influence, and the belfry on the S gable is the only later addition. Unfortunately no frescoes survive in the interior; this is doubly regrettable, as features such as the generally high quality of the masonry, the quite elaborate door framing and the attractive brick pattern in the top of the drum of the cupola suggest that the founder's means would have been sufficient to have initiated an interior of comparable richness.

This quiet village, with its contrasting churches and only a few km. S of Limin Khersonisou, makes a rewarding objective for a half day's excursion.

Axos   Αξός

(*Nomos:* Rethymnon.)
Five churches,** of which two are roofless.
The three most interesting are:

1) Church of Agia Irene. (Locked; key in first shop to N).
Easily seen beside the main road that traverses the upper part of the village.

The first feature of this church that you will notice is its quite elaborate cupola, carefully restored in recent decades, with a small arcade around it below the tiling; looking further it can be seen how there would originally have been twelve colonettes round the drum, and their supporting corbels are still in place. More importantly, it can be seen that this small but attractive church in fact began as a centrally planned, domed Greek cross inscribed within a massive, almost square, base; this is partly concealed by the separate pitched roofs over the N and S arms and W door. What is exceptional is that the E bay was later extended to form a single hall nave, so leaving the original cruciform nave to serve as a narthex. The relative dates of these two phases may not be far apart; the first building is probably later 13th/14th C, and the second of 15th C; the interior is bare plaster, with the surviving fresco fragments left in the apse too feint to be an accurate guide as to its date.

2) Basilica of Agia Paraskevi. Roofless and unenclosed.
This ruined 3-aisle basilica is just below the main road that runs through the upper part of the village. Its three apses are still standing, and they indicate that this building began as a single-nave hall church, to which chapels were later added to N and S; this enlargement was not accompanied by an extension to the W, so the proportions of the interior are now almost square, with a large narthex running across all three aisles. As with Agia Irene, the period over which these changes were made may not have been very long; the original building may have been 12th C, and the lateral chapels added during the 13th – 14th C; there are some quite impressive fresco fragments on the S wall which are probably 14th C.

3) Church of Arkhangelos Mikhael. Roofless and unenclosed.

Descending further into the village, you will find the quite formidable N wall of this church overlooking the main plateia. It is immediately clear that this is a double-nave church, and the building detail indicates a date well into the Venetian period – probably 15th C. It has been an impressive building, and such features as the finely cut cushion caps on the piers dividing the two naves indicate a building of some quality. While the immediate indications all suggest that this is one of the few churches built as a double-nave structure ab initio, with the wall height appearing too great for a single nave with a later addition, there are a few indications that shed some doubt on this unified plan. The naves are not quite identical in width, the S apse is at a slight angle, and a corbel for roof vaulting on the N wall is considerably lower than that on the S; these features do not prohibit a unified building history, but encourage a critical viewer to decide the matter for himself. There are traces of fresco in both apses, but too slight to help an enquirer.

Biranepiskopi   Βιρανεπισκοπή

(*Nomos*: Rethymnon).
Church of Agios Dimitrios.* Partly ruined, doorless and can be entered.
Leave the village by the road signed to Elefthera; take the second road on the right, and you will see the church 1 km. further on the right, occupying a broad looping bend in the road.

Now abandoned and partly ruined, this quite sizeable church, set in open country, must have been the seat of the local bishop, and probably a 14th C foundation. In form it is a triple-nave basilica, but a small, domed chamber has been built on to the SE corner; this may have been a funerary chapel, but there are no frescoes in this or any other part of the interior. A peculiarity of the interior is that in the dome of the added chamber and in the barrel-vault of the S and central aisles a considerable number of ceramic tubes have been set; one explanation for this could be that the building was converted for use as a Turkish bath, and this might also have involved the construction of the SE chamber.

Although clearly just a shadow of its original form, this must at one time have been quite an impressive building, and would repay conservation. There are the negligible ruins of another basilica in the vicinity of the village, and it may be that this foundation was a later replacement for the bishop's seat.

Bizari
Βιζάρι

(*Nomos*: Rethymnon).
Ruined basilica of Servitos. * Fenced, but can be entered.
In the village turn right opposite the Post Office, and some 800 m. down this road take a side track signed (inexplicably) to ELLINIKA; a short way down here, beside a reservoir, is the basilica.

This was the site of a sizeable Roman town; however, the substantial remains of quite a large triple-nave basilica that you find here, with walls rising to a considerable height, is thought for various reasons to be 8th C. There is just a trace of the synthronon left, and although no caps are now to be seen, five of the eight columns that lined the nave are still here, and of particular interest at the entrance to the presbytery are the cleanly cut slots for the erection of marble screening slabs. The presence of two small, rounded apses flanking the main apse is one of the reasons for proposing an 8th C date, and although not properly visible now, the excavations revealed in the S of the three apses the stepped recess of a tiled font; this would further confirm the relatively late date of the basilica, as in earlier centuries the font would have been housed in a separate baptistry.

This is one of the three or four most interesting basilica sites on Crete, and you should have it to yourself. (The small church on the summit of a hill at the edge of the village is of medieval date, but has little of interest to show.)

Bizariano (Pigi)
Μπιζαριανό (Πηγή)

(*Nomos*: Irakleion).
Church of Agios Panteleimon. **
(Usually locked – see below).
Two turnings to the S of village of Pigi are signed to "Byzantine church and Paradise Tavern"; the dirt roads each run uphill for some 600 m. before reaching the church on its shady hillside terrace. If the church is locked the landlady of the Paradise Tavern just below to the W will ring the bell in a way that summons the man with the key, and she will be anxious to offer you refreshment while he comes.

The church is remarkable in several ways: considering its rural location it is large, even for a 3-aisle basilica; it has the most lavish use of spolia in the area (where it is not uncommon); and the formation of the NW column of the church from four caps must be unique. The spolia provide us with the main clue to the church's history; the fragments on the exterior of the S wall are 6th/7th C, and the caps may be 5th/6th C, so it must be assumed that an EC basilica formerly stood here. Its rebuilding may have taken place in the 11th or early 12th C, and certainly must antedate the coming of the Venetians; the substantial triple-arch window in the main apse, with other details of masonry, suggests the earlier date. The remaining frescoes on the interior are later (13th / 14th C), but impressive, with the Communion of the apostles in the apse and standing saints on the N wall being particularly effective. The reason for the column being made from caps must be a matter of surmise.

This is certainly one of the more outstanding churches of the island, and should not be missed.

Dories   Δόριες

(*Nomos*: Lasithi.)
Church of Agios Konstantinos and Agia Eleni.*
Locked; key with papas in nearest house to NE.
Easily seen on right of the road on entering the village from Elounda.

Although this church was at one time the katholikon of a monastery (some older surrounding monastic buildings are still visible) it has been rebuilt, and the only reason for recommending this visit is the unusual quality of the icons still kept here. A large icon of the Virgin Pantanassa has a partial silver *reza* and a painted frame with portraits of the apostles; although there is some overpainting this is still very impressive, and its later 14th C date makes it the earliest icon in Crete. A less interesting and somewhat later icon of the Crucifixion is attached to the reverse. The other focus of interest is the pair of large doors in the 18th C iconostasis painted with figures of Christ the Great High Priest, and the three Doctors of the church; they are fine quality Cretan painting in a style very close to that of the great 16th C artist Michael Damaskinos.

The church has been fitted with a complex modern alarm system, which gives an indication of the value in which these icons are rightly held. Their location in a relatively isolated village church gives them a far more convincing and realistic context than a modern museum would provide.

Elounda   Ελούντα

(*Nomos*: Lasithi).
Floor mosaic of EC basilica.** Gated but open. (See Pl. 1).

After traversing most of the village going N, take acute right turn, and follow the road over a causeway towards three windmills; the mosaic is 100 m. further on.

The surviving floor mosaic can be easily seen, and is the finest and most complete in Crete. The area that you will find preserved inside a low wall must have occupied the central nave of a triple-nave basilica, and has been dated by style to the second half of the 5th C. Its richly inventive design, including areas of both geometric ornament and figural panels with lively families of dolphins, also contains three inscriptions; these provide the names of individuals who must have been the patrons of the scheme, although no clue as to date. In the large central roundel, the texts mention the mosaics as the gifts of Theodoulos, Epiphanios and Antaxios, while the frame of one of the dolphin mosaics simply says: 'Heliodoros makes this donation for his own salvation'.

For a number of reasons this is a highly rewarding visit to a site that is only minimally developed; the method of preserving the mosaic area by surrounding it with a low wall is particularly successful and has the advantage of allowing a slightly raised view-point.

Episkopi (Kissamos)   Επισκοπή (Κίσσαμος)

(*Nomos*: Khania.)
Church of Arkhangelos Mikhail (rotunda).**
Usually open daily, morning and evening.
Well signed with a large notice on the main road coming S from Kolimbari.

The design of this church is unique in Crete (and indeed virtually so among all the Greek islands), and its relative fame means that it has been made quite easy to find. The original rotunda was probably built in the 7th / 8th C, and externally its most striking feature is the massive dome formed in five concentric steps. The prevailing opinion now is that at some later date (perhaps late 10th / 12th C) this was surrounded by quite extensive building forming flanking aisles, a narthex and chapels providing SE and NE corners; as this has naturally detracted from the monolithic character of the original structure it seems most logical to regard it as a later phase of the building, rather than as a single unified concept. The entrance is now at the SE corner and you only enter the rotunda proper after going through to the narthex. Here the height of the cupola seems almost exaggerated by its parabolic internal profile, and the deep openings in the walling of the original rotunda disclose its massive thickness; the electric light now installed is essential to appreciate the forms of the building. The closest comparison must be with Agios Giorgios in Thessaloniki, which is a palatial building of undeniable magnificence, but the rotunda here is much more modest in scale and the massiveness of the cupola construction suggests a less experienced building team.

There is a small area of mosaic floor in the SW sector of the rotunda, but this appears too fragmentary a basis for a supposition that the site was originally occupied by an EC basilica. The excavations outside the E end certainly show no signs of such an origin. There are fragmentary frescoes from three different periods, the earliest probably 10th C, and others from the 12th, but all too damaged to be of great significance. As to the date of the rotunda, it seems most probable that it ante-dates the Arab invasion of 824; the surrounding building can then be dated to the period after the reconquest of the island by the Byzantines in 961, and may be as early as the late 10th C. The name certainly implies that this was the seat of a bishop, and the expansion of the building can again be associated with the return of Byzantine rule and the re-assertion of diocesan organisation that would have occurred at this point.

The inherent interest of this unique building makes it one of the few essential objectives in the area W of Khania.

Episkopi (S of Mourtzana)   Επισκοπή

(*Nomos*: Rethymnon).
Church of Agios Ioannis.** Roofless and doorless; can be entered.
Just beside the road in the centre of the village, on the right if approaching Mourtzana.

This must at one time have been one of the most impressive churches in Crete, much smaller than Gortys but with its finely cut limestone apse giving it an exceptionally rich appearance. (The road here would, of course, have been carrying the main traffic along the N coast of the island, now superseded by the modern coast road.) This expenditure was due to the fact that it was one of the first foundations made after the purchase of the island by the Venetians in the early years of the 13th C, and they no doubt wished to create a sufficiently powerful impression. An important clue to its later appearance is the lintel over the door in the N wall, which bears the date CDLXVIII and the escutcheon of a bishop Sorreto. While the design can be said to show slight Venetian influence, the main forms of the original building must be regarded as Greek; outside, the lower arcading of the apse with the restrained decorative insertion of brick in the lower arches, and inside (as you will see) the five cupolas that were part of the original building, are all completely Greek.

But confronting the finely cut limestone of the upper row of windows it is clear that we are looking at what in a Western cathedral would be called a clerestory, and the finely chiselled cutting of the cusps over the blind niches of the upper storey will be due to the 1568 renovation. The caps of the main window seem possibly to be re-used pieces from an earlier building, and there is certainly a templon fragment inserted in the exterior of the S wall which probably came from a church here prior to the 13th C. Entering the S aisle the proportion of the interior seems unexpectedly broad for its length (almost square, in fact), but there would have been a narthex that is now demolished. There are still blind cupolas over the N and S apse chambers where the apses still stand, and there would formerly have been two more over the W ends of the aisles; the spacing of the four piers that supported the main cupola indicates a very substantial scale (it was still standing early this century). Frescoes surviving in the N (prothesis) cupola are of a 14th C painting of Pentecost, but those in the central barrel vault and the S cupola are now illegible, although Gerola saw a Virgin with angels there. The 1568 renovation also provided the two new windows in N and S walls.

This village is a rewarding objective, as besides the impressive church there are extensive 17th / 18th C farm buildings across the road to the S in remarkably fine condition, with an olive press still in use, and which the farmer's wife is anxious to display. They could well have been attached to the church and so provided for the bishop's farming needs.

Evangelismos   Ευαγγελισμός

(*Nomos*: Irakleio).
Church of the Evangelismos (the Annunciation).*
Coming from Kastellia go through Arkhangelos, and in 3 km. you will reach Evangelismos on a low hill.

The church is in the centre of the village (key in the house across the road from the NW corner, or in the kapheneion close to N side of the church). The most striking feature of the building, which is of a basically cruciform plan, is the massively monumental character of its exterior, with a very high transverse vault and a huge buttress absorbing the single apse; the height of the cross vault is emphasised by being narrower than the E and W cruciform arms. There are no later additions other than the E buttress, and there can never have been a dome. The interest here, besides the unusual vaulting, lies principally in the frescoes which cover much of the upper W vault and on what may be a tomb in the S wall; you will find a number of Genesis scenes, including very individual renderings of Adam and Eve in Paradise, the Communion of the Apostles, and the Second Coming occupying the middle of the vault. These can be dated by style to the mid 14th C, and this is probably also the period of the church's construction.

Fourni   Φουρνί

(*Nomos*: Lasithi).
Church of Agios Ioannis Theologos.*
Easily found at the upper (SE) edge of the village; key above the door or at nearest house.

The interest of this simple, three-aisle rural church is the relative rarity of a design of this kind, with a raised central roof and side aisles without apses or windows. Either it was built as a standard single nave hall church, to which side aisles were added at an early stage, or it is a rare type (for this location) of a three-aisle church (a tiny 'basilica') completely unaltered by such additions as a narthex or side chapels. There are no frescoes and its proportions (of a width that is almost half as much again as its length) are easy to read. Whatever its original design, its date must most readily be put in the mid 14th C.

Frankokastello.   Φραγκοκάστελλο

Med: Castelfranco. (*Nomos*: Rethymnon).
Venetian fortress.* Gated but open. (See Pl. 21).
Easily seen from the road that follows the S coast, a 3 km. (signed) detour brings you directly to the fortress.

The sandy coast is quite shallow here, and this made it an easy beach for pirates' landings; their raids became so troublesome that the Venetian Senate (via their ambassador) was petitioned by the local populace to provide protection. The result was the building of this fortress in 1371-74, located beside the sea to ward off the raids. Gerola published a photograph which shows that at the turn of the century a Venetian lion and the escutcheons of the Querini and Dolfin families could be seen over the entrance. At first sight it is hard to imagine that what you see today is of this date, but closer inspection largely confirms a 14th C origin. Its four-square plan (some 60 m. x 35 m., including the projecting corner towers) is very simple; the well-cut quoins speak very much of both the period and the Venetian builders.

The walls are not particularly massive, and they have a sentry-walk all round the interior at the height of the continuous castellation, but no significant provision for even modest artillery (compare it mentally with the later sophistication of Rethymnon or Irakleio). The interior has remains of successive phases of building, some of it almost certainly Turkish, but what gives the fort a feeling of being much later is a sequence of openings cut at 2 m. height in the walls facing on to the sea; these are already present in Gerola's photographs, but they will be Turkish as they have pre-cast concrete lintels, and were clearly for use as military look-out points. Without this wholly un-medieval feature, the entire design becomes far easier to see as a strong-point that only had to house a small garrison and withstand random pirate assaults, but no well-organised military siege; these walls would soon have collapsed under even modest cannon fire. Again, the function determined the form, and so a 14th C date would seem to be completely correct for most of this unusually well-preserved fortress.

Gortys / Gortyna   Γόρτυς / Γόρτυνα

(*Nomos*: Irakleio).
Basilica of Agios Titos, Roman odeion, remains of second basilica.*** Enclosed site, open every day 8.30-15.00; entrance charge.
Travelling E from Phaistos, you cannot miss the huge mass of the E end of the basilica of Agios Titos standing 15 m. high beside the road.

For the Byzantinist this must be the prime architectural site in Crete, its importance due to the traditional association with St Titus and the immensely impressive ruins of the church dedicated to him here. From a number of New Testament references we know that St Paul sent his disciple of this name on various missions to Epiros and Dalmatia, and left him behind in Crete to appoint elders in each city, but it is the 4th century scholar Eusebius who provided the principal source for the importance of Titus here, as he wrote that Titus was appointed to be "bishop of the churches of Crete" (*Hist. Eccl.*, 3.4). Titus was traditionally buried at Gortys, which under the Romans was the capital of the island, where his remains were venerated for many centuries. He is the patron saint of the island, and the 15th century Florentine Christoforo Buondelmonti was told, when he visited Gortys c. 1418, that Titus was a descendant of Minos. Although his head was taken to Venice by the Venetians for safe keeping after the Arab invasion, where it is still kept in St Mark's, when Sir Richard Guylford visited here in 1506 he wrote: "In Candy also is the olde churche where of Tytus was bishop... I sawe the grave of sayd Tytus".

The huge church here was built to a highly complex plan, which contains elements of both a basilica and a domed Greek cross; so much of the bema is still standing that the E end needs little imagination to restore it to its original form, with the curved surfaces of niches flanking the entrances to the broad central apse from the small lateral apses and their adjoining chambers, probably pastophoria. In the main space of the naos the bases of the two W piers still define the huge extent of the dome, and the apsidal forms to N and S of this space would have expanded and enriched this space still further. The ambo in the Historical Museum, Irakleio would have been sited centrally in this area. But the W end would have been the most visually complex part of the church, with a deep W gallery continuing round to N and S on both sides above the side aisles and the inner and outer narthexes and atrium extending the building even further to the W; foundations of this area are all still visible. In spite of this great expenditure, the decoration may have been relatively simple; you can see some capitals and a fragment of carved marble from the original templon with formalised vinescroll ornament in relief, and the ambo (as can be seen in the Historical Museum, Irakleio) would not have been a spectacularly ornamented piece. No mosaic tesserae have been found to suggest a more sumptuous interior; the lament of Buondelmonti, that he saw "1500 columns of marble or stone, upright or fallen," can be taken as an exaggeration. The sophistication of the design, however, does suggest a building team from a major centre either in Asia Minor or from Constantinople. The grave that was here in 1506 is no longer present, and no inscriptions survive to give an accurate date, but the design and decoration as a whole suggest an initial construction date in the 6th century (Krautheimer suggests very late 6th century). Earthquakes brought much damage on the city of Gortys, and its destruction was completed by the Arabs in the late 7th century; the church was re-dedicated in the 10th century on the recovery of the island.

Among the extensive classical survivals on this site which it is well worth examining are those to the NW of Agios Titos; here the extensive excavations of a Roman odeion, last reconstructed in the 2nd C AD, are impressive and must provide a point of comparison with the similar survival at Kampos on Ikaria, where it was built into another palatial structure. Beyond is the famous curved arcade which displays the unique 5th C BC Law Code of Gortys carved in a row of stone tablets.

Besides this there are not only further classical remains on the nearby acropolis, which was probably fortified in the 7th / 8th C, but also three further excavated Christian buildings can be seen of the six that are known to have existed here. Two of these are now too overgrown to make viewing very rewarding, but the ground plan of a third large basilica indicates the long term importance of this locality. Almost opposite the site entrance is a road signed to Mitropolis, and in the angle of this and the road running past Agios Titos are the overgrown foundations of one of these complex buildings. Some 300 m. further on down the minor road you will find that it passes straight across the transept of a recently excavated major basilica, with its extensive floor area occupying both sides of the road. It is enclosed by a fence and nothing is now standing here, but huge broken columns and a fine 5th C cap suggest considerable magnificence, although you will find that areas of floor mosaic are gravelled over. This may have been an earlier bishop's seat (hence the name of the nearby hamlet) which suffered destruction, as a result of which the present church of Agios Titos was built. You might also wish to view a further substantial ruin which appears some 50 m. into a field to the East.

The extent and interest of Gortys means that if possible you should allow at least a clear half-day to fully absorb what the area has to offer.

Irakleio   Ηράκλειο

Med: Candia (*Nomos*: Irakleio).

From 827 the city was the site of the first capital of the island under the Arabs, who on their invasion established their headquarters here as Chandax; it was this name which provided the medieval Candia, which came to be used for the whole island. (It has actually only been the modern administrative capital of Crete since 1971.)

The Historical and Ethnographical Museum.***
Open 09.00-17.00, Sat. 09.00-14.00; closed Sundays and holidays; entry charge.

The handsome neoclassical house, close to the seafront and with its entrance facing the Xenia hotel, which has been the home of the museum for several decades has now been given a large and well-designed modern extension that much increases its capacity.

To the right on entering is an excellent large-scale model of the city, and you are strongly advised to start by absorbing what can be learnt from the commentary, as it provides an invaluable orientation for the history and topography of Irakleio.

Thereafter, the medievalist should begin by viewing the sculpture collection in the basement of the old building. Besides some good but unspectacular classical pieces there is a considerable range of EC and later sculpture which is well displayed and will extend understanding of buildings elsewhere in Crete. Among the exhibits is the 6th C ambo from Agios Titos, Gortys, and although partly reconstructed its simple marble forms should be held in mind when visiting this premier site; it is perhaps surprising that such a grandly spectacular interior should have such a relatively simple centrepiece, with the broad, lozenge-shaped mouldings enclosing a relief of a single small bird. A collection of caps includes some fine 5th C examples, and there are some interesting Greek and Latin sepulchral inscriptions. Among the secular sculpture here are three medieval well-heads; these are intriguingly problematic, as they all seem to date from before the Venetian arrival, yet there is no known tradition for monolithic, carved Byzantine well-heads of this kind. Venice, on the other hand, which had nothing but well-water, with no springs or running water, had many hundreds of such well-heads; the design and decoration of all three here seem possibly to be more likely to derive from this long Venetian tradition (an art form in its own right) than from any other, and so one must conclude that they were most probably imported – either before or after the Venetian arrival. The two more richly carved (one is square, with hunting scenes and two animals drinking, the other rounded with a tree and a figure holding a shield) are probably 12th C, and the third, with very simple arcading, 10th/11th C.

On the floor above are displays of 13th C frescoes from the church of Agios Giorgios, Amari, which as a small, domeless, single-cell church is typical of many that are found in Crete, a range of 13th-14th C detached frescoes, and some icons and part of the iconostasis from the Panagia Gouverniotissa, Potamies. Perhaps the most exceptional area of the collection here is the display of Byzantine and Venetian jewellery, lead seals, Byzantine steatite reliefs and cast bronze figures. There is also on view an outstanding collection of Byzantine, Arabic and Venetian gold and silver coins: about 100 gold nomismata dating from the emperor Nikiforos Focas (the re-conqueror of Crete in 961) but concentrating on the 11th and 12th C, with many further Byzantine silver and copper coins, and coins of the Venetian doges Giovanni and Andrea Dandolo and Giovanni Gradenigo. Further cases display seals, bread-stamps and a mould for casting medallions; bronze candelabra and a 6th C hanging disc for lights from Gortys are also here, as well as much medieval ceramics, mainly with Italianate forms and glazes.

Finally, with a room to itself on the ground floor, is displayed a painting by the island's most famous artist son: Domenikos Theotokopoulos, or 'El Greco'; he has succeeded here in creating a charming genre scene of travellers being greeted as they arrive at a completely Byzantine version of the Justinianic monastery of St Catherine at the foot of Mount Sinai.

The upper floor is given over to displays of ethnographic material, and historic documentation of episodes such as the German occupation of Crete in World War II.

A visit here cannot be recommended too strongly, as there is no other chance to see such an exceptional collection of sculpture, *ars sacra* and coins anywhere else in Crete or in any other of the Greek islands.

Just some 60 m. to the E of the Museum there rises the roofless but impressive shell of the main Dominican foundation in Irakleio, **St Peter Martyr***. Built originally in the first half of the 13th C, but much repaired, it is easily the largest relic of the city's medieval past, and although it is closed and under permanent restoration, enough can be seen to form a strong impression of the impact that the mendicant orders must have made; it was converted to being the mosque of Sultan Ibrahim in the Turkish period. Beyond the E end an area called 'Castelli' is being excavated to a substantial depth, and pottery from before the Arab invasion has been found.

Beyond to the W and down beside the harbour are the 16th C Venetian Arsenals, built on an immensely impressive scale to allow each enclosure to hold a galley and its oars.

The church of Agia Aikaterini of Sinai.***
Open Monday – Saturday 9.0-13.00 and Tuesday, Thursday & Friday 17.00-20.00. Closed Sundays and holidays; entry charge.

This mid-16th C church houses what is called an **Icon Collection**, but following an expansion and re-hanging of the display, what is now on view approximates more to a comprehensive museum of Byzantine art. Besides offering an opportunity to view a major collection of icons that demonstrates the development of some of the main phases of Cretan icon painting, there are some fresco fragments and a number of MSS and liturgical artefacts that broaden the context for which the icons would have been created.

Starting from the W end of the N wall there are three fine 15th C icons, with that of Christ being perhaps the most impressive in quality, but another with a miracle scene of St Fanourios and the Virgin coming to the aid of seamen in a storm, painted below a Gospel scene, which is perhaps the most unusual. These are the main icons from the Byzantine period, but the extension of the N crossing into what was the Byzantine church of Agioi Deka allows for an interesting display of 14th C frescoes from the church of Patsos, Amari; that of the Communion of the Apostles, with the magnificently adorned robes of three church fathers, is particularly impressive. The displays of later church silver and vestments (manikia, epigonatia and a small epitaphios among them) are of high quality. But the pride of the collection is the sequence of icons by Michael Damaskinos on the S wall; he was born in Irakleio c.1530, and died here some time after 1591, and is rightly regarded as one of the two or three most important of all post-Byzantine icon painters, and this is the largest concentration of his works. Among the three most noteable and profound of them is perhaps the first on the E end of the S wall, depicting the 1st Council of Nicaea; Constantine and Pope Sylvester preside, while above, St Peter of Alexandria converses with the small figure of a youthful Christ in torn robes, who refers to the heretic Arius, seen below; the date of 1591 makes this the last dated work of the artist. That of the Holy Liturgy again exemplifies the function of the icon in presenting a range of ideas in one image; the different ranks of angels (powers, thrones, archangels, etc.) flank the central image of the Trinity, while above three angels carry an epitaphios (an example is displayed in the case to the left) as it is borne in the Good Friday services. The icon of the Virgin in the Burning Bush is another of these major panels, and linked strongly with this church; the subject came to represent the Virgin Birth, and here is surrounded by episodes of Mosaic OT history and the burial of St Catherine on Sinai, while the poet St John Damascene comments from the right. The other three icons are for reasons of condition and later overpainting perhaps less impressive, but all demonstrate the artist's ability to fuse western and Byzantine imagery into a unified pictorial language.

This is undoubtedly an outstanding collection of Cretan icon painting, not possible to match anywhere else. Icons by Cretan painters are known from documentary evidence to have been exported in huge numbers, particularly to Venice, and what is here forms a unique record of this strong island tradition.

As mentioned above, the city's buildings offer few survivals from its medieval past; the Archaeological Museum occupies the site of one of the larger Franciscan houses in Crete, but a smaller W monastic church, **St Mary 'dei Cruciferi'**, stands at the corner of Odos Markou Mousourou and Odos Diktaiou Antrou. This was a mendicant order of the 'Crutched Friars', or 'Cross-bearing Friars', an order, suppressed in 1656, whose members wore a prominent cross on their habit, but the church is sometimes called 'St Mary of the Crusaders'; the interior, although keeping its original triple-nave proportions and columns during its time as a mosque, is now completely modernised and serves an Orthodox congregation, but N and S exterior walls still retain corbels which would have been the supports of monastic buildings, those on the S probably a cloister roof. There was also a hospital for the old here, which received many legacies.

The other main survival from Venetian rule is the imposing church of **Agios Markos**, opposite the Morosini Fountain, which is now used as an art gallery; it was the original 'flagship' church of Venetian Crete in the 13th C, but after many vicissitudes, including vandalism during World War II, it can now only be regarded as a modern reconstruction, although Venetian tombs are displayed at the E end.

The most evident part of the Venetian fortifications is the fortress of the **'Rocca al Mare'** reached down a broad jetty protecting the Inner Harbour. Although the original building was 13th C, what you see today dates (according to the inscription over the N entrance) from 1523; it is worth visiting (open every day 09.00-17.00, entry charge), as although the design of its cavernous ground floor chambers is dominated by the need for heavy artillery, it has a fully authentic quality and is largely unrestored by the Turks or later. The cannon emplacements and observation points continue on the upper level, and lions of St Mark face both land-wards and sea-wards; it was never taken by the Turks in 1669, being surrendered with the rest of the city.

The huge Venetian land fortifications, built mainly in the late 16th-17th C, receive little attention, although from the air are immensely impressive and withstood the Turkish siege for 21 years; modern building encroaches further and further upon them, making it mostly impossible to assess what are certainly post-medieval constructions.

Itanos   Ἴτανος

(*Nomos*: Lasithi).
Ruins of EC basilica.★ Unfenced and open.
There are quite good road signs to this site close to the NE tip of Crete, but the basilica itself is unmarked.

You will find this rather a dispersed site, and the basilica (the chief survival) is some 200 m. N of the arrival point; it overlooks a small bay on the further side of the small headland on which ruins of other early buildings survive, and it is possible that this was also a temple-site in classical times. There are many fallen columns and other spolia, and the plan of the church as it now appears is that of a broad, three-aisle basilica, its main apse embedded in the hillside but with clear foundations of semicircular exedras to N and S of the centre aisle. This has been explained by the ruins being those of two superimposed churches; the first church would have been a triple-aisle EC basilica in the tradition of those on other sea-side locations (e.g. Khersonisos, Sougia and Elounda) and would have been of quite broad proportions; this must have collapsed, as at some later date a domed church with the same lateral semi-domes as at Gortys was built so that it just occupied the central aisle. The period in which this occurred is unknown, except that it most probably post-dates Agios Titos at Gortys; it could therefore be either an 8th / early 9th C building of the time before the Arab invasion, or of the 11th / 12th C after their expulsion (in this respect being comparable with Episkopi, Kissamos). There are no decorative elements (caps, templon fragments, etc.) left at the site to fill out the picture left by the ground plan, although a small fragment of floor mosaic was excavated near the W end. The dedication of the church is unknown.

The remoteness of the site means that it is little visited, but the journey is well worth making and the remains here reward a leisurely examination.

Kadros   Κάδρος

(*Nomos*: Khania).
Church of the Panagia.★ Normally locked; the key is kept at farmer's house immediately adjoining to NW.
Travelling S towards Palaiokhora, take a small, poorly surfaced road on the left which climbs to the hamlet of Kadros; the turning to the church runs slightly downhill on the right 1.3 km. from the main road (if you reach a sign to the Archaeological Site you have come too far).

This single chamber hall church is surprisingly large for its rural setting, and offers as its main interest a largely complete fresco scheme covering much of the interior; its condition is quite good. There is an inscription to the left of the door above the figures of Constantine and Helena, and what may be a donor figure on the right, but neither gives an accurate date. The style is strongly reminiscent of other mid-14th C schemes, however, and among the fairly predictable range of subjects is a graphic image of the Betrayal, and a scene of the Torments of the damned but lacking a full scene of the Last Judgement.

Kalamas   Καλαμάς

(*Nomos*: Rethymnon).
Church of Agios Giorgios.*
In the centre of the village; key kept in lock.

There is an element of surprise in coming across this quite impressive building in such a modest village, but its unexpected sophistication can be explained by its being the seat of the local bishop in the centuries after the Byzantine re-conquest of the island. Its basic 11th C structure of a centrally planned inscribed-cross design has had a narthex added later (probably in the 12th C), and a large exonarthex built on later still; the drum of the dome is unusually high and a further interest is provided by the sophisticated use of a W arch to replace the two W piers that would otherwise have supported it, so increasing the visitor's sense of space on entering. An unusual external tomb occupies the N side. Its interior is mostly plain, but fresco fragments survive in the W vault of scenes from a St George cycle, and both prothesis and diakonikon have retained portraits of bishops in their vaults which are contemporary with the church's foundation. This emphasis may be due to the function of the church as the former bishop's seat.

Kefali   Κεφάλι

(*Nomos*: Khania).
Church of Sotiros Christou.*
On entering the village travelling due W, a concrete path leads down to the left beside the first building you come to; the church is some 100 m. down the path. The key may be in the door; if not, ask at the kapheneion.

The church here is a simple barrel-vaulted hall, and its chief interest is in its frescoes, which are dated by an inscription to 1320. Their subject-matter is for the most part quite standard, but their style is surprisingly refined, and this gives them considerable power even though their condition is patchy. Scenes on the N wall of a large Anastasis and of the Three Maries at the tomb, with a military saint on the N arch are all particularly notable.

A visit here is recommended as providing experience of a comprehensive and securely dated fresco scheme, which is usually easy of access.

Kera   Κερά

(*Nomos*: Lasithi)
Moni Panagia Kardiotissa.★★ Normally open 8.00-1.00 and 15.30-19.00.

Easily seen down a 50 m. side-road to the right on entering Kera from the direction of Mokhos.

Although the building history of this much-visited convent is quite complex, with four phases of construction, they are all confined to the 14th C, and a careful restoration in the 1970's has consolidated the whole ensemble. The exterior has a much richer use of brick and tile than most Cretan 14th C building, particularly in an arcade on the W front and round the windows. You enter the most recent part of the building, the narthex, and can move freely past two piers into the main area of the naos, which formed the third building phase; the absence of a cupola means that this area, its three aisles making it broader than it is long, is free of any other piers or columns. The bema is the earliest part, dating from the early 14th C and forming little more than a chapel with three small, curved apses, and a further small chapel added in the NE corner may have been added as pastophorion. The frescoes have suffered some losses, but those remaining are impressive and readily visible, with some outstanding feast scenes; interesting is a small cycle of eight scenes of the Infancy of the Virgin in the bema, although two are broken into by later building, and the Ascension in the vault of the bema displays real grandeur; these are all early 14th C and hint at the exaggerated qualities of the Palaiologue art of the capital during this period. The fine figure of a female donor on the SW pier must commemorate the inception of some part of this ensemble.

Allow time to dwell on the various features of this convent in its peaceful valley, as it is one of the better preserved and accessible of the monastic buildings on Crete.

Khania   Χανιά

Italian: La Canea. (*Nomos*: Khania)

This town was effectively a Venetian foundation, and although it shared the centuries of Byzantine and (later) Turkish rule with the rest of Crete, it is the Venetian presence that has left the most substantial survivals. A 16th C traveller has left a disparaging account of life in the town, "which was the most evil-smelling he had ever known": at three o'clock in the afternoon a bell was sounded, and this was the signal for every household to empty its chamber-pots out of the window into the street below, and no fine was incurred if anyone below was in the way – they had been warned!

A Venetian kastro was built here in the 1250's, and in 1300 more money was voted by the Senate for its upkeep. The town's attractions were also evident to the Genoese, who managed to wrest it from the Venetians and hold it from 1266 to 1290. The **Venetian ramparts*** effectively enclosed the entire town, and substantial portions of them can still be seen down much of the length of Odos Sifaka. The re-use in them of classical spolia, including column drums, recalls the kastro on Naxos; this section may well have been constructed on the foundations of any Byzantine fortifications there may have been. Other sections of their 3 km. length, built in the 16th C, can be seen elsewhere, and perhaps most impressive of all are the huge vaulted structures of the arsenali by the harbour, comparable with those in Irakleio, each constructed to house one of the famous galleys. Churches built by the Venetians are also still in evidence, and Gerola lists 26 of which records exist; S. Rocco, with an inscription of 1630, is prominent but now disused, but the smaller Agioi Anargyroi nearby is still in use; its double nave design may account for its continued survival through Venetian and Turkish rule.

In 1898 Khania was made the first capital of an independent Crete, a rôle that it only gave up in 1971.

Khania Archaeological Museum.**
Open 8.30-15.00. Closed Mondays. Entrance charge.

For a medievalist, it has to be said that the building here is the most interesting feature. The display is modern and varied, with some fine individual exhibits, but is almost entirely of classical material, and inside some Byzantine and Venetian coins are all that can be seen from the post-classical period. The building itself, however, is the former 14th C church of San Francesco and formed the focus of quite a substantial Franciscan house.

The building was used as a mosque during the Turkish period, and its appearance has become complex over the centuries as additions were made; its initial plan seems to have formed quite a long nave with five bays, but the roof now has three sections, all of slightly different heights, and a series of small chapels down the N side was not balanced on the S. A substantial campanile occupied the SE corner, but the W wall is modern, and late last century Gerola's plan shows a further extension to the W of some 10 m. (now destroyed) which incorporated a minaret; the way the aisles vary in width over each section underlines the variety that the alterations have brought about, and the date of 1606 on a corbel in the W section confirms the sustained Venetian interest. Be sure to visit the pleasantly shaded courtyard occupying the S side of the exterior; besides the base of another minaret and a washing place, there are some good 5th C caps and the bowl of a Venetian fountain with four escutcheons.

Khersonisos   Χερσόνησος

(*Nomos*: Irakleio).
EC basilica on the headland acropolis. ★ Unenclosed.
A sign on the main road, which you can only see if you are approaching from the W, points to "Harbour and Byzantine Basilica"; follow the sea-side road through to the headland and you will find the ground plan of this large and superbly sited basilica.

Its dedication is unknown (it is referred to by archaeologists as Basilica B), and it was dated by Orlandos to the late 5th century. Now the remains are confined to a clearly defined ground plan and some areas of exposed floor mosaic and terracotta tiling – the mosaic fast eroding; the bases of eleven columns down each side of the nave indicate the aisle divisions. Two exceptional features of this fine site should be mentioned: one is its great size, with the threshold of the inner narthex to the apse measuring 37 m. and making it almost precisely as long as Agios Titos, Gortys; it would have seemed even larger originally, as there are also foundations of an outer narthex and a further structure added to the N side. The second is the finely carved classical marble sarcophagus lid dating from the 2nd century AD which was used as the base of the Christian altar here; it is not known how common this useage of pagan spolia for something as significant as an altar might have been, or if indeed any importance should be attached to it.

It should be mentioned that there was another early Christian basilica at Khersonisos, almost as large, and also with extensive floor mosaics; this (Basilica A) was on a site in the grounds of the modern Eri Beach Hotel, immediately beside the tennis courts. The site is now derelict.

Khersonisos must have been a thriving centre in late antiquity, with its two large basilicas serving an extensive population. Basilica B takes its place as one of the foremost of the early Christian sea-side sites in Crete, larger than Elounda and more prominent than Itanos.

Khora Sfakion   Κώρα Σφακιόν

(*Nomos*: Khania).

The main function now of this small fishing town is a staging post in the Samaria Gorge outing, but if you have the time its winding lanes disclose two **medieval churches.** One, which may well have been 13th C, is now ruined and abandoned, but the other, probably 14th C, is in use and has two unusual free-standing Venetian tombs in its churchyard which could well be 15th C. The most prominent feature of the town in the later medieval period was its kastro, which occupied a rocky outcrop overlooking the harbour from the W. Gerola gives no record of it before 1526, when it was strengthened by the Venetians, and in 1589 it is called a *palazzo fortificato*, implying a building more like the kastro of Astypalia. Its ruins can still be seen among trees looking down from the road descending into Sfakia from the E.

Khromonastiri   Χρομοναστήρι

(*Nomos*: Rethymnon).
Monastic church of Agios Eutykhios / Metokhion of Perdike.
Open and unused.
The road winds up through olive groves to the village some 11 km. S of Rethymnon; on your left before reaching the centre of the village a sign ("Perdike Metokhi") points down a badly surfaced track; after 1.5 km. you reach this site, where some farm buildings and a barking guard dog perpetuate the function of the metokhion.

The remote and idyllic valley is a tranquil setting for this 11th C domed, inscribed-cross church; the interior space is divided in an unusual way, with the piers supporting the cupola attached to the N and S walls and so intruding into the naos, and emphasising the E to W axis. There has been no substantial alteration made to the building, and some shadowy frescoes in the apse (an impressive deesis and standing saints) hint at what must originally have been an imposing interior.

Kitharida   Κιθαρίδα

(*Nomos*: Irakleio.)
Church of Panagia Eleoussa.
Closed and unused.
This very small village is not marked on all maps; to reach it, at S end of village of Pyrgou take a turning W signed to Pentamódi, and Kitharida is

some 5 km. further down this road as it winds down through vine-clad slopes. The church is on the S edge of the village, virtually surrounded by fields.

Fortunately it is the exterior of this church which offers all the interest, with two features of real note; there are no frescoes or other internal decorative features. The first form of the building as it now stands seems to have been a centrally-planned inscribed-cross design, but with the E end given particular emphasis by having a small cupola over each of the three equal apses – highly unusual in Crete, particularly in such a rural locality. A photograph from earlier this century shows a fourth, larger, cupola over the crossing; this must have collapsed, which explains the rather temporary-looking modern roofing of the naos. The transverse narthex is clearly later, and this is quite common, but very distinctive here is the display of 14 ceramic bowls set into the masonry of the W end wall; three of them are exceptionally good Hispano-mauresque ware of 15th / 16th C. All this indicates a role of some importance not suggested by the modern isolation of the village; the original church must have been not later than 13th C, and the narthex of the early 15th C, from which time the apparent importance of the village must have diminished.

The combination of this unusual church in its beautiful valley and with its unique ceramic decoration makes this a highly attractive objective, and within easy reach of Irakleio.

Kournas   Κουρνάς
(*Nomos*: Khania.)
Church of Agios Giorgios.*
Locked; key in the kapheneion on the left side of the bend in the road going to the church.
Easy to reach from the Khania-Rethymnon road, passing the only fresh-water lake in Crete; the church is prominent, and easily seen if you look up to the left of the road that winds up into the village.

The first sight that you will have of this church is of its four apses that look out over the approach road to the village; three of them are original to the late 12th C three-aisled church, and the fourth is that of a large parekklision added to the N side probably not long after. Apart from its quite striking exterior and position, the chief interest here is provided by the surviving 12th C frescoes which are of unusually impressive quality; the main area where they are left is in the apse, where the Communion of the apostles is painted above figures of bishops, with some other fragmentary scenes. The real sense of restrained but dynamic movement contained in the figures of the apostles approaching the patterned altar must be the work of a 12th C artist who had experience of major metropolitan trends, and is very reminiscent of the more extensive frescoes in Myriokefala.

Although not great in extent, the quality of what is left here means that it should not just be seen by those with more specialist interests; this is also a church that is easily found and readily accessible.

Kritsa   Κριτσά

(*Nomos*: Lasithi).
Church of Panagia Kera.***
Open 09.15-15.00 (Sundays -14.00); entry charge.
Signed on the right of the road from Agios Nikolaos, 1 km. E of village of Kritsa, at Logari.

This church has been adopted as the chief showpiece of Cretan church painting, and this public enthusiasm is indeed justified. Now supported by broadly spreading buttresses, the building grew in at least two phases between the 13th and mid 14th C; starting as a domed hall church, the two flanking chapels were added later, that on the N being dedicated to Agios Antonios and the S to Agia Anna. But it is the interior which provides the overwhelming interest here, with a mass of frescoes representing several phases of work between the 13th and 15th C. Among the many riches here you might particularly look out for the following: in the central nave the broad drum of the cupola has a largely unique fresco scheme, formed initially round the four heavily rounded cross ribs (itself a highly unusual feature, suggesting Venetian influence). The spaces between them have been used for four feast scenes, and instead of the Pantocrator in the summit you will see that the presence of the ribs obliged the artist to substitute four angels. The centre aisle displays the most vivid and sophisticated style in the building, with clear Palaiologue influence, although the Last Judgement contains soldiers with Frankish escutcheons on their shields. Unusually fine are paintings of the Ascension in the bema and of the Entry of the Virgin on the N side of the centre nave. On the S side of the centre aisle close to the door are striking, although less sophisticated, scenes of the Massacre of the Innocents and of Paradise. A full-length figure of St Francis on a N wall pier is unexpected in this context, as is the image of Salome in the N vault carrying the Baptist's head on her own.

The extent and quality of the frescoes here demands a leisurely visit, but the church is not large and in season becomes crowded, so be sure to arrive at opening time.

Kyriakoselia
Κυριακοσέλια

(*Nomos*: Khania).
Church of Agios Nikolaos.★★
Locked; the key is kept in the first house on left on entering the village of Samonas, above Kyriakoselia. (See Pl. 3).

This 11th / 12th C church is notable on two counts: its striking exterior is exceptional, with the richest use of decorative brick found in any Cretan building, and its interior is covered with an impressive range of frescoes, some dated by style to c.1200 and others to 1230-1236. The approach, as you descend through orange and olive groves, is also exceptional; it is surprisingly rare to be able to see a Cretan church from this kind of distance. The building is basically a single-apse, domed hall church, its profile dominated by the tall drum with eight deeply-framed, brick-arched windows; the window of the apse was originally triple-light (though now much reduced) and still shows a decorative dog-tooth brick surround, and the N and S arcades now have had their brickwork restored; the large later narthex only slightly detracts from the powerful impression of this outstanding exterior. The frescoes form an unusually complete scheme, from the cupola with Christ Pantocrator 'Antifonites' of 1230-36, the Ascension and other standard subjects to the many saints' portraits in roundels and areas of pattern ornament. The style of the frescoes is more reminiscent (even in areas of wear and damage) of centres nearer to CP which received fresco decoration in the Komnene period, than most of what can still be seen in Crete.

Lampini
Λαμπινή

(*Nomos*: Rethymnon).
Church of the Panagia.★
Locked; ask for key in the nearest house in the village to the NE.
Follow sign N to Karines / Lampini in middle of the village of Myxorrouma; the church can be seen from about 1 km. away as you ascend from down the valley.

The church is tall and quite substantial, built on a Greek cross plan and with the bays to N and S projecting; the surrounding space is generous and welcome. Its relative sophistication must be due to its having been the seat of the bishop of Lappa, and its 14th C date is reflected in the generous external arcading of the walls and elaboration of the brickwork in the drum of the cupola; if the 20th C plaster rendering were removed from the lower parts of the exterior we might well see further decorative use of brick. Only the form of the main apse is reflected on the exterior, with the much smaller apses of the lateral chapels absorbed in the thickness of the E wall; the dome is carried on four piers. The frescoes inside are mainly of two phases in the later 14th and 15th C; they are quite extensive, but not in readily visible condition. More easily seen in the main body of the church are the frescoes in the S bay, which include the quite rare subject of 'Christ Elkomenos', and in the W bay, further Virgin scenes; in the apse the fresco of the Virgin with four bishops below, and (in the diakonikon) her entry into the temple can all be identified.

This is again one of the Cretan churches where the external aspect is one of its chief attractions, and (given its high visibility) it would be a good subject for a restoration.

Liliano   Λιλιανό

(*Nomos*: Irakleio).
Church of Agios Ioannis.★ Unlocked and open.
Take turning signed to Liliano on road out from Kastelli, but only some 50 m. along this road and almost in the angle of a crossing you can see the church on the right close to a military airfield, partly hidden among olive trees.

Although there is no internal decoration here, this is an unusually interesting example of a three-aisle basilica. It was built with the re-use of some classical spolia (relatively rare in Crete), and you can find two Ionic caps in the nave and two with acanthus foliage. The later narrow, barrel-vaulted narthex also carries six earlier inscriptions, and it is easy to see a number of ancient cut blocks in the N and S walls interspersed with the local stone. The present nave seems unlikely to be earlier than 11th C (Gerola thought 12th -13th C), but it is quite possible that it replaces an earlier building, and, if this is the case, the four columns that survive here may have been used to support a cupola; certainly their siting in the nave forming an exact square suggests that they may have had some such previous function. The narthex is clearly later, and so may be 13th C, but again the spolia built into it may also in this case have been present in an earlier building.

This is the kind of church building that gives rise to more possibilities the longer that you look at it, and so will reward a leisurely visit.

Meronas
Μέρωνας

(*Nomos*: Rethymnon).
Church of the Panagia*. Locked; key with the papas across the road.
Travelling SW from Rethymnon you will find the church to the left of the road as you reach the village.

While the design of this three-aisled church shows Venetian influence, its principal interest lies in its Byzantine frescoes, dateable by style to c.1400 and some recently uncovered. The unusual variety of subjects include, among more standard themes such as the Martyrdom of St George, the Parable of the ten virgins, cycles of the Life of the Virgin and the Akathist hymn (this one of only six such cycles in Crete), and the even rarer scene of the infant Christ depicted above the altar.

As in many other churches the level of lighting is quite low, so to be able to appreciate the frescoes try to time your visit here when there is strong daylight.

Meskla
Μεσκλά

(*Nomos*: Khania).
Church of Metamorfosis Sotirou*. Unlocked.
On entering the village from the N, and before crossing the first of three bridges, turn left up a small, steep road; the church is 80 m. along this road on your left.

The church is a simple, barrel-vaulted, single-apse hall, without a cupola, but it offers the interest of having frescoes dated by a donor's inscription to 1303; the patron was a monk named Leontios, and his inscription also gives the names of the two artists who worked here as Thedodoros son of Daniel and his nephew Mikhail Veneris (possibly a form of the Venetian Venier?) Most of the frescoes are now rather poorly preserved, but the condition of the painting of the Transfiguration (the dedicatory feast of the church) that faces you as you enter by the N door is good and this makes a powerful impression, intimating what the ensemble once was like; the monastic saints in the soffit of this niche, Antony and Leontios (the patron saint of the donor) are also in a better state than the rest, and (were it not for the inscription) the quite pronounced linearity of the style here might have suggested a later 13th C date. The narthex is a somewhat later construction, and its frescoes are probably of the 15th C, with a graffito on the S wall of 1471.

Although this church is modest in size, the interest of its frescoes well repays a leisurely visit. If you return to the main road and continue up to the upper end of the village you will find, immediately outside the W door of a large modern church (the Panagia), a small chapel, now disused; the site is of interest in that the modern church is on the site of an EC basilica, and the chapel until recently retained some areas of floor mosaic. These (which may have been of a baptistry) have now been removed, but suggest that the ensemble must have been of some importance in earlier centuries.

Megalo Khorafia / Stylos   Μεγάλο Χωράφιά / Στύλος

(*Nomos*: Khania).
Church of the Panagia Serviotissa. ★★ Open.
Travelling N on the road between these two villages, the cupola of the church appears in open country on the left, some 300 m. from the road and isolated among lemon and orange groves; a foot track leads to it in 10 minutes.

This impressive church used to be the katholikon of a monastery founded by monks from the Monastery of St John the Divine, Patmos, shortly after the foundation of their own monastery in 1088. Patmos itself received an imperial chrysobull, and (to judge from the exceptional quality and scale of the building) the emperor Alexios I Komnenos (1081-1118) would again have been involved here. The building is a domed, inscribed cross, on an almost central plan, with only the three apses extending the E end beyond the outline of a square; the height of the central arch of the external arcades to N and S is exceptional. It has been sensitively restored from quite a dilapidated state, and in general its metropolitan origins mean that it stands out from the great mass of middle Byzantine Cretan churches; the drum of the cupola has a rich use of brick dividing the eight arched windows, and the central E window, with its two arched lights separated by a column and with minor brick ornament over it, is a classic example of its type at the turn of the century. The interior is devoid of frescoes, but is unaltered save for a modern iconostasis.

A visit here is recommended as, although there are no frescoes, the building itself sets a standard of architectural accomplishment against which you can set many other churches of a comparable period.

Moni   Μονή

(*Nomos*: Khania.)
Church of Agios Nikolaos. ★★ (See Pl. 20).
Coming from Palaiokhora, call for the key at the first house on your left on

*entering the village; you will be directed down a rough track across a small
ravine which leads to the church in about 5 minutes.*

Agios Nikolaos is quite a small, early 14th C hall church in a wooded,
rural setting; it is an unsophisticated building, but its interior offers one
completely unique work. The main feature of exterior interest is the
cylindrical free-standing campanile which may well be contemporary
with the church, and must be virtually unique in the island. Inside, the
frescoes are dated by an inscription to 1315, and form one of the eight
known works of the artist Pagomenos; the inscription names five monks
as the donors. The frescoes are mostly in indifferent condition, but what
makes this one of the outstanding interiors of Crete is the painting that
confronts the visitor on entering by the N door. Here a giant head of St
Nicholas, preserved in brilliant condition, gazes out with awesome
intensity, its scale and grandeur making this one of the most memorable
visual experiences that the visitor to Crete can undergo. Pagomenos
retained such an unerring sense of scale, proportion and siting in
creating this huge image that, although clearly of exceptional
dimensions, it still comes as a surprise to find that the head is almost
four times natural size. As might be expected there is a cycle of scenes
from the saint's life above, but although they clearly have been of
impressive quality, only two of them are now properly visible. It is the
head and shoulders of the saint beneath that dominates the entire
building.

Although lacking the variety and richness of interiors such as Kritsa,
in its particular way this is one of the prime examples of Cretan art and
amply rewards (and deserves) a careful visit.

Moni Faneromeni   Μονή Φανερομένη

(*Nomos*: Lasithi).
Usual monastic hours.
*Well signed from the coast road between Agios Nikolaos and Siteia, climbing
for 5.9 km. from the turning will bring you to this isolated monastery.*

Although the monastic buildings are mostly modern, the foundation is
certainly a late medieval one; the katholikon built on to the cave (which
is the miraculous cause of the monastery's existence, when an icon
appeared there) is in all probablility a medieval foundation. The frescoes
are mostly 18th C, but a graffito of 1465 indicates an earlier layer; there
are two good late icons on the 18th C iconostasis.

In general, the associations of this site and its spectacular setting,
with the impressive outlook from its terraces, are more evident than

surviving features from the medieval period, but it still repays a visit as part of the monastic heritage of W Crete.

Moni Kaliviani   Μονή Καλιβιανί

(*Nomos*: Irakleio).
Chapel of the Panagia Kaliviani. ★ Open.
Signs just E of Faistos direct you to the large and thriving orphanage here, of which the modern buildings can easily be seen from the main road; the visitor has to go round the outside of the large modern katholikon to find this small 14th C chapel.

The most interesting feature of this simple, single-chamber chapel is that it retains a complete and undamaged 14th C masonry iconostasis, many that have survived having suffered some loss; the dog-tooth ornament round the pointed opening into the bema is closely comparable with the decoration round the exterior of the W doors of a number of churches of the Venetian period. Even more rarely found is what is clearly a contemporary fresco image of the Pantocrator painted on to a layer of plaster on the N side of the iconostasis, and now protected by a glazed screen; this seems to have been a standard image for this location, possibly 'transposed' from its usual place in the apex of a cupola. A second layer of fresco must be 15th C, with painting in the apse and upper parts of the main ceiling vault, although very sooty.

This chapel seems to be little known, and the ease with which it can be found and visited commends it as a rewarding objective.

Moni Toplou   Μονή Τόπλου

(*Nomos*: Lasithi).
Now used as a **museum.** ★★
Open 09.00-13.00 and 14.00-18.00; entry charge.
Sited beside the road that runs close to the sea linking Siteia and Itanos, towards the E tip of Crete.

Most of the monastic buildings here are of 15th or 16th C date, and although still of interest it is the katholikon, dedicated to the Panagia, which should be the initial focus of a visit here. The building itself is a double-nave structure of the earlier 14th C, and the frescoes in the N of the two naves, although rather feint, are also of this date. Their subject-matter is not in any way unusual, but the vigorous style of the Palaiologue artist can still be felt.

The monastery was the beneficiary of patronage and bequests by

1. CRETE. Elounda, floor mosaic with dolphins; 5th century.

2. AIGINA. Palaiokhora, Church of the Metamorphosis, frescoes in the vaulting.

3. CRETE. Kyriakoselia, looking down on the church of Agios Nikolaos.

4. CRETE. Aradena, church of Mikhail Arkhangelos viewed across a gorge;
one of the more remote Cretan sites.

5. CRETE. Anydroi, church of Agios Giorgios Anydriotis, fresco of St George, the dedicatory saint of this church.

6. IOS. Palaiokastro, church, with outlook to Irakleia and Naxos.

7. KARPATHOS. Pigadia, reconstructed ruins of the basilica of Aphote.

8. KASTELORIZZO. Fortress built by the Hospitallers,
with the Asia Minor coastline beyond.

9. KEFALLONIA. Moní Sisia, interior of church of the Franciscans, damaged in 1953.

10. KHALKI. Kastro, looking SE to Rhodes from the sentry-walk.

11. KYTHERA. Cave of Agia Sofia, 12th century frescoes by the painter Theodoros.

12. NAXOS. Church of Agios Mamas.

13. RHODES. The country church of Agios Nikolaos Fountoukli, looking west.

14. SIKINOS. Episkopi, a church converted from a classical building.

15. TILOS. Moní Agios Panteleimon, with its observation tower.

Venetian families in the 16th and 17th C, and the results of this period of relative prosperity are now displayed in a small museum; the conversion of the monastic buildings to this function has been done with some sensitivity, and the presentation is of a good standard. On view are some 50 icons, some of them signed examples of 15th (the date of the earliest example, an icon of the Koimisis) to the 18th C, a range of artefacts and a quantity of embroidered vestments and ecclesiastical silver. Bibliophiles may be interested in a display of Venetian printing of liturgical books of the 16th to 18th C, and a copy of Suida's 3-volume Greek and Latin Dictionary (Cambridge, 1705) is unexpected. A quantity of engravings and lithographs associated with Greek monastic life is also on view.

A visit here offers the biggest variety of interest in E Crete, and the museum content must be second only to Patmos and Irakleio among the Greek islands.

Myriokefala   Μυριοκέφαλα

(*Nomos*: Rethymnon).
Former monastic church of the Panagia. ⋆⋆ Unlocked.
The village is sunk in a hollow of the surrounding mountains, and the church, located prominently at its centre, cannot be missed.

This used to be the katholikon of a monastery, of which some of the surrounding buildings still survive; the foundation is an early 11th C one by the local saint, John '*O Xenos*', who was influential in developing Cretan monasticism. The exterior of the ensemble has been recently intensively modernised, but the interior of the church has mercifully been carefully conserved. The original katholikon was a domed, cruciform, centrally planned building, to which two narthex chambers were added later. The interest here lies in the frescoes, of which there are two layers. The earliest is dated by a poorly preserved inscription in the S arm of the crossing to not later than 1020, which makes this among the earliest fresco painting in the island; now rather fragmentary, those in the cupola (the Pantocrator and prophets round the drum) are from this phase, as are the images of the evangelists Matthew and Mark in in the S arm of the crossing. Paintings of the second layer, dating to the later 12th C, are much better preserved, with the heads of Christ and two apostles in the Entry into Jerusalem on the S arm of the W vault being of memorable quality, and the whole scene more visible than the cupola frescoes; from this phase also are the other Passion scenes, including the damaged but intense scene of the Lamentation, and the sequence of bishops in the apse.

Both the origins of this monastic church founded by the most significant figure in Cretan religious life after the recovery of the island in 961, John 'O Xenos', as well as its frescoes, make this one of the more important of the smaller churches in Crete.

Pigi: see Bizariano

Platania   Πλάτανια

(Nomos: Rethymnon).
Church of the Panagia.* Locked.
Coming from Bizari, the church is just above the road on the left in the middle of the village and opposite the kapheneion; if you call there a child will be sent to fetch the papas who has the key.

The church here is quite a small, barrel-vaulted, single chamber of the later 14th / early 15th C, but its frescoes are of this date and are relatively complete. The vault and upper register are now very obscured by soot, but the lower register contains some impressive images; besides some more usual scenes are particularly powerful representations on the N wall of St George and St Demetrius on horseback, with St Michael, another 'warrior saint', and six further standing saints along the S wall. The fragmentary inscription by which the church is dated can be seen over the W door.

This is a good example of a modest village church of this period which in this area is relatively unusual in that it has neither been enlarged, nor had its frescoes over-painted.

Plemeniana   Πλεμενιανά

(Nomos: Khania).
1) Church of the Panagia Myrtiotissa.* Open.
Beside a bridge on the edge of the village (on the left if coming from Palaiokhora) a sign to the church points down a footpath; the church is 100 m. down this path beyond some farm buildings.

This small and very simple, barrel-vaulted hall church would have been a private foundation of the late 14th – early 15th C, and the *ktitor* is portrayed on the right of the fresco of the Koimisis. The frescoes cover the interior, but are not easy to see as heavily encrusted; they appear to be contemporary with the building and never re-painted. Their style is unsophisticated but has an impressive directness that emphasises the rural nature of the setting here, and a large inscription over two saints on the S wall is too obscured with dirt to read. Surprisingly, the door jambs are formed from two re-used marble columns, which suggests the prior presence of an older church in the area.

2) Church of Agios Giorgios.★ Unlocked.

If coming from Palaiokhora, the church is on your left shortly after entering the village, and although only about 20 m. from the road is not very visible; it has a newly tiled roof.

A larger church than the above, but still a simple, domeless hall space of which the chief interest is its fresco decoration. This is dated to 1409/10 by an inscription visible on the N wall, in which the emperor Manuel II Palaiologos (1391-1425) is mentioned, and celebrates the patronal saint with a sequence of lively and colourful paintings of his life and miracles. On the S wall you will see scenes of him rescuing the princess while trumpets are blown from the town walls, and later brought before a ruler, put in prison, and then martyred on a spiked wheel; on the N wall the saint is on horseback with the boy from Mytilini riding behind. The style, although not sophisticated, is unusually vigorous and the artist shows a fine sense of using the wall spaces to the best advantage. The interest in the legend of St George has resulted in a displacement of the usual image of the Virgin in the apse, where only the Pantocrator is painted, and only a small image of the Virgin in Paradise appears on the S wall.

The paintings here are some of the most personal and colourful in W Crete and the two churches in this village provide a contrast that makes it a rewarding objective.

Potamies   Ποταμιές

(Nomos: Irakleio)
1) Church of the Panagia Gouverniotissa.★★ Locked (see below).
Coming S from the coast, some 300 m. before you reach the village there is a battered sign on the left of the road that points up a dirt track (past the church of Christos Sotiros, see below) to the Panagia; if a custodian is here he will charge you for entry and let you in, but if he is not you will have to ask in the kapheneion in the village.

The modestly sized, compact church of the Panagia Gouverniotissa is all that is left (save a few derelict buildings) of the monastery that occupied this broad terrace site; its plan is a Greek cross and the cupola is unusually prominent, with eight lancet windows and external arcading.

Do not miss the richly decorative carved surround of the W window – a clear indication of Venetian influence, and quite foreign to Byzantium. There are no additions or significant alterations, so the extensive frescoes that cover the interior are mainly undisturbed, although generally not in very good condition. The elements of a restrained and rather provincial Palaiologue style that they display, with some Italian elements visible here and there, particularly noticeable in the drapery, places them all in the first half of the 14th C; among the large range of subjects, the Pantokrator in the cupola, the Virgin Platytera in the apse and a striking sequence of Passion scenes all repay seeking out, with the more unusual episode of Peter's attempt to walk on the water being vividly captured. The painted sanctuary doors, part of the iconostasis and a group of icons have been removed from here and taken to the Historical and Ethnographic Museum, Irakleio.

In various ways the peaceful and isolated location of the church here makes it a rewarding objective.

2) Church of Christos Sotiros.*
The same custodian with the key of the Panagia can also let you in here.
Although not nearly as impressive as the Panagia, it is worth having this small, domeless hall church opened while you are in the vicinity. It too is a 14th C building, and although much less ambitious, its frescoes represent a more rural version of the same period as those in the monastic church, and are largely unaltered.

Protoria   Πρωτόρια
(*Nomos*: Irakleio).
Church of Mikhail Arkhangelos.* Unlocked.
Easily seen on the W edge of this small village in a little plateia.

This attractive and quite massive little church is difficult to assess, in that its detail suggests it is 13th C, but the proportions and design argue at least in part for a considerably earlier date. It is domeless and has three apses, of which the central one projects some 3 m. beyond the side apses; a deep narthex more than doubles the interior space, and were it not for the coherence of the masonry it could be suggested that a small, earlier single-chamber chapel was later expanded with the addition of two lateral apses and a narthex, but this does not seem to be the case. It is also possible to imagine that there may once have been a cupola over the central bay of the narthex, but no signs of one survive. The doorway in the S wall of the narthex has typical Venetian detail. There are no frescoes inside, and the fabric has been carefully restored, allowing the visitor to take a careful look at the whole.

An intriguing and enigmatic building which repays a thoughtful visit.

Pyrgos   Πύργος

(*Nomos*: Irakleio).
Church of Agios Giorgios and Agios Konstantinos.★ Unlocked.
The church is easily seen, its N wall facing directly on to the road at the upper end of the village.

The dual dedication of this modest-sized church is due, as usual, to its double nave plan; as far as the heavy external whitewash allows, it seems that the whole building is homogeneous, and the two naves (the N dedicated to Agios Konstantinos and the S to Agios Giorgios) are certainly equal and symmetrical. Gerola's plan indicates the remains of E and W walls of a third nave to the N, and a blocked up way through to it; if this was the case it would have occupied ground where the modern road now runs. Inside, a low arched opening links the two naves; in other respects the two spaces are discrete. The church has two inscriptions, one by the W door of the N nave, the other close the apse of the S nave; both name the same donor, but the latter is dated to 1314-1315, and is an early example of rhymed inscription, copying the form of a liturgical prayer. The donor is named as Giorgios Pakhnoutys, who says that he "renewed the church from its foundations" in memory of his mother, Helena. The frescoes are not in good condition, but can be dated by the inscription, and so provide another guide to the development of styles in this period of Cretan painting.

Roukani   Ρουκάνι

(*Nomos:* Irakleio).
Church of Agios Ioannis.★★ Unlocked.
Only about 250 m. from the village centre, but unsigned and quite well hidden; as you reach the edge of the village travelling S look for a rough track ascending through fields at an acute angle to the right; the church is in a hollow in the hillside 100 m. up this.

It is certainly surprising to find a church of this scale and sophistication in such an isolated spot, and there must be aspects of its history that are now lost which might have explained these factors; it is certainly the result of monied and informed patronage, which could afford builders of the first rank, and there would surely have been an explanation for its obscure location here. In form it is an inscribed cross and now has a tall, broad drum supported on quite slender piers, although Gerola's photograph of c.1905 shows this to have been a modern replacement; the height of the cross-vaults contrasts with lower tunnel-vaults over the corners. The exterior (which is all original) shows a greater use of brick than would normally be expected in this area, with effective use of it made in conjunction with local stone in the external arcades on both N and S facades. No frescoes survive on the interior, but this partly emphasises the purity and economy of its building technique, which must be late 11th to 12th C, although with the cupola restored.

The recent restoration has left this impressive and accessible church in a condition that amply rewards a careful visit.

Sarakina   Σαρακηνά

(*Nomos*: Khania).

1) Church of Mikhail Arkhangelos* (between Sarakina and Kontokynigi). Locked.
Start by entering Sarakina and getting the key at the Pantopoleion next to the kapheneion; then return 500 m. S down the valley to where a newish concrete path leads down on the left to a bridge over a small stream (a sign is only visible if coming from this direction).

The church is the simplest of domeless, barrel-vaulted chambers (recently externally re-roofed), with the interior space divided by just one transverse arch, but it has inside quite a complete fresco scheme, and a masonry iconostasis. The latter, of which not many survive in the island, is damaged with the loss of some of its arch, but the paintings on its plaster surfaces (Virgin and child on N side, Christ on the S) still survive. These, and the frescoes on the walls and vault, which must be mid-14th C, are in a direct and vigorous style, and have passages of considerable power; the figure of St Michael on the N wall and the varied heads of the apostles in the Ascension in the vault of the bema, with the figure of St Antony on the inner face of the iconostasis, are among the best preserved. Also striking in this modest interior is the scene over the W door of Joshua at Jericho, with the trumpets being blown (a torch will help here). The building and its frescoes must be contemporary, and although the latter have suffered some damage through the centuries, neither has been added to or renovated.

Although not immediately impressive, this little church deserves and repays time spent in examining its highly personal fresco decoration.

2) Church of Agios Ioannis.*
Unlocked.
This is in the village, below the level of the road, and 15 m. down a track opposite the kapheneion.

Here a mid-14th C hall church has had its W end extended considerably, but the frescoes remaining in the E end, although in a rather damaged state, are contemporary with the building. Besides paintings in the apse and bema, there is a vigorous rendering of St George on horseback, and in the barrel-vault such remaining scenes as the Entry into Jerusalem and Anastasis suggest what the interior here must once have been like.

This is both larger, if less complete in its interior, than the other church of Mikhail Arkhangelos a short way down the valley, but is still well worth looking out.

Sfakion: see Khora Sfakion

Siteia   Σητεία

(*Nomos*: Lasithi).
Kastro.* Locked, and cannot normally be entered. Unsigned.
The Kastro is easily found at the highest point in the town.

It is hard to realise today that Siteia was once an important and thriving Venetian colony, mentioned frequently in the Venetian Senate; its location so close to Turkish lands meant that it was given priority treatment when the Serene Republic was disbursing funds. The Kastro was already in existence here by 1211, but was very damaged in the earthquake of 1303; a substantial sum was provided by the Venetians for it to be re-built with a keep at the highest point and with walls reaching right down to the harbour and enclosing the entire town. This is the form in which it was first recorded in a 17th C drawing, but it had already been sacked by Khaireddin Barbarossa in 1539, and it was largely destroyed in 1651 when the Turks finally occupied Crete. The only part of this extensive kastro that survives is one of the massive towers (in effect, a self-contained fortress) that has been heavily restored; it must have been one of the highest, and is now prominently sited on rising land at the N edge of the town, easily visible from the road beside the harbour; all the fortified walls running down to the sea have now gone, but a viewing is recommended as it provides an opportunity to envisage the original character of one of the most substantial Cretan fortified colonial strongholds that the Venetians built. (Perhaps only those of

Irakleio and Rethymnon were on a larger scale.) Its form is a polygon covering an area of some 100 m. x 80 m., and the problem here is to establish how much of what can now be seen is a survival from the original construction. Gerola regarded the whole building as it now appears as Turkish, but this seems unlikely, as if the Turks had needed a fortress of this kind they would not have destroyed the entire Venetian defences. The most likely answer is that substantial parts of the masonry here could be original but heavily restored, with just corner turrets probably added at a later period; to the NW a separate small fortress adjoins it which must be Turkish work of 18th C or later, and has been modernised in relatively recent times. The function of the Kastro as providing a bastion of Venetian defence and observation for the E end of the island is very clear, but there would seem to be little need for the Turks to make any substantial investment in their defences here.

Even in its present state it is certainly worth seeking out the Kastro, and it is to be hoped that in due course greater local interest will be taken in it and it can be made available for regular entry and closer inspection.

Sklaverokhori   Σκλαβεροχώρι

(*Nomos*: Irakleio).
Church of the Panagia.** Locked.
On entering the village from Kastellion the church is beside the road among vineyards on the left; the key is kept in the first house on the left beyond it.

This is a mid-14th C hall church with an attractive but unremarkable exterior, found in a rural setting that will have changed little over the years. What is exceptional here is the interior, where there are frescoes remaining of unusual quality and brilliance; the only date attached to the church is a graffito of 1481, but the frescoes are certainly 14th C, and probably contemporary with the building. Notable are feast scenes in the N part of the vault – Raising of Lazarus and Entry into Jerusalem, with in the bema scenes of Pentecost and the Entry of the Virgin into the Temple – the latter seems at one time to have been the church dedication, and interesting features in the fresco include the robe worn by the priest and the architecture of fantasy in the background. The later extension of the church to the W would have entailed the loss of further paintings. The style of this fresco scheme is remarkable in Crete for the powerful sense that it gives of closeness to a major metropolitan tradition; the Palaiologan revival in the arts that gathered strength during the 14th C in CP is very clearly reflected in this fine, if modest, interior; the particular qualities of Palaiologue style – the exaggerated gestures and movement in the figures, the towering rocks in landscapes and unreal and bizarre forms in the architecture – can all be found in the frescoes of this modest village church.

For artistic interest this is the outstanding interior in this area, and is worth making a considerable effort to visit it.

Sklavopoula   Σκλαβοπούλα

(*Nomos*: Khania).
1) Church of Agios Giorgios.* Locked.
When entering the village from Kalamios, this church is close to the road on your left, close to the school; the key is held at the farmhouse just downhill from it.

The village has a military origin, as it was originally populated by Slav mercenary soldiers who had assisted the Byzantine emperor Nikiforos Fokas in the recovery of the island from the Arabs in 961. This probably explains the village's name and the dedication of this, its main medieval church; it is now considerably higher and more spacious than might be expected in quite a remote location, but this may be due in part to the fact that the S wall and much of the vault is later, due no doubt to physical collapse. The church would always have been a simple hall space, roofed now with a slightly pointed vault; it must originally have been a later 13th C building, and the first of the two layers of the fresco has an inscription addressed by the artist to the celebrant at the liturgy: "Remember, O priest, Nikolaos the lector and peasant, the image-maker", and dated by an inscription to 1290-91, with the second about a century later. It is of interest that the inscription is in the centre of the apse, where it could readily be seen by the celebrant at the altar. Although not without some damage, the frescoes provide considerable interest; the Virgin Platytera in the apse exemplifies the refinement of the style, which suggests the presence of an artist from a more sophisticated milieu than might be expected here. On the N wall military subjects painted in the second phase dominate, with St George and St Demetrios on horseback, and the archangel Michael; at the start of the vault above them an interesting sequence of three scenes from the life of St George gave the artist scope to exploit this military interest, with soldiers carrying shields painted with black and white chevrons. This knowledge of W heraldic useage (quite foreign to a Greek audience) is repeated in the Crucifixion scene over the W door, where the Roman centurion Longinus also holds a similar shield. There are several more points of interest in this well-lit interior, which repays careful viewing.

Two further churches here are both rewarding to visit, but locating them lower down and across the hillside amid olive- grown terraces is more easily achieved under the youthful (paid) guidance of children from the next farm down the hill, who will bring the necessary keys with them.

2) Church of Sotiros Christou.* Locked.

This small hall church has the simplest of exteriors, with only four bowls set in its W facade to offer slight relief. Its interior is covered in fresco which, although mostly in poor condition, remains readable, and is again from the later 14th C, although by a less sophisticated artist than that in the larger church of Agios Giorgios. There are some striking and imaginative vignettes to be sought out here. An impressive full-length figure of a female donor on the N wall stands holding a model of the church, with a beautifully painted and luxuriant plant growing beside her; although the head is damaged, this must rank as one of the most individual of such images in Crete. Also unexpected given the scale of the interior is the striking group on the S wall of four saints all on horseback, of which only the titles of George, Demetrios and Constantine are still visible; a large image of the Pantocrator (somewhat damaged) occupies the conch of the apse instead of one of the more usual types of the Virgin), and (again on N wall) two infancy scenes of the Holy Family are followed by a miracle scene of Christ's adult life. The interior here suggests considerable intervention by the donor to create a freshly personal combination of conventional subject-matter.

3) Church of the Panagia.* Locked.

This is the smallest of the three churches here, and its form is again a domeless hall, with just two transverse arches across its vault. The paintings inside are complete but mostly in poor condition, with those in the apse being best preserved. Their style shows them to be painted in one phase and dating from the late 14th to early 15th C, and this is confirmed by an incomplete inscription which names the donor as one Alexios; there are glimpses of Palaiologue detail, particularly in the architectural backgrounds, which link the artist to a more metropolitan origin than is the case with either of the other two churches here. While the frescoes in the apse are of quite standard subject-matter, with a fine image of the Virgin Platytera, the S wall carries unusual scenes of Paradise including Abraham and the Virgin with the young Christ child, and the apostles above in two groups of six as they appear in the Last Judgement; these features are unexpected given the greater sophistication of the artist's style.

All three of these churches have something different to offer, and collectively they represent a varied and interesting range of the styles that can be found in medieval painting in one quite remote village in W Crete.

Sougia   Σούγια

(Nomos: Khania).
Church of Agios Panteleimon (Basilica A).* Locked; the key is held at the reception desk of the Hotel Pelikassos.

This newly built church is located on the edge of the village, 50 m. from the sea, and the area of abraded pebbles that you cross to reach it shows that the sea was once much closer. The site is of a large, triple-nave EC basilica on which the modern church has recently been built in such a way as to preserve much of the original floor; the dedication seems also to be recent. The main survival (besides an EC capital next to the entry gate) is a substantial area of fine mid-6th C mosaic flooring that occupies the E end of the central area of the church. Besides abstract patterning there are panels depicting birds and antelopes, and the variety and good condition of the survivals here makes them some of the most memorable in Crete after Elounda.

The remains of two other basilicas (B and C) are known in the area to the E of the village, but little of them can be seen. Rewarding visits can be made on foot from the village to the site of the ancient Lissos to the W, where there are medieval churches of **Agios Kyrikos** and the **Panagia**, and to the E where a sea-side chapel dedicated to **Agios Antonios** has fresco paintings dated by an inscription to 1382-83. Although none of these has the importance of the EC mosaics in Sougia itself, they make the village with its resident pelican a worthwhile centre.

Spilia   Σπηλιά

(Nomos: Khania).
Church of the Panagia (Presentation and Koimisis).* Unlocked.
Coming N from the coast towards Episkopi, this small church is signed at the far end of the village, beyond the large modern church; it is on the left, above a small open area, and is quite easy to miss from the road.

This simple little domeless, hall church is attractively sited among trees, but their shade makes for a dark interior; its fresco decoration, which is largely complete, with just a few areas of damage, provides the chief interest here. The subject-matter of the paintings is conventional, but their style is of interest in that they have been dated by style to the 14th century, and an early graffito of 1401 confirms this.

It is certainly worth stopping here if going through to the unique church at Episkopi 7 km. to the N, but it is adviseable to have a torch.

Stylos (church of Agios Ioannis) see: Megalo Khorafio

Thronos   Θρόνος

(*Nomos*: Rethymnon)
Church of the Panagia.** Locked.
The church is beside the road in the middle of the village, and cannot be missed; the key is kept at the house four doors downhill to the N on the opposite side of the road.

The village of Thronos occupies the site of the ancient Greek town of Sybrita, and this simple hall church is of interest for three quite separate reasons. In the first place it is clear without even entering it that it is built on the site of an EC basilica, which must have risen near the centre of the classical settlement; this had three aisles, and the church occupies part of the N aisle and presbytery. The mosaic floor of the S aisle of the original basilica is first seen outside the S surround of the church, where it has been left open to the elements; the mosaics are dated by style to the 5th C. (Also outside, note how the fragment of an early marble templon has been found a new use as the doorstep of the adjacent house.) Secondly, it is not common to find outside the territories of the Hospitallers a set of W escutcheons carved in relief placed as prominently on a Greek church as is the case here; their presence forming the lintel of the W door may even be the first aspect of the building that you will notice, with the arms of what may be the Calergi family flanking a shield with a decorative cross. Thirdly, inside the church there are further areas of the 5th C floor mosaic, mostly in better condition, but the frescoes are relatively complete; there has been some partial cleaning, and although the rest suffer somewhat from general dirt they form quite a unified scheme. The usual feast scenes are impressive, and perhaps the most striking area is a sequence of four female saints on the S wall by the entrance. They are the work of more than one hand, and we have no help from any inscription or graffito, but they are probably late 14th C, and this makes it likely that the whole building is of this date; certainly the attractive cable ornament carved round the doorway would support this.

So on several counts this modest church, with both external and internal interest, makes a very interesting and worthwhile objective.

IKARIA   Ικαρία

Med: Nikaria.
Island group: S Sporades. (*Nomos*: Samos).

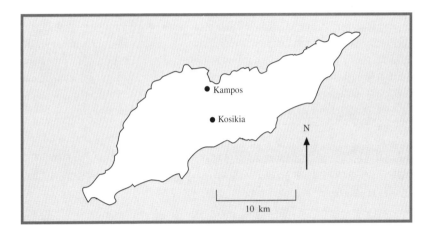

T his quite fertile and well-watered island lies somewhat stranded between the E fringe of the Cyclades and the much larger island of Samos. Its relative isolation gave it a largely different history from the islands of the Archipelago, and although archaeologists have uncovered 5th C buildings which speak of some prosperity then, it goes unmentioned by the main medieval historians. The lack of any sizeable natural harbour must always have affected its development, the modern one at Agios Kyrikos being largely man-made.

The fortunes of Ikaria became linked with those of its neighbour Samos, and to a lesser extent with Chios; the island was governed by the Latin emperors in CP from 1204 to c.1225, and then by the Greek emperors from c.1225 to 1304, first from Nicaea and then from CP; it then came intermittently, with Samos and Chios, under the rule of the Genoese, with the family of Zaccaria in control until 1329 and again from 1346 to 1362, with a short period of Byzantine intervention between 1329 and 1346. The Genoese then had to scale down their interests in the Aegean, largely through the activities of pirates, focussing most of their effort in consolidating the richest island of Chios, and Ikaria was handed over to the lesser Genoese family of Arangio, who ruled here as counts from 1346 to 1481. Little is known about this family, but when the Spanish traveller Ruy de Clavijo called here in 1403 he reported that the ruler of the island was then a woman, who would have been of the Arangio dynasty. For just 40 years, from 1481 until 1522, it was held by the Knights of Rhodes as the most northerly of their outposts, and fell then (with Rhodes and the other Hospitaller islands) to the Turks who retained control until 1912, with just two years of Venetian intervention (as in Chios) in 1694-95.

Unlike the other islands which they had governed, on Ikaria the Genoese have not left us any physical survivals of their presence; while the Zaccaria and Arangio families spent almost 120 years here, where their stronghold may have been located can now no longer be identified. Neither Kampos nor Koskinas show any secure evidence of their presence (or even, in the case of the latter, with the Hospitallers).

Kampos   Κάμπος

Substantial secular ruins ('Palatia'), an 11th C church and small museum. (See Pl. 22).
Ruins gated and locked, but quite visible; church and museum locked; museum key kept in shop/kapheneion opening on to the road immediately below.

This small complex close to the N coast offers what must be one of the most interesting and almost unique medieval sites in the Aegean. The tall ruined buildings are on the right as the road winds up towards Kampos from beside the sea shortly after leaving the little harbour of Evdilos. The church and museum are some 100 m. further on, on the right.

The original identity and purpose of the ruins (known locally as the **'Palatia'**) are at first sight puzzling, and there is certainly room for speculation on the history and original function of this building, constructed as it is from local stone with carefully cut pale limestone quoins, and rising in parts to two storeys. Some of the remains descend to the road, but to see most of what is there you have to scramble up a bank; although fenced off, it is easy to see all the main features.

It is known that there was a Byzantine town here, and the most complete surviving element contains what in a church would be reminiscent of quite a spacious curved synthronon facing towards the sea, with, in the wall above it, a large carefully filled-in window. This, it has been suggested, was an *odeion* with probable Roman origins that was still used in the 4th/5th C, and if so is a virtually unique survival of this building form; the only comparable building in the Aegean islands has been excavated on Crete at Gortys. The concept of the odeion originated as an area for spectacles or plays, and was later used as a law court, and it may have been as the latter that it served here. (The flooring has been covered in by the usual protective gravel, so any mosaics cannot be seen.) Some 4m. in front of it is a high wall with two arched openings left from a series opening onto an upper storey; at no point does brick appear to have been used. This and other buildings adjacent would seem most probably to be later, and the received opinion on the whole complex of quite imposing and expensive buildings is that it was later used as a palace for the local governor or commandant, which was altered and added to several times before falling into disuse. This certainly seems the most probable kind of explanation, but it is unlikely that it was used by the 14th – 15th C Genoese governors.

The earlier history of the settlement here may be a clue, as it was the ancient Greek Oinoe or Oinon and was a place of some importance; as the name suggests, it was famous for its wines – as famous, indeed, as Samos. It could be that the local governor wished to perpetuate a pre-Christian secular ruler's palace, but the visitor is free to speculate further on what lay behind this impressive ruin.

Continuing uphill to the village you will find the medium-sized **church of Agia Irene** a short way off the road up to the right. You approach the W entrance through a classical form of archway and across a small courtyard; to the left, on the N side of this open space is a small area of EC floor mosaic which has been dated by style to the 5th C, indicating that this was the site of an EC basilica, with this space perhaps already serving as an atrium. The church has a broad, octagonal drum supporting its cupola; the interior is innocent of frescoes, and the cupola is supported on piers, not columns, with virtually no decorative sculpture. Its form is consistent with an 11th C date. There is quite a quantity of minor spolia in and around the church, again suggesting an earlier EC foundation here.

The small **Museum,** reached up a flight of steps from just beside the gateway, is devoted almost entirely to a small display of pre-Christian exhibits; from the medieval period there is just one Byzantine copper coin on view.

Kosikia   Κοσικιά

Byzantine castle of Koskinas. ★★ Gated but open.
Coming from Evdilos you first see this castle high up against the skyline to the NW; the nearest village of Kosikia is due SE from the castle. It can also be approached by a series of dirt roads (all unsigned) from the SW; the last km. is a steep climb on foot, and you will be at almost 1000m. at this point, with predictably extensive views.

This was in existence before the arrival of the Genoese in 1346 (see below), and so can be compared in some respects with e.g. Apalyrou on Naxos; it must represent a Byzantine citadel which has been subjected to later modernisation by the Genoese occupants. Once you reach it you will find the outer enceinte complete and in place from N to S, with a sheer drop on the E. The inner enceinte encloses an area of some 40m. x 20m., and there is the base of a small circular tower at the E end of the enclosure (for its occupant, see below), but much of this quite limited space is taken up by a chapel that has mostly survived in a good state of preservation; only the W end has collapsed and been replaced by a later wall. The ribs supporting the barrel vault are exposed as in many other island churches, and brick has been used sparingly in the door arches; the projecting apse is rounded. It is most probably contemporary with the original building of the castle, and so must be a Byzantine construction, although no fresco painting survives.

The function of the ensemble is somewhat enigmatic; the sea is visible to both N and SW, but neither Chios to the N nor Patmos to the SE can readily be seen. So while a magnificent expanse of the island can be viewed from here, beyond its use as an observation and signalling station it is hard to see the reason for its construction. Even if this was known to be the case, the geographical position of the island on the extreme NW point of the S Sporades and with no visual contact with the Cyclades or the Turkish mainland means that at least for the period that the Hospitallers were here it must have acted as the most northerly point of their signalling system. However, the construction is clearly earlier than the late 15th C, with a date in the 11th-12th C being most probable, and this must imply a Byzantine origin; certainly the masonry is completely consistent with this date. If this is the case, the castle here corresponds well with that at Apalyrou on Naxos, which is on an equally remote mountain top, and must represent a typical Byzantine solution to this need. It is possible that the Hospitallers were present here during their tenure of the island, but if they were they left no signs of their presence.

As late as 1874 a traveller was able to write down a ballad, which he heard an Ikarian singing, that narrated "The taking of the Frourion of Ikaria at Koskinas" by the Genoese. It began: "Anathema on the Genoese and on the Weaver-of-deceits / who went to surprise the castle of Ikaria," and goes on to tell how, having landed at Fanari and marched all night to the castle "well renowned and pictured in Constantinople and in Venice", the Genoese first had one man stick daggers into the wall and so make a ladder up which he climbed; however, a Greek girl on top of the tower threw down tiles (perhaps the local schist slabs) reciting the while the belligerent blank verse of the song, and so prevented entry by this means. Also inside the castle was a rejected lover of the damsel, who was persuaded by the Genoese that if he gave them the keys of the gate they would hand over the damsel to him; he agreed to this betrayal, and so by this means they took the castle. While obviously not an accurate account, this ballad with its colourful details must contain the elements of the Genoese subjugation of the island, and is an interesting reflection both on the antipathy to the occupying power and its persistence for so many centuries.

IOS   Ἴος

Med: Nio.
Island group: Cyclades (SE). (*Nomos*: Cyclades).

Although to a modern eye the rocky island of Ios is as attractive as any of the Cyclades, during the medieval period it was regarded as one of the least well endowed islands of the Archipelago; its position did not give it any special strength, the land was particularly poor for agriculture and there was little water and no natural mineral wealth; its fine harbour was its only resource, but even this became a mixed blessing, as pirates later found it an ideal refuge.

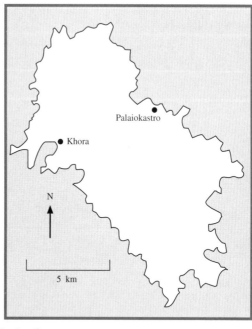

Passed over without mention by the medieval historians, its status began to change with the establishment of the Duchy of Naxos in 1206, when it was numbered among the eleven islands of the Duchy. Recovered by the Byzantines later in the 13th C, it came again under Venetian control c.1300 when a family from the lagoons, called the Schiavi, captured Ios and held it as a fief of the reigning Duke of Naxos. By 1397 it had reverted to the Crispo family, and had been alotted on Francesco Crispo's death to the fifth of his sons; in the treaty between Venice and the Sultan of 1419 it appears in the list of islands that are acknowledged to belong to Venice. Its population had dwindled to such an extent at this time that the ruling lord, Marco Crispo, is said to have populated the island with Albanians that he brought in from the Peloponnese. In the 16th C the island passed by marriage to another Venetian family, the Pisani, but nothing could eventually withstand the onslaught of the Turkish admiral Khaireddin Barbarossa in 1537, who brought Ios and five other islands into permanent Turkish occupation almost three decades before the last of the islands of the original Duchy succumbed.

In Khora there is now little remaining of its medieval past; there was at one time a kastro built at the summit by the Venetian lords, and scattered fragments of its walls can still be found, but nothing of any size survives. An Italian visitor in 1494 reported that there were so many of the local inhabitants living there, using it as their sole protection from pirates, that it was overcrowded and smelly.

Khora

1) Double-nave church of Agios Panteleimon and Agios Ioannis Theologos.*
Easily located on Odos Astronauton Armstrongk.

The same local need for modernity that must have encouraged (or, if ordered by the Turkish *pasha*, compelled) the replacement of so many of the Aegean island churches with modern buildings, here no doubt allowed the earlier destruction of the kastro, and took the more positive form of re-naming in the 1970's this street of the Khora, where you can see that the tradition of double-nave churches has persisted.

The simple church (the key held in nearest house to the E) is probably 14th / 15th C in origin, and as usual each of the two barrel-vaulted naves has its own dedication; that to the N is Agios Panteleimon and that on the S Agios Ioannis Theologos; there is no internal decoration, although a classical column and base has been re-used inside. One is slightly higher than the other, and it is possible that they were not built at the same time; although they are now both dedicated to Greek saints, they probably date from the period of Venetian occupation, and so have originally had one Latin and one Greek dedication.

2) Church of the Panagia Frankklissa.*
Easily seen from the road that winds up to the summit of the Khora outside the original housing area, it is on the N edge of the town, and stands out from all the others as not being covered in thick whitewash; it has to be reached from the paved footpath inside the boundary wall.

As its name implies it was almost certainly taken over as a Latin church, but its design is certainly Byzantine; this means that it might be dated from before the Venetian dominance in the 13th C. The basic design is that of a dome over an inscribed cross, and the nave is extended westwards; the exterior of the drum is notable for a succession of small blind niches. It appears to be permanently locked, with no key available, and is certainly untended and semi-derelict, reinforcing the impression of apparent former Latin ownership which has not been replaced. It is known that in the 17th C a RC priest was sent to Ios to minister to the spiritual needs of pirates and other mariners who had settled here, and their families, and this may have been adopted as his church; there was never a RC bishop here. If the above surmise on the past history of this church is correct, this could be an unusual example of a Byzantine church (probably 12th C) being adopted by the Latins, and then abandoned rather than returning to Greek use. The only characteristic that is not answered by this is the slight Venetian character of some of the carved detail, which would imply a 14th/15th C date. If this church was used by the Latins ('Franks'), it was probably for only quite a brief period.

Palaiokastro

Ruined castle★★
Unenclosed. (See Pl. 6).
This isolated cliff-top castle is spectacularly sited on the E coast, between Psathi and the bay of Agia Theodoti. Take the new dirt road that has recently been built, and follow signs to Psathi; when the road divides take the left fork (the right goes steeply downhill), and in 1.5 km. you will reach a levelled parking area. Palaiokastro is then some 15 minutes' walk up a steep track, with immense views over the island and NE across the straits towards Irakleia and Naxos.

None of the early travellers in the Aegean mention this modestly sized but quite prominent kastro. The single enceinte encloses a polygonal area some 100 m. x 60 m., and surviving stretches of wall still have a sentry walk and castellation; there are still ruins of considerable buildings within the walls, including quite a large cistern and what was probably a small church, although no traces of a tower or keep survive. Except for a later chapel and several store-houses, the building seems largely to be all of one period, but evidence for a date is difficult to find. One opinion is that it is part of a 12th C Byzantine system of maritime fortifications, but there is very little comparative material to justify this. Alternatively, given the island's history, a date in the years around 1400, when the Schiavi gave way to the Crispi, could be suggested.

Having reached here you will not want to leave in a hurry, and can speculate on the reasons why this should have been built; certainly not easy to service either from land or from the sea using the small bay below, and not large enough to shelter a substantial number, its main use must have been for observation. While no doubt Byzantine sea-routes used these lanes, it is easier to visualise the Venetian overlords needing to be able to look towards Irakleia and the chief island of their archipelago, Naxos; the Crispi would no doubt have wished to keep in signal contact with their newly recovered island. In this it corresponds more closely with the majority of smaller kastra, such as that on Amorgos, and does not suggest the quality of cultivated ease that one feels the Querini enjoyed in the kastro on Astypalia, or the capacity to house the numbers that existed there.

ITHAKI

Ιθάκη

Med: Dulichia, Itacha, Thiachi, Val di Compare.
Island group: Ionian / Eptanisous. (*Nomos:* Kefallonia).

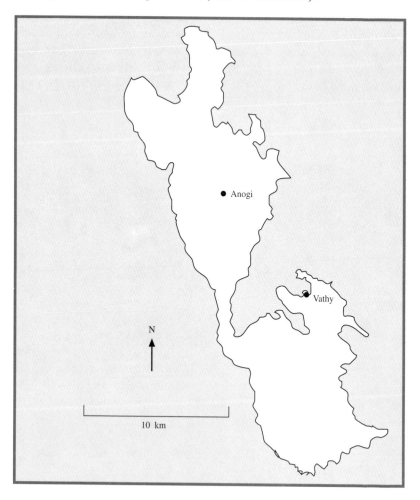

If there is one association for which this beautiful and rocky island is famous it is, of course, with the Homeric hero, Odysseus. Thereafter, the island disappears from Greek writings of all kinds, and it was only two millennia later, when the Normans from Sicily invaded Greece in 1185 AD, and the nearby islands of Kefallonia and Zakynthos where occupied by their admiral Margaritone of Brindisi, that Ithaki re-entered Hellenic history. When Margaritone invaded and annexed the two larger islands, he did not mention Ithaki in the title that he adopted, but it soon became linked with its two larger neighbours in the many documents that cover the later history of this much coveted Ionian grouping. Although Venice could have claimed that her rights were implied here after 1204, as the Deed of Partition named Corfu, Zakynthos, Leukas and Kefallonia as awarded to the Republic, the Senate seemed content in 1209 with the title of 'Palatine Count of Kefallonia' devolving upon Matteo Orsini, who just had to acknowledge their overlordship.

By 1264 Riccardo Orsini was announcing his title as 'Lord of Kefallonia, Zakynthos and Ithaca'. Like other Ionian islands, Ithaki was to come under the control of the Angevin dynasty when in 1324 John of Gravina, the prince of Achaia, conquered the 'County of Kefalonia' from the Orsini; it remained under their suzerainty until 1357 when it was given by Robert of Taranto to Leonardo, the first of the Tocco family from Benevento to take on the grand title of *Comes palatinus Cephaloniae, Ithacae, et Jacinti*.

It was the strength of Venice that so often remained the critical factor in the survival of the Ionian islands; by 1449 (and so four years before the fall of CP) Leonardo III Tocco had lost all his mainland possessions in Epiros, but the knowledge that Venice would fight to protect her islands of Kefallonia, Zakynthos and Ithaki meant that they were left in relative peace.

In 1479 Ithaki was laid waste by the admiral of the ageing sultan, Mehmet II, who was trying to consolidate his hold on the many islands of the Greeks that he no doubt felt by now should have been under his control. By 1504 we know that Ithaki was uninhabited, and the Venetians (then still owning Kefallonia and Zakynthos) had the island re-settled by offering highly favourable tax terms to anyone from the two larger islands who would come; it then remained until 1797 as a relatively prosperous island fragment within the sprawling Venetian empire.

[An engaging traditional explanation for the medieval name of 'Val di Compare', which is certainly much used in the documentation from the 12th C on, is said to derive from an Italian sea captain, seeking shelter at night in a storm, who was driven ashore on Ithaki. Seeing a light shining through the darkness near the sea-shore, he approached and found it came from a hut where a baby had recently been born. The parents asked the stranger to be the child's godfather (*koumparos*) at the christening next day, and so the name was given to the seaside valley, and hence to the island.]

Anogi   Ανώγι

Church of the Panagia. Locked; key held in the kapheneion a few m.
W from the W end of the church
Taking the road round the bay of Molos into the N part of the island, the
village is some 10 km. from Vathi; the church is beside the road on a bend in
the street traversing the village.

The form of the church is of the standard Ionian type of a simple
domeless hall some 20 m. long, and with a later barrel-vaulted roof. Its
chief interest is provided by the virtually complete scheme of fresco
decoration which entirely covers its interior walls; they are in good
condition, and have not undergone any significant re-painting. At first
sight these could well be 15th C, but the more conservative style of this
area would suggest a century later. In the nave they are arranged in four
rows, with the top zone (slightly truncated by the later roof) formed
from 26 NT scenes, mainly of the Passion, the second from 34 scenes
chiefly of the life of the Virgin, with some saints' martyrdoms, the third
a sequence of heads of saints and the bottom row from full-length
standing figures of saints. The templon is of masonry and dated 1650,
with only the topmost part later; the apse painting of the Virgin Platytera
is of a less usual type and is probably of 17th or even 18th C.

   This church offers an excellent opportunity to examine in situ a
typical interior of the Ionian islands, and is very comparable with that
from Valimes, now re-erected in the Museum in Zakynthos.

Vathy / Perakhora - Palaiokhora

Church shell with frescoed masonry templon. ★★ Unenclosed.
Take the road S out of Vathy and follow signs to Perakhora; after traversing
this whole village the road continues to climb until you reach a sign to
Palaiokhora. Leave any transport near to the derelict later church on the
right, and take a stony track leading up and due N along the mountainside.

At the end, in a few minutes, is the roofless church, oriented N/S due to
the terrain, and marked by a later belfry. Its form would have been a
simple wooden-roofed hall space; all fresco decoration there may have
been on the walls has gone, but there are considerable frescoes in the
apse, some still in quite fair condition; the main interest here, however,
is the templon of rendered brick and tile, some 4.5 m. high and with
three openings, which still displays an almost complete fresco scheme.
This represents one of the best preserved examples of masonry
iconostasis decoration in all the islands; that in Agia Barbara in

Palaiopolis on Kythera is as complete in form, but has lost all its imagery, while several in Crete have survived, but are all smaller or more damaged. It is crowned by a row of 14 rounded fresco images of the twelve apostles, the Virgin and John the Baptist, all in half-length; the centre space is now empty but would have had an image of Christ. Below these, the four piers of the templon have frescoes of St John the Evangelist (who was thus most probably the patron saint of the church), the enthroned Virgin, Christ as the Great High Priest (a subject developed in the post-Conquest period) and St John the Baptist. The conch of the apse is occupied by the Virgin Platytera, with four bishops in the area below and the *Akra Tapeinosis* in a niche of the prothesis, as usual.

All the frescoes are of the same period, and in the absence of any inscription we can suggest two possible occasions that would provide a period for their creation. The church and its frescoes could have been in existence from shortly before the sacking of Ithaki by the Turks in 1479 (see above), or it could have been a creation of the new population arriving after 1504. In either case, we have an interior that has survived some 500 years without any significant modernisation. Given the historical conditions just mentioned, and the tendency of island populations, as they start to feel more secure, to move down towards the sea, it seems most probable that this church was quite recently built in 1479, that it escaped destruction by the Turks, and that when further new development took place after 1504 this higher area was abandoned. The belfry could have been added soon after 1504, just before this move downhill started to occur under increased Venetian protection. The style of the decoration is consistent with a date in the 1470's, and the ensemble suggests an interpretation along these lines.

This ruinous but highly interesting survival is very well worth seeking out in its peaceful hillside setting, as it presents such an authentic glimpse into church interior furnishing in the period after the more open templon had been superseded, and before the arrival of the omnipresent high, gilt wooden iconostasis.

The small scale of Ithaki meant that the ruling counts always lived on Kefallonia or Zakynthos, so there never was a fortified kastro to offer protection for the population, although you may read elsewhere of two 'Venetian forts' guarding either side of the mouth of the harbour of Vathy. From boats arriving at Vathy and passing the NE headland, two cannons can indeed be seen projecting from what could be a small fort. However, closer inspection reveals only a modern low wall on which two late 18th or early 19th C muzzle-loading cannons have been fixed, their breech ends resting on modern concrete blocks at ground level. One is

Venetian and one British, and may be a survival of the Greek War of Independence, possibly taken here from Mesolongi on the mainland, where there are still numerous British cannons. The only construction on the other side of the harbour mouth visible from the water turns out to be a pair of ruined windmills.

KALYMNOS   Κάλυμνος

Island group: Dodecanese / S Sporades. (*Nomos*: Dodecanese).

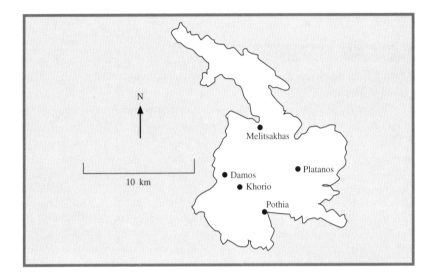

L ying between Leros and Kos, and so one of the most northerly of the Dodecanese, the island goes unmentioned by the medieval historians of the Aegean, although the presence of the major early basilica at Damos would suggest that it had been of some importance. When governed from CP it formed part of the Aegean *theme*, and later, in the 1250's, Kalymnos and Leros formed part of the Nicene empire under the Laskarid dynasty. Its significance was at once clear to the Hospitallers as soon as they were established in Rhodes, and it was under their control by 1315, at the same time as Kos and Leros; thereafter it formed part of the defensive chain of the Knights. The inhabitants must have enjoyed quite good agricultural conditions, as in 1403 Ruy de Clavijo, on his way to visit Tamurlane, commented on the grain production of the island. In 1457 The island was laid waste by Mehmet II as part of his intended subjugation of the Aegean, and was finally surrendered to the Turks, with the other Hospitaller possessions, in 1523. The surviving buildings reflect clearly the island's medieval history, with EC and Byzantine churches and Hospitaller castles all indicating phases of its past.

The main town and port is now Pothia (or Kalymnos), from which one road follows the coastline to the E and arrives at the smaller harbour of Vathi; the other runs NW inland to Khorio, which was the medieval capital, and then on to the W coast. The town centre of Pothia itself has no monuments to offer, but both the castle of Khrissokhera and the spectacular ruin of the church of Christ "Lemniotissa" are within an easy walk or few minutes' bus ride of the harbour.

Pothia

Kastro Khrissokhera. Ruins of Hospitaller castle.**
Gated but open.

This is not the largest, but it is the most prominent medieval building here, being easily seen from the sea, and is only about 2 km. inland, on the outskirts of Pothia and not far off the road to Khorio. Turn off to the left where a smaller road is signed to Vlykhadia or Vothynoi, and where you can see three windmills striding up the steep hillside; the track and steps to the Kastro start from near them.

The eye is immediately caught, when looking up at the fortified wall of the castle that faces SE down towards the sea, by three pairs of knights' escutcheons, and (even allowing for the freedom with which these were sometimes used) they convey the continuing interest and investment by the Hospitallers in this medium-sized castle. Not all are identifiable, but one of them is of the Spanish Grand Master, Anton Fluvian (1421-37), another of the Venetian Querini family (possibly installed here by the admiral Fantino Querini, governor of Kos in the 1440's), and another rather flamboyantly carved is probably the most recent addition. You will be able to detect at least three different phases of masonry; the earliest of these is in a technique that is almost certainly 12th C Byzantine, with ceramic filling in the mortar; other areas above this must be later additions or repairs.

It would appear from this that the Knights of Rhodes (who we know in any case to have been holding the island in 1403) took over an existing Byzantine castle and strengthened it for their own use, probably in the 14th or certainly the early 15th C. The fortifications occupy the whole of the uneven summit of the rock, but the area is not extensive; this could never have been a place of refuge for any sizeable mass of the local population, nor could it have housed a major garrison; its function must always have been to serve as a look-out and signalling position, with good views over the sea channel to Kos and towards the huge Knights' castle at Antimakhia, as well as NW inland towards Khorio. The town itself is mostly out of sight, but the sloping extent of Pera Kastro above it is fully visible. The small modern chapel no doubt perpetuates an earlier building, and there are the remains of a small tower.

Khorio

Pera Kastro: Large fortified kastro; numerous churches.*
Gated, but normally open access.
Continuing up the broad valley from Pothia, you will reach the large village of Khorio after about 5km. There are virtually no directions to the Kastro, but after winding up through the narrow lanes and streets to the right of the road you will eventually come to a long flight of steps; these will bring you to the gateway of the Kastro, set in a curtain wall with frequent towers.

Once inside you will find yourself at the foot of a large sloping area with a jumbled mass of ruins stretching steeply uphill. Almost the only maintained buildings are now churches, and there are more than a dozen – all modest in size and barrel-vaulted; there are no timber roofs. Looking back down towards the sea it is easy to pick out the much smaller kastro of Krissokhera, and the contrast in function becomes very clear: the area enclosed here is clearly sufficient to contain a sizeable local population in the event of attack by any hostile force of either Turks or pirates. It is hard to tell the date of any part of the ensemble; the churches are all simple and largely undecorated, with just a few fresco fragments showing through the whitewash, and one building bears a simple but enigmatic escutcheon on its wall. It was probably in existence before the arrival of the Knights, and the arms of one of the last Grand Masters in Rhodes, the Italian Fabrizio del Carretto (1513-21), looking out in relief from the E wall across the valley to the other kastro, show their continued interest. The stronghold was maintained and occupied into the 18th C, as danger will have persisted up to that period. There is no strong evidence of Hospitaller attention here, although they may have assisted in its development.

These two castles should be visited as they represent well their differing functions, and so allow us to gain some understanding of the dynamics of medieval existence on the island.

Damos

Church of Christ Lemniotissa ("of Jerusalem").
Apse of a large basilica.** Gated but open. (See Pl. 23).
The road from Pothia to Khorio rises after some 3km. to a low crest; just before reaching the crest four whitewashed steps lead up from the left side of the road to a metal gate.

Here, out of sight of the road and adjoining a jumble of chicken sheds, is one of the most impressive examples of EC church building in the

Dodecanese. All that you can see now is a large single apse, some 7 m. across, with a triple-arcaded window, but the scale, precision and finish, with lavish use of marble, all make it immensely impressive, and you immediately feel that you are in the presence of what was once an important building. A local tradition holds that the founder was the emperor Arcadius, 395-408AD, who built it after visiting Jerusalem – hence the name – but we have not been able to confirm this, and this date is too early for the mosaics – see below.

The main structure and synthronon is built of finely-cut marble blocks and the conch is formed from very accurately set thin bricks; much of the marble is re-used spolia, with classical Greek inscriptions still occasionally visible. (These have been identified as coming from a temple of Apollo at Myrties.) Just where the nave arcading joins the apse is the beginning of a simple decorative band of vine rinceau cut in relief in the marble, and this would presumably have run the length of the nave. The 1937 excavation of this site by the Italians revealed that there were side aisles about 2 m. wide, and although there is now no trace of secondary apses, a modern chapel occupies the space to the S of the main apse. The aisles were floored in decorative mosaic (now no longer visible) depicting animals and trees; the 6th / 7th C date given to these must serve as the best evidence for the date of the ensemble; the nave was paved in marble. The exterior of the apse has a course of finely-cut marble dog-tooth ornament, and this crisp classical detail emphasises the contrast with the tumbledown nature of the chicken sheds which occupy the area of the nave and N aisle.

The scale of this building would suggest quite a major settlement here, and its location, looking both inland and towards the sea, and perhaps later guarded by the Byzantine castle, would suggest a considerable local population. Allow time for a leisurely viewing of this rather neglected site and the one now following, as they are almost adjacent and repay a speculative visit.

Damos

Ruins of 6th C church of the Evangelistria / Agia Sofia.*
Excavated, overgrown site.* Gated, but open.
Walking some 60 m. back towards Pothia through olive trees and past a heap of large excavated classical marble spolia, some with inscriptions, you will find this enigmatic site.

Although much less is left to view than at the large basilica nearby, the ground plans and remaining walling make this a rewarding excavation to view. The original building here was a simple triple-apse basilica, with the S apse and the base of the central templon still visible; a broad narthex can also be located, and the mosaics here, depicting fishes and geometric interlace ornament, although partly protected by netting and gravel, can still partly be seen. At some point the basilica must have been largely destroyed, as you will see the curved walls of a chapel that was built in the space between the chancel enclosures and the narthex. Possibly at the same time the main apse was apparently enclosed by a much smaller wall, re-using old building blocks; this can be found as a feature of the design in other EC basilicas on the Turkish mainland, but here it seems later. Much of the spolia excavated here has the been identified as coming from a nearby Greek theatre, as the curve of the marble seating can still be seen. The impression made by the site is one of long occupation during the course of which the function of the building changed, and with it its form; two tombs were found within the church ruins and many more in the vicinity, suggesting an extended period of occupation.

Melitsakhas

Ruins of 5th C basilica of St John.★ Unsigned; gated but open.
This site overlooks the small harbour of Melitsakhas, and is some 100 m. above the sea, looking across to the island of Telendos. It is out sight of the main road that runs from Pothia and continues up the W coast towards the only tourist development on the island; to reach the church turn left off the main road as it approaches the summit of a small hill just before arriving at the first recent housing of Myrties, and you will find the basilica on a terrace on the further side of this hill.

The original EC basilica was quite small (some 17m. from nave threshold to the apse). Two broad aisles flanked the nave, and there seem to have been carved marble slabs erected between the four columns down the nave, as one of them is still in place; excavated spolia include window columns and caps, one with peacocks carved in relief. The synthronon is still in place in the apse, but the large window above has been filled in. The narthex still has interesting mosaics in situ, with an inscription praying for the reader to help Anatolios, the founder, although these are now covered with the protective gravel of the local ephorate.

A modern small funerary church (as so often) occupies the site of the S apse of the basilica, and beyond this the remains of a second (12th C?) chapel lie adjacent to it; this would suggest that when the EC basilica fell into disuse its place was taken by this more modest, single-nave church, and the E end of the basilica was used for other purposes. This is an isolated site with considerable interest and atmosphere and the outlook across the sea below to Telendos is spectacular.

The road on through Myrties and up the coast offers views across to the island of **Telendos.** This was not visited as the crossing can only be made at all easily in season, but the surviving remains of an **EC basilica of Agios Constantinos** and the relative rarity of an EC cemetery formed from a number of barrel-vaulted chambers make a visit worthwhile. There are no medieval survivals on the road up through Arginontas.

Platanos

Churches of Agios Antonios, Agios Nikolaos and Taxiarchis Mikhailis.**

The two former usually open; key for the third in house above road close to Agios Nikolaos.

The other centre of medieval activity on the island was in the fertile valley reaching inland from Vathi, with its small well-sheltered harbour. Two modern churches in this locality have been built over EC basilicas: that of **Agios Anastasios** was built over the 'Basilica of the Resurrection' (*tis Anastaseos*) on the S arm of the bay of Vathi, and that of **Agia Irene** occupies the site of another of unknown original dedication on its N shore. Both are of some interest, but if time is limited you would be advised to visit first those discussed below.

The road runs W inland, passing through Platanos after about 1 1/2 km, and traversing walled groves of fruit trees. It was probably in this fertile shallow valley that in 1403 Ruy de Clavijo saw the evidence of grain production that impressed him. All three of the churches are on your right, beyond the village; the road runs parallel with a low cliff, and the churches can be seen from the road but have to be reached by paths that strike upward and go behind the cliff.

Agios Antonios, the first you will see after appr. 1 km, is small and undecorated, but the second one, **Agios Nikolaos**, also a simple, barrel-vaulted chamber has frescoes in the nave and apse; although in poor condition and relatively conventional in treatment, they could be 12th C. Easily the most interesting and extensive among the other survivals in the valley is the church of **Taxiarchis Mikhailis**; for this, either continue on the track behind the cliff, or follow the road until you see a low wall of sandstone blocks that formed the base of a pre-Christian building, perhaps a fort. This construction, now largely overgrown, forms part of a terrace on which a substantial three-aisled EC basilica was built; the church occupies part of what was the S aisle, but there are extensive remains of other parts of the basilica. (Even if the key-holder is out these make the site well worth visiting). The three doorways of the original basilica still have lintels in place, and as you pass from the substantial narthex into the nave you will see that graves have been excavated just inside the SW door. A massive marble roof section from a Greek temple was used to form part of the templon of the main apse, and other classical spolia indicate that this was a temple site. The most enigmatic part of the building remains is a long, narrow chamber, originally barrel-vaulted lying along the length of the basilica on its N side; it has a separate wall built only some 4 cm. from the external wall of the basilica, and windows open straight from this space into the basilica. This seems too narrow to have been anything like a parekklision, and is certainly too long for a funerary chapel, so may have been some kind of communal hall or refectory, but this too is not a convincing explanation. The small 13th/14th C barrel-vaulted church is now the only part of the complex still in use; it had a large apse window that is now filled in, leaving now no windows at all. The wooden iconostasis has been removed, giving an authentic and uninterrupted view of the apse area. The frescoes that cover most of the interior are expressive in style, and are varied in date; those inside the chancel arch and the apse are in best condition, with fine images of the Pantocrator above a series of bishops. The S side shows feast scenes of the Nativity, Entry into Jerusalem and a fragment of the Anastasis. Do not leave the site without exploring the surroundings to the SW, where there are secular buildings constructed against the ancient walling.

The many centuries encompassed by the buildings in this rural area make it a fascinating and rewarding locality to explore, and there are a few lesser, more scattered remains that you may come across in the valley.

KARPATHOS   Κάρπαθος

Med: Scarpanto.
Island group: Dodecanese (S). (*Nomos*: Dodecanese).

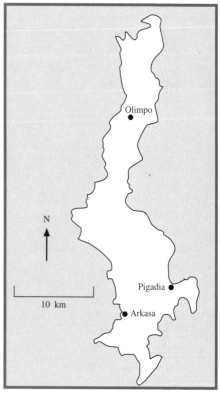

Although of an area the same as Kos, Karpathos, lying at the S end of the chain of the Dodecanese, is of such an extended shape and its terrain is so ruggedly mountainous that it has remained one of the least desired and least exploited among the inhabited islands of the E Aegean. Its position on the sea route between the two largest islands of Crete and Rhodes did give it some importance to the maritime powers, but the medieval historians of the Aegean are silent on the island; it is not until the Fourth Crusade that its name begins to appear in written sources. Unmentioned in the 1204 Partition, it is said to have been held in fief from the Latin emperor by Andrea and Lodovico Moresco, members of a Genoese family; a century later, in 1306, it was seized from them by a Venetian, Andrea Cornaro, and it was from that family that the Hospitallers seized the island, probably in 1312, as part of their campaign to establish Rhodes as their new home. The Venetians, who were never friends of the Order unless it suited them, were in a position to show their hostility to this action, and after sequestering money of the Knights that was in transit through Venice, Karpathos was handed back to them in 1316. It was still in Venetian hands in 1419, as in the treaty of that year between the sultan and Venice 'Scarpanto' was one of the islands explicitly regarded as belonging to the Republic. It was occupied by the Turks from the mid 16th C.

A note of local colour comes from the 15th C traveller Christoforo Buondelmonti, who complained that the inhabitants of the island were very unpleasant to meet as they all worked producing resinous pitch, which was smelly and stained them badly.

Karpathos town (Pigadia)

Extensive remains of EC basilica of Aphote. Unenclosed. (See Pl. 7).

Taking the road out from Karpathos travelling N towards Pigadia, some 2 km. after the last houses you will find the ruined basilica of Aphote (Agia Photeine?) to the left of the road and some 30 m. from the sea.

This was a medium sized EC basilica (about 24 m. from threshold to synthronon), and had quite lavish screens and columns of imported marble; its roofing would have been of wood. The entire ground plan is visible, and two columns and caps and the very fine templon screens (although partly fragmented) have been reconstructed. The exceptional size and quality of the marble reliefs here contrasts with the terra cotta tiles of the floor, which are partly still in place; there is no trace of mosaic. Could it be that the two reliefs were brought here having been first installed elsewhere? They are 2.32 m. wide, and leave a gap of only 87 cm. between them, which appears distinctly narrow. A further contrast is also provided by the surviving masonry of the apse which, relative to the interior furnishings, is of quite rough quality. There are some graves in the S aisle and remains of other buildings to the N (perhaps a baptistry?) (The cruciform font in the garden of the Atlantis Hotel in the town may have come from this site.) Both side aisles are slightly lower than the central nave, and the ensemble conveys a feeling of being the result of more than one building phase.

Be prepared to spend some time in this tranquil site adjoining the beach, as you will find its inherent interest repays an unhurried viewing.

Arkasa

Extensive EC floor mosaics, 4th – 6th C. Unenclosed.

Just before reaching the village by the road descending from Menetis, a sign on the left points towards the church of Agia Sofia (formerly Agia Anastasia) about 1/2 a km. away, where the small modern church now stands some 30 m. from the sea.

All the mosaic floors left here (two sections were removed by the Italians to the Archaeological Museum, Rhodes) are in the open and immediately adjacent to this church, except for one area to the W which has been roofed. This is a complex site, with mosaic floors partly superimposed from three different buildings, and the encroaching weeds do not make it easier to distinguish the different phases. The first area that you reach is some 6 m. square and to the N of the modern church; this is known as the basilica of Alypos as the inscription reads: 'Lord, help your servant the presbyter Alypos who made this work'. The mosaic is not an ambitious one, using only four colours and quite simple abstract patterns, but is thought to be later 4th or early 5th C, which would make it one of the earliest mosaics of this extent in the Aegean. It was partly overlaid by the mosaic floor of the NE area of the later 5th C basilica of Agia Anastasia, which also has inscriptions, although very damaged (it is sometimes referred to as the basilica of Ciros). This area, to the S and W of the modern church, is both more extensive (some 24 m. long) and more inventive, combining large circular motifs with other more varied ornament; parts of the central nave are still quite well preserved, although partly overgrown with weeds. A third, smaller church was built some 200 m. to the W in the late 5th C, and is known now as the basilica of the bishop Eukharistos from his dedicatory inscription; it is the floor mosaic of the bema from here that is one of the exhibits in Rhodes. It is of interest that the most decorative and complex area of mosaic was reserved for the immediate surrounds of the altar. There are a number of EC caps and column fragments in the vicinity here, but there is no indication of their original home. Some 10 m. to the W another section of mosaic, in much better condition, is now protected by a simple barrel-vaulted chamber.

Allow time for a leisurely visit here, as the site still offers substantial surviving areas of mosaic flooring, and working out the levels of the three basilicas underlines the continuity of EC building on this seaside locality before the Arab threat.

Ano Lefko on the road to Mesokhori near the island's W coast, has (for its location) a modestly sized but surprisingly elaborate church to offer, with the unusual dedication of **Agios Giorgios tou Notara;*** it is on the right of the road a short way before the left-hand turning down to Kato Lefko. It is a 12th C building, but its exceptional design incorporates five domes, which must make it almost without parallel in the islands. The frescoes are of the same date but are much damaged.

The whole of the N part of the island is one of the most savagely inhospitable and mountainous of the inhabited Aegean islands; it would have been amid this grand but desolate landscape that over 100 Turkish raiders (according to Buondelmonti's 15th C account) starved to death when the boats by which they had arrived were burnt while they were marauding inland. Certainly, the many rocks protruding in the dirt road that runs N to Olimpo make it inadviseable to use an ordinary town car. Those who travel it will be rewarded by a magnificent and rugged coastline, with steep mountain slopes descending abruptly into the sea.

Olimpo★★ offers so many characteristics of a medieval Aegean village that it should be visited for its forms alone, although the considerable medieval remains that it must have retained until recently have now been largely eroded. A 12th C church of Agios Onoufrios mentioned earlier this century cannot now be identified and may have largely collapsed, and most of the fabric of the medium-sized church of the Panagia in the middle of the village appears to be mainly 19th C; however, the iconostasis is 18th, and some fresco fragments are probably 17th C. Some of the earliest survivals in the village may be among the 40-odd windmills on the surrounding hills. This must be one of the most remote villages in all the islands, where the local women still wear traditional costume as a matter of course (and where, incidentally, family inheritance still descends from mother to eldest daughter). The well-signed "Museum" at Olimpo is the only such collection of folk material we have experienced where every single item is priced and for sale.

The most interesting building in the area is the small church of **Agia Anna★,** reached down a turning to the right of the dirt road which descends from Olimpo to the port of Diafani (enquire for the key at the kapheneion there); its interior offers a substantial area of aniconic fresco painting, of which other examples in the islands exist principally on Naxos, but also on Ikaria and Crete. These are now usually thought to be of the 10th-11th C, or even 12th, and as the example here has no inscription it has for the present to be seen as part of this post-iconoclast survival of aniconic church decoration.

   The tiny off-shore island of **Saria** to the N retains a number of ruined buildings at Palatia among which there must be some medieval survivals, and the small church of Agia Sofia is built on the site of a 5th C basilica, but access is seasonal and expensive and it was not visited. This applies to an even greater extent to the church of **Agia Irene** some 5 km. N of Mesokhorio on the W coast, which is said to have Byzantine origins and some frescoes, but which can also only be reached by sea; on 5th May boats leave from Levkos beach in the morning and remain for the day's celebrations; for the rest of the year this must remain unvisited except by the determined specialist.

KASTELLORIZO   Καστελλόριζο

Med: Megisti, Castrum Rubeum, Castellum Ruzum, Castel Roys, Castel Rugio, Castelrosso and (briefly) Castel Alfonsi.
Island group: Dodecanese (E). (*Nomos*: Dodecanese).

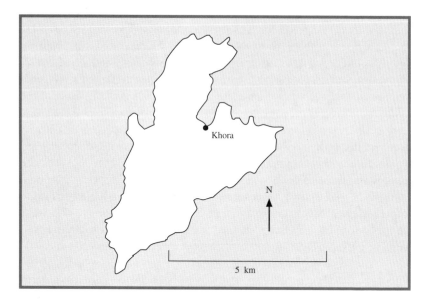

Although geographically isolated from the main group of the Dodecanese (its only link is now an administrative one) and really just a small rocky island off the coast of S Turkey, Kastellorizo has always maintained a distinct identity as part of Greece. Its position so far to the E of any other of the Aegean islands meant that whoever held it had a tempting foothold on the sea routes to Cyprus and the Holy Land, which they were in a position to provide for and protect. It was also well placed to give warning to any W powers of the possibility of a hostile Turkish presence.

The Knights of Rhodes were quick to realise this, and although they are only recorded as having occupied the island by c.1340, they were probably there before then. A pilgrim to the Holy Land of that date, Ludolph of Sudheim, wrote of the very high and strong castle here, and how the Knights sent signals of smoke by day and fire by night between here, Rhodes and Kos. When Nicolas de Martoni visited here in 1395 he was told that the islanders owned vineyards on the Turkish mainland, and that a truce with the local Turks permitted their farming them; you will see how close the mainland is, and commercial collaboration (strictly unofficial) is said to still exist today.

Another leader who was quick to see the potential value in having a foothold on this small island was Alfonso V, king of Aragon, Naples and Sicily (1442-1458); he was anxious to keep the Turks out of the Adriatic (even for a time entertaining an ambition to re-establish a Latin empire in CP with himself as emperor) and appointed himself the protector of both the Knights of Rhodes and the kingdom of Cyprus. An indication of the importance that the Hospitallers attached to the island is contained in the message that the Grand Master, Jean de Lastic, sent to the people of Lindos on Rhodes in 1440, threatening with the gallows any man of Lindos who did not join a ship to go to war against the Sultan of Egypt who was attacking Kastellorizo. In 1444 a Turkish attack on the island was successful, and the castle is said to have been destroyed (although see below). In 1450 Alfonso V received permission from the Pope (Nicholas V) to occupy the island to protect it from Turkish annexation, and the castle was taken over by Alfonso's admiral, Bernard de Villmarina; in 1452 he advised Alfonso that the castle tower was dilapidated, and the king told him to re-build it and install an escutcheon on it displaying the arms of Aragon. To the annoyance of the Knights he even renamed the island Castel Alfonsi.

It was due to its medieval importance that it came to be called 'The Castle in the East', as before the coming of the Knights it was only known as Castel Rosso – a misleading name as neither the soil nor the rock is red. The name of Megisti ('the biggest') that it is still sometimes given is due to the small archipelago of 11 rocky islands which no doubt once joined it to the Turkish mainland (a small chain of these would still encourage a moderate swimmer to reach the coast not far away); of these Kastellorizo is simply 'the biggest'. It has suffered drastic depopulation, with some 20,000 dwindling to under 200 during the last fifty or so years (there were about 700 in c.1400).

Kastellorizo / Megisti

Partly ruined 14th/15th C castle. Unenclosed. (See Pl. 8).
The prominent Kastro guarding the harbour and the straits beyond is the only surviving medieval building on the island. It is reached by an easy track up from the landward side (the piles of stone rubble you pass here were houses until the 1940's).

Both its site and its approach make you at once aware that it is very much a seaward-facing fort, with no major inland defences. It was built in two parts, of which the main square tower is easily the most prominent, and you will reach this first. The forms are very simple, and indicate that the main function of the fort would have been to act as a look-out post and guard for the channel that separates the island from the mainland. The summit of the tower encloses an area of some 10 x 15 m., and provides a perfect view of the sea approaches and the coast of Turkey beyond; it must have been from here that fire and smoke signals would be sent and received, warning of the presence of Turkish shipping.

It is not certain when the castle would have been built, but it was probably quite early in the 14th C after the Knights had occupied Rhodes, and an examination of the masonry of this main tower shows clearly that in its original form it had vertical walls. At a later date, which was probably in 1450, there was a broad talus built on to this which extended the base by some 10 m. or more all round, but the top few courses of the original, vertical walls were left exposed; the masonry of the quoins is of a noticeably more refined character on the later building than on the original. The fact that the original, earlier walls can still be seen here projecting above the later additions must imply that the castle was not really 'destroyed' in 1444, although it may have suffered some other damage. The addition of a talus would have been the work of Alfonso's admiral, Bernardo di Villamarina, and represents a standard 15th C form of adaptation to an existing earlier fortification which had vertical walls (similar to Antimakhia on Kos.) It could well have been that he needed to exaggerate the damage done in order to acquire funds for his work of modernisation; there seems in any case to be no signs of significant damage to this part of the fortress.

The lower, N facing outworks, reached by scrambling round the W side of the main tower, are now partly ruined, but it is still possible to establish their main structure. There would have been two rounded towers (still partly present) linked by a curtain wall running at a slight angle to the seaward wall of the main rectangular look-out tower; this formed a modest enclosure which still retains the remains of a cistern and which was even small enough to have been partly roofed. The original entrance to the main look-out tower would have been from this enclosure; you will see that a rectangular space still exists on the seaward wall of the fort that would presumably have held the relief escutcheon of Aragon that Alfonso had demanded; the entrance was probably just below this.

Museum.★★ Usual hours; small charge. Closed on Mondays.
The small Museum is housed in an old, semi-fortified house just below the Kastro.

Besides some of the more standard local ethnographical material, there are several items that make this well worth visiting. There is a small but quite impressive group of 17th C frescoes detached from the walls of the local church of St Nicholas; these indicate how the present reduced state of the island's population and economy is actually relatively recent. Also on view are a number of fragments of EC marble sculpture from the destroyed church of Agios Giorgios Santrape, although none are of great distinction. (The small area of floor mosaic that was reportedly found on the site of this church now seems to have disappeared.) What is unique here, however, is a collection of 30 near-perfect Byzantine ceramic plates that were retrieved from a wreck in one of the island's bays. The very personal and inventive semi-abstract slip underglaze decoration is an unexpected feature of secular ceramic art; when first published in 1986 these were dated to the mid-13th C, but opinion now is that they may be slightly later. The usual result of long immersion in sea-water is for objects like these to have lost some or all of their glaze, and to have accumulated barnacle growth, but this group has not suffered in either of these ways, and their fresh inventiveness could surely not be matched in any other museum. An exceptional, and even unique, display, earning this museum its **.

So while the medieval attractions of Kastellorizo are limited in number, they still make the island a rewarding one to visit, and walks inland will reveal such survivals from the Turkokratia as the deserted buildings of an 18th C monastery. A visit to this island is warmly recommended.

KEA Κέα

Also: Keos. *Med*: Zia.

Island group: Cyclades (W). (Nomos: Cyclades)

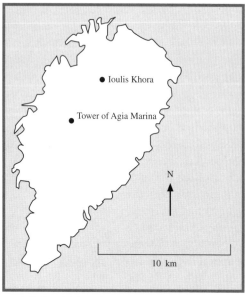

Kea is hilly but well-watered, and was from antiquity regarded as one of the best-endowed of the Cyclades. Like so many of the islands, it is unmentioned by any medieval historians until the Fourth Crusade altered the whole pattern of the Aegean. From 1204 its position affected the course of its later history, as it is within easy sight of the coast of mainland Greece; it was no doubt for that reason that the archbishop of Athens, Michael Akominatos, exiled by the Latins in 1206, spent his unhappy last years here, from where he could see his beloved Attica. Lying on the outer fringe of the Cyclades meant that the island did not form part of the original Duchy of Naxos under the Sanudi, probably because it would have been harder for the dukes of the Archipelago to maintain control from Naxos.

It was to be through the efforts of a Venetian, Domenico Michieli, assisted by Pietro Giustiniani, that Kea was annexed to the minor princedom of the Venetians Andrea and Geremia Ghisi, who had occupied Tinos and Mykonos, as well as Skyros, Skopelos and Skiathos. (It is a comment on the character of these island dynasties that in theory, according to the Deed of Partition, both Tinos and Skyros belonged to the Latin emperor in CP, and should never have been occupied by Venetians.) Kea, with all these islands, had been recovered for the Byzantines by the Lombard admiral Licario c.1276, but during the war between the Byzantines and Venetians that began in 1296, the Ghisi were able to recover Kea, along with Amorgos and Serifos. The proximity of the island to the mainland also meant that the Catalans, after their occupation of Athens in 1306, did not neglect to plunder it.

In the 1419 treaty between Venice and the sultan Mehmet I, Kea is named among the islands that are acknowledged as belonging to Venice. It was to be as late as 1499 that Kea came by chance briefly to the forefront of Aegean politics when the ruling Duke of Naxos, Francesco III Crispo, went mad and murdered his wife. As his son and heir, Giovanni IV Crispo, was no more than eleven years old, a Giacomo I Gozzadini, who was then baron of Kea, was elected as a temporary governor of the whole Duchy of Naxos. Kea would have come under final Turkish occupation in 1566, with much of the rest of the Archipelago.

While the island may have enjoyed some relative prosperity, the fact that it now offers few medieval survivals, with no substantial Byzantine building left to see, must be due in part to its peripheral position; regarded as part of the archipelago by the powers on the mainland, but never a full member of the Duchy of Naxos, it lacked the protection that other islands might call upon.

Ioulis / Khora   Ιούλις Χώρα

Gateway and wall of 13th C Kastro. Permanently open.
On leaving the Plateia and entering the pedestrian area, follow signs up a broad walkway directing you to 'Hotel Ioulis'.

The kastro here was almost certainly built by Domenico Michieli c. 1210 after he had occupied it under the Ghisi, but it was largely dismantled late in the 19th C. Before then it would have been the most substantial survival from the medieval period that the island offers, but it is now much diminished. The first part of it that you will see is a section of Hellenic wall on your left, on the large blocks of which the 13th C builders erected some of the wall of the Venetian kastro; for some reason this was left standing when the rest was demolished. A short distance further on you will reach a wide, low arch spanning the path; this was the fortified entrance to the kastro, and is some 20 m. deep. It was probably spared from demolition as later building has provided it with domestic housing above, and it is devoid of any gates – although the channels that may have guided a port-cullis can still be seen. Once you have passed through the gateway you are in the grounds of the Hotel Ioulis, a relatively modern building.

Tower of Agia Marina.

Hellenic tower with ruins of medieval monastic buildings.* Fenced but open.

The tower can be seen from the road from Ioulis to Poisses, where a sign points down a winding dirt road to the right.

Although this huge Hellenic tower is pre-Christian, it is included here on account of the medieval monastery that was built adjacent to it. Now it provides easily the chief interest here, surpassing in its original scale even the massive tower of St Peter on Andros; although the latter is more complete, the three storeys of that on Kea, which can be seen where the E wall has fallen away, make it the largest in the Aegean. The technique of dry stone building to this height, with carefully-set steps leading from floor to floor, still appears miraculous. The ruins to the E of the tower are those of monastic buildings that existed here in the medieval period, but there is too little left to allow for the suggestion of even an approximate date. The fabric of the church of Agia Marina (unlocked) is relatively late, although an earlier foundation can be assumed. When Theodore Bent visited the monastery here in 1883 he was told that the monks had had their cells in the tower, and that its partial collapse had only begun when King Otho visited it around the middle of the century and had asked for a stone with some carving on it to be removed from the wall of the tower so that he could take it back to Germany, and that this had caused instability in the whole structure.

It would be a pity to leave Kea without visiting this quiet valley with its immensely impressive ensemble, which (like Episkopi on Sikinos) survives as a relatively rare example of a major classical building having been adapted to the needs of Christian monastic life.

KEFALLONIA　　　　　　　　Κεφαλλωνιά

Med.: Cephalonum, Cephalinia, La Chipolignie, Zeffalonia.
Island group : Ionian / Eptanisous. (*Nomos*: Kefallonia).

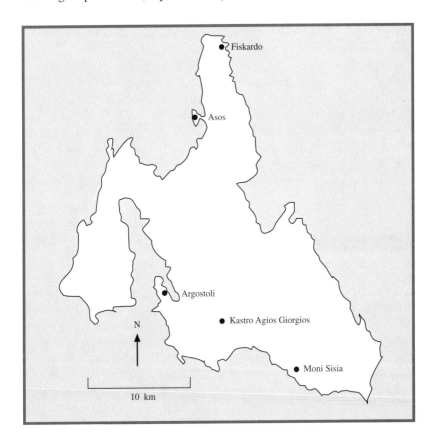

The name of this fertile and well-watered island, the next largest of the Ionian group after Corfu, was said to be due to the profile that it presented to sailors coming from the S, to whom it appeared to resemble a man's head (*kefalos*). In common with the other Ionian islands, the proximity of Italy and its distance from CP shaped its medieval history at all stages. In the early centuries the island was an important link with Byzantine possessions in Italy, and subsequently it took on a frontier role in preventing Arab infiltration into the Ionian sea.

Coveted and raided later by both Normans and Venetians, in 1185 it was eventually taken by the admiral Margaritone of Brindisi for William II, the Norman king of Sicily. Its fortunes were thereafter to remain closely linked, with its neighbours of Zakynthos to the S and Ithaki to the N, to the W powers. Matteo Orsini, who had married the daughter of Margaritone, became 'Lord of the Ionian Islands' in 1194, founding a dynasty that would survive until 1339; that of the Tocco succeeded in 1357, the last of whom, Antonio, ceded Kefallonia and Zakynthos to the sultan Bayezit II in 1485. Venetian interests in the Ionian sea were always very strong, however, and they had made sure that in the Deed of Partition of 1204 Zakynthos was listed as being allocated to the Republic; while they might tolerate other Italian rulers the ownership of Turkey was a different matter, endangering all their sea routes to the Levant, and in 1500 they seized the islands, to retain them until 1797.

Although the British were later in occupation (1809-64), following a French and Russian presence 1797-1809, it is predictably the long Venetian presence that is best reflected in the surviving secular buildings of Zakynthos.

Asos   Άσος

Venetian castle.* Gated but open.
Easily seen and reached from the road running up the W coast of the island.

Although not built in the medieval period, this entry is included as this castle is (with the Kastro Agios Giorgios) one of the two surviving major buildings that commemorate the long Venetian presence on the island. The magnificent prospect that this castle presents as you look across from the coast road, and before descending to the isthmus which joins it to the main land mass of Kefallonia, is really the most descriptive, as well as the most spectacular. From no other point are you able to see so much of the building at once, and it is easy to follow the line of the fortified enceinte as it runs right down to the lower cliffs on the N end.

Once you have climbed the steep dirt track up to its walls (not recommended for town cars) you are confronted by a huge fortified Venetian rusticated gateway; the building dates are given by a plaque here with the date of 1595, and over the second, inner door of this curved entrance, with a finely set ashlar vault, is the date of 1611. The interior of the castle, after this impressive arrival point, is perhaps something of an anticlimax, although an attractive one. The Venetians in effect did little more than enclose the greater part of the summit of this huge rock, and the interior presents a pleasantly rural scene of partly cultivated land with farm cottages, vineyards and collapsed terrace walls;

the only substantial internal building is a strongly fortified redoubt on the SE extremity. The building of this very sizeable castle must have been undertaken with two objectives in mind: the small harbour of the village of Asos, at its foot (overlooked by the redoubt), would have been well protected, and the interior space could both have sheltered a very large part of the island's population in times of danger as well as providing safe agricultural land.

A visit here makes a rewarding objective if you are travelling N to Fiskardo, and the coast road passes through some of the finest coastal scenery in all the Ionian islands.

Fiskardo   Φισκάρδο

Substantial ruins of a basilica.★★ Unenclosed.
The port here formed from a small inlet was used by many ships overtaken by storms when crossing from Ancona, and it is on its N shore that the ruins stand isolated and exposed, in full view of the village across the harbour.

This small settlement is named after the duke of Apulia, the fair-haired, blue-eyed giant Robert Guiscard (a son of Trancred of Hauteville), who died here in 1085 at the age of 70, the last of the great Norman 'robber brigands' to make war in Italy. Robert had already made one military incursion into Greece, and was embarking on another when, already stricken by an epidemic that was probably typhus, he died at this small harbour where his boat had put in to shelter from a storm, and which was later to be named after him.

The ruins on the headland here are of a substantial, triple-nave, single-apse basilica, measuring some 25 m. from threshold to apse; there may have originally been a five-light apsidal window. It has no narthex, but the most striking (as well as the most interesting) feature of the design remains the pair of large towers at each corner of the W facade of which the ruins still rise to several metres; the strangely shaped door openings that these display are only part of the range of interesting and unusual features here, but before discussing them further it is worth mentioning that the whole structure appears to be built at one time, constructed of local stone but with tile courses inserted – the four courses in the apse strongly reminiscent of Byzantine practice.

Twin towers became a distinct feature of EC churches in Syria and Anatolia in the 6th and 7th C, but this appears to be their only appearance in Greece. They were also a symbol of secular power in the early medieval period, being a feature of palace facade design in Rome and other parts of the early medieval world where this association was understood or emulated. Their appearance here has produced the suggestion that this is an 11th C building, the product of Guiscard's son, Roger Borsa, wishing to create a memorial to his father's memory which gave expression to his imperial ambitions. However, archaeologists now accept that this must be an EC basilica, but incorporating (for reasons so far unknown) the twin-tower facade associated with Syria and Anatolia.

With the views across the straits to Ithaki only some 3 km. away, the isolated ruins of this substantial basilica fully deserve and repay a leisurely visit.

Kastro Agios Giorgios   Κάστρο Άγιος Γιόργιος

Heavily fortified castle. ★ Closed.
The rocky hill-top here can be seen from a considerable distance, and the large castle on its summit housed the medieval and the Venetian capital. On the left of the road that climbs up to the fortress is the ivy-clad shell of a ruined church, where the apse still retains some of its original fresco decoration.

The foundation date of the castle is unknown, but it is mentioned in an interesting document concerning land holdings in the island that was drawn up in 1264, so it may well have been begun during the 12th C by the first Orsini rulers. Now nothing survives from before the 17th C, and the greatest impression to the modern viewer is provided by the truly awesome array of massive outer defences of the Kastro which dominate the whole area and are 17th and 18th C Venetian work; the town below, which used to serve as the capital of the island, was abandoned after an earthquake in 1757. The plan of the castle is a rather pointed oval, with four towers and a massive bastion at one apex with prominent machicolation.

When visited, the gates were locked pending the appointment of a state custodian, but even so, the impressive exterior can be fully appreciated and in any case dominates the character of the few remaining buildings inside the castle. At the towering entrance the slits through which ran the chains of a drawbridge are still evident, and the three flamboyant escutcheons on the bastion beside it will be of the Venetian governors: from left to right they are of the Grimani, Foscari and Balbi families, and the fourth, higher up and with the initials B C is of the Contarini. There was only minimal destruction in the 1953 earthquake, but of the various buildings within the fortifications the earliest is said to be the church (now roofless) which was an early 17th C foundation.

Even without entering this is a worthwhile objective, and when it is open on the appointment of a guardian it will provide a spectacular and memorable visit.

Sision: Moní Sisia   Μονί Σίσια

Ruins of Franciscan conventual buildings. ★★ Unenclosed.
(See Pl. 9).
Travelling on the coast road down the broad SE promontory from Argostoli, the new monastery of this name (now dedicated to the Panagia) is signed down a steep narrow road towards the sea; continue some 300 m. beyond where the road ends at the new monastic buildings and you will reach the ruins of a medieval ecclesiastical complex left as they fell in the earthquake of 1953.

At first sight you might think that you were here looking at the ruins of a neo-classical church building, and the date of 1849 in the metalwork over the door could be thought to confirm this; however, once you have entered the shell of the church (now roofless) through the door in the N wall and then passed through to the open area beyond, you will find that you are standing in a space that has all the characteristics of the courtyard of a W conventual cloister, albeit heavily overgrown. Even the well-head is still in place here, occupying the centre of the rectangular cloister area, and with cobbled paths radiating from it. At this point the name of the location here, Sision, should be recalled, as it derives from the original dedication of this complex to (Saint Francis of) Assisi. The buildings (which are still quite extensive) were arranged so that the church formed the N side of a square, with other conventual offices on the other three sides; the roofless hall to the E may well (by comparison with other early Franciscan houses) have been the friars' dormitory. Returning to the church building, it can be seen how earlier decorative roundel windows were reduced or blocked up and larger windows were made and given new frames in the 19th C renovation, and the whole interior coated with a new layer of plaster; under this it is possible that some original fresco decoration may survive. The niche to the N of the altar is particularly interesting; falling plaster reveals it to have been a double niche which has been reduced by raising the bottom member and filling in one side, and now the remains of a fresco of the *akra tapeinosis*, the Man of Sorrows, can still be seen; this was the standard subject to be found in the prothesis of a Byzantine church, and confirms the impression that one is standing in a church that was originally built for the celebration of the Roman rite, but became transferred to

Orthodox use.

The completely un-Byzantine form of the ensemble is confirmed in an affirmation by the priest and traveller Christoforo Buondelmonti, who was here c.1418 and wrote that when he was travelling on the island he visited Sision where there was "close to the sea a church of St Francis that he built himself, and there we attended worship with reverence." This comment is of great interest as he was clearly repeating a local tradition, and means that Franciscan friars were still in residence. This confirms the derivation of the current Greek name, which can clearly be traced back to that of St Francis of Assisi, and on the departure of the Franciscans the name of their Order lived on here as Moni Sisia. The Franciscans probably left in the brief period of Turkish occupation of 1485-1500, as Greek monks would have been preferable to Italian Franciscan friars for the Muslim power.

The date of the original foundation will probably never be known for certain, but Franciscans were already established in CP by 1220, and it has been suggested that Saint Francis, whose ship took refuge in the island when a storm arose while he as on a sea voyage from Ancona in 1219, could indeed have visited this place. Although not proven, this is an attractive hypothesis, and there were certainly no less than 14 Franciscan houses in 'Romania' by 1400.

While there are comparable ruins of W monasteries on the Greek mainland, this is the most interesting of those on the islands, and the only one outside Crete; it remains surprisingly little known, and a visit here offers a unique and highly rewarding experience in a dramatic coastal setting, and should not be missed.

KHALKI   Χάλκη

Med: Carchi, Carystos.
Island group: Dodecanese. (*Nomos*: Dodecanese).

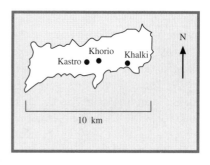

T
he fortunes of this small, rocky island off the W coast of Rhodes must always have been linked closely to those of its larger neighbour during the medieval period. Historians do not mention it at all, and its main claim to distinction is recorded by the traveller Buondelmonti, here c. 1418, who wrote that this was a place where St Nicholas was said to have rested after a tiring voyage *(ex itinere fatigatus)*; minimal EC remains at sea level and inland, including within the Hospitaller castle, show that it was inhabited at that period, but Khalki must have remained largely depopulated for much of the medieval centuries. In 1366 a citizen of Rhodes, Borrello Assanti, was given charge of the island, with that of Piskopia, on payment of 200 florins and on condition that he built a tower with a cistern on its even smaller neighbour, Alimnia; it is not clear what defences were then in existence on Khalki, although it could be assumed that the acropolis above Khorio was fortified in some way.

The Hospitaller castle here (see below) seems to have largely been built in the later 15th C, suggesting that the presence of the Knights had brought about a measure of security. However, the island would certainly have come under Turkish occupation on the withdrawal of the Hospitallers from Rhodes in 1523.

Hospitaller castle.★★
Extensive ruins of castle enclosing ruined Byzantine church. Unsigned at any point. Ungated and open. (See Pl. 10).
A good concrete road leaves the town going SW, and reaches a monastery gate after some 3 km. of uphill gradient; traverse the monastery courtyard and follow a stony track up to the castle.

Three factors are clear before even entering the original gateway: you will have passed large numbers of ruined dwellings on the way up here, and the inland khora (now Khorio) here was evidently (as in many other islands) the home for most of the island's population through the medieval centuries and into recent times. The harbour-side settlement will mostly be relatively modern. It can also be seen that several courses of large dressed stones in the base of parts of the castle enceinte show that there was an existing pre-Christian fortification here; this re-use of sites and building from classical times was quite a common feature of Hospitaller castles and can be seen on Alimnia, Symi, Tilos and elsewhere. Thirdly, an escutcheon in relief over the gate shows the arms of the Grand Master Pierre d'Aubusson (1476-1503) quartered with those of the Order; while not always an accurate guide to dating, it can be said that d'Aubusson was very proud of being made a cardinal in 1489, and (as in Antimakhia, Kos) the cardinal's hat tended to be included in his escutcheon after this date; the fact that it is absent here may therefore suggest that the building of this castle took place between 1476 and 1489. Certainly the extensive castellation still to be seen on the N wall is fully consistent with this kind of date, and this castle may have been part of the concerted campaign of fortification which also included his work at Symi and left over 50 of Aubusson's escutcheons in the walls of Rhodes. It is possible that the castle may have been built here to reinforce the much smaller one on Alimnia, from which the view of the Rhodes coastline was more limited.

Once inside the gateway the visitor finds himself in a guard room (now roofless) some 5 m. square; this is the only point in the castle where cannon embrasures can still be seen, but there are only three and of relative simplicity, implying that heavily armed attack was not anticipated. The masonry suggests that this may have always been an ante-chamber to the pre-existing structure, as the gateway from this into the main enclosure is formed from huge monoliths that must have survived from the Hellenistic structure, and cannot have been part of the Knights' building. The main enclosure is a rough oval, some 90 m. x 40 m., now mostly full of rubble from collapsed internal buildings. The wall of the enceinte is still complete for much of the N sector, and parts elsewhere, and seems to follow the classical walling; the sentry walk can still be used here for 30 m. or so. A substantial square-section tower occupies the centre of the N wall, with a latrine beside it, and a five-sided tower is opposite it to it on the S wall, looking towards Rhodes; a substantial cistern, with its lining and most of its roof still intact, lies almost between them, and a deep well has been sunk to the W.

But the most prominent feature of the interior is a medium sized church, occupying the area close to the N wall. Its rather bulky exterior is due to the fact that its original form seems to have been enclosed, or at least reinforced, by later stonework. It can easily be entered through a doorway in the S wall of the narthex, and the nave, now filled with rubble, was clearly once barrel-vaulted; the roof has collapsed and there are no signs of a dome here, although the narthex retains the springing of squinches. Inside the nave you can find a number of cases of further reinforcement of the structure, and among the rubble there are even some marble fragments of EC building such as window members. The interior of the church still retains areas of Byzantine fresco on three walls and the apse, although now much damaged; it is these which provide evidence for the dedication of the church to St Nicholas. Besides a colourful band of fictive marble at ground level, and standing saints on the S wall, which include bishops, one of whose titles can just be read as St Gregory Thaumaturgos, there are above these some miracle scenes; these include a clear image of a saint, who must be St Nicholas, steering a boat at sea. This is the only known image of an episode in the saint's *vita* when sailors called on him during a storm, and he arrived and took the helm, saving the ship from being wrecked. The tradition that St Nicholas, when tired from a journey, rested in the khora on Khalki was repeated by Buondelmonti: *in summitate oppidum,... ubi Nicolaus sanctus, ex itinere fatigatus, resedit*. It must be this tradition which lies behind the fresco cycle and makes St Nicholas the most likely dedication of the church. The style of the frescoes suggests a date in the Palaiologue period, or slightly later, and this could be explained by their being linked to the later 15th C building of the castle itself.

The sequence emerges of a pre-Christian fortification within which an EC church was later built; a Byzantine church replaced this at some point probably in the 12th or 13th C. The Knights later used the site for their castle, probably not before the later 15th C (although conceivably initiated, like Alimnia, during the 14th), and reinforced the church building, at the same time as the interior received its frescoes. In this way the ensemble is comparable with the Hospitaller castle on Tilos, enclosing its Byzantine church. The visitor to the castle here can therefore find four different periods of building located on this single hill-top site.

The function of the Hospitallers' castle here was probably two-fold; its size would indicate that it was intended to shelter quite a substantial number of the island's population (housed in nearby Khorio) in times of danger, and its position looking across to Rhodes and the Knights' castle of Kritinia would provide them with a further signalling base. It may be that the castle here was intended to support and amplify the purely observational intention behind the smaller castle on Alimnia (see p. 10).

Allow a clear half day for a visit to this exceptional site, as much of the range of interest here only becomes apparent on picking an unhurried path over the heaps of stony rubble.

Two other abandoned monasteries can claim attention, both reached by continuing to climb the road past the Kastro.

First reached is that of **Taxiarchis Mikhail Panormitis,*** where the church in the monastic buildings is usually locked, but it is possible to glimpse some damaged frescoes; the earliest are aniconic, and probably 10th C, with some later scenes of the Dodecaorton that are dated to the 12th C. Some classical spolia indicate that there was pre-Christian use of the site.

Continuing back along the track to the W, in about an hour of walking in magnificent scenery you will reach the buildings of the monastery of **Agios Ioannis Prodromos**; although highly picturesque, the main medieval interest is to be found in the small church of the **Panagia Enniameritissa,*** a short distance the NW. The interior has frescoes dated to 1367 by an inscription, although not in good condition, and the use of EC spolia is evidence of an early settlement here.

Leave plenty of time for this excursion; the surroundings will have altered little over the centuries and the interest of the two localities will reward the unhurried visitor.

It is from the dilapidated church of Agios Zakharias, in the country to the N of Emborio, that the 14th C frescoes were removed that are now in the Byzantine Museum, Rhodes.

KIMOLOS Κίμωλος

Island group: Cyclades (SW).   (*Nomos*: Cyclades.)

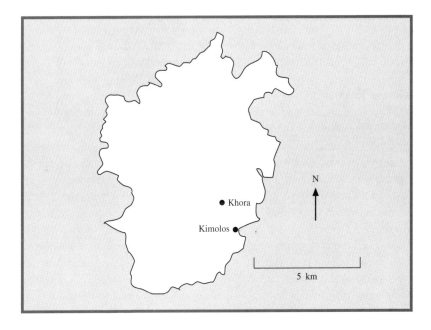

A lways linked with its larger neighbour of Milos, Kimolos with its volcanic soil cannot have been blessed with any very special riches during the medieval period, either natural or man-made. Although Pliny tells of silver mines here, and when Pitton de Tournefort was here c.1700 he calls it "silver island" (*Argentière*), this source of wealth must have by then been long exhausted. He reported that there were then no natural springs, the only water being rainwater conserved in cisterns, and so agriculture was always difficult on the unproductive land; only the fuller's earth that it exported brought some new wealth into the island's economy. Unmentioned in earlier medieval histories, its name does not appear in the Deed of Partition of 1204, but Marco Sanudo ensured that it formed part of his new Duchy of Naxos, passing later in the 14th C to the Crispo family. With the death of Francesco I Crispo in 1397, and with the division of the Duchy among his five sons, Kimolos (with Milos) formed part of a separate baronial fief with allegiance to the Duchy of Naxos. Its lack of an early fortified kastro meant that it must have been a target for pirates, and there were periods when it became uninhabited. It was later adopted by the Gozzadini, a Bolognese family who became completely Hellenised, and who maintained some form of feudal presence on Sifnos, Folegandros and Sikinos as late as 1607; Angelotto Gozzadini sent his sons in that year from Kimolos to Rome for their education in the Collegio Greco there, but in 1617 they were swept away by the latest Turkish advances.

The medieval interest on Kimolos is entirely focussed on the Khora, about 1.5 km. inland from the harbour on an easy uphill road.

Khora: Kastro**.

This very much deserves a visit, although very different from the heavily fortified remains that the Venetians have usually left behind. Rather it is an enclosed area of two-storey domestic buildings that in character is strongly reminiscent of the similar kastro on Sifnos, the home of the da Corogna family. Indeed, according to an 18th C writer who was told so by the inhabitants, the traditional origin of the kastro here is that it was founded by twelve families who came here from Sifnos in the late 16th C to seek a freer life than they would have enjoyed in their native island; however, there is much better evidence that it was the Gozzadini family who were later on to adopt Kimolos as their home, even leaving inscriptions here. What you will now find is a high walled rectangular enclosure, roughly trapezoidal in plan and with a greatest dimension of some 80 m.

You enter it by one of the arched openings in the surrounding wall (these must have been gated during the centuries of its most active life) and immediately you are in a street of quite substantial town houses. They are noticeably well built, retaining much of their original masonry, fine marble quoins and external steps leading to upper floors. The whole area is built to a much more regular plan than the streets of the Greek part of the Khora which you will have just left, or indeed of other kastra such as those of Naxos or Mykonos; most of the upper floors are reached by an external staircase from the street, and a strong sense is given of an early essay in estate planning. This must be entirely the work of planners and builders with heavy Venetian influence, and be the result of the original annexation of the island by a W family. There does not now seem to have been a central administrative building or palace, such as is left on Sifnos, nor does the ensemble seem to have been defended in any conventional sense; there is certainly no surviving castellation, nor any sense that such defences were needed. After a few minutes here you feel that you might be in a rather neglected old town in the Veneto or Friuli rather than on an Aegean island. It was apparently not strong enough to withstand a raid by pirates in 1638, when it was badly burnt, but recovered later in the century and remains today as a little-known but highly interesting example of Aegean urban planning.

The impressive church of **Agios Chrysostomos***, also in the Khora, is the other main point of interest on the island (key held just across the road in nearest house to the S). It lies just a few m. to the N of the Kastro, is unusual in having its exterior of local stone without any rendering, and has its own surrounding wall enclosing a courtyard. It is of medium size (quite large by Cycladic standards) and its interest lies both in its overall plan and in some well-preserved detail. The former has been created to give it a virtually double nave, divided internally by a broad arcade; there was previously a narthex right across the W end, and a rather squat octagonal drum supports a relatively small cupola. This would suggest that it may be another example of a church built to house both the Latin and Greek rites, and this impression is reinforced by the unusual carved decoration framing the S door and a double window in the S crossing, which would seem more at home in a medieval W context. The period of its building is difficult to determine, but the position of the church outside the Venetian kastro combined with its possible use by Latin as well as Greek congregations suggests a 13th / 14th C date; certainly this would seem the most probable period.

The combined interest of this church and the unique qualities of the Kastro, make the Khora of Kimolos a highly rewarding visit.

KOS

Κως

Med: Ico, Karia, Lango, Stanchio; *Turkish*: Istankoy).
Island group: Dodecanese. (*Nomos*: Dodecanese.)

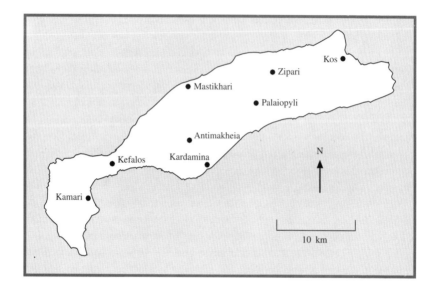

The largest of the Dodecanese after Rhodes, Kos was an island of considerable religious and political importance throughout the EC centuries; the bishop of Kos, although a suffragan of Rhodes, participated in major church councils from the 1st at Nicaea (of 325) onwards; the only other Greek islands so represented were Rhodes, Limnos and Corfu. It was governed from CP by officials of the rank of *droungarios*, and during the 12th C members of the imperial family controlled the island. After 1204 in the Deed of Partition Kos was actually awarded to the Latin emperor, but from the start he was never able to exercise control and the island at that stage came under the rule of the Genoese; c.1225 the navy of the Byzantine government in exile in Nicaea and its emperor John Vatatzes occupied it, as he did also Lesbos, Chios, Samos, and Ikaria, which then all formed part of the Nicene empire.

In 1304 the island came again under the control of the Genoese in the form of the Zaccharia family, before being included (with Leros) as part of the agreement under which the Hospitallers took over Rhodes as their main base in 1306-9. They did not actually occupy the island until 1315, and then their presence was interrupted for some 18 years from c.1319 when the Turks were again in control, but after c.1337 another phase of relative importance began with the re-assertion of the Knights' presence; it would have been under them that the Latin bishop Oddino was installed here in 1343. At this time the clear Byzantine interest in maintaining influence in Kos was reflected in Andronikos III (1328-41) raising the island to the status of an archbishopric. The Hospitallers eventually built here the most massive of their castles outside Rhodes, and its siting at the NE tip where it faced across to the Turkish coast only 5 km. away was certainly a gesture of defiance intended not only for the benefit of their Muslim enemies there, but also to show their Christian allies in the W that they were acting as a bulwark against Muslim aggression. Outside the castle, the island was quite vulnerable, and in 1457 and 1460 a Turkish force under the young sultan Mehmet II had attacked and sacked the island, as part of his intended subjugation of the Aegean, but he found that he was unable to take the castle on either occasion and withdrew. It was only after the fall of Rhodes in 1523 that Kos came finally under full Turkish subjugation.

The medieval survivals of Kos form a fair reflection of the island's history, being divided between some exceptional EC sites, a few Byzantine churches and the massive military buildings of the Hospitallers.

Kos town

Med: Narangia.
1) Hospitallers' castle (Kastro Neratzias).★★★ Enclosed and gated; usual museum hours and entrance charge.

The overwhelming reason for the Knights to develop the town of Kos would have been to provide a base from which they could defy the Turks, and it was therefore to be expected that the town would be subjected to periodic retaliatory attacks from these hostile neighbours. In order to guard themselves against these assaults the Knights had early on built a massive protective wall, the considerable remains of which you will find as you approach the Castle to the E of the harbour (*Mandraki*); this was built 1391-6 under the Grand Master Heredia to defend the City of the Knights, and was the first area to be enclosed in this way, taking in the market and part of the harbour area.

The Castle itself is easily the most prominent medieval building in the town, and its harbourside position makes it an inescapable landmark. You enter it now by a bridge leading from the original Knights' enclosure and arriving at a doorway in the outer enceinte. There would originally have been a drawbridge, and even today the entrance starts on the original stone-built walk-way and has its last section in wood – although longer now than earlier this century in order to make space for a wider road below.

The area that you enter first would have been among the later parts to be built. When the traveller Ruy de Clavijo visited here in 1403 he crossed what he called "a lagoon of sea-water", which was in fact a moat. "You enter the castle across a bridge which spans the ditch which is filled by sea-water", he wrote. He must at that date have been entering the first enceinte to what is now the massive construction on a roughly rectangular plan that occupies the central area of the castle, and which you will reach later. The modern visitor approaches the entrance which is under a piece of decorative Hellenistic sculpture set over the door, in the form of a row of theatrical masks; the quartered arms of Emery d'Amboise (1503-1512) indicate the relatively late construction of this area. (While not always a precise guide to building dates, the many knights' escutcheons here, as elsewhere, can be used as a guide to building activity.) More classical spolia can be found used in this way in Kos than any other of the Knights' castles, of which the severity usually has little relief beyond the inevitable escutcheons. This mode of entry makes it harder to grasp the general plan of the castle, which is a rough quadrilateral, with a double enceinte, but now has quite a complex interior arrangement. The complexity of the whole site is due to the fact that its growth took place in several phases and over more than a century; the many reliefs of Knights' escutcheons on both the exterior and interior walls are alone evidence of the interest of successive Grand Masters and governors of Kos.

Surprisingly, there is no evidence of building here before about 1450 other than the testimony of Clavijo; the date below a triple escutcheon prominently sited on the central building is 1454, and the Venetian governor, Fantino Querini, was involved at this point until his fall from grace, but a start may have been made as early as the time of the Grand Master Juan Fernandez Heredia (1377-96). The visitor now arrives on the S terrace of the later, outer enceinte, and a staircase leads to an interesting collection of sculpture, mostly fragmentary, from classical and medieval periods, with a number of Knights' escutcheons; much of the former may have come from the *Asklepieion*. The nearest bastion to this SW corner is part of the latest phase of the building here completed in 1514 and named after the Grand Master Fabrizio del Carretto, who employed fellow Italians in its design and construction. This, and the corresponding one to the NE looking across towards Bodrum, would represent the most up-to-date military engineering of the period anywhere in Europe, with ample provision for artillery and cleverly angled, smooth masonry to deflect incoming cannon-balls. Coming down from this level you can penetrate the inner enceinte through an entrance passage roofed entirely by ten massive granite columns, which again must be classical spolia; the triple escutcheon over the entrance is of the Grand Master Pierre d'Aubusson (1476-1503). (These are also on the outer massive NW bastion overlooking the harbour). The inner area is dominated by the massive four-square structure with corner towers which was the original castle of the Knights; two sets of escutcheons are on the N and NE aspects, one dated 1476 and another with the arms of the Grand Master Giovanni-Battista Orsini (1467-1476). It is of interest to record that the usual garrison at Kos consisted of 25 Knights Hospitaller, ten Latin men-at-arms, 100 foot-soldiers, a doctor and apothecary, and a galley with banks of 20 oarsmen.

The best way to gain an impression of the ensemble is to use the continuous walk-way round the battlements; you will find a deep enclosed area in the NE corner with steps leading down to a lower level, where three archways have now been blocked up – possibly once a watergate or loading area for the galley maintained here. The overall impression of the inner bailey is one of quite frequent and sometimes extensive re-modelling during the period of its use, but the Turks do not seem to have felt the need to continue this process; it was to oppose them that the castle had originally been built, and once they were in possession here it no longer had a role to play.

The exterior walls of the enceinte also display more Knights' escutcheons; one of these facing out to the NE (although upside down, and so presumably re-set) is of the Venetian Fantino Querini and dated 1445. He was an admiral and governor of Kos 1436-1453 and was much involved in building the castle, although in 1453 he was dispossessed and imprisoned by the Grand Master Jean de Lastic.

2) The Knights' enclosure.
Not far from the entrance to the Castle, on the corner of Leoforos Hippokratous and Odos Giorgiou II, is a relatively modest, partially fortified building on a square plan. It must have formed part of the land defences of the Knights' enclosure, and its chief interest is that it retains three fine escutcheons of the Knights over its door; these have usually only survived on more prominent buildings, and that on the left, of three towers, could be that of Grand Master Heredia (1377-1396) in a reduced form, and so perhaps before he was elected Grand Master. This adjoins a small area of overgrown parkland SW of the harbour front, and behind the buildings of the Akti Miaulithis was the area of the Knights'

enclosure, and you will find the two churches here of **Agios Giorgios***
and (somewhat larger) **Agios Ioannis*,** both built with copious use of
spolia and both in use (the latter normally open, although without
particular internal interest). While probably only dating from the last
decades of the Knights' presence here, they are comparable to the many
such small churches built in Rhodes during the same period.

3) EC basilica and baptistry in frigidarium of Roman baths.*
Fenced enclosure, but can be entered.
Among the extensive remains of Hellenistic and Roman buildings in the
town, the Western Excavations contain the most striking survivals, with
mosaics and even some wall paintings from the classical period. The
frigidarium of the large baths complex here was converted into a basilica
in the 5th C, and the best preserved part of this is the baptistry. A marble
doorway has been re-erected, and the marble steps descending into the
baptismal font to E and W are still in place; the floor area has extensive
mosaics, but these have unfortunately been covered with protective gravel.

Among the EC monuments on Kos this is not the most impressive,
but it does demonstrate an interesting adaptation of a classical building
to 5th C Christian use.

4) EC basilica in the Asklepieion complex.**
Enclosed; usual museum hours and entrance charge.
*Some 4 km.SW of the town, beyond the village of Platanos, is the highly
impressive excavation of the Asklepieion; this has now been made the
principal tourist attraction on the island, with a huge car-park.*
It is certainly a grandly spacious Hellenistic site, and it would have been
surprising if EC builders had not been active here. To the left of the vast,
monumental staircase that faces the visitor the walls, some 8 m. high, of
the large triple nave of the church dedicated to the **Panagia tou
Alsinou** rise towards the left (NE) corner of the first of the terraces; the
three large apses are partly buttressed, and the ground-plan and walls of
a baptistry survive to the SW corner. There are some large fragments of
marble slabs with relief carving, but otherwise no decorative features
survive. The scale of the ensemble is very impressive, and in this respect
is in keeping with its neighbouring classical ruins. The date is uncertain,
but it must be no later than 5th to 6th C

Zipari   Ζιπάρι

EC basilica and baptistry with extensive floor mosaics. *
Unsigned; ruined and enclosed, but can be entered.

This site lies only some 30 m. to the E side of the road from Kos town, and at about ¹/₂ a km. before you reach the crossroads in the centre of the village of Zipari, but is easy to miss due to being on a lower level than the road; it is approached down an unsigned farm track descending steeply from the road.

This is, with Agios Stefanos, the most rewarding of the EC sites on the island, with its extensive floor mosaics neither transported to Rhodes by the Italians nor covered in protective gravel. The basilica, dedicated to St Paul, is of medium size (some 21 m. from threshold to apse) and is dated by the style of the mosaics to the late 5th / early 6th C. The mosaics of the basilica floor are quite ambitious in design, with figurative themes such as birds enclosed in large, swirling abstract frames with flower forms filling the corners; the condition is still quite good, although encroaching weeds have caused some losses. The outstanding feature here, however, is the baptistry building in the SE corner of the complex, much of which still stands (it is the top of this which is all that can be seen from the road); it is square in plan and must have had a small dome, as the pendentives are still partly present. The font is sited so that the catechumens could step from its marble surround through a doorway and into the N aisle of the basilica. A further complex of rooms lies to the N, and these also have mosaic floors, although their function is not evident.

This is an impressive and atmospheric site, which provides a particularly clear indication of the layout and character of the basilica and its baptistry when it was functioning; you will almost certainly have it to yourself.

Palaiopyli   Παλαιοπύλι

Ruined village, three churches (one ruined) and ruined castle.**
Unsigned; churches open and castle unenclosed.
Some 4 km. on the road SW from Zipari take a left fork to reach Pyli in about a further 2 km; the route to Palaiopyli is down a left turn close to the modern church. The ruins of the old town lie mainly concealed behind a steep mountain that you reach on the left of the road after about a further 2 km.

Before starting the ascent of the main track, a short walk down a path leading E brings you soon to a medium-sized hall church with large narthex, with the unusual dedication of the Purification of the Virgin (it is unlocked). The interior is of standard Byzantine design for the Dodecanese, with the barrel-vault rising to a slightly pointed apex, but it is exceptional in that the ribs strengthening the roof are supported on corbels which in turn rest on re-used classical columns, standing free from the wall. It could be as early as the 14th C, but the frescoes are of 15th / 16th C; they are now in a poor state, with the apse holding those in best condition. This church probably served the needs of the village until it became deserted with the move of the population down to Pyli.

Returning to the track that winds up through the ruins, after about 10 minutes you will reach a smaller, very simple hall church dedicated to the Archangel Michael (it is unlocked). The floor is only of earth, but the frescoes are 14th / 15th C and show a range of Passion scenes, saints, bishops and with the Pantocrator over the altar; there is also a wall tomb and a narthex has been added. A number of fragments of classical spolia suggest that this may have been a temple site. This chance survival of a very modest rural church must represent countless others that have disappeared.

The stronghold at the summit (in essence an acropolis) is at the top of a steep but manageable path, which for some of the time is clearly that used by the medieval inhabitants. It is worth making the ascent for at least two reasons besides the magnificent views. On the way up the track passes through what was the narthex and naos of quite an elaborate, domed Byzantine church; the dome itself has long collapsed, but the elaborate herring-bone brick patterns set in the shallow blind niches of the W front show that it was a 13th / 14th C building of advanced design and expensive execution. It would seem to be the only medieval building on the island built solely of brick (presumably imported), and its presence must be the result of wealthy patronage. From 1249 Kos, with Lesbos, Chios, Samos and Ikaria formed part of the empire of the exiled Greek government in Nicaea, and we know that c.1258 a Byzantine *kephali* (governor) had been appointed to Pyli called Ioannes Steriones; it could well be that he was the patron of this quite impressive church, which would represent the taste of the Nicene Laskarid court at that time. Its presence and elaborate design can only be explained by some such association. The later addition of a stone-built gateway adjoining the W entrance makes it clear that the collapse of this church took place while the acropolis was still in use; there was a very serious earthquake on Kos in 1495, and it could well have been this that caused the destruction of this highly interesting building, of which the ruined W front was then adapted to provide an additional fortified barrier on the steep ascent to the summit.

Once on the summit the reason for building a citadel of this kind is at once apparent; the range and scope of the surrounding sea and land that can be observed from here is enormous, with Kalymnos clearly visible in the NW and the Turkish shore to the NE, with lower parts of

Palaiopyli to the S. The purpose of the original stronghold here was probably as a refuge for the local inhabitants when pirates or Turkish raiders attacked, but it is also perhaps no surprise to find a finely carved escutcheon of the Knights of Rhodes detached but lying close to the path; beside the Hospitallers' symbol are the arms of the Venetian Querini family; this suggests that Fantino Querini, governor of Kos 1436-53, was involved here as well as in the main town. (Buondelmonti, here in c.1418, called Pyli *Peripatos*, but makes no mention of the Knights.) The island was in the hands of the Hospitallers continuously from 1337, and with the huge Hospitaller castle at Antimakheia, only 6 km. to the SW, the fine visibility of the castle here would have made it a valuable link in a signalling chain to warn of any danger.

Antimakheia   Αντιμαχεία

Hospitallers' castle. ★★ Enclosed but can be entered.
Although this castle can be most easily seen from beside the sea at Kardamaina, it is more easily approached from the village itself; some 3 km. S of the village of Antimakheia down a dirt track running due SE, the massive walls of this large castle come into view.

Three features of its design and construction become evident almost before you enter; it was originally built to face sea-wards, with the land falling rapidly away towards the shore at Kardamaina, leaving the W approaches from inland relatively vulnerable. This must have been the cause for a later modernisation, whereby the land-ward walls were made much stronger with the addition of a broad talus, reaching up to within some four metres of the castellated summit of the original walls; thirdly, and most prominent of all, is the huge redoubt that must have been built at the same time as the talus was constructed, and was to protect the old N entrance from frontal attack. Among the escutcheons here is one above the entrance in the enceinte on your left as you enter the redoubt, which bears not only the arms of the Grand Master Pierre d'Aubusson, displayed proudly beneath his many-tasselled cardinal's hat (awarded him by the Genoese pope Innocent VIII in 1489), but also the date 1494.

Once inside the area enclosed by the walls the function of the entire castle becomes much clearer. There is first the huge area enclosed, which is at once evident – it is some 400m. from E to W and about 120m. from the N entrance to the S enceinte; there would be space for many hundreds here, at least for a limited period. Next you will probably be struck by its relative emptiness; there is a small church building almost opposite the entrance, another larger one towards the E end of the complex, and a sequence of ruined chambers along the S wall where the Knights could look directly across the straits to their colleagues in the kastro close to the harbour on Nisyros. But most of the area here is empty, with only traces of earlier buildings quite sparsely scattered; the chief function of this large enclosure must surely have been to act as a refuge for the protection of the local population in times of danger.

The smaller church (open) in the centre of the compound is a simple hall in form, and has traces of fresco remaining inside; its exterior displays a fine triple armorial which includes the arms of the Italian Grand Master Fabrizio del Carretto (1513-21) with the date 1520 – only three years before the final departure of the Knights from Rhodes – and a large cistern adjoins the N wall. To reach the larger church to the E (Agia Paraskevi tou Kastrou) you have to traverse areas of ruined building, but it is itself in good state. It is a barrel-vaulted, stone-built chamber with four broad ribs supporting the vault and a finely-cut stone apse; it is probably of 14th / 15th C, but the two W ribs are supported on earlier, broken caps that still have free-standing cut interlace on their corners. Remains of frescoes on W wall are probably contemporary with the foundation. Integrated into the exterior of the apse is a fine double row of pointed arcading, and a long chamber (now roofless) running the length of the S wall may have been a chapel or meeting space; on its W face is a superbly cut grey marble relief with d'Aubusson's arms, but it loses something of its impact by being mounted upside down.

It is along the S wall, looking down to Kardamaina and over to Nisyros, that one feels that the most daily activity would have taken place. A sequence of ruined chambers and low towers line this section of the enceinte, with a higher tower rising to the SE. The whole sector would have been easily seen from the castle at what is now the Panagia Spiliani on Nisyros, and signals could easily have been passed.

There remains the question of the overall building history of the castle here. It is known to have been attacked in 1457 for 20 days by Mehmet II, who was unable to take it and suffered heavy losses, and so must have been fully established by then. The date of 1494 must refer to modernisation by d'Aubusson; the arms of d'Amboise are a correct guide to the addition of the talus and the redout, which would be the main building of the last thirty years of the Knights' presence on Rhodes. In the context of their history in the area this would seem to be consistent with the scale and importance of Antimakheia, which must have been an important link in the communications between Kos (and even Bodrum on the mainland, built by 1408), Nisyros, Tilos or Symi and Rhodes, and the Knights would have wanted to give it full support. It seems more probable that by the time of the death of Philibert de

Naillac in 1421 there would have been a fortified building of some kind here, and that the operations marked by the later Knights' escutcheons were concerned with reinforcement and expansion. There may have been limited modernisation by the Turks, but the position cannot have been of great interest to them and they have left it largely untouched.

Kardamaina   Καρδάμαινα

Ground plan of EC basilica of Agia Theotis. Enclosed but can be entered.

A development of newly built apartment blocks and shops is the unlikely setting for the remains of the 5th C EC basilica of Agia Theotis. The site is only a short distance NW of the town centre, immediately opposite the Aeolus Travel office, and is set at an angle to the modern street grid. The nave is some 25 m. from threshold to apse, and is clearly marked, but none of the floor mosaics here have been preserved and the ground area of the nave is covered in gravel; likewise no spolia have been left here and no walls survive to any significant height. This is one of three EC basilica sites in Kardamaina and its vicinity, and emphasises the significant status that Cos must have had in the EC period.

Agios Stefanos   Άγιος Στέφανος

Ruins of two EC basilicas.★★
Unenclosed.
The two adjacent basilicas here, on the coast due E of Kephalos, form one of the outstanding natural EC sites in the Dodecanese. They are reached from the road running due W and near the coast, and access is just beyond a large new holiday complex some 10 km. from the airport.

Fortunately this intrusion of the modern world has not seriously detracted from the atmosphere of this sea-bound site where the waves are never more than a few metres away. The N basilica is the first that you will reach, but it is in fact slightly the later of the two, and for several reasons it can be preferable to visit the further one first.

The S basilica, which has been dated to the later 5th C, has a very complete plan: atrium (washed by the sea), with rock-cut steps up to the narthex, with a baptistery at its S end, and a nave with nine pairs of marble column bases; there are numerous fragments of carved marble, including part of a marble ambo and one entire column re-erected. This was clearly built with ample funds, which procured this imported material and supplied the extensive mosaic floors.

There is a contrast in this respect when you approach the N basilica; it was built with less lavish resources, but is somewhat larger (some 17 m. from entrance to the synthronon). The four piers down each side of the nave suggest that marble was not now available in these quantities; there are just fragments of a marble templon, now re-erected, which may have been re-used from an earlier building. The caps of the nave piers are less refined and of less special material. A point of interest here is the baptistry: this is a square chamber, with an unusual site outside the E end of the church, overlooking the rocky shore and with its marble-lined font still intact.

This one of the three or four richest EC sites in the Agean, and your visit should not be hurried.

Kefalos   Κέφαλος

Castle ruins. Unenclosed.

Overlooking the bay here, and some 50 m. above the sea, is this small, ruined fortress of the Knights. The siting is easily explained by the view across to Nisyros to the SE and towards Kalymnos to the NW; signals could readily have been passed to and from this point. It is possible that it was one of the earliest of the Knights' fortified structures on Kos, and that its modest size meant that it was eventually superseded by the much larger castles at Antimakheia and Kos town; there is no secure evidence of its date, and its ruins are now much abraded, but it was probably a later 14th / 15th C building. The site is spectacular, and the local terrain of soft, pale sandstone has been eroded by wind and rain to form cliffs displaying caves and shallow ravines.

Kamari   Καμάρι

Church of Panagia Palatia. Unenclosed.

On the left of the road running SW from Kephalos towards Agios Ioannis is a track with a sign to 'Panagia Palatia'; the building can be glimpsed from the road at about 50 m. distance. Although only a small and simple chamber, and now roofless, it was constructed from massive blocks that must have originally formed a classical temple; carved triglyphs are still visible, and the footing of the altar is formed from the base of a fluted marble column. Remains of an adjoining chamber (too elongated for a typical narthex) lie to the W, and traces of the original temple plinth can be found among the agricultural terracing nearby to the NW. Its date is impossible to establish with any precision, but it must

surely have been here before the arrival of the Knights, and could well
be 9th / 10th C.

The site is spectacular, overlooking the bay and with the ruined
castle of Kephalos to the NW, and it is rare to find both the site and the
materials of a classical temple given such a directly Christian form.

Mastikhari   Μαστιχάρι

Ruined EC basilica of Agios Ioannis.★★ Enclosed but can be
entered.

This site lies just above the beach and close to the newly built Hotel
Achilleos, which is passed by the road that follows the coast about 500
m. inland. However, the easiest and most attractive way to approach it is
to walk W-wards along the beach from the little port of Mastikhari for
just under 2 km; the shoreline rises some 10 m. above the beach which
means the site itself cannot be seen, but the enclosing fence is visible.

The basilica, which has been dated to the first half of the 6th C, is of
three naves and of medium size (some 22m. from threshold to
synthronon) and had nine pairs of columns. It was endowed with an
unusually fine series of mosaic floors, and it is to be regretted that these
have for the most part been covered over with gravel, as they incorporate
a rich series of diverse and colourful designs which include birds and
animals, and a number of inscriptions. One of these is a dedicatory one
of the *presbyteros Kyriakos* and his wife. Traces of a staircase towards the
W end of the S aisle suggest that there would have been a gallery, adding
to the impression of scale and wealth, and the centre of the nave was
occupied by an ambo. However, a few surviving caps have very simple
incised crosses, with a generally unsophisticated level of finish,
suggesting a contrast with the lavish mosaics.

A notable feature of the plan is a substantial structure to the S
forming three rooms; they were entered either from the diaconicon or
from a door in the S wall of the middle room, and suggest that they
functioned in connection with the duties of the clergy. On the other side
the baptistry lies adjacent to the NE corner, and has an unusually
complex plan which shows that each corner was formed into a niche,
which must have enriched the spatial experience of anyone entering the
chamber. Also of interest is the way that the chamber from which the
baptistry was entered, and which still has the benches of the
catechumens round its walls, is the only area not floored with mosaics,
but with plain terracotta tiles, still visible. This must surely have been
intended to emphasise the moment when the candidates for baptism

crossed the threshold from where they had been awaiting the act of initiation, to enter the enriched surroundings of the baptistry with its complex spaces, small cupola and richly colourful mosaic flooring. Note too the apse in the E wall, not balanced by another in the diakonikon on the S side; the catechumens would have faced this across the sunken, marble-lined, cruciform font (which is still to be seen) when they entered the baptistry, but its imagery has regrettably perished. The usual three steps lead into, and out of, the font.

This is another very rewarding EC site, from which the outlook across the straits to Kalymnos will not have changed significantly over the centuries. The community which the basilica served must have lived in the immediate vicinity, and several trial excavations have uncovered traces of housing even beyond the modern hotel building.

KYTHIRA   Κύθηρα

Med: Cerigo, Serigo.
Island group (nominally): Ionian. (*Nomos:* Attica).

Palaiopolis ●
● Pente Pigadia
● Agios Giorgios tou Vounou
● Agios Theodoros
● Perlegianika
● Areoi
Mylopotamos
Agios Dimitrios ●
● Livadi
N
● Pourko
● Khora
● Kapsali

10 km

T he individual character which Kythira has retained into modern
times must be due, at least in part, to the two factors of its
position and its terrain. As it lies in almost complete isolation
from other islands and within sight of the southern-most tip of the
Peloponnese, its ties with the mainland were often stronger than with
any island group. From time to time it was linked administratively with
Crete, where in the later 14th C their governor was elected, rather than
in Venice, and occasionally its fortunes became linked to the Ionian
islands, but today it is administered from Piraeus. In addition, the quality
of the land of its interior was so poor that it could only be made to yield

the most meagre crops, and so it was not coveted for any intrinsic value. It was just the presence of two harbours that made it from time to time a desirable location, and then mainly as a base for other operations. Traditionally Christianity was brought from the Peloponnese to the island in the 4th C by a holy woman, the Osia Elesse, and there was certainly another missionary here in the 10th C (c.950), Osios Theodoros. According to his Life he found the island depopulated (indeed, that was the reason for his going there); this was due to Saracen raids from Crete, but these ceased after the recovery of Crete by the Byzantines in 961. Details in his Life tend to confirm that the poor terrain of the island contributed to its having little importance until the later medieval period; he was eventually buried at the site of the Monastery that now bears his name (see below). Some church building began from this period (there is only trace of one building prior to this point) but it seems only to have been from the 12th C, under a Greek family from Monemvasia, the Eudaimonoioannis, that it started to be significantly repopulated. The Fourth Crusade does not seem to have changed life on Kythira as much as elsewhere in the Aegean, as in 1238 the island was offered as a dowry for his daughter by Nikolas Eudaimonoiannis on her marriage to Marco Venier, the son of a feudal lord of Crete who was of Venetian origin. The Venetians (in one form or another) were to provide almost the only foreign presence in Kythira until the late 18th C. The name of Venier gave another dimension to Kytheran legend, as it linked them with Venus, whose island (in mythological tradition) this was, and they adopted the grand title of 'Marquises of Cerigo'. An 18th C association was in this way born, which has given us (among other delights) the painting of *The Embarkation* by Watteau. This idyll is in complete contrast with the reputation of the Venier family, who became something of a law unto themselves, but still called on the Venetian government for help when needed. (An example of this came in 1353 when a law suit was brought by a Marco Venier; his father, Bartolomeo, said he had been offered Kythira if he married the daughter of a "Greek lord" there. The marriage was celebrated, and Marco was born of the union, but when the Greek lord found that Bartolomeo already had a wife in Crete he ejected him; the suit was being brought by Marco, who was made consul at Khania in recompense.)

A hiatus of Byzantine control had occurred from 1275, with an archon appointed from Monemvasia; control was too difficult to maintain from CP and, with Monemvasia so close, probably unnecessary. Monemvasia was always the island's most powerful neighbour, and the metropolitan there was granted in 1293 a chrysobull giving him the title of 'Exarch of all the Peloponnese' and eight suffragan bishoprics, one of which was Kythira. By 1307 the Venetians were back in control – or at least the Venieri, although the course of their family history seldom ran smoothly. In 1354 the island was governed by no less than five brothers of this family, but they rashly supported the Cretan rebellion of 1363, two of them being executed for their part. Venetian oversight was to remain until 1797, with only a three-year spell (1715-18) of Russo-Turkish presence. The island and its protection must have been a drain on Venetian finances, as (for example) in 1398 the senators were asked by the *castellan* for money so that he could repair the castle here, and in 1450 their help was requested in dealing with some Catalan pirates who had raided the island and stolen two small galleys. However, the continuous W presence meant that Islamic influence in the island was virtually non-existent. The British administration of 1805-63 seems to have been largely benign as far as the medieval history of the island is concerned; they built the lazaretto still found beside the inner harbour, and the archive housed in the castle at Khora is, for this period, one of the most complete in Greece, and full of local interest.

This varied political past is reflected in the way that the most prominent buildings that you will find in the island were originated by both Greeks and Venetians with, later, the British. Characteristic building materials are a coarse brown limestone, which was used, where funds allowed, for vaults and wall facings, and frequently for simple door and window surrounds, and a grey volcanic rock which is almost invariably rough hewn. Brick is very seldom seen, and would have to have been imported. There was an almost complete lack of classical building in Kythira, with only the remains of a temple to Aphrodite being reported in the 19th C; re-used classical columns or caps, so common on the mainland and elsewhere, are only seldom seen on the island.

Kythera is unusually rich in small country churches, no doubt partly due to the fact that there was never any significant Turkish presence; elsewhere it was common for the local pasha to insist on a new church replacing an existing one, with the result that so many medieval churches were intentionally, if reluctantly, demolished. There are over thirty rural churches, many with some frescoes surviving; some are difficult to locate, and others are too damaged to be mentioned here, but the most rewarding to visit are included. As there is no clear or recognised route for touring the island, the sites are given here in a simple alphabetical sequence.

Agios Giorgios tou Vounou and Agios Nikolaos.
Two hill-top churches on one site, one with floor mosaics.**

Unsigned. Keys held at monastery of Agia Moní.

Take the road E from Aroniadika, in the direction of Avlemonas; the mountain of Agios Giorgios will come into view E of Agia Moní, with the two churches at its summit, reached up a winding dirt road.

This superb mountain-top site overlooking the small harbour of Avlemonas is the most Eastern point of the island, and has some of its earliest Byzantine remains. Of the two modestly sized Byzantine churches you will find at the summit, neither is now in its original form. The earlier is that to the E, and bears the dedication of the site, Agios Giorgios tou Vounou; there may have been a small monastery here, built on later, but now with nothing remaining. It is a very simple barrel-vaulted chamber with a small rounded apse which originally had two windows; one is now blocked and the other reduced in size. A later extension has been added to the W. The building is a problematic one to date on the basis of its very simple masonry, but the main attraction here is provided by the floor mosaics, which are of outstanding interest; if these were part of the original decoration of the church they must provide the main clue to the period of the original building, but doubt has been expressed as to whether they are contemporary with it. Areas that still survive (they are unprotected) show mosaics of secular subjects, with a striking and colourful figure of an archer or huntsman on horseback; he wears a Phrygian hat and draws back his bow to its fullest extent. Adjacent to him is a leopard, and a fragment that shows the hooves and head of a horse or mule. Further fragments indicate a border with roundel decoration, and elsewhere a standing figure enclosed in a decorative circular motif. There is little to offer as a comparison with these mosaics, but most estimates of their date focus on the period around the 7th C, and certainly (even in their fragmentary state) are of the greatest interest. The problem that they raise relates partly to the general condition of the island at this period which, according to current knowledge, seems otherwise have been too poor and underpopulated to support relatively lavish decoration of this kind. However, coins of Justin II (565-578) and Maurice (582-602) were excavated a short way below to the SW at Kastri, so our perceptions here may be at fault. It could also be suggested that the mosaics were already in place here before the present church was built over them.

The second church, dedicated to St. Nicholas as well as to the Panagia Myrtiotissa, was originally almost square, with two small, rounded apses. Its low cupola is carried on well-cut limestone squinches, and it has had a W extension built that doubles its size. Its date is hard to determine, but it may be prior to the 10th C. Its interior has no decorative interest.

It was just outside the harbour at Avlemonas, below, that the ship carrying some of the sculptures taken by Lord Elgin from the Parthenon sank; the cargo spent some 18 months on the sea-bed before being raised and taken on to Malta. This mountain-top site has therefore much to offer, and be prepared to devote a day to reaching and entering the church.

In open country NE of Agios Ilias. Άγιος Ηλίας.
Church of Agios Dimitrios *
Leave the road 3 km. to the E of the village, and then on foot by easy track.

There is nothing to prepare you for the sight of this small but impressive stone-built church, of which the most prominent feature is a broad drum for the dome that takes almost the full width of the naos. It has been quite recently restored, and the remaining frescoes are probably in two phases of early and late 13th C, although the building itself could well be earlier. You can see a fine depiction of the church's dedicatory saint in half-length in the conch of the apse; this is certainly a Kytheran tradition, which you will find in numerous other churches on the island. This figure of St Dimitrios, with the bishops below, is of the earlier of the two layers of fresco.

Agios Theodoros   Άγιος Θεοδώρος
Monastic church.**
In use; usual monastic limitations on hours of viewing and on dress.
Signed to the W off the central road joining Kastrianika and Potamos, not far from Logothetianika; just 50 m. down a dirt road.

This must be the site of the chapel erected by Osios Theodoros in the later 10th C and dedicated to SS. Sergius and Bacchus. An attractive courtyard is formed by the two-storey monastic building (?18th/19th C), the well-preserved shell of an early 19th C schoolroom built by the British, and the impressive katholikon on the S side. The latter is the only Byzantine building here, but it is the largest of this period on the island. It is entered from the S side, and the initial impression is of a fairly conventional inscribed cross design, with a high octagonal drum, rendered and whitewashed; its interior uses no columns, and the cupola and walls are mainly colour-washed. Close to the N door is the tomb of Osios Theodoros. The decorative interest is confined to two fragments of (?)12th C fresco in the N bay, and then, most interestingly, to what now serves as a narthex, but is usually entered from the naos and S aisle of the church. It clearly was in fact a self-contained, barrel-vaulted chamber, perhaps intended as a parekklision of the present katholikon, but oriented N/S. It has a masonry screen across its N end with 11th/12th C paintings of prophets, which are in quite good condition. It is now dedicated to SS. Cosmas and Damian, and there is a possibility that it may even have pre-existed the katholikon as part of an earlier foundation, although its orientation does not support this.

As one of the most historically important sites on Kythera, and one of the easiest to visit, this should not be missed.

Araioi   Αραίοι

Church of Agios Petros.*
After turning W off the main road just N of Dokana, the village is some 4 km further on; take a narrow concrete road running back E for about 1 km.

It is a surprise to find this quite impressive 12th C church, of medium size, in a position of such isolation. Built of undressed local stone its design is a conventional domed, inscribed cross; it has no additions and its recent re-pointing is the only restoration. It has three equal apses and (as always on Kythera) no columns are used. Some frescoes are still preserved inside, with the most impressive being a half-length figure of St Peter in the conch of the apse; it is probably early 13th C, and below it is a long donor's inscription. The isolated setting and the undisturbed and attractive forms of the building make this a rewarding church to visit, although entry can be difficult; its location may have an explanation in some earlier, possibly pre-Christian, association.

Khora / Kythira

(signposts have the former name and maps the latter.)
Castle, churches and museum.**

The fine harbour below the rocky headland here must always, in spite of its visibility to the local pest of pirates, have made it one of the most desirable strongpoints on the island. The whole locality is dominated by the massive buildings of the Venetian castle, now kept ungated; this must have originated in the 14th C, but even by 1398 the *castellan* of Kythira was being granted a considerable sum by the Venetian senate to repair the castle here; no doubt other repairs and expansion took place over the years, and most of what is now visible was probably built in the

16th/17th C. Two churches are enclosed within its courtyard, built adjacent to each other near the tip of the headland. The larger of the two, the Panagia Myrtioditissa, is a Venetian church built as a simple, high hall, probably 15th/16th C with a later iconostasis. The dedication, 'Our Lady of the Myrtle', must have been perpetuated from an earlier building, as she was the patron saint of the Kytherans, and they founded another church with this dedication in Monemvasia. The smaller church beside, however, the Panagia I Orfani, a simple medieval, barrel-vaulted chamber, has quite extensive fragments of 13th/14th C fresco; their condition is poor, but their presence in this site indicates the co-existence of local Greeks and their Venetian governors.

While in the area of the fortress, a short walk down below its NW ramparts will bring you to a group of seven small churches; all are of the Venetian period, and are kept locked, except for the ruined Byzantine church to the E of that of the Panagia Mesokhoritissa, and dedicated to Agios Demetrios, of which the N wall has fallen away. The S wall and apse survive, where the 13th/14th C fresco fragments of the Communion of the apostles have finely painted heads remaining which are the work of an artist of considerable distinction.

The medieval holdings of the small local **Museum** on the NW edge of the town are not extensive; there is a small display of Byzantine coins, and some medieval Venetian ceramics. The main displays are of classical ceramics and 19th C memorial tablets collected from the British cemetery below the castle, which provide a vivid and human dimension to the existence of the members of the 19th C garrison and their families.

Kapsali   Καψάλι

Hermitage cave/chapel dedicated to Saint John.*
Locked; keys kept in Kapsali.
The whitewashed frontage is easily seen high on the cliff face overlooking the inner harbour; first collect the keys from one of the last houses on the left as you start the walk up from near the 19th C lazaretto.

The cave hermitage is cut into the cliff face, some 100 m. up a steep footpath and steps; a local tradition has it that St John Theologos wrote part of the Revelation here. The interior has an 18th/19th C screen and icons, but two inscriptions cut in marble tablets let into the gateway over the steps suggest a Byzantine origin for the ensemble. It is a rewarding objective, representing as it must many such hermitages in the islands; in summer you would be advised to make the visit either in the early morning or late afternoon, as the track up is fully exposed to the Aegean sun.

Livadi   Λιβάδι

Church of Agios Andreas; frescoes.★★
A short way up a side road in centre of village; key held at house on the left of the track up to the church.

The church, which has a picturesque setting, is built on an inscribed cross plan, without use of columns, as usual. The central of the three rounded apses is larger, and there is a slight distortion in the W sector of the cupola suggesting that the more extended W bay may have been a later alteration, although the external masonry does not indicate this. The design suggests a late 10th/11th C date, and this is largely confirmed by the surviving frescoes. Although there are large losses, some were clearly by artists of considerable sensitivity. The main areas to be seen are in the bema and the prothesis, where the earlier of the two phases of painting survive; the earlier is thought to be of the date of the church, and the later of the 13th C, with two further layers of post-Byzantine painting. Particularly fine are figures from the Ascension in the bema, and over the conch of the apse is an unusual theme of a cross between half-length figures of David and Moses; the highest quality fragments are on the N wall of the naos.

The church is very accessible, and these frescoes are among of the most distinguished left on Kythera.

Mylopotamos   Μυλοποτάμος

Kastro and cave hermitage with frescoes.★★ (See Pl. 11).

Although now displaying a fine baroque Venetian gateway (even if partly obscured by the obtusely placed school built by the British), the Kastro here certainly has medieval origins. Much of the masonry of its defences must have been used for later building, and its interior now consists of a few stone-built houses and some small church buildings; the latter, some of which are later 15th C, with one dedicated to the Transfiguration, have been recently reinstated after long neglect, and are usually kept locked. The interest of the site is the experience that it offers of a small medieval stronghold that has not seen later development of any extent, and if you can effect entry there are some impressive fresco fragments.

A dirt track signed to the left in the village leads down to the **Cave of Agia Sofia** some 3 km. away. (The cave is gated, and is currently open three afternoons each week.) The setting of this remarkable site is superb, overlooking the sea and W coast of the island from some 120 m. above the shore. The artistic interest is focussed on a masonry screen about 20 m. inside the cave which carries some well-preserved frescoes; these have usually been dated to the late 11th/12th C by style, and a recent specialist opinion of late 13th C certainly seems too late. To the left of the central opening of the screen are three standing figures of SS. Sofia and her daughters Elpis, Pistis and Agape (Faith, Hope and Charity), with a bust portrait of St Panteleimon on the far left; on the right are a figure of St Theodore and a fine rendering of the enthroned Christ between the Virgin and St John the Baptist in intercession, with a figure of St Theodosius on the far right. There are further frescoes of St Nicholas and the archangel Michael, and (very unusually) the signature of the painter can still be seen in an inscription with small characters between the Virgin and Christ; the inscription forms a simple invocation: "God, help thy servant Theodoros the painter and his wife and child." Although he could not be called an artist of great sophistication, these figures nevertheless have a very real and direct presence and convey a strong sense of scale in the wild surroundings of the cave; their condition is the best of any of the Byzantine frescoes on Kythera.

For several reasons this cave in its spectacular setting is one of the most interesting and rewarding sites on the island.

Palaiokhora   Παλαιοκώρα

Extensive ruins of Byzantine town; churches and houses. ★★★
Reached down a stony dirt track some 5 km. E from the main road close to Vamvakaradika; only one church is locked.

This ruined town (sometimes known also as Palaiokastro or Palaiopolis), with its buildings clustering vertiginously on a craggy spur at the junction of two deep and rocky ravines, is one of the most interesting and rewarding such sites in all the islands of Greece. For while its scattered ruins recall those of Palaiokhora on Aegina, and indeed those of Geraki and even Mystra in the Peloponnese, here they form an almost complete 'time-capsule', as the town was never revived after its sacking by the Turkish admiral Barbarossa in 1537. It seems to have been mainly developed from the mid-13th C, although it was probably founded in the late 12th C, and so it offers a chance to experience an island capital as it developed over some three centuries. Never re-inhabited and not later used extensively as a quarry for building materials, there is a unique opportunity here to explore a later Byzantine town, with its remains of many public and private buildings.

The choice of site, close to the E coast but out of sight and (at some 200 m. above the sea) out of reach from it, must have been governed by the need to avoid observation and attack by pirates, with safety being the pre-eminent consideration. It is known that Barbarossa captured and destroyed a castle that was here, and this must have provided the main communal refuge, with parts of some outer defensive walls. There are (as in the sites mentioned above) a striking number of churches, and these tend to be better preserved than the houses; 22 can still be identified here, of which the dedications of three are still known. By contrast, about 50 houses have been recorded in an archaeological survey. The building form which predominates for the churches is a simple, single-cell, barrel-vaulted space, while most of the houses seem to have had a roof that was almost flat, but supported by beams; protection was not by tiles (there is no clay on the island) but by slabs of schist laid on the beams. There is frequently little differentiation in scale to distinguish secular from ecclesiastical use, but some of the churches have a narthex, and about half were built with a blind arcade.

The first building that you will see on arrival at the site is the church of **Agia Varvara**, slightly below and to the left of the track to the main site. It is untypical in that it is built as a modest-sized, domed, inscribed cross design and it clings to the upper margin of one of the ravines; the relative crudity of its exterior masonry, with two faceted apses flanking a large central one, does not prepare one for the quite grand impression made by its interior. There are no columns, the cupola being carried on wall sections, but the impressive effect is created by a substantial and finely proportioned masonry templon screen which stretches across all three apses. Although some of its original plastering has fallen away (revealing some use of brick – rare on Kythera) sufficient is left to show how (as in Palaiokhora, Ithaki) a later Byzantine screen would have been decorated. The six shallow, round-topped recesses either side of the central opening contained images of the Dodecaorton, which were still present in a photograph taken earlier this century. This must represent a stage in the development of the iconostasis before it became usual to have one of wood, and even higher. It is a problematic church to date, but is probably of the late 12th/ 13th C.

On entering the area of the town you will first find the church of the **Panagia** or the **'Kyra tou Forou'**, which is the only church normally kept locked; it has been restored, with a disfiguring modern roof. Also very evident here is the high wall section of a ruined building that must have been part of the kastro, but of which the precise function has eluded the archaeologists.

Penetrating further and wandering through the ruins of the town as it clings to the sloping sides of its rocky spur, you will find the remains (some largely complete, but a number partly ruined) of many further churches and houses; on such a rocky and precipitous site uniformity was impossible, and you will find great variety in orientation and distortions of normal building type due to the uneven terrain, with even in two cases the apse being sited in the longer wall; two are built adjacent and almost end-to-end, their barrel vaults slightly offset. Frescoes can still be seen in ruined state in some of them, but none of those left has a cupola, and it may be that Agia Varvara was for some unknown reason exceptional in being built to a more widely used design. Building seems to have gone on here at least into the 15th C.

Also outside the area of Palaiokhora, to the E and just N of the bed of the Palaiopolis river, not far from the excavation of the classical site at Kastri, is the ruined church of **Agios Panteleimon**. This is of interest in that it has been shown that in its original form it was most probably a three-aisled, single-apse basilica, and that its present form is the result of successive re-buildings; it originated possibly in the 5th C and the latest re-construction is thought to be of 7th C date, perhaps following destruction in an Arab raid (the site is more accessible from the sea than the rest of Palaiopolis). This would make it one of the last churches to be built on the island before its depopulation and abandonment; when repopulation began safer sites were chosen, further inland and within less easy reach of the sea.

For Byzantinists Palaiokhora must be the most interesting and rewarding site on the island; its history and setting put it in a class of its own on Kythera, and its remoteness may be some protection from fuller exploitation. Allow at least a day for absorbing what this unique survival has to offer.

Pente Pigadia   Πέντε Πιγάδια

Two adjacent churches of Agios Blasios and the Panagia.*
Locked; ask for the papas in the village.

This and the following entry concern the rarely met phenomenon of 'twinned' adjacent, double-apse country churches. While double-nave churches are not uncommon in islands with a RC element in their population, these are built as two distinct buildings, domeless and of the simplest design except that they have the further feature of each being provided with two equal apses. They both retain some frescoes, if rather damaged – probably 13th C; the most unusual is in the church of St Blasios to the S, and shows the warrior saint, Theodore, on horseback; he is usually represented standing. A standing figure of St Mamas, holding a sheep, is in better condition and represents well the rustic style of the artist. In the N church, the Panagia, the condition of the frescoes is better, and they may all be slightly later; the enthroned Virgin and child in the apse is memorable, as is also the pair on the N wall of SS. Myron and Basil.

These churches may represent the interest taken in the island after 1275 by the rulers in Monemvasia, and the increased population that this brought about.

Perlegianika   Περλεγιάνικα

Two adjacent churches of Agios Andreas and Agios Giorgios.★
Locked; ask for the key at nearest house in the village.

Like the churches in the previous entry, these two small, domeless hall churches are unusual in two ways: not only are they linked but they also both have two equal apses. Built using only local stone, both still offer some frescoes, although they is considerable damage, and they both appear to have been painted in the 13th C in a direct, if rustic, style. The N church, dedicated to St Andrew, offers a particularly impressive image of the Triumphal entry, and in that to the S a memorable fresco of the Crucifixion survives from a Passion cycle.

Although just outside the village this pair of churches is rewarding to seek out, and even if entry cannot be achieved the exterior characteristics can only be matched elsewhere in Kythera at the previous entry.

Pourko   Πούρκο

Church of Agios Dimitrios.★★ (See Pl. 25).
Locked; key in one of nearest houses in Pourko.
Easily seen when looking down from the road up to the monastery of Agia Elessis, some 150 m. to the S.

This small building must be the most bizarre of the medieval survivals on Kythira. Although its modern rendering and roofing convey a sense of uniformity, it must in reality be the result of the amalgamation of three chapels (one of them domed) with a slightly larger church (also domed). All four buildings thus amalgamated have different orientations; the most complete of the churches it incorporates is oriented with its double apses to the N, while two others, to the E, one also with a double apse are more conventionally sited, and a fourth, single-apse unit joins them together. There is no agreement on why this unique structure should have come to be in its present form, but it surely cannot have been planned; its appearance must be the result of piecemeal development.

The fragmentary frescoes on the walls of the main church are the result of three phases of painting; those of the bishops in the apse are probably c.1100, and the others slightly later. The larger of the chapels has a dedication to St Nicholas, and an inscription gives the donor as one Nikolaos Kontodonatos, and (exceptionally) names the artist as Dimitrios of Monemvasia; a date can be read as either 1095 or 1100, and the damaged frescoes here must be of that period. This represents an interesting product of the close ties that existed at this period with the Byzantine stronghold of Monemvasia. There is a further phase of post-Byzantine painting dated by an inscription to 1707.

One of the more accessible churches on the island, and unique in form, this should not be missed.

KYTHNOS   Κύθνος

Med: Thermia, Fermene.
Island group: Cyclades (W) (*Nomos*: Cyclades).

I n spite of the thermal springs which gave Kythnos its later name of Thermia, its landscape is one of the most arid of the Cyclades, with most of its interior covered in brushwood *maquis*. Like a number of the smaller Cycladic islands, Kythnos is not mentioned by any of the medieval historians of the Aegean, and it was only with the chroniclers of the Fourth Crusade that it begins to enter history. It was one of the many islands unmentioned in the *Partitio Romaniae* of 1204, but from

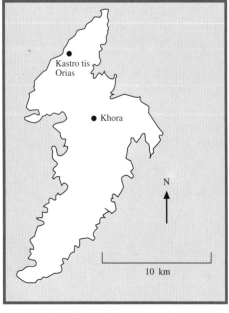

1207 was brought into the embrace of the Sanudi as one of the eleven islands forming the new Duchy of the Archipelago; the Castelli, a family from Treviso on the Venetian terra firma, became their vassals on the island in c.1322, but in 1336 Nicolo Sanudo awarded the barony of Kythnos to the more powerful family of the Gozzadini, of Bologna, who he no doubt considered would be more able to give him support in time of need. They held six other islands, and there is perhaps some irony in the fact that they were to survive on them as late as 1617, some fifty years after the Turks had occupied the rest of the islands of the Duchy, before they were finally handed over to the Turks.

It is of interest that Kythnos (with other smaller islands of the Archipelago, but not Naxos) had suffered a severe attack by the Aragonese admiral Roger de Lluria in 1292. It may well have been the relative lack of security of its position, on the fringe of the islands of the Duchy and close to the mainland of Attica, that allowed it (like Kea) to change hands quite readily; it was never to be one of the most desireable of the Aegean properties.

The island now has only a few survivals which illustrate the ebb and flow of its medieval history. The most significant movement of the population of the island occurred in the early 17th C, when the population centred on Kastro tis Orias left the stronghold there and the modern Khora was developed; this would seem to have begun before the arrival of the Ottoman Turks in 1617, as the church of Agia Saba in Khora has an inscription over its W door of 1613, with the arms of the Bolognese family of Gozzadini, that must have been erected shortly before the Italian withdrawal. Previously the island capital had been the inland village of Driopis, and this is now the only visible relic (other than the impressive fortifications of Kastro tis Orias) of all the centuries of colourful W personalities who peopled the medieval island.

Kythnos town / Khora

Church of Agia Triada.★
The church of Agia Triada is in the centre of the village in a small plateia just below the police station, and cannot be missed.

Although the village church here is now completely modernised, its core of a broad cupola supported over an open crossing on lateral arches to N and S, forming a domed hall, appears certainly medieval. The features of a broad cylindrical drum carried on a slightly raised crossing can readily be matched with other 11th C churches; both the E and W bays may have been extended, and this would be consistent with the need to enlarge an existing earlier church when the population increased in the 17th C. The original masonry has all been plastered so that it is only the outline forms of the building that convey its origins as a product of relatively sophisticated middle Byzantine church building from before the arrival of the Latins.

Kastro tis Orias / Kastro tis Katakefalos   Κάστρο της Όριας

Deserted ruins of fortified capital.★★
Unenclosed.

Just before entering Loutra from Khora take a rough dirt road signed to 'Kastro', and fork right in 100 m.; the road eventually enters a 'goat-alley' with dry-stone walls either side, most suitable for walking, but possible with the most rugged of vehicles. This takes you in some 5 km. to a rough but manageable foot-track that starts when the Kastro comes into view. (A right fork leads to the church of Agios Giorgios, of which more later.) To walk from Loutra would take approximately 90 minutes each way.

The rough foot-path leads round the side of the mountain to enter the Kastro from the SE through a re-built gateway. The building that you see first is in fact a relatively late small church (open) but it is built from the stone of the ruins so appears older. Its dedication is given on a plaque inside as *Agio Eleouso Tokastro*, which may represent a dialect form of the Greek title 'Panagia Eleousa tou Kastrou' (Our Lady of Compassion of the castle). The summit of the mountain, from which Kea is easily seen, has the ruins of many buildings, including a small but deep cistern to the NW that still has its plaster lining intact; there is virtually nothing left of an enceinte. But the most striking building here is just below the summit to the NW, and is an almost complete barrel-vaulted chapel some 8 m. in length; its W wall has collapsed, but the interior, with two broad supporting ribs, is intact and displays considerable areas of surviving Byzantine fresco painting. Besides figures on the S wall you will see two impressive feast scenes in the S bema and in the apse is a damaged image of the Virgin surrounded by a patterned circle. The style is reminiscent of the less sophisticated 14th C Cretan painting, and both style and layout are certainly Byzantine rather than reflecting any Venetian practice. This building must have been used by the local Greek population here, and again illustrates the relationship that existed between them and their Venetian rulers; this was undoubtedly the strongest and best defended point on the island, and underlines how in times of danger the local Greek islanders made common cause with whoever was the ruling W power at the time to defend their stronghold, just as the Hospitallers were to do in the Dodecanese.

This question must also relate to the medium-sized **church of Agios Giorgios** that you can see from the Kastro across open country to the E, and where a visit is well worth the 10-minute detour on the way back; it is located among farm buildings and is unlocked. The broad dome is carried on lateral arches over the crossing, so making it a domed hall, and although all the interior detail is the result of an 1865 renovation, the church is clearly of the same type and period as Agia Triada in Khora. For a church of this scale to be built in the 11th – 12th C implies a considerable Greek population existing outside the immediate confines of the Kastro, and underlines the shift in population that must have taken place before the Turkish occupation.

LEROS   Λέρος

Med: Lero.
Island group: Dodecanese (N) / S Sporades. (*Nomos*: Dodecanese.)

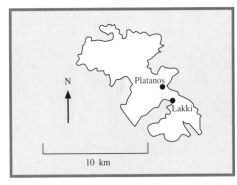

This small and quite fertile island forms the most northerly link in the chain of the Dodecanese as they spread towards Lipsi and Patmos. Although with some EC remains, it is passed over without mention by the medieval historians, and it is not mentioned by name in either the 10th C listing of islands in the Aegean theme or the Deed of Partition of 1204. It was one of the conquests of the Byzantine government in exile in Nicaea, which was in possession by 1254, if not earlier, and Leros would then have been governed from CP until c.1309, when the Hospitallers had secured their new headquarters in Rhodes. Following this new annexation, Leros was taken over by the Knights, and it was really only when they started to establish a defensive system running up the Turkish coast that the island became an outpost of some importance. The islanders seem to have retained some loyalty to their emperor, however, as in 1319 they revolted against the rule of the Hospitallers, saying that they had been too overbearing (see below). The island remained in W hands until the fall of Rhodes in 1523 (in fact handed over on Dec. 31st, 1522), when it came under permanent Turkish occupation.

Platanos   Πλάτανος

Hospitallers' castle and church of Panagia tou Kastrou.★★
Castle gated but unlocked; church open Tues & Sat. 9.00-12.00, Wed. & Sun. 14.30-16.30.
The Kastro is easily the most prominent landmark on Leros; from the Plateia in Platanos it is reached up a continuous (signed) stairway of some 800 m.

Its siting was clearly intended to be able to overlook the harbours of both Agia Marina and Lakki as well as the channel across to the Turkish mainland. It had been built by 1318 and was already part of the

Hospitallers' defensive and signalling chain by then, but in 1319 their garrison here was killed by a force of two thousand local Greeks who had revolted against their rule, and declared their support for the Byzantine emperor. It was to be another of their number, a bombastic Saxon noble called Albert of Schwarzburg, who recovered the castle here the same year and reinstalled a Hospitaller garrison. In 1403, when relations with the local population had improved, the traveller Ruy de Clavijo visited and was impressed by it, noting that it was "a very strong castle, built high", and c.1417 Christoforo Buondelmonti reported that every night all the inhabitants of the island retired inside its walls for safety. In 1470 the island was attacked by Turkish forces under their victorious sultan Mehmet II, as part of his campaign to subdue all the Aegean, but although they ravaged the island they were unable to take the castle. The origins of the castle are said to have been Byzantine; this may well be true, but it is hard now to pinpoint evidence of Byzantine builders here: what you will find is overwhelmingly a product of the Knights of Rhodes.

Inside the first gate and outer fortifications the space is dominated by the recently restored church of the Panagia tou Kastrou. It is quite a simple hall church, said to have been adapted from the castle armoury, with a single faceted apse and no cupola; an attractive open loggia has been added on the W and N sides. The only evident survivals of the Byzantine period here are some fragments of carved marble; two (as so often the case) probably come from a dismantled templon: one is over the main entrance and carries quite a long inscription, and the other is built into a modern structure to the E of the apse, while other spolia can also be seen, including what may be the fragment of an ambo. The church contains a well-preserved collection – it can hardly be called a Museum – of later icons, silver and some printing, but little of medieval interest.

Further on is a second gateway and a tunnel through the thickness of the inner fortification; the masonry of all the castle is of quite roughly cut local stone, but part of the barrel vaulting here is of fine ashlar worked with exceptional skill. A chamber that may have been a second, smaller chapel opens into the thickness of the walls on the left here, gated and locked; a small, apsed recess facing the gate may well have once been painted, but the plaster is now bare. Passing through this you will find a third gateway leading up into an inner keep, but this is occupied by the Greek military – the modern successors to the Knights (entrance and photography forbidden); the view from this level still offers a fine impression of the superb outlook and strength of the location, and underlines how six centuries later its position is still important. While the great majority of the building must be high quality 14th C work of the Knights and kept in good condition, a few superficial additions such as the rifle slits in the castellation may be Turkish or even Italian.

This is a spectacularly sited castle that has been maintained in fine condition; among the Hospitaller castles it must count as of middling scale, and as their furthest outpost to the N it must always have been of great use as a lookout and signalling station, but with added capacity for sheltering the local populace and housing a small garrison.

There are reports of up to six sites on Leros with minor evidence of building in the EC period, but the only one with significant surviving remains is the following.

Lakki   Λακκί

Church of Agios Ioannis Theologos.*
Locked; key in nearby house to N.
Leaving Lakki by the road to the airport, about 1 km. from the harbour, on the right and above the road you will find this church with its W front looking out over the local countryside.

Its exterior, with some 19th C modernisation, is unpromising, but the site is probably EC in origin, and an EC cap on the W terrace offers confirmation of this. A view of the completely plain interior shows that the piers which were the original sole supports of the cupola have been built into walls which now form a nave of very western character, with just two openings into the N and S aisles; the S opening has a carved lintel which may have come from the templon (now completely replaced by masonry), and an 11th C window in the N wall certainly shows a middle-Byzantine phase. The roofing of the sanctuary appears to be groin-vaulting, however, and the general picture seems to be of a medium-sized 11th/12th C Byzantine church (itself replacing an EC one) that was substantially altered at a time when W influence, presumably from the Knights of Rhodes, was strong. The later 11th C phase is supported by a local legend that the church was the result of a visit by Osios Christodoulos, the founder of the great monastery on Patmos, raising funds for his new institution there.

This church repays a visit by an enthusiast in that it is an interesting demonstration of what could happen to an early Greek church building during the period of Western presence in the Dodecanese. There were no doubt many other such 'westernisations' that have been subsequently demolished and re-built as later Greek churches.

LESBOS   Λέσβος

Med: Mitylene, Metellini.
Island area: E Aegean. (*Nomos*: Lesbos).

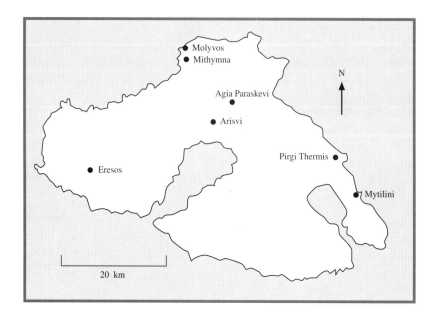

T his relatively fertile island is the next largest in area of all the
Greek islands after Crete, and its position close to the coast of
Asia Minor and the busy port of Smyrna (Izmir) gave it an
added importance for much of the medieval period. Although the island
was raided and plundered successively by Arabs in the 9th C and Turks
and Venetians in the 12th, it was retained mainly under Byzantine
control until 1204. Awarded to the Latin emperor Baldwin of Flanders
in the Deed of Partition, it remained in W possession for just 20 years,
being re-taken by the Byzantine emperor in Nicaea c.1225.

A period of Genoese rule began in 1355, and was to last 107 years,
when the island was taken over by a freebooting member of the Gattilusi
family, Francesco; he achieved this with the help of the young and
ambitious but (at the time) retired Byzantine emperor, John V
Palaiologos, who promised him the hand of his sister, Irene Palaiologina,
in marriage, if he helped him to recover his throne. With the help of
Francesco he achieved this, and his reward of marriage to Irene
Palaiologina was duly bestowed; she took the name of Maria on her

marriage. What was more, she brought to him, as her dowry, the island of Lesbos; at a stroke he had realised his ambition of founding his own new principality in the Aegean and had entered the charmed circle of the Byzantine imperial family.

Under the Gattilusi a period of stability allowed the island to prosper for over a century; in spite of the easygoing nature of his arrival, Francesco was to become an international figure on the diplomatic scene, accompanying his brother-in-law John V to Rome in 1369 and witnessing his signature on his formal confession of the Catholic faith before pope Urban V. But the island's prosperity under its six Gattilusi dukes, combined with its position so close to the Asia Minor coast, meant that it was an early prey to the young and ambitious sultan Mehmet II; from 1449 the dukes paid an annual tribute of 3000 gold pieces, and in 1458 the younger brother, Niccolo Gattilusi deposed and imprisoned his brother Domenico and then had him killed. After increasingly desperate calls for help, the last duke, the fratricidal Niccolo Gattilusi, with his castle at Mytilini being pounded by six huge cannon, finally handed over the keys of the city to the sultan on September 17 1462. It was to be only in 1912 that the Turks would finally surrender the island.

(The 15th century traveller Christopher Buondelmonti gives the colourful story of one of the Gattilusi princes who was spending the night in a tower on the island while hunting, and was bitten on the hand by a scorpion; his cries brought so many of his entourage into the room that the floor gave way and they were all killed in the resulting collapse.)

An assumption could be made from this brief sketch that the main medieval survivals among the island's buildings will be military rather than ecclesiastical, and it would be largely correct. While the remains of over 40 EC basilicas have been identified, their remains are in most cases too fragmentary, remote or (in the case of mosaics) covered over to warrant an individual entry, and churches that survive from the Byzantine period are also very small in number. The principal survivals that you will see are all the product of the Genoese lordship of just over a century, with subsequent Turkish modernisation.

(The visitor to Lesbos should know that the island has a more developed industrial life than almost any of the other Aegean islands except for Crete and Rhodes, and traffic tends to be heavier due to a road system, developed by a British engineer, which is nearer to mainland standards.)

Mytilini   Μυτιλήνη

Large fortified castle.
Enclosed and gated; entry fee if open. (See Pl. 26).

The massive Kastro must be the largest to be found on any of the islands after those of Rhodes and perhaps Limnos, and occupies a prominent, steeply rising site from which it dominates the town and port.

There was a Byzantine castle here long before the island belonged to the Genoese, but almost all that you can now see must be the result of building by the Gattilusi from c.1355 onwards, and then extensive modifications and additions by the Turks. The plan is an elongated polygon, with a massive enceinte and several immense towers; there does not seem to have been an inner keep. The modern entry to the bailey is at the E end, initially through Turkish outworks.

Once inside the walls, the character of the builders is established by a heraldic relief that you can see on your right on a plaque high on a tower to the NE; a single-headed eagle, a BBBB arranged in a cross (usually said to stand for Βασιλεύς Βασιλέων βασιλεύων βασιλευούσι, but both this suggestion and its meaning are still debated) and the Gattilusi "scales". A late Roman fragment of a gladiator below must be a further indication of the Gattilusi outlook. This whole area was probably that destroyed by an earthquake one night in 1384, when a tower of the castle in which Francesco Gattilusi, his wife and three sons were sleeping was shattered; they all perished in the ruins except for one of the sons, Jacopo, who was found next morning by a neighbouring farmer below the walls close to some windmills. He was at once made duke in succession to his father, and re-named Francesco. The heraldic arms here may commemorate the subsequent re-building, although 20 years later the Spaniard Ruy de Clavijo, on his way to the E, reported seeing here "great castles fallen in ruins". On the ground in front of the entrance and ticket office is another carved heraldic relief, only partly completed; this has been broken across, and it has been suggested that this was intended to be a sarcophagus, and that the fracture occurred while the carving was in progress (but see below).

It would have been in the castle here that Francesco I installed a mint to produce coins for his new principality; they also were inscribed with the arms just mentioned, and give his name and title as FRANCISCUS GATTILUXIU DOMINUS METELINI.

Near to the entrance is the complete ground area of a small church, with some column bases and the E wall, and with part of a staircase to a gallery; this has recently been identified as a Latin church, although there are indications that it may have been originally Byzantine, but later converted by the Genoese. It is recorded that Francesco Gattilusi built a church dedicated to St John the Baptist, and that he was buried in it "in a tomb that he had ordered"; this church is most probably the one just mentioned, and it is possible that the sarcophagus near to the entrance (see above) above was his "tomb". Following the track downhill to the NW, passing major Turkish buildings, you can reach a small outer courtyard, now enclosed by later Turkish walling. This may have earlier been the main entrance, as it displays a prominent marble plaque with the heraldic emblems of the Byzantine imperial eagle, as the symbol of the Byzantine princess Maria Palaiologina (wife of Francesco Gattilusio from 1355), the "scales" of the Gattilusi and the Palaiologue monogram, as on Samothraki and Thasos; a fine inscription gives the date of 1373 and states that a "...*Gatelux... fecit fieri hoc edificium.*" Much of the main enclosure is heavily overgrown, but tracks allow some inspection of the perimeter wall; this must for the most part have been adapted by the Turks, and has extensive provision for artillery. A further enclosure running downhill to sea level to the NW is entirely Turkish and cannot normally be visited. (In 1912 an archaeologist reported that the presence of the Turkish army still quartered here prevented him from looking at or recording at all closely anything beyond the entrance gate; this provides an interesting comment on the continuing strategic importance of the castle here.)

As the town buildings intervene extensively between the castle walls and the harbour (as at Kavalla) the best overall view of the Kastro can be gained from the road beside the sea just to the N of Mytilene, and looking back towards the town; even in the 17th C engravings were being made from this viewpoint.

A combination of severe earthquakes and unsympathetic later occupants means that history has not dealt kindly with the other pre-Turkish survivals on Lesbos. There must have been a considerable number of Byzantine churches which have not survived. As it is, the military buildings of the Genoese provide the main documents of the island's medieval past.

Agia Paraskevi   Αγία Παρασκευή

Restored EC basilica and 15th C Genoese bridge. (See Pl. 30). This village near the centre of the island has little to offer in itself, but it is the point of departure for visiting these two sites:

The basilica of Khalinados is some 4 km. to the E down a hilly dirt road, and is a good, if partial, example of the many such buildings that existed in Lesbos by the 6th C. The site is remote and the setting very rural, but as the columns and caps that have been re-erected here give a strong impression that must be allowed speak for the many basilicas that have not received this attention. The dedication of this (as in most cases) is unknown.

The bridge of Kremasti* can be found at about 4 km. to the NW down a dirt road (keep on asking, as there is no sign). It must be a later 14th or 15th C structure built by the Genoese, and is in remarkably good condition. It is about a metre wide, with no parapet and its delicate stonework seems completely unrestored; its single, steeply arching span of some 15 m. must rely on interlocking masonry to carry its loads. The river bed that it crosses is now dry, but it must be a virtually unique survival of such a feature, of which greater numbers must have existed at one time.

Arisbi   Αρίσβι

Small ruined Byzantine fort.*

Just before entering Kalloni from the E a historically important cross-roads is now located at this village, where the main roads meet as they traverse the island from E to W and N to S. About 1 km. outside the village due E a dirt track leads for about 2 km. to a low hill beside the River Tsikni on which are the ruins of a small Byzantine fort. The remains are not sufficient to provide a date, but its function must have been to control the traffic on these two roads that cross the island, and it is one of the few such survivals of Byzantine rule here.

Mithymna / Molyvos   Μήθυμνα / Μόλυβος

Substantial Genoese castle.** Enclosed and gated, but can be entered.

The Kastro here provides, with that of Mytilini, the chief survival of Genoese presence in the island, and this no doubt typifies their priorities. Its position above the town means that nothing could pass down the straits between Lesbos and the Asia Minor coast without being observed from Mithymna; its siting and structure, however, although powerful are not impregnable, and had this been the main intention a fortified structure on Cape Korakas or Cape Faros, to the E, would have been more appropriate. The choice of this site may therefore have been influenced by considerations of observation and signalling.

Its form is that of a broad polygon, some 90 x 70 m., and it occupies a site overlooking the town and small harbour. You enter the outer defences through a gateway with a Turkish inscription, and on the route between that and the main entrance to the bailey you can see remains of previous fortifications which must be Hellenistic or earlier. Although these continue to be visible inside, all the main buildings and surround of the bailey are nevertheless Genoese, with some later Turkish adaptations, mainly for the use of cannon; it never received from them the attentions that were lavished on Mytilini. There does not seem to have been a keep, and the general aspect of the castle here is somewhat reminiscent of that of Lindos, on Rhodes. It served the Gattilusi as a stronghold more than once when other parts of their large island were invaded, and it was, for example, in this castle that in 1450, after a long siege by the Turks and when the inhabitants were on the point of surrender, that Orietta Doria, the lady of Dorino Gattilusi, put on male armour and appeared among the defenders, leading them to a surprise victory over the amazed Turkish besieging army.

Pirgi Thermis   Πύργοι Θερμής

14th / 15th C Byzantine church. ★
Some 10 km. along the road running NW from Mytilini beside the sea, a paved road leads off to the W for 150 m. to the Panagia Tourloti.

This is one of the very few Byzantine churches in the island that has retained its main forms; it is a modestly sized church with three apses, and a dome carried on four piers. The plan was originally a square, but a large narthex was added in the (?) 16th C – perhaps for use as a schoolroom. The windows in the N and S walls were originally a triple arcade, although are now modernised, but there are two classical marble relief fragments, both of hunting subjects, still mounted in the S wall of the narthex. The exterior here has all the interest – the interior is, alas, modern throughout.

The EC enthusiast might wish to explore the sites of three quite large basilicas which were all excavated in the 1920's; however, they are unsigned and difficult to find and there is little now to be seen. Two are at **Eresos:** the Basilica of Agios Andreas Kritis, and the Basilica "of Afentelli"; and the third at **Ypsilometopos,** in the N of island, where the floor mosaic of the basilica of Agios Demetrios has an inscription by "Anatolios, who made the mosaics".

LIMNOS Λήμνος

Med: Stalimene.
Island region: N. Aegean. (*Nomos*: Lesbos.)

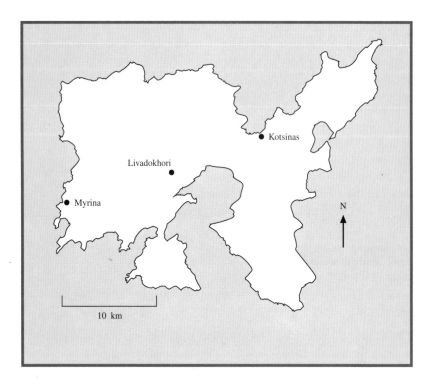

The siting of this island close to the mouth of the "Passage of Romanía" (i.e. the Dardenelles) gave it, with Samothraki and Fokaia and after the loss of Asia Minor, an importance to the Byzantines that was disproportionate to its other attractions; it was always clear that whoever held the island could control the sea routes between CP and Thessaloniki. As early as 325 the island was represented by its own bishop at the first Church Council in Nicaea, when the only other Greek islands so distinguished were Rhodes, Kos and Corfu. In 902 the island had (in spite of its location in the N Aegean) been plundered by a Saracen fleet, and it was no doubt a realisation of the problems that would result from the Arabs establishing a foothold so close to CP that caused the island to be raised to a metropolitan see under Leo VI (886-912); in 924 the Arab fleet was conclusively defeated off Limnos by the Byzantines.

The Venetians, never slow to scent a commercial advantage, arranged with the island's archbishop in 1136 that they should be granted a chapel at the port of Kotsinas (see below). Although awarded in the Deed of Partition of 1204 to the new Latin emperor, the island became, from 1207, a domain of the Venetian family of Navigajosa; when the first Duke, Philocole, died in 1214, the island was divided in half, with his son ruling one half and his two daughters the other. This arrangement continued until 1276, but then Michael VIII, of the Greek imperial dynasty returning to CP, was able to re-establish possession.

With the rise of the Gattilusi family in the N Aegean, and correspondingly weaker Byzantine power, it came under their control, with Jacopo Gattilusi (Lord of Lesbos) ruling there 1414-1419. In the later Byzantine period it was used as an inducement and reward for favours, and in 1453 it was the stated price required by Alfonso V of Aragon for his help against the Turks, as well as (reputedly) being promised by the emperor to the Genoese general Giustiniani Longo if he assisted in successfully repelling the Turks from the walls of CP. Probably because of its strategic value the Genoese did not succeed in holding it until 1453, but even then it was only in their hands for under two years as the rule of Nicoló Gattilusio was so unbearable that the inhabitants sent a secret plea to the sultan, Mehmet II, offering him the island if he would send one of his pashas to come and rule them instead.

This was forestalled when, in 1456, a papal force under a cardinal Lodovico Trevisan arrived and occupied Limnos, Samothraki and Thasos, installing governors and garrisons in all three islands in the name of Pope Callixtus III. This was part of a papal crusade to recover CP from the infidel, and under his successor, Pius II, a completely new religious order of knights was founded; formed largely in the image of the Hospitallers, its headquarters were to be on Limnos and it was called the Order of Our Lady of Bethlehem. A papal nuncio, John of Navarre, was a governor here 1461-65, but the sultan, brooking no further interference, took over all three islands, but gave Limnos as an appanage to Dimitrios Palaiologos. The island was fully in Turkish hands by 1470, and we hear no more of the new papal order centred here. Although the Venetians were to return there for two periods in 1464-79 and 1656-7, its value to the Turks always brought them back.

The harbour sheltered the British fleet in 1914 before the disastrous Dardenelles expedition, and at least one prominent gun emplacement on shore must date from this period.

The balance of the island's surviving buildings, running from the EC centuries to the 15th C and after, and with an outstanding castle, form a fair reflection of its history.

As there is no clear route within the island, the locations are given in alphabetical sequence.

Kotsinas (Kokkino)   Κότσινας (Κόκκινο)

Ruins of Byzantine / Venetian castle.★ Unenclosed.
The small mound where a modern bronze statue of the 15th C Greek heroine Meroula has been erected, make the site of this castle on the N coast easily visible.

This must have been an important harbour as it was here that (as mentioned above) the Venetians began to establish themselves as early as 1136, and in 1397 Kotsinas became the headquarters of the Venetian garrison which then built the small castle here, almost certainly expanding an existing Byzantine building. Its associations in later Byzantine history are strong, as it was to here that the despot Constantine Palaiologos, who was to become the last Byzantine emperor, brought from Lesbos his young Genoese wife, Caterina Gattilusi, in August 1442. (They had been married in July of the previous year, his first wife, Maddalena Tocco, having died in 1429.) He was on his way to CP, and had put in to the harbour here; some submerged remains of the foundations of a jetty are still visible. The Turks found out that he was there and besieged the port and castle for several weeks with their fleet, but eventually had to abandon the enterprise. The stress of the blockade caused Caterina to become ill, and she died here following a miscarriage; she was buried on the island at the classical Greek site that was then already called Palaiokhora.

The church itself is of only slight interest, but there is substantial masonry surviving in and around the hill on which it stands; partial excavation has revealed some chambers, and a walk beside the sea below the hill reveals lengths of the walling of the castle just 2 or 3 m. from the sea; they are eroded but are certainly original. This would appear to be an excellent prospect for a thorough excavation, which might then make it possible to distinguish Byzantine from Venetian elements in its construction.

A visit here is recommended as the outlook from this small harbour, looking out across the bay of Pournias, cannot have changed significantly since the 15th C, and the few houses to the SW do not impinge on the quiet and remote atmosphere here with its strong associations.

Livadokhori (near to)
Λιβαδοχώρι

Church of the Panagia built in a farm-yard on the site of an EC basilica.★★

Both farm-yard and church open. (See Pl. 29).

Turn due N opposite the sign to Livadokhori, and follow the dirt road past an army camp; continue for 2.1 km. and the farm entrance is then on your right.

The first surprise here is to find two erect columns of Proconnesian marble from an earlier church facing you across the farm-yard as you enter it; these are some of the survivals (now used in the porch of a later church) from what must have been a substantial three-aisled EC basilica, which, judging by the marble flooring of the ground plan, projecting far into the modern farm-yard, could have been some 25 m. long. The present church, which occupies the central nave of the older building, is probably 18th C, but built into the wall over the entrance is a marble beam with a damaged inscription and what may be a date (1078), but even the 19th C German epigraphers are not sure. It could well be 11th C, and this must also be the approximate date of what is perhaps the rarest and most interesting item here, found on the S side of the yard.

This is a major piece of well-preserved decorative carving on a hollowed-out grey marble monolith, now used as an animal trough but which must originally have been a sarcophagus. Some 2 m. long, its carved decoration of five finely cut roundels is 11th/12th C, and the crosses among the relief decoration tend to confirm its function as a sarcophagus. (There is another of very comparable proportions and decoration in the museum at Bursa in N Asia Minor.) Spolia of various kinds lie around, and in the floor of the apse of the church, which still retains the bishop's masonry throne, parts of an 11th C templon are embedded in the cement. This ensemble is known locally as the 'Metropolis Farm', and it was clearly the seat of a bishop in the middle Byzantine period.

This site has been given ★★ on account of the unique combination of a completely rural context for what seems to have been a substantial 11th C bishop's residence retained on an EC location; where else in Greece could one find a farm-yard furnished with marble columns, carved Byzantine marble animal troughs and the residue of an episcopal estate?

Myrina
Μύρινα

Kastro.★★ Currently ungated and open.

This hugely impressive stronghold occupies a massive rock joined by a low neck of land to the shore; it must, after Acrocorinth and Monemvasia in the

Peloponnese, count as one of the best endowed natural fortifications in the Aegean. There is no one view point from which its qualities can be assessed, but studying it from both the main harbour to the S and then the sea shore to the N will give an initial impression of its character; this is amplified by viewing it as you approach Myrina from the sea.

Entry to this imposing site is up a winding, stony path from the harbour side of the headland, and arriving at the NE extremity of the Kastro. It occupies the whole of the summit of the huge outcrop of rock that dominates both the coast and the interior at this point, and the area enclosed is some 160 x 90 m.; the complex fortifications exist on many different levels and cover the whole of this irregular mass.

The earliest building here to survive is of the 7th C BC, and small amounts of walling from this phase can still be seen on the left as you enter the first areas of the main fortification and on the N face of the highest area. There would have been Byzantine activity here, but the defining phase of building was that of the Venetians. It is worth recalling that the Byzantine emperor Michael VIII, besieging this castle, was unable to dislodge the Venetian 'Grand Duke' Paolo Navigajoso who was holding out here with 700 men; the emperor in vain offered Navigajoso 60,000 gold hyperpera if he would hand the castle over, and this was at a time of low imperial finances. Even after the death of the Venetian leader and when the siege had gone on for three years, his widow, a sister of Marco II Sanudo, Duke of Naxos, departed taking with her the lead from the roof of the palace where she had lived as Duchess.

Little of the internal building that was present then can now be identified, and most of what can now be seen of this construction is Genoese work, building on to existing Byzantine walls, and will date from the presence of the Gattilusi here in the 15th C, or immediately after 1453, during their short residence. It would in any case seem certain that it is prior to the Turkish occupation, and either the Genoese of the Papal forces would have had the greatest interest to invest in this kind of fortification. The artillery positions built on the E sector overlooking the other side of the headland will certainly be Turkish; the same must be said of the large roofless building encountered quite early on during the ascent: the tall wall niche and remains of a spiral staircase in an added minaret confirm it as the remains of a mosque. Towards the NW tip of the headland (looking straight over to Mount Athos) there is an almost complete, roofed building some 16 m. long sunk in a walled surround and adjacent to a complex of underground, barrel-vaulted chambers – all of which can be entered; the latter is probably Venetian but the former also seems Turkish.

Allow plenty of time for visiting this formidable fortress with its many layers of occupation and use, and return if possible for a second visit, as it is a complex site which will not reveal all its aspects in one viewing.

The contents of the small **Museum** in Myrina, which faces the beach to the N of the Kastro, are almost entirely classical; besides a few Byzantine copper coins displayed on the first floor, a marble base block just inside the gate has a 5th C BC inscription of the *boule* of Athens on one face, but a cross in relief on another indicates its re-use during the medieval period.

MILOS

Μήλος

Med: Melo

Island group: Cyclades (SW) (*Nomos*: Cyclades).

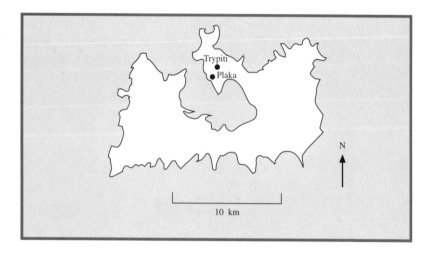

Milos had a geographical position of some importance as it was the first island of the Cyclades that mariners would reach after rounding Cape Malea in the SE of the Peloponnese on their way to the many ports of the Aegean, and thence to CP. Its large bay provided one of the safest harbours in the Cyclades, and the island was unusually rich in minerals and enjoyed the benefits of fertile land; several sources also refer particularly to the mill-stones which were among its most regular exports. During the 7th-8th C there is further evidence of the prosperity of Milos in that it was among the few islands which sent its own bishops to the 6th and 7th church councils in CP and Nicaea.

In spite of its natural endowments, the medieval survivals of the island are slight, and after a flourishing EC period, the island seems to have been abandoned between the later 9th and 12th C; this desertion may well have been caused by Arab raids during the later 8th/9th C.

Its fortunes after the Fourth Crusade and the *Partitio Romaniae* were initially the same as many other of the Cyclades, becoming one of the islands of the original Duchy of Naxos, of which the archbishop furnished a Latin suffragan. During the 1260's, however, when Byzantine rule was being re-imposed from CP in a number of the islands, the relative proximity of Milos to Monmemvasia, which was one of the securest strongpoints of Byzantine rule, meant that it was one of the most active islands in rejecting Latin occupation. A Greek monk headed a revolt and drove out the Latins from their castle, which would probably then have been that at Plaka, but also perhaps at the modern Zefyria (see below) and briefly held the island until the duke, Marco II Sanudo, returned with sixteen galleys and quickly re-took the island and re-installed one of his family in control; the châtelaine of the new régime rejoiced, incidentally, in the name of Donna Cassandra Sanudo. It was again the short distance from the Peloponnese and the Greek mainland that caused Milos to be the subject of a punitive raid in 1316; this time it was the Catalan Company under Alfonso Fadrique, who were then establishing themselves in Attica and who had been opposed by a relative of the Sanudi, who landed and carried off some 700 of the island's inhabitants.

Milos returned to Venetian control later in the century, and it was the island's bishop who was sent to Venice in 1383 to gain legal consent for the new Crispo dynasty to succeed as dukes of the Archipelago; later, while under the Crispo dukedom, the island is mentioned by name in the treaty of 1419 between Venice and the sultan as one of the islands acknowledged as belonging to the Serene Republic. Milos followed the rest of the Archipelago into full Turkish occupation in 1566.

As might be expected, the island's buildings which survive from its quite turbulent past are in the main either from the EC period or secular building from the centuries of the Duchy of the Archipelago. The chief focus of interest is to be found on the E-most of the two broad and rocky promontories that embrace the fine harbour, formed from the crater of the extinct volcano that make up the island. During the later medieval period the population of the island was located either in Zefyria (formerly Millo), on lower ground somewhat inland from the middle of the bay, or Anokastro (near Plakes); the buildings of the former (also known at one time as Palaiokhora) have been used as a quarry since the 18th C, and the locality now offers little of interest, but the castle at Anokastro (or just 'Kastro') still has some surviving ruins.

(The Museum in Plaka is devoted to pre-Christian exhibits, and has no *medievalia* on show).

Trypiti   Τρυπητή

EC catacombs, 3rd / 4th C.★★ Gated, but entry daily during usual visiting hours except Sunday & Friday; free.

EC baptismal font. Unenclosed.
Following the road W through Trypiti, the catacombs are well signed to the left

on leaving the village and are reached down a long flight of steps.

No other such excavated area for multiple Christian burials has been discovered anywhere in Greece, and these catacombs are rightly claimed to be unique in the Aegean. The closest comparison is probably with those in Malta, but the much harder kind of limestone there has resulted in a more cramped layout than is the case with those at Trypiti. The excavated area has been cut from the soft, volcanic tufa, and the friable nature of this material no doubt accounts for the rounded forms you will find. The first 30 m. of the complex is lit by electricity and so can be visited, but beyond this area the galleried tunnelling is roped off.

The first published account in 1843 described a total of a dozen 'galleries', with some 1,500 to 2,000 burials, but already there had been wholesale robbing of the sarcophagi; distinguished visitors to the island were said to be allowed to select, open and empty a grave here. By the time that Theodore Bent visited Milos in 1884, when he wrote of five galleries entered from four separate entrances, there was not one grave that had not been despoiled.

The visitor today is restricted to only a small proportion of these in the lit area. The individual burial sites take the form of either simple niches cut into the tufa, or *arcosols,* the term for where a recessed arch has been cut into the rock over the burial shelf. It is clear that six of the *arcosols* that are visible have had a plaster rendering with painted imagery, but most regrettably these have been obscured by grafitti and soot deposits from candles – now replaced by the electric lighting. (Bent describes many inscriptions and paintings). The general character of this site is one of simplicity, even of poverty; while other decorated *arcosols* are said to survive they cannot be visited, and those here must be taken to be typical, and can never have been of any refinement. The lack of any surviving decorative features makes it impossible to give any firm date, but it is most probable that the catacomb here was in use during the 3rd and 4th C, and may have been begun earlier than this. The out-dated view of the catacombs as hiding-places for the persecuted, now long discredited, will again be shown to be untenable by what you will see here.

It is surprising that no other catacombs in Greece are known, but the uniqueness of these makes a visit here even more rewarding. However, the locality has yet further interests.

Looking steeply down towards the sea a large ancient Greek theatre can be seen from several view-points; the audience, as so often, must have enjoyed an outstanding natural outlook, in this case looking over the bay formed from the core of the volcano which created the island. If, instead of descending the steps to the catacomb entrance, you continued walking towards the sea you would in a few metres pass the site of the discovery in 1820 of the famous marble statue of Venus, now in the Louvre. Continuing, after some 40 m. the ground rises on your right to a low terrace, and here you will find (quite unsigned and unenclosed) the remains of an **EC baptismal font**. It is damaged and has lost all traces of the baptistry that must once have enclosed it, but the sunken, cruciform shape, with some of the original marble lining still in place, is immediately clear. There would have originally been a basilica and baptistry building as well, and this, with the catacombs below, speaks of the vigorous Christian community that existed here from the early centuries.

Plaka: Kastro (Anokastro or Apanokastro)

Castle ruins and two churches.★
Castle unenclosed; churches normally locked.
A separate, steep hill to the N of Plaka is crowned by the remains of the medieval castle site, and retains five churches at different points; it cannot be missed.

You climb it by a paved stairway named as the Odos Genethlion Theotokou, which passes the church dedicated to the Panagia Thalassitra, the largest of the group. This is a fine domed basilica, superbly sited on a broad terrace; it is probably 14th/15th C in origin, and must in any case date from the period of Venetian occupation; it was restored in 1694, when the belfry was probably added. The interior has no special attraction, but the size of the church suggests the importance of the locality in the late medieval period; during the centuries of Venetian dominance the bishop lived at Anokastro, and this could well have been his cathedral.

Continuing up to the summit you will find a small plateau of some 30 m. square, which must have been the chief vantage point and heavily defended. Another small church, the Panagia Skiniotissa (or Koimisis) occupies the central area; although this was traditionally where both W and Greek rites were celebrated, it used to display a relief with an image of the Venetian ruler's wife, with Latin inscriptions; this can no longer be seen, and the present building certainly does not date from before the 16th C. All that is left of the fortifications occupy the perimeter of the summit. The original castle here was probably built by the first duke of Naxos, Marco I Sanudo, when he annexed Milos in 1207. Although it was, with the kastro at Zefyria, the main refuge for the islanders during the 13th-16th C, the kastro here could never have housed large numbers, and there was also a house of Franciscan friars here in the

15th C of which no trace can be identified. There has been recent consolidation, but the site was clearly not regarded by the later Venetians of the Duchy (or, later on, by the Turks) as being worth the expenditure of major modern fortification, and there are no signs of provision for cannon. The enthusiast may wish to look for a fragment of what could be part of the 13th C kastro to the SE, downhill from the main site.

With its undoubted distinction of being able to offer the only Aegean catacomb, Milos is both an attractive and interesting island to visit, with notable survivals from classical and post-classical periods.

MYKONOS Μύκονος

Med: Micone.
Island group: Cyclades (NE). (*Nomos*: Cyclades).

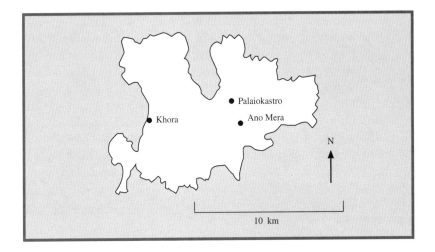

Mykonos is one of the more arid of the Cyclades, and although its terrain is not particularly mountainous, agriculture has never been productive here. Not mentioned by the medieval historians or in the Deed of Partition of 1204, it may have been its unproductive soil that caused Marco Sanudo not to annex it himself when he founded his duchy on nearby Naxos in 1207. It was left to an equally enterprising pair of Venetians, Andrea and Geremia Ghisi, who decided that they would create their own lordship, to occupy Mykonos and the nearby island of Tinos. They soon added Skopelos, Skyros and Skiathos to their holdings, so founding the second largest of the Venetian dukedoms.

It was not to last as long as the Duchy of Naxos; the family links died out with the death of Giorgio III Ghisi in 1390, and so Mykonos and Tinos were bequeathed to Venice. In a move that would allow them to retain control and draw an income from it, the Senators in 1406 put the two islands up to auction. Every four years thereafter a governor arrived whose bid had been successful, and he would collect what revenues he could, paying an agreed sum to the Republic and keeping the rest for himself. In 1430 this system changed, with direct rule from Venice being imposed, and with governors on two-year contracts directly answerable to the Senate. It was this system that was still in force in 1537 when the Turkish admiral, Khaireddin Barbarossa made Mykonos one of his prey during his campaign of destruction and annexation. From that year Mykonos was occupied by the Turks, although Tinos was to remain with Venice until 1715.

To put the operation of relatively tolerant Turkish rule into perspective, however, it should be said that the link with both Venice and Tinos that lasted throughout the island's medieval history is perpetuated in one of the very rare public papal inscription still surviving in the Aegean; it is dated 1677, and you can see it prominently over the door of the RC church at the entrance to the modern village. In it Pope Innocent XI confirms Angelus Venier as bishop of Tinos and Mykonos, and the Ghisi arms in marble relief above confirm the Venetian association.

A final observation could be made about the pelicans of Mykonos. A colony of them was already here in 1689 which fascinated the English traveller Bernard Randolph; with his companions he measured the liquid capacity of the expanding lower pouch of the beak of a dead bird, and wrote that after pouring in twelve quarts of water there still seemed to be spare capacity.

None of the ecclesiastical buildings on Mykonos can now demonstrate a medieval origin, with even the metropolis church of the Theotokos Pigadiotissa being clearly later, but fragments of the '**Kastro**' walls on the promontory can still be glimpsed which may go back to the 13th or 14th C. The most authentic part of the kastro substructure can surprisingly be found in the basement of the **Folklore Museum** (open Monday-Saturday 17.30-20.30, Sunday 18.30-20.30); the entrance is at ground level, and the display of folk material continues into the cellar of the large house next door. Located as it is right at the tip of the promontory, this was clearly built over the site of the kastro, and one wall of the cellar here is taken up with the substantial arched foundations of the Venetians' building, which has otherwise almost entirely disappeared.

Palaiokastro   Παλαιοκάστρο

Remains of castle enceinte.*

Taking the road out towards Ano Mera, the hill-top site comes into view after some 5 km. Take the signed turning to the left, and leave transport at the 18th C Moni Palaiokastro.

The track to the Kastro leads up past the convent, which is reached in about 10 minutes. Now only a dry stone enceinte encloses an area some

60 m. x 40 m., and a late chapel crowns the hill-top. This is the near centre of the island, and would have been the main refuge of the islanders during the medieval centuries (and later), but does not bear traces of having been a determined Venetian fortification; they seem to have been content with their kastro on the town headland, and, as so often, preferred to be close to the sea. It is worth noting here that in 1689 Bernard Randolph wrote of Mykonos: "This island is very near the Road from Constantinople, and Egypt, and seldom is free from Privateers." It would presumably have been here that the island's population gathered to defend themselves when the dreaded ships were sighted.

Ano Mera   Άνω Μέρα

Moni Tourliani.★ Rural monastery; usual monastic hours of opening. *Situated right on the village street, the quite imposing entrance to this monastery cannot be missed.*

The general layout is impressive, and corresponds to the traditional arrangement of a free-standing katholikon in a courtyard surrounded by the monastic buildings. As it now appears the fabric of this quite large and prosperous monastery is of 17th-18th C; any painting from a previous building has disappeared, but the presence of re-used earlier columns and some other spolia would suggest that it was originally a medieval foundation. This could well be another example of Turkish insistence on replacing ecclesiastical buildings, rather than permitting duplication.

Given the paucity of medieval survivals on this popular island, a visit here is recommended.

NAXOS

Νάξος

Med: Acsia, Naxia, Nixia (also Dionisiada, on account of its fine wines). Island group: Cyclades. (*Nomos*: Cyclades).

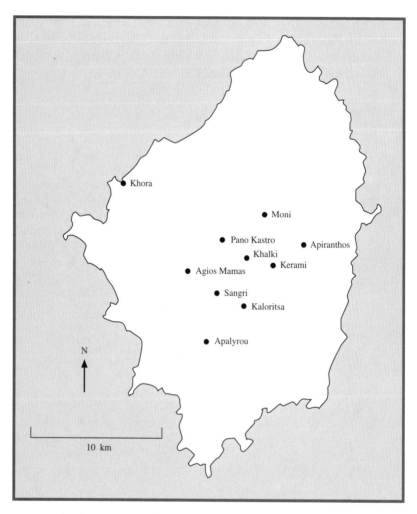

The island of Naxos could be said to have two secure claims to fame: the first is the natural beauty of its interior which meant that from earliest times it was regarded as the most favoured of the Cyclades, and even today its mountain slopes display more green and thickly wooded expanses than anywhere else in the Archipelago. From Herodotus onwards all writers on the island have found some way of expressing their admiration, with such poetic titles as 'the pearl of the Levant', and this can indeed still be used when describing this, both the largest and the richest of the Cyclades during the later medieval period. The second claim concerns its medieval history, when it became the centre of the most enduring of all the various dukedoms initiated in the Aegean by the Latin invaders.

Its position made it an important staging post on the sea route between CP and Crete, and in 1083 its status was enhanced when its bishopric was raised to being (with neighbouring Paros) the seat of a metropolitan 'of Paro-Naxia'. But it was after the Fourth Crusade that Naxos was to take on a more special identity, first as the seat of the Duchy 'of Naxos', and later 'of the Archipelago': its total lifespan could be said to cover 362 years, and it knew 21 dukes from two dynasties. As a result of this prolonged W presence, the island has today one of the larger RC populations of the Aegean islands, and Italian names still survive in some numbers.

In one of the stranger omissions of the *Partitio Romaniae* Naxos is not specifically mentioned, but (whatever reason might be suggested for such a major absence) Venetians were not slow to decide that its relative richness and desireability had marked it out for them. Even before 1207 a band of Genoese pirates had seized occupation of its mountain-top castle of Apalyrou, but these did not deter the individual adventurers setting out to carve out their own domains. One of these was Marco Sanudo, the nephew of the shrewd old doge who had been present in CP throughout the Fourth Crusade, Enrico Dandolo; he embarked with a band of kindred spirits to take over Naxos and establish their own rule there. After a five-week siege of the castle stronghold his conquest was rapid and complete, but he decided to reject all Venetian control, and only recognise the suzerainty of the Latin emperor in CP, Henry, who awarded him his title of Duke. Sanudo gathered ten other islands under his control and so established what was called first the 'Duchy of Naxos' and later 'of the Archipelago'. From 1207 this new Duchy held the islands of Paros, Antiparos, Milos, Kimolos, Ios, Amorgos, Sifnos, Sikinos, Kythnos and Syros.

In 1248 suzerainty of the Duchy was transferred to William II Villehardouin, prince of Akhaia, and, after the Byzantine re-conquest of some islands in 1278 had failed to capture Naxos, the duke became a vassal of Charles I of Anjou. In 1383 Duke Niccolo II died violently, probably the victim of assassination, and the Sanudi were replaced by the Lombard family of Crispo, but it was to be only from 1418 that the protection of Venice was invoked by Giovanni II Crispo, who then ruled as a vassal of the Serene Republic. It was just over these years that

Buondelmonti visited Naxos, and he commented on the lack of men in the population, which obliged many women who wished to marry to die childless; the shortage of manpower was no doubt a factor in the appeal to Venice.

There was later to be direct rule from Venice for two periods when the native Greek population, suffering from too harsh treatment by their dukes, appealed for protection; one of these was from 1494-1500 and the other 1511-1517, when Francesco III Crispo, having apparently gone mad in 1510 and murdered his wife, was held in Santorini. He died in 1511 and as his son was only eleven, Venetian rule was called upon for six years until he was old enough to assume the title. Unlike many of the islands, Naxos did not succumb in the campaign of Barbarossa in 1537, and it was only in 1566 that the Turkish sultan, Selim II, after accepting the surrender of his island from the last Latin duke, Jacopo IV Crispo, cleverly appointed a rich and resourceful Portuguese Jew, Jacopo Nasi, as titular duke of the Archipelago, whose notional rule as the last holder of the title lasted from 1566 to 1579, although he never set foot in his dukedom.

In spite of its long and colourful political history during the medieval period, Naxos now has far more to offer in the way of ecclesiastical treasures (particularly Byzantine) than of reminders of its secular or political past. The persistent W presence has left a distinct mark on the architecture of the island, with its landscape offering numerous double-nave churches and some grand Venetian semi-fortified mansions, but as arrival will almost certainly be at the capital and port of Khora (Naxos town), the monuments there, and other military survivals, will be mentioned first.

Khora (Naxos town)

Remains of Venetian Kastro and RC Cathedral.★★

As the winding alleys of Khora rise so steeply towards the Kastro that you arrive at its centre without having seen it as an ensemble, it is adviseable first to walk out along the short causeway to where the giant doorway of the temple of Apollo dominates the harbour. Looking back towards the town from here gives a much clearer idea of the siting and scale of the Kastro than can be gained from climbing up to it through the town. Equally informative is the view of the town from the sea, as boats approach or leave the harbour. Although only one of the twelve towers that once defended it, with some sections of its original walls, still stand, its bulk and aspect are still impressive. When it was first built it stood virtually alone, and it was in subsequent years that the *borgo* grew up below it, with its curving alleys still following the line of the original walls.

Although there may have been some Byzantine building here before 1207 to defend the harbour, the only surviving features all date from the Venetian occupation. Of the two routes up to the Kastro, the N one takes you past the so-called 'Tower of Sanudo' which is the only major part of the 13th C defences to survive, and through the only remaining gateway (the Trani Porta) into the enceinte. Here, on a rather shapeless Plateia, the mass of what must have been the keep of the original castle, sometimes called the 'Sanudo Palace', rises to some ten metres. This, and any adjacent castle buildings that have not survived in recogniseable state, were home to the 21 dukes who ruled here for over three and a half centuries; here cases would have been judged according to the 'Assizes of Romanía' and here too, no doubt, was the mint that produced the coinage of the Duchy of Naxos; here, too, the Sanudi and the Crispi would have lived, married, given in marriage and died, and (in the case of the 18th duke) gone mad. The tower is kept shut, but its exterior has a massive and forbidding aspect even in its truncated state.

To the N of this, and almost filling the Plateia, is the large **RC Cathedral**, open at 6.0 p.m. each evening; the original dedication was to the Assumption of the Virgin. Its continued existence and scale are due to the large RC presence in Naxos which arrived with the Venetians and which persists to the present day. The original building formed part of Sanudo's castle complex, and was endowed by him with a staff of seven canons. Although it is now in effect a 16th C building (a lost inscription over the door recorded its consecration in 1589 by archbishop Raphael Schiati), it was restored in 1865 and again last century; over the doorway can still be seen (partly obscured) four armorial escutcheons which have been identified as being (from left to right) of the della Craspere family, of the Crispi family, of the Venetian Republic, and of the Sanudo family (the colouring of the last would have been of silver with a blue bar). They were probably carved and installed c.1579 under the Venetian archbishop Domenico della Craspere.

The interior, quite recently restored, presents a conventional basilica plan, and used to have many more 17th/18th C memorial tablets in its floor than it does now; their disappearance during the raising and re-laying of the floor is to be regretted as they document with great clarity the continuing Western presence (particularly Venetian) in the island. As it is, there remain at a few steps to the NE of the entrance door the arms of the Genoese family of Grimaldi, who now survive in one of the last Mediterranean princedoms as the ruling dynasty of Monaco; members of the family still lived here in the 20th C. The dukes were (perhaps surprisingly) not buried here, but in a burial ground outside the Khora, and some tomb fragments were still being reported as visible in the 19th century.

But by far the most interesting work here is the altarpiece, which in 1962 was found to be of a full-length figure of the Virgin Eleousa with a small votive figure of a bishop at her feet (previously it had been obscured by a silver revetment and was thought to be of the far more common half-length type). This beautiful and unique work presents a series of problems; its style represents a complex integration of Western and Byzantine art, and the diminutive kneeling bishop, denoted as John of Nicomedia, has a prayer to the Virgin inscribed in Greek above him, but wears his pallium *alla romana*; there are two layers of paint in some places. It is most probably early 13th C in date, but has been described as 12th C. On the reverse of the panel is a later full-length image of St John the Baptist. It would be of the greatest interest if the origins of this altarpiece could ever be conclusively established.

This is a surprisingly rewarding church to visit, offering as it does some unique artistic evidence of the powerful and continuous W presence in the island, and the fertility that can rise from the meeting of the two traditions.

Two further military survivals on Naxos will be described here:

Kastro Apalyrou   Κάστρο Απαλύρου

Ruins of castle.★★ Completely unsigned and unenclosed.
On the main road to Khalki branch right at the prominent Venetian tower of Bazaios; after about 2 km. turn left on to a stony track, and the castle is on the summit of the mountain to your right; after 1 km. leave the track and the scrambling, pathless climb up to the castle (in view most of the time) takes some 45 minutes and you will then be at over 400 m.

The seat of Byzantine rule in Naxos had traditionally been located here, towards the S of the island, and away from the sea; Byzantine presence here has been confirmed by finds of coins of the emperor Leo III (717-741). This is not the kind of location that was usually favoured by either the Venetians or the Genoese, but the latter may well have initiated their attempted annexation by establishing themselves here because it would then have been the strongest point in the island. The strength of its position did mean that it took Marco Sanudo five weeks to dislodge the Genoese before he could establish himself here in 1207; he would certainly have needed an existing stronghold from which to launch his takeover of the island as he had burnt the galleys that brought his band of adventurers, and the substantial castle remains here strongly suggest that this was where he originally located himself. The kastro above the harbour at Khora would then not have been built. The siting of Apalyrou is typical for the Byzantines, sufficiently high and far enough inland to provide good visibility and security, but it was too far from the sea and harbour to be coveted by Venetians.

The castle occupies the entire summit of the mountain, its enceinte forming an oval some 200 m. long with the flatter sides running due E/W; there seems not to have been a secondary, outer enceinte, and the most prominent surviving feature as you approach is a substantial tower on the NW outwork. This guards the shoulder of the mountain which must always have provided the only approach route, as it still does today. You will find a number of cisterns still in existence, some quite large, suggesting that in times of need it was intended to shelter quite a numerous population, and there are remains of a number of other buildings across the slope inside the walls; quite a substantial church straddles the mountain ridge, and its three apses can still be seen close the E wall. The absence of any clear signs of later alteration suggests that Sanudo abandoned it as soon as he could. It seems clear that these are the remains of a Byzantine island stronghold, in use over several centuries, and probably last strengthened in the 12th C, with little or no occupation after c.1210. As such this is a relatively rare example, as most local Greek strongholds of this kind were either developed into more substantial castles, or were sufficiently near to other centres of building to have been used as a quarry or simply built over. The isolation of Apalyrou has always been retained, and must account for its relative completeness today.

This must rate as an important example of Byzantine military building, and the climb here is rewarding in every way.

Pano Kastro / Epano Kastro   Πάνο Κάστρο / Έπανο Κάστρο

Ruins of castle.★★
Unenclosed.
Signed from Khalki down a good dirt road; it is some 45 minutes on foot from Tzingalario and stays in view all the time.

The jagged remains of this castle can be seen breaking the skyline for a long distance around this central mountain range. The steep climb up to it rewards the energetic with outstanding views over much of the island and as far W as the sea. It must have been a substantial structure, and was clearly intended to dominate much of the interior; contrasting with

Apalyrou, which was probably also intended to protect the local population from attack, the construction of Pano Kastro was by Venetians, and may have been initiated to impose or maintain some order on the local Naxiote population of the island interior. One episode of revolt is recorded when Marco II Sanudo enraged the populace by overthrowing the altar of a local saint, Agios Pakhys, who was venerated for his health-giving powers – particularly for making thin babies and men become fat – but there were likely to have been others. A date in 1250's or 1260's is most often suggested for the initiation of this castle. The reason for building a new stronghold here rather than modernising the castle of Apalyrou was probably connected with the location of the latter so far to the S, from where it would have been much more difficult to exercise control.

The remaining parts of Pano Kastro are now very scattered; before even entering what would have been the enceinte the visitor finds several small churches of various periods on the lower slopes. One of the largest remains is met early on and is a substantial defensive tower; the design of this must be Venetian in origin, and the same design can be found in several other locations in the islands where Venice held sway, including Paros and Kythira. Its firing apertures for six cannon suggest it is late 15th/16th C, and it may survive from the Venetian presence of 1511-1517. Further up the remains are earlier, and the walling in the W sector looks as if it could be part of the earliest building here. The enceinte had six towers, three half-round and three rectangular, and two plaster-lined cisterns can still be seen, one 17m. long, various half-ruined fragments still stand, with the arcaded walling of quite a substantial hall or church the most prominent feature of the original enclosure.

In its own way this must be regarded as a relatively rare example of Venetian fortification, as its inland siting is so unlike their traditional practice; again, the independence of the Sanudi from direct Venetian control may well lie behind the ensemble here.

Venetian mansions.
A prominent and picturesque feature of the island is the presence of a number of very substantial mansions (now often called 'Towers') erected by Venetian landowners; they can be found in the countryside and in some villages, and can easily be picked out by the decorative castellation which crowns their walls, and was perhaps intended to be reminiscent of the Doges' Palace in Venice. Typical examples are those of the Bazaios family on the right of the road to Khalki, that of the Gratsias family in Khalki itself, and that of the Bellonia family near Galanado, which retains adjacent to it a small double-nave church (for

which see below). That of the Bazaios is thought to be the oldest, while that of the Gratsias indicates well the later integration of Venetians into the island's life, with three escutcheons in relief, and an inscription of 1742 in Greek naming a ΒΕΡΝΑΔΟΣ ΜΠΑΡΟΤΖΙΣ; their presence is also evidence of the tolerance of the Turkish power then in occupation. While some may have elements that go back to the 15th century or even earlier, most must be later, and the armorial bearings over their gates often bear dates in the 17th or 18th C. These mansions cannot normally be visited.

Churches.
Scattered and fragmentary remains exist of five EC basilicas, but the most pervasive interest for the medievalist in Naxos must however be its numerous Byzantine churches, many still with fresco painting. Thirty-six have been identified, but either the fabric or the frescoes in many of these are too damaged to repay seeking out except by the specialist; nevertheless in no other Aegean island except Crete or perhaps Kythira can such a range and quantity of Byzantine frescoes be seen, ranging from the 7th to the 14th C and later. Some churches are quite easy to find, while others, particularly those among the olive groves of the Tragaia plain where they are remote from any road or track, can be both very hard to locate, and even when found, their position is hard to describe; that of Agios Giorgios Diasoritis, which has some fine frescoes, is omitted for this reason. Many can be seen, but are not of sufficient interest to enumerate here individually; an example is beside the track that leads off the road to the castle of Apalyrou, described above, where a recently restored 10th/11th C church is representative of numerous other modest middle Byzantine churches.

Another feature of the Naxos landscape is the phenomenon of small **double-nave churches**, which can be found in considerable numbers; none are of exceptional individual interest, and many are quite late, but collectively they represent an interesting local feature. The traditional explanation for their appearance is that they offered the opportunity for Orthodox and RC congregations to share the same building, and this is probably correct; each nave usually carries a different dedication, in some cases one nave is domed and the other not, and they tend to be found in rural situations. Some are certainly medieval in date, but none have retained frescoes of any interest. This tradition may represent a particular social development of the island's countryside.

The Byzantine churches described here represent a selection which has been arrived at on the bases of accessibility, visibility and inherent interest. The arrangement that has been adopted is first to select four of the most prominent and outstanding of the churches which are also relatively easy to locate. Some less accessible churches will then be described, but the enthusiast with plenty of time might wish to combine both groups.

The first group is: Agios Mamas of which the nearest village is Kato Potamia, the Panaghia Protothroni at Khalki, the Panagia Drosiani (near Moni), and Agios Nikolaos at Sangri.

Agios Mamas. (Unenclosed, derelict and doorless.) (See Pl. 12).
This substantial domed church, lying near the bed of a shallow valley, is visible from several points to the E of the road that winds through the hills between Galanado and Sangri; it can only be reached by foot, either from Kato Potamia or by scrambling down over rough ground from the road.
Although it is the only church in this group with virtually no surviving decoration, its substantial scale (some 8 m. across the N and S arms of the crossing) has given it some importance and attracted the suggestion that it was the seat of the Orthodox metropolitan of the island before the arrival of the Venetians. Its plan is an early type of the domed, inscribed-cross design, with the short but broad, equal-armed cross. Its large, high dome (with eight windows) is supported on four piers, with the four corner spaces roofed by barrel vaults; the broad, cylindrical form of the main apse is the only damaged part of the main structure, and its size emphasises how the side apses are little more than niches – the N one has the only surviving fresco fragment (probably 12th C). The builders have used spolia from earlier periods: the window divisions would seem to be EC in date (one has fallen into the naos) and classical Greek frieze fragments have been built into the E corner piers of the main apse and over the N door exterior. There is a large narthex built on at the W which may be c.13th C, and must in any case be later than the church itself as there is a blocked window high in the W wall. The narthex has a double barrel-vault supported by a massive pier, and it would have been larger before its N bay disappeared. An arcosol in the SE corner survives from a tomb here.

A date is hard to determine, but from various indications the main structure is most probably later 9th or 10th C, with the narthex and belfry some four centuries later. Its scale, relatively good condition and early date make this one of the most architecturally interesting of the Naxiote churches, as well as being finely sited. It was still in use in 1707, when Antonio Giustiniani, then the current Latin 'archbishop of Naxoparos', had his name inscribed as donor of a gateway he had erected here.

Do not be deterred from a visit here by the terrain, as it is one of the most significant and rewarding of the Naxiote churches.

Khalki   Χάλκη

The Panagia Protothroni.**
In the centre of the village; the key is held by the papas, who lives some 500m.
down the side road that leads away from the church, in a house on the right.

This can now be regarded as the most important, from the viewpoint both of its history and its frescoes, of the numerous churches on the island. Its architecture has been fully studied and its five (or more) layers of wall paintings restored; it also has several dated inscriptions that give an unusually accurate idea of its history.

The plan of the church is now that of an inscribed cross with E and W bays extended; there is quite a deep narthex flanked by separate chambers forming two parekklisia. Before entering you might wish to examine one of the most important inscriptions, now built into the ledge on the W front below the later belfry (binoculars needed); it is cut into a piece of marble of which the decorative bosses suggest that it was first used in a templon (presumably taken from inside this church), and asks the Virgin to protect the individuals, including the Bishop Leo and the Protospatharios Niketas, who renovated the church in 1052. It is fairly certain that in its earliest form the building was a basilica, and that the cupola was a later addition, perhaps of the 8th-9th C or slightly later.

Once inside the church, the lengthy nave area is very evident; the cupola is supported on wall sections forming narrow piers, with no columns used. The synthronon in the apse indicates the church's early role as the seat of a bishop. It is at first hard to establish the characteristics of the various layers of fresco; those in the cupola are some of the most homogeneous, and are probably mid 11th century, of the period of the inscription on the exterior and forming the third fresco layer. Their subject-matter is highly unusual, with 14 saints, prophets and archangels ranged round the drum, rather than the more usual choir of angels. The most artistically impressive are those on the S wall of the sanctuary where the Annunciation is the most complete and visible and must represent the work of a major artist; these date from the late 12th C and constitute the third fresco layer. Earliest must be the paintings in the apse, where a small masonry episcopal throne still survives; though damaged, there is a section depicting a group of the apostles approaching the centre which is thought to be pre-iconoclast art, going back to the 7th C. If this is correct, it must represent the date of the original foundation, and is in any case the earliest layer; recent restoration has revealed fragments of aniconic decoration here that must date from a later phase, possibly 10th-11th C. Also from this earliest group are quite well-preserved feast scenes in the vault of the S crossing of the Annunciation, Visitation, Presentation and the Forty Martyrs of Sebaste. The figures of SS. George, Philip and Akindynos in the NW parekklision are also very impressive, and their style suggests the early 12th C.

As this is one of the most prominent churches on Naxos, and has the greatest range of frescoes, an early visit here is recommended as being particularly rewarding, as well as helpful when viewing other churches.

Moní   Moví

The Panagia Drosiani.** (See Pl. 31).

Coming from Khalki, just round a bend at 3 km. S of village, a small sign points 20 m. E of road up a steep path; it is normally locked, but a lady selling needlework is often there who lets visitors in. A torch is adviseable.

This small church dedicated to the Birth of the Virgin, with its unique ground plan, must be one of the most unusual in the Cyclades. It is all that survives of a monastery that gave the nearby village its name, and it probably served as a cemetery church, although this does not explain its orientation, with the apse due SE (in spite of this, reference will be made to parts of the church as if orientation was standard). An initial tour of the exterior will take you past the apse, which is the earliest part of the building; it retains its original trilobed form, with a central dome and an absidiole to N and S of the main apse, and a simple hall parekklision built on to the W. But the strangest feature awaits you as you reach the N side, where two tiny domed chapels project at an angle to the NE.

On entering the church, these small chapels become more prominent, and a third one (without even the small apse window that the others have) can be seen buried in the masonry between them. They must relate to the funerary function of the building. Each of these two chapels, as well as the main apse, retains a small masonry throne in the curve of the apse – a feature of many Naxiote churches; these seem too small to accommodate a human being, and may have held an icon. Four inscriptions survive (all undated) naming donors of frescoes, possibly relating to the cemetery function of the church; that in the dome (for example) asks for the salvation of Andreas, his wife and their children.

There are a number of areas of fresco remaining, dating from at least three periods; easily the most exceptional (perhaps unique in the Aegean) is that in the dome, where you will see two images of Christ Pantocrator within roundels, one youthful, holding the Gospels, and the other older holding a scroll. The main apse fresco of the Virgin Platytera, and that of the Virgin Nikopoia with the SS. Anargyroi in the N absidiole, are also impressive, although rather abraded; the depiction of St George on horseback on the S side of the crossing is of interest in showing him with the boy from Mitylene riding behind him, and there are a number of other fragments, some of impressive quality.

When can this attractive but enigmatic little building with its various fresco layers be dated? Its oldest part is certainly the apse and cupola area and some specialists regard this as going back to the pre-iconoclast period of the later 6th or early 7th C, or even earlier, citing a number of features such as the dome fresco and other elements of the decoration; while this may be the case, an 8th-9th C date also seems possible, and is supported by the relatively humble and remote character of the whole ensemble, which would suggest a less advanced artistic outlook. Later fresco layers, such as the Virgin from the deesis and parts of the W parekklision, with the subsequent chapels on the N side must in any case be later additions, perhaps of the 12th C; the St George on horseback cannot be earlier than this; the small belfry was probably the last element to be added.

Allow plenty of time to study this absorbing and enigmatic small building, on which many questions still remain open.

Sangri   Σαγκρί

Agios Nikolaos. ★ Normally locked; key held by the papas in one of the nearest houses in the village.

Opposite the most easterly of the two windmills on the E edge of the village a dirt track leads downhill, soon becoming a deep mule track; follow this for some 300 m. and the church will come into view, SE of the village. (Do not be confused by another church some 200 m. further E, the Panagia Arkholou, of which the interior is less interesting. There are also several other churches in the vicinity.)

The rough stone exterior, recently restored, shows this to be a domed, single-aisled structure, with the dome carried on engaged pilasters; the only windows are the four in the drum. Three fresco layers have been established here, of the which the third, the most pervasive and best preserved, is dated by an inscription in the apse to 1270, although an area of damage allows us only to know that the wife of the donor was called Irene. To this phase belong all the extensive scenes of the dodecaorton, of which the Nativity and Baptism, in the vault adjacent to the bema, are two of the most prominent and best preserved; the former includes the relatively rare figure of the piping shepherd, and the latter an unusual personification of the river Jordan. Rarely found, particularly in a rural location such as this, are the tetramorphs and cherubim in the pendentives; fragments of the two earlier fresco layers are confined to the N wall, where there are two superimposed images of the Virgin, the upper one with the Christ child, but they are too fragmentary to allow more than an approximate guess at their period, which is probably late 11th to 12th C.

The above are representative of some of the foremost of the Naxiote churches; those of Agios Giorgios Diasoritis in the Tragia plain, the Panagia at Giallou in the S and Agios Ioannis at Adisarou, have been omitted as being difficult to locate and not offering any special characteristics. Below are details of five more which are of less artistic importance but each of which has something to recommend it as an objective. There is no particular significance in the order.

Kerami   Κεραμή

Agios Ioannis.★ Locked; key at nearest house in the village.
Most of this village, between Khalki and Filoti, lies above the main road; from Khalki, take the first turning left into the village and follow the lane round past the large Venetian mansion; the church lies in a field at the further edge of the village.

Stone built and recently restored and strengthened, this small, squat church has a basic simplicity of construction; the low drum, carried on simple engaged corner piers, supports quite a flat cupola and the character of the whole is of rural directness. Until the W narthex was added the interior would have been even more limited. Although damage has caused considerable losses, there is ample evidence that the artist here was of considerable ability and vision; in particular, the sequence of angels in the drum of the cupola conceived as holding a roundel inscribed with a text, and the image of Christ Pantocrator within it, would be impressive in any context and is quite unexpected in this rural setting. Striking, too, are the frescoes of warrior saints in the N tympanum and St Mark in the NE squinch. No inscription survives to provide a firm date, but the style of the remaining frescoes on the interior surfaces (all of one phase) has been thought to date from the second half of the 13th C, although some passages, such as the head of Christ Pantocrator in the cupola, could readily be associated with the style of at least a century earlier.

Both relatively easy to find and impressive in its simplicity, this small church offers a highly worthwhile detour.

Kaloritsa   Καλορίτσα

Cave church of the Panagia Spiliani / Kaloritissa.★ Unsigned; gated, but the exterior can readily be seen on W slope of Mount Prophetis Elias.

On the road from Galanado to Khalki, after branching right at the prominent landmark of the 'Tower of Bazaios', in 350 m. a dirt track leads off to the left; after passing a farm it peters out in goat tracks, but the ruined buildings of an abandoned monastery outside the cave can be seen above, and provide a focus for the climb up; 30 minutes should bring you there.

The abandoned monastery of the Kaloritissa that occupies a terrace in front of the cave still has a cupola, invisible from below, which conveys something of the earlier fame and importance of this cave church. Behind this the high cave opening leads down some 30 m. into a spacious cavern converted into another church, dedicated to the Nativity; from these natural surroundings a nave and sanctuary have been formed, with a synthronon and masonry throne as its focus. A gate and grille close this off, but it is quite possible to see the remaining fragments of painting, the wood and plaster templon and the plastered apse cut from the rock carries a complete fresco scheme. This portrays the Virgin and child between two angels and St John the Baptist and the prophet Isaiah, with the standing apostles ranged below; although not in good condition, these are of considerable interest as being dateable by style to the mid-10th C, and indicate the breadth of the artistic tradition then current on Naxos. There are further fresco fragments, somewhat later, on the right-hand wall just outside the gate which allow further evaluation of the style of those inside the cave. Do not miss a smaller inner chapel on the N of the cave, with a cross painted on its plastered apse; previously this had had a fresco layer superimposed, probably in the 13th C, depicting a military saint, and on this account the cross here is thought possibly to date from the iconoclast period of the 7th-9th C.

The steep climb here rewards the energetic with a site of threefold interest; besides the experience of a cave hermitage which must at one time have been of sufficient fame to attract substantial numbers of visitors, there still exist its 10th C frescoes, and the 180 degrees of its magnificent outlook take in a fine profile of Paros, in full view across the straits.

Near Vourvouria, appr. 2 km. SW of Khalki.
Church of Agios Artemios.★ Unsigned and locked; key held by the local farmer, living nearby to SW.
In view in open country on left of the road from Sangri to Khalki; stopping

at the nearest point close to a small bridge appr. 3 km. before Khalki, it is some 10-15 minutes' scramble over trackless rough, but level, terrain.

The main interest of this church, which is of modest size, and with a squat cupola supported on a low drum, is provided by its remaining fresco decoration: it is a good example of the minor local tradition of aniconic (or non-representational) art which existed on medieval Naxos and a few other Aegean islands. Here the main areas of patterned fresco are confined to the vault of the bema, where the simple colour range has been used to produce patterns which are partly reminiscent of decorated tiles; squares can be seen filled with a limited range of repeated patterns, with scrolls and lozenge forms in adjacent areas and leaf forms in the apse itself.

When first published, examples of this kind of decoration were assumed to date from the iconoclast period of the 7th-9th C, and the reign of the emperor Theofilos (829-842) has been associated with the painting in this church; he is known to have espoused Islamic decorative art, and the forms you see here are certainly reminiscent of Arabic work. (A more remote example on Naxos, in which birds are depicted, is the church of Agia Kyriake, near Kalloni.) The opinion now is, however, that they should be regarded as a form of continuation of the iconoclast tradition in decorative art that survived in rural areas in various parts of the Aegean in the 10th to 11th C; similar fragmentary survivals have been found in small rural churches on Karpathos, Rhodes and Crete. Even on Naxos, recent restoration in the Panagia Protothroni, Khalki, has revealed an aniconic fresco laid over an earlier figurative layer.

Apiranthos Απείρανθος

Churches of Agios Pakhomios and **Agios Giorgios.** (Open when visited.)
These two domed and linked churches are easily seen, looking down into the valley to the right from the road arriving here from Filoti; follow a concrete track down from the main road.

The smaller of the two, Agios Pakhomios, has a greater amount of its fresco decoration surviving, and the style of this suggests that it was probably the first built, and may well be 12th C; this is supported by its E window (now partly blocked up) which is larger. Points to note include the unusual feature of two deep niches in the apse, some fine vegetable ornament in the NE squinch and a well-preserved figure of St Michael in the N lunette; the drum (taller than its neighbour) also retains some of its frescoes.

Agios Giorgios, also a domed, inscribed cross, has a substantial later parekklision down its N side, with a separate door. Few frescoes survive inside, and the most unusual feature is a masonry screen of three arches, which provides the E support of the cupola, creating a structural iconostasis. The date of the church here is established by an inscription as being 1253-4, and it was presumably built at a period when its neighbour had become unable to serve the local needs.

The tranquil setting here invites an unhurried visit to this unusual unit of two linked churches.

NISYROS   Νίσυρος

Med: Nisera.
Island group: Dodecanese. (*Nomos*: Dodecanese).

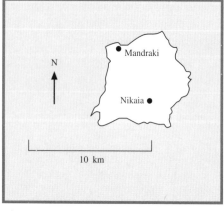

This small volcanic island, within easy sight of the Turkish mainland and the Knidos peninsula, receives no mention by any of the medieval historians of the Aegean. In spite of having a reasonable harbour and a later reputation for producing much fruit (particularly figs), the island was clearly not coveted by the major invaders of the 13th C, and it is only with the arrival of the Hospitallers on Rhodes that its name enters history.

Its position meant that they naturally saw it as providing a useful strategic link in their defensive and signalling chain between Rhodes and Kos, and by 1316 the island was already under their wardship; in this case they came to an arrangement with a family from Ischia, the Assanti. The Grand Master Foulques de Villaret wished to reward the two brothers of this family, Giovanni and Buonaiuto, for the help they had given to the Order, and although they were really little more than pirates, gave them the vassalage of the island on condition that they provided the Knights with an armed galley of 120 oars. The Knights clearly kept a close watch on the Assanti, and in 1340 they confiscated part of the island from Ligorio Assanti and sold it to his cousin Giacomo; again, in 1347 the young sons of Giacomo, Chiqui and Niccolo, were allowed to commute the galley service for an annual payment of 200 gold florins. This general arrangement was still in force in 1374 when Bartolomeo Assanti died without heirs, and it was awarded to a Hospitaller Knight, Domenico d'Alemagna; his obligation continued as the annual fee, although in that year there had been a revolt against the Assanti by the local populace, who must in any case have had to pay the due in whatever form it took.

In 1433 the island was given in fief by the Hospitallers to the Venetian admiral Fantino Querini, who was governor of Kos, and styled himself Lord of Nisyros and Kos until his disgrace and imprisonment by Jean de Lastic in 1453; with Leros and Kos, it was decimated by Sultan Mehmet II in 1457 as part of his campaign of subjugation in the Aegean, and would finally have come under full Turkish control with the fall of Rhodes in 1523.

There was demand for the sulphur produced by the volcano here (which is still active today) and from at least the 14th C it was bought by merchants who called at the island. The mining of the sulphur was one of the local industries, and the volcano produced its own legend: a Russian abbot called Daniel, who visited here on his way to Jerusalem in 1106, was told that the bubbling sulphur of the volcano was "the torment of Herod", indicating a tradition of long-term activity of the volcano.

In spite of their long connection with the island the Assanti have left us no physical reminders of their presence; unlike the Querini on Astypalaia or the Da Cognara on Sifnos, we can today visit no single building of any kind with which they can be associated. (It is perhaps surprising that they did not adopt and modernise the extensive ancient ruins of Palaiokastro just inland from Mandraki (see below.) Although minimal mosaic remains of two EC basilicas have been found in the area of Mandraki, the most prominent survival is associated with the Knights; the Assanti have come and gone with their only record as vassals being in the Knights' archives, now in Malta.

Mandraki   Μανδράκι

Hospitaller castle remains, enclosing a rock-cut church.★★
Gated and locked; key in a house close to bottom of steps (be sure to get it before starting to climb the steps).
The castle and the church it encloses are both easily seen from the harbour, the church displaying a particularly prominent title.

1) The Moni Panagia Spiliani is at the top of a rocky outcrop adjacent to the W end of the village, and is reached up a long flight of steps, carefully numbered. It consists of a series of three chambers excavated from the rock, which no doubt accounts for their eccentricity of shape, but for a medievalist the interior is disappointing. Some small marble columns may be re-used classical spolia, and the doorway that leads through from the long narrow vestibule to the naos is framed by carved marble members that are certainly Byzantine, and probably 12th/13th C, and may have originally formed part of a templon. This suggests that the church ante-dates the castle enclosing it, rather than being a later transformation of the castle chapel. Otherwise, the iconostasis and all visible detail is late, and gives no further clues.

2) **The Kastro** must always have been quite small, confined by the bluff of rock that it occupies, and can never have held more than a very modest garrison. It is now quite fragmentary, but what is left must be substantially the work of the Knights of Rhodes as on the highest remaining part is a triple escutcheon, with another on the wall facing the sea, although both are now too eroded to be deciphered. This must have been intended to form part of the chain of observation and defensive outposts linked to Rhodes, and so most probably dates from some point in the mid-14th C. In this connection it is interesting to speculate why the knights did not make use of the massive and still highly impressive remains of the 3rd/4th C BC stronghold on the acropolis above Mandraki as the basis of their castle, as they did later on Khalki and Alimnia. This is less than half a km. inland, is higher than the Knights' Kastro, is vastly more substantial, and must count as one of the outstanding ancient fortified towns of the Aegean. The answer may well lie in the fact that the large castle of the Knights at Antimakheia on Kos is easily visible from their small stronghold at Mandraki, but not from the old acropolis; if so, it would again suggest that visual contact played a significant part in their defensive strategy. Position and visibility were more important than either size or brute strength.

The 14th C pilgrim Niccoló da Martoni reported three castles here, and this was repeated by the 15th C traveller Buondelmonti, who claimed in his *Isolario* that when he visited there were three more castles on Nysiros besides these two; in 1905 Dawkins and Wace found remains of a third at Nikaia, called Parkettia, but this cannot now be seen. The eroded rock formations in the locality can produce startling effects that from a distance resemble man-made fortifications, and Buondelmonti did not have the benefit of binoculars.

Nikia   Νικιά

Cemetery church with frescoes*.
Just outside the SW edge of the village, reached down a paved track and located some 40 m. beyond the cemetery; kept open.

The two churches in the hill village of Nikia (SE of the central volcano) are quite recent, but just outside and below the village cemetery is an interesting small, simple, barrel-vaulted church, half buried in the hillside. Windowless, with an earth floor, and only some 5 m. in length,

6. THASOS. Limena, Kastro walls, where the Genoese builders re-used Classical materials.

7. ASTYPALAIA. Maltezana, floor mosaics of the basilica of Karekla, beside the sea.

18. CHIOS. Convent of the Nea Moní, mosaic of the
Anastasis in the north vault of the katholikon.

19. CHIOS. Sklavia, church of the Panagia Krina;
its design closely reflects that of the Nea Moní.

20. CRETE. Moní, the church of Agios Nikolaos, with a giant head of the saint painted in 1315 by John Pagomenos.

21. CRETE. Frankokastello, the Venetian castle built to give protection from pirates to the local inhabitants.

22. IKARIA. Kampos, 'Palatia', a secular building of possibly pre-Christian origin.

23. KALYMNOS. Damos, church of Christ 'Lemniotissa',
traditionally founded by the emperor Arcadius.

24. CHIOS. Church of the Panagia Sikilia, a detail of typically Chiote brickwork.

25. KYTHERA. Pourko, church of Agios Dimitrios, where four churches are combined.

26. LESBOS. Mytilini, dynastic symbols of Genoese and Byzantine families united over the gateway of the Kastro.

27. SAMOTHRAKI. Khora, inscriptions in the wall of the kastro which combine Gattilusi and Palaiologue dynastic emblems.

28. THASOS. Kastro, Grimaldi escutcheon of 1434 now installed on the village church.

29. LIMNOS. Livadokhori, a 12th century sarcophagus in the farmyard beside the church of the Panagia.

30. LESBOS. Kremasti, a bridge built by the Geonese exemplifies their contribution to the island's economy.

31. NAXOS. Moní, church of the Panagia Drosiani, perhaps dating from the 7th century.

32. PAROS. Paroikia, wall of Venetian kastro formed from fragments of Parian marble from a classical theatre.

33. SAMOTHRAKI. Palaiopolis, towers built by Palamede Gattilusio overlooking the sea.

the interior is nevertheless covered with frescoes that would seem from their style to be of 14th/15th C. date. Although now adjacent to a cemetery there is no evidence of a funerary theme running through their subject-matter; only the siting of the Anastasis on the W wall may be evidence of this function. There is no inscription. The condition of the frescoes is mostly not very good, but considerable sophistication can be found in a number of passages; on the N wall the paintings of the Koimisis, Transfiguration and Baptism, and on the S wall that of the Raising of Lazarus are all particularly impressive. There are traces of an earlier masonry iconostasis, now vanished, which also suggests a relatively early date. It is no doubt the out-of-the-way location of this interesting and attractive chapel which accounts for its survival when the main churches of the village were replaced.

PAROS

Πάρος

Med: Pario, and

ANTIPAROS

Αντίπαρος

Island group: Cyclades. (*Nomos*: Cyclades).

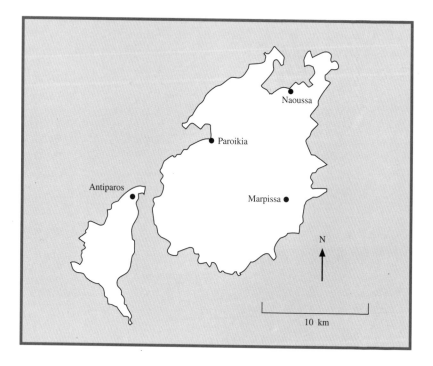

T he 'marble isle' of Paros, lying near the centre of the archipelago, might have been sometimes overshadowed by its larger and more fertile neighbour of Naxos, but its position always meant that it retained some importance in its own right. Its landscape is not mountainous by Aegean standards, and it must be a source of surprise that the famous marble that was quarried here, known throughout antiquity for its brilliant, crystalline whiteness, is not mentioned by any of the medieval writers.

The medieval history of Paros shares several features with other Aegean islands, in that it suffered during the 9th C from Arab attacks, and was for some periods virtually deserted. Nevertheless by the late

11th C it had a bishopric shared with Naxos (as the diocese of Paro-Naxia), which was one of the suffragans of Rhodes. Unmentioned in the Deed of Partition in 1204, it was natural that when the neighbouring island of Naxos became the seat of the new duchy under the Sanudi in 1207, Paros, as the closest and one of the best endowed neighbouring islands, should at once become one of the eleven islands of the dukedom. It also inevitably shared the problems that arose as the Duchy prospered, and although it was not recovered by the Byzantines after 1261, and prospered with Naxos under the Dukes, it was (with Antiparos) to be made the price for settling disputed claims to Andros; thus in 1389 the lordship of Paros was made over to the Sommaripa family. Originally from Verona, they had come to the Levant with the other Venetian families, and were to be one of the longer-lived of the western dynasties. Paros suffered a major Turkish attack in 1416, just before Buondelmonti's visit, and the Florentine traveller's account of life at that time makes depressing reading, with the bay at Naoussa used by pirates to repair their boats and the population much diminished; however, in the treaty of 1419 that brought peace between Venice and the sultan, Paros is explicitly said to belong to the Republic.

In 1517 after an attempt by the Duke of Naxos, then Giovanni IV Crispo, to usurp, it was decided in Venice that the sister of the last baron had the best claim to take over the island, so in 1520 rule of Paros passed to Fiorenza Venier. In 1531 it was again another sister of the last male ruler who was held to have the best claim, and in 1535 Cecilia, wife of Bernardo Sagredo, took over the rule. It was inevitable that during his campaign in 1537 Khaireddin Barbarossa would try to take Paros, and although initially he was unsuccessful, with Sagredo holding out in the small but well defended castle above Marpissa; provisions ran out, however, Sagredo capitulated and the islanders were either killed, sold into slavery or (if they were young boys) enrolled as janissaries. Two sources put the loss in population as high as 6000. In the treaty of 1540 it was acknowledged as under Turkish rule, but for some reason the sultan must have handed the island back to the Duchy as in 1560 Paros was still numbered among the sixteen island possessions of the Dukedom. Although after 1566 the Portuguese Jewish banker Joseph Nasi, nominated by Selim II as Duke of Naxos, was until his death in 1579 the titular ruler of Paros with the rest of the duchy, any real power was already in Turkish hands.

There are still several monasteries functioning on the island, but the period of greatest activity for these was in the 16th/17th century, when over thirty were founded. None of those that survive antedate the Turkish conquest. The main development of the small port of Naoussa

also took place in the 17th and 18th C, with the founding of a school
staffed by Capuchin friars and it was for a time a centre of RC teaching.
The focus of medieval interest is the island capital of Paroikia, with
a major Byzantine church and two survivals of Latin presence.

Paroikia: Παροίκια

1. Cathedral of the Panagia Ekatonpilianí / Katapolianí. Παναγία Εκατονπιλιανί / Καταπολιανί.★★★

On the N side of the town, set some 200m. back from the sea, the façade (in fact the W face of an atrium) is disconcerting as it has more in common with a Venetian palazzo than a cathedral.

This is not just the most interesting and distinguished building on Paros, but must be among the three largest and earliest church buildings in all the Greek islands. Its name, literally 'of the hundred doors' may be a corruption of Katapoliani, 'below the town'). A glance at its complex plan shows that it is formed from the amalgamation of four different structures: the main space of the naos is provided by a large central cupola supported on piers, with adjacent barrel vaults radiating out to form a cross; those to N and S are slightly shorter than those forming the bema and nave. To the N of the large bema a small basilica, Agios Nikolaos, has been absorbed, and to the S a further smaller chapel is used as the diaconicon. Through an opening in the wall of the S arm of the naos a bridging passage connects with another structure, now of basilical form, providing a baptistry with a sunken, cruciform font sited in the apse.

It is easier to understand the interior if, instead of first entering the central door in the completely inappropriate Venetian palazzo facade, you go round to the S side and up the incline behind (towards the Museum) from where the full spread of the various parts of the building can be appreciated. The three successive apses, with the baptistry providing the fourth, and the massive central cupola (invisible from the entrance) can all be seen at once here in a unified view.

With this in mind, the visitor can enter the spacious courtyard, on the far side of which rises the imposing cathedral facade. This space is in effect an atrium, with raised colonnades on three sides; an assemblage of caps is displayed along the S wall, some from the 4th/5th C, but a series most probably from the 10th, and perhaps associated with the reconstruction after a known earthquake at that period. The lofty exonarthex retains two substantial Venetian tombs of the 17th C, with the remains of members of the Condili and Mavroyennis families.

On entering the main body of the church (there are three doors from the narthex) the full scale of the massive central space is evident; there are galleries with marble slabs bearing simple but impressive reliefs, many with monograms. With the exception of some later frescoes in the squinches and bema, the entire wall and vault surfaces of the interior are now undecorated; only the slightly varied colours of the well-cut ashlar blocks go some way to relieving the generally rather severe impression made by this unusually monochromatic interior. Its sombre character is due to its restoration by Orlandos in the 1960's, when he recovered its original Byzantine forms from a Venetian baroque interior, but without introducing any colour. The high marble iconostasis remains, and is a Venetian product of 1611, but even here it is possible to see that the incised ornament is carved into columns which may well be classical. The bema has a somewhat cramped quality, as the rounded benches of the large synthronon in the apse reach down towards the columns of a substantial ciborium over the altar; the caps, though damaged must have been very fine 5th C work, and the columns seem, surprisingly in the island of Parian marble, to be veined in a way that suggests that they came from the Sea of Marmara. In the S arm of the crossing you will see an unusual feature for a church interior: the head of a well that is still in use.

It is only at this point that you will reach, adjoining the NE of the main building, what is in effect a basilica in its own right, dedicated to Agios Nikolaos. The re-used classical columns that line the nave have been extended to raise the height of the gallery, and a cupola rises over the nave. This was probably the first building on the site, and another synthronon in the apse offers confirmation of this.

The S parekklision, serving as the diaconicon, is formed from a much smaller, domeless chapel dedicated to St. Philip, and there is another narrow chamber beyond this dedicated to the SS. Anargyroi.

A further feature of the greatest interest is the almost separate structure to the S. Although now a domed basilica, with its cupola supported on piers, it could well have first been a simple baptistry built to a central plan around the sunken font. While there are many other such separate baptistries located close to their main church, the cruciform font here must be one of the largest in the islands, and although its decoration with crosses is of rather uncertain date, it cannot be later than the main church building alongside.

As for chronology, to propose a sequence in which these buildings were erected must involve some speculation. It has been suggested that there was originally in fact a 4th C basilica on the site, but of the surviving parts it seems most probable that the earliest is Agios Nikolaos; the main church was then built to accommodate increased congregations and house a larger council in the synthronon. The forms of the cupola and the structure as a whole suggest a date in the mid 6th C, and this must also be given to the baptistry in its original form. At some later date (perhaps in the 10th, after earthquake damage) the baptistry was enlarged with a domed nave to accommodate its own congregations. The siting and forms of the S parekklision suggest that it may antedate both the main church and the baptistry, but certainty is hard to achieve here.

The interest and complexity of the Panagia Ekatonpiliani needs at least one return visit, which will be amply repaid.

2) Kastro.
Remains of Venetian castle.* (See Pl. 32).
The only elevated ground close to the sea was used by the Venetians c. 1260 for the construction of their castle; it must have been an impressive building when it was complete, and even now its surviving parts amply repay a visit. It must have dominated the entire town, and all the streets in the vicinity still follow the lines of the original walls. The most prominent feature is the substantial NE corner tower; constructed very largely from classical spolia of Parian marble, assembled largely without mortar; many column drums are set in horizontal rows, and huge rectangular blocks said to have originally been the seating of a theatre leave numerous gaps which have been adopted by the local pigeon population as nesting holes. Some 50 m. of wall can be traced running S from the tower, much of it now embedded in houses (and two small churches) built into and onto the re-used classical fragments. On the summit of the low hill the 17th/18th C church of Agios Konstantinos, which no doubt replaced a medieval church, looks out over the sea, with some fine Iznik tiles forming a cross on its facade. A reconstruction of the Kastro has suggested that it was originally built out several metres further to a point across the modern sea-side road and reaching to the water's edge or beyond, but the evidence for this is hard to find.

Entries on the two other Venetian castles on Paros, at Marpissa and Naoussa, are given below.

3) 'Treis Ekklisias'. Τρείς Εκκλησίας.
Taking the road to Naoussa, the site is on the left of the road, some 2 km. from the centre of Paroikia; it is fenced but permanently open.
The 'Three Churches' after which this site was named were excavated in the 1960's, but there is now little to show other than of archaeological interest, as only the ground plans of the three EC structures previously

here can still be seen. Among other finds made during the excavation were fragments of a large and richly carved EC ambo, but they are not on view, and must presumably be in the Museum vaults.

Marpissa   Μαρπίσσα

Castle ruins.⋆ Unenclosed.

The small town here, on the E of the island, is dominated by a steep conical hill, Mount Kefalos, with the later monastery of Agios Antonios hugging its summit; Tournefort actually calls it "le Fort de S. Antoine", and it is sometimes referred to simply as "Kefalos". If you continue on the road past the town and stop where vehicles can be left in an area on the right, a steep path leads uphill to the castle ruins.

This brings you in about 15 minutes' walk to just below the summit, where the remains of the castle that is thought to have been built by Nicolo I Sommaripa (1462-1505) look out over the dramatically impressive channel that separates Paros from Naxos; there is now no enceinte, but a few barrel-vaulted chambers mark the site of what must have been a modestly-garrisoned but well-defended kastro. It is of interest that it was to here, rather than to the castles at Paroikia or Naoussa, that Sagredo came to defy Barbarossa; so while it not only offered the site from which signals could be sent across to Naxos – perhaps even to the castle of Apalyrou – it probably had the most up-to-date and strongest defences of the three castles on the island. You can even find here two cisterns surviving with their lining; these must have provided the water supply that had run dry in 1537 when Bernardo Sagredo had to capitulate to the besieging Turkish forces of Barbarossa.

Naoussa   Νάουσσα

Small Venetian kastro.⋆ Unenclosed.

The 16th C Venetian historian Paolo Paruto recorded that in 1536 the castle and harbour "on the N side of Paros" belonged to the Venier family, before passing in succession to the Sagredo. The small port of Naoussa must surely be what he is referring to, and there is indeed a small fortress here still to be seen located at water level, guarding the harbour mouth. It is almost circular in plan, and there are seven apertures for cannon, although there is hardly space for all of them to be in use simultaneously, and there must have been living quarters for any garrison elsewhere; the remains of a small tower beside the entrance suggests that this was also a look-out point. The date of the ensemble is most probably in the first quarter of the 16th C. From the expression used by the historian it is probable that there was another, larger kastro further inland which was where the family and defending forces were housed, and which has now disappeared. The design of the sea-level fortress is matched almost precisely on Kythira at Avlemonas, and – much higher up – on Naxos at Epanokastro.

ANTIPAROS

The visitor to Paros might enjoy taking the short ferry journey across to **Antiparos**, the small island to the W, where the few ruined remains of the Kastro can still be seen at the end of the winding village street as it climbs gently from the quiet and peaceful harbour. These are the only medieval survivals on the island, and are now so minimal that an island entry was not justified, but Antiparos was named in 1207 as part of the Duchy of Naxos, with its fortunes initially following those of its larger neighbour. It was hard to defend from the usual predators of pirates and Turkish raids, however, and by c.1440 it had been unpopulated for many years, but around that time a member of the illustrious family of the Loredano, who had become the son-in-law of Crusino Sommaripa, lord of Andros, took the island over and re-populated it. The ruins of the castle that he built there can still be seen, and in its original, mid-15th C form it would have appeared as a hollow square of housing round a central fortress. In the 18th C the Loredano arms could still be seen over the gateway, but now all that survives are a few arches and a large buttress, although the modern street plan no doubt echoes that which became established when it was built.

PATMOS Πάτμος

Med: Sanctus Joannes de Palmasa.
Island group: S. Sporades. (*Nomos*: Dodecanese).

This small, rocky island off the coast of Turkey and at the N end of the chain of the Dodecanese has few natural advantages; its unfertile land, poor water and lack of a deep natural harbour meant that it attracted no attention in the early medieval centuries. Yet this neglect must be a matter for some surprise; not only are Patmos,

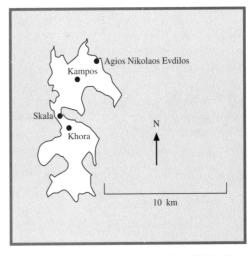

Crete and Rhodes the only Aegean islands named in the Bible, but Patmos has the ultimate prestige of being the stated location for the writing of the Revelation of St John – the Apocalypse; for centuries it was even regarded as being where he also wrote his Gospel. Yet only one EC basilica seems to have been built here, and there is no evidence of any significant cult of the saint until 1088, when almost a millennium of neglect was reversed with the emperor Alexios I Komnenos granting to Osios ('the holy') Christodoulos from Bithynia, who had been an abbot in Latros, permission to found a monastery here dedicated to St John Theologos. The entire subsequent fortunes of the island, which was at that point uninhabited, are closely linked to this foundation.

By the time of the Fourth Crusade the rapidly growing prestige of the monastery allowed it virtually complete independence; not listed in the Deed of Partition of 1204, the Venetians left the island and its monks largely to themselves and allowed them a number of privileges. Although the increasing wealth of the monastery made it a target for some pirate raids, its defences must have been sufficient to withstand attacks of this kind, as some of the monastic treasures have a continuous known history within its walls from the 12th C. In the 1270's the island is known to have been protected by the Byzantine emperor, and the Hospitallers never used the island as a base; they may indeed have been made unwelcome there, as their presence could have attracted Turkish reprisals. Perhaps as a result of this, the Turks offered very little interference to the monks, although the island's relative isolation would have made harassment relatively easy; Buondelmonti, writing c.1418, emphasised this as being worthy of comment.

Patmos and its monastery submitted to Turkish domination at the time of the fall of Rhodes in 1523, so becoming among the earlier of the Aegean islands to accept Muslim rule, but Turkish tolerance continued to be exercised through the centuries of Ottoman dominance in the Aegean.

Khora: Monastery of St John Theologos. ★★★
Opening hours as for a working monastery.
It is impossible to miss this towering fortress, dominating the centre of the island and reached by foot through the village of Khora.

Were it not for its unique significance as the island where Saint John Theologos wrote the Book of Revelation, Patmos would never have achieved the eminence that it now enjoys among the medieval sites of Europe. Yet although the island is crowned by this, the most famous and prestigious monastery of the Aegean islands, with an international fame that makes it the goal of thousands of visitors each year, they have to be content with only portrayals of the saint, as no relics of St John have been preserved. It was only with the late 11th C foundation of the monastery by Osios Christodoulos that attention and wealth came to be focussed on the island. Christodoulos must have had great organisational gifts, and besides the building of the monastery, assisted by many privileges and a chrysobull from Alexios I, he saw the economic regeneration of the island as an essential element of the future prosperity of the monastery. He left behind three sets of Rules for the monastery, written 1091-93, but an attack by Turks in 1092 caused him to flee, and he died on Euboea in 1093.

The original foundation was first established in two periods of building; between 1088 and 1093 (during the lifetime of the founder) the katholikon with the cistern below it, the refectory in its early form and some of the monks' cells were built. Also to this first phase belongs a substantial part of the massive defensive walls, although there is not full agreement as to which areas date from this phase. In the 12th C a second period saw the building of the narthex of the katholikon, the parekklision of the Virgin and the second, enlarged form of the refectory. Throughout, there is a strong impression of gradual expansion that has been confined within the area of the massive walls, and so has entailed building in spaces that in other monasteries are left open. During the 16th and 17th C, with the monastery's fame securely established, more chapels were built, and other additions and modifications made, and after an earthquake in 1646 the walls continued to be strengthened; the huge escarpment round the NE end of the monastery dates from just after this event.

The layout of the monastic buildings is unconventional by Greek Orthodox norms; after negotiating the curved, fortified entrance the visitor arrives in the main courtyard, but the facade of the katholikon closes the E side, as the building itself does not offer the usual free-standing form. This facade with its open arcade encloses the exonarthex of the katholikon, and it is an indication of the continuous growth that the monastery has undergone that, with most of the rest of this courtyard, it dates from as late as 1698. Also characteristic is the incorporation of various earlier elements in the exonarthex: a re-used 5th C cap can be seen (perhaps from the EC basilica reported to be here before the monastery was founded), the balustrade is clearly formed from the marble columns of an earlier templon, and there are small classical columns said to come from a temple of Artemis. At right angles to this, to the N, is an impressive two-storey arcade (known as the tzaphara) also from the extensive late 17th C building phase, and all constructed from finely dressed local stone.

Entering the inner narthex you will encounter the most impressive and revered icon in the monastery; it depicts St John Theologos and is basically a 12th C work, but the gilt metal book that he holds with the opening words of the fourth gospel in enamel is probably a 15th C addition, while the gilt and enamel halo, evidently re-used from another icon, may be the earliest part of the ensemble. Once inside the body of the katholikon the first impression is that this is a traditional monastic domed, inscribed-cross plan, but there are some differences which make it more unusual. While the narthex itself is a later addition (a monastic church would normally have an integral narthex), the barrel vaults to N and S of the main space of the naos run transversely rather than the more usual way of E to W, and are almost uncomfortably high. The quality of masonry, where it can be seen, is unrefined, and the general impression is that in spite of its imperial support, the katholikon did not enjoy the attentions of builders from CP; compared with the airy grandeur of the Nea Moní, Chios, of some 40 years earlier, this is a distinctly cramped and provincial interior. You will find that the frescoes have sustained considerable losses, and some are hard to see on account of soot, but they all date from c.1600. They are thought to be the work of an artist or artists from Crete, brought by the enlightened Cretan

Nikiforos Chartofylax, who was abbot here from 1580. Among the less usual subjects here is a fine image on the N wall of St John in the cave, and among full-length monastic saints is the portrait of St Christodoulos (he was later canonised). Much of the interior detail and icons are later, with the richly gilded iconostasis of 1820 one of the most recent.

Two parts of the katholikon are extra to this main space and adjoin the N of the katholikon. One is the parekklision of the Virgin (or Theotokou), entered through a doorway in the N wall, which is thought to have been built c.1180; its masonry shows a more highly finished character, it is better lit and its walls carry the earliest frescoes in the monastery. These highly impressive paintings, in a sombre and restrained style of great power, were revealed after the removal of 18th C frescoes in 1957-63, and are contemporary with the building (few survive from the roof vaulting). Among the less usual subjects you can see prominently on the W wall an impressive miracle scene of Christ healing the woman with a bowed back, and there is a general emphasis on miracle scenes in this chapel, with an exceptional number of portraits of church fathers and patriarchs associated with Jerusalem. As when this was built and decorated the katholikon would probably have displayed a more standard range of feast scenes, this chapel could be seen as focussing on aspects of the founder, who after his death was credited with a number of miracles. It has also been suggested that a bishop Leontios, who had been abbot on Patmos 1157-58, and was patriarch in Jerusalem from 1176, was the patron of this chapel and its decoration, which would explain the prominence of personalities associated with Jerusalem among the portraits. Finally, you can see that the quality of the marble flooring of this chapel is of considerable refinement, and that the flooring of the katholikon is also of marble and could be said to be its most sophisticated feature; this has prompted the suggestion that Leontios also had the floor of the katholikon renewed when he built the parekklision.

The other chamber to the N is entered from the narthex, and although dark and much less impressive, counts as the most sacred part of the monastery: it is the chapel of Osios Christodoulos. The relief carving on the saint's sarcophagus under its modern wood canopy is an example of good, if unspectacular, middle Byzantine decorative style, and it seems fairly certain that this would have been installed as part of the later 12th C building campaign. It supports a silver-gilt reliquary containing the saint's relics; this was made in 1796 in a Greek workshop in Smyrna, and the relief of the dormition of the saint is clearly based on the scene of the Virgin's koimisis. Opinions on the date of the chapel itself vary between the 12th C and c.1600 (the date of the iconostasis), but the probability would seem to favour the earlier period. The frescoes are again of c.1600, and although hard to see, contain a representation on the E wall of the death of Osios Christodoulos that follows the usual form of such portrayals.

The visitor can enter two further parts of the monastery. One is the refectory, which in its first form had been given a wooden roof; now, penetrating round to the S of the katholikon, you will pass a hollowed-out tree-trunk some 3 m. long, resembling a boat, which was used for kneading the monastery's bread. Passing this, you can enter the impressive space of the refectory, re-modelled in the 12th C with a stone vault and a small cupola; a long marble table occupies the centre, and it is worth recording that the dimensions of the space here exceed those of the katholikon. Some frescoes remain on the walls that would have been painted at the time of the 12th C re-modelling, and although some are in poor condition they are expressively painted and well lit; the scenes from the Passion, the Communion of the apostles and the Appearance of Christ at the sea of Tiberias, with St Peter in the water, are particularly effective. Their style sometimes shows more movement and vigour than those in the Parekklision of the Virgin, but they are in general sufficiently close to be the work of the same artist or team; the style of the fine standing figures of bishop saints, which include St Kyprianos and St Dionysios the Areopagite, is closer to that of the parekklision. Also displayed here is another carved marble relief from a sarcophagus, comparable to that of Christodoulos, brought from elsewhere in the monastery.

The other area of the monastery that can be visited is the new Treasury. Here an exhibition has recently been set up in which manuscripts brought from the library (which cannot usually now be visited), icons, silver and vestments are well displayed; no secular museum could show the visitor such a richly varied assemblage as can be found here. The items are accompanied by brief descriptions, but among the fine array of exhibits these should not be overlooked: from icons of the Byzantine period, an 11th C mosaic icon of St Nicholas with a broad silver frame is a particular rarity; and it would be hard to find two more outstanding 13th C icons than those of St James Adelphotheos and St Theodore Tyron in any museum; of the many icons from the post-Byzantine period, that with the traditional (if apocryphal) subject of the greeting (O ACΠACMOC) of the saints, Peter and Paul, dating from the later 15th C is highly unusual in both its circular form and its subject, and that of the complex subject known as "In thee rejoiceth" (*Epi soi khairei*) by Theodore Poulakis of 1670-90 represents the later tendency by icon painters to develop extended liturgical themes.

The extensive array of liturgical objects in precious metal form a clear reflection of the developing fame and wealth of the monastery. They come from many parts of Europe, with works originating in Moldavia, Romania, Russia, Georgia, Italy (particularly Venice) and CP, although only minor items are earlier than the pair of flabella dated 1468. This has been a part of the monastery's possessions that was very vulnerable to dispersal, with many items from an inventory of 1262 already missing by 1300. As it is, we find that the bulk of the rich and elaborate vessels, book-covers and other liturgical objects of great splendour arrived here in the 18th C or later, and by this period international baroque and rococo styles, while increasing its richly decorative impact, give a more international character to the collection.

This is less the case with the numerous liturgical vestments on display; two epitaphia, two epitrakhilia, and an epigonation, all of the 15th C, are among the earliest items, but even 18th C examples of these retain a greater sense of their Byzantine origins. If one is to be singled out it should be the epigonation embroidered with an image of the sleeping Christ child and angels with a flabellum and instruments of the Passion; this complex symbolism, involving OT and NT sources concerns the redemption of the world, and is referred to in the Orthodox Easter services.

The library on Patmos has always been one of the most famous parts of the monastery's inheritance; an inventory made in 1200 lists 300 manuscripts, of which 110 are thought to be still here, and while lax librarianship may have allowed 190 to wander (some as far as British public collections), an account of 1801 tells how the abbot sold five Byzantine MSS to an English cleric as he thought they were of less interest and value than his newer, printed books. There are now some 890 MSS and over 2,000 printed books, as well as over 12,000 documents relating to the monastery's history. Among the latter, pride of place must go to the chrysobull of Alexios I initiating the foundation of the monastery. The fine selection of illuminated MSS on view represents only a fraction of the library holdings.

The monastery will be the prime motive for any visit to Patmos, and if there is one area within it which most repays a return visit it is perhaps the parekklision of the Virgin; further time spent here will allow you to experience the authentic quality of this interior, which now reflects better than elsewhere the original qualities of this historic ensemble.

The Cave of the Apocalypse.★★
Irregular opening times, with no advertised routine.
The small, stone-built complex surrounding the cave is on the left on the way

up to the Monastery of St John from Skala, and cannot be missed.

Although unmentioned by Osios Christodoulos in his account of the founding of the monastery, this became the traditional location where St John wrote the Revelation, and like most other such hallowed sites its appearance has been altered over the centuries. The first adoption of the locale was almost certainly in the 12th C, well after the foundation of the Monastery on the hill-top above. The centre of the ensemble is a linked double church, and what you will see today is known from an inscription on the iconostasis to be a late 16th C creation of one Parthenios Pangostas and the monk Germanos. The two parts are formed from a single chamber dedicated to St Anne, and (to the S) the cave itself, dedicated to St John Theologos. It is worth mentioning that the habitually sceptical Pitton de Tournefort, who visited the cave c.1700, and whose engraving of its interior is almost certainly the first visual record of it, admitted that it is probably where the Apocalypse was written.

The artistic survivals here are, it must be admitted, slight. Apart from the 16th C iconostasis, the only wall-paintings were discovered in 1973 in the sanctuary of the cave itself, beyond the iconostasis; they are considerably damaged and have much graffiti, but have been dated by style to the mid-12th C and constitute the best document for the first adoption of the cave. The best preserved is an image of St John dictating to the deacon Prochoros, who writes down the first words of the Revelation; the painting lacks the distinction of the 12th C frescoes in the monastery, and it is difficult to penetrate the sanctuary to see it, but if you can you will have seen the most authentic element in this famous complex.

Kampos   Κάμπος

Small triple church.★ Locked; key in one of nearest houses to the S. *Coming from Skala, fork right as you enter the village, and this interesting small complex is on the left of the road as you leave the village for Ag Nikolaos.*

The dedications of the three small, barrel-vaulted churches joined together are to the Anastasis, Agia Triada and the Panagia; their grouping suggests that they may have been built on the site of a triple-aisle EC basilica. The roofing of each is different, suggesting that they were built at three different dates; their interiors offer no medieval decoration of any kind, but the group could well date from the 12th – 13th C, and makes a worthwhile stop on the way to Agios Nikolaos Evdelos.

Agios Nikolaos Evdelos

Small rural church.* Locked; key held by Monastery of St John.
This little country moni on the N coast is reached at the end of a dirt track, about 1 ¹/₂ km. beyond Kampos village; take the right fork at entrance to the village, and left when the track later divides.

The appearance of this small, barrel-vaulted hall church, with a parekklision on its S side and no apse windows, suggests a later period for its building, but it is believed to have been founded in 1087, and (if this is correct) it is slightly older than the great monastery of St John. Its claimed origins as the earliest building on the island has earned it a *. It has no internal decoration of any interest, but its site, overlooking the sea and a small fisherman's jetty, is impressive.

Later churches on the island include the Church of the Holy Apostles of 1603, and three further monasteries founded in the 17th C.

PAXOS / PAXOI   Παξοί

Island group: Ionian / Eptanisous. (*Nomos*: Corfu).

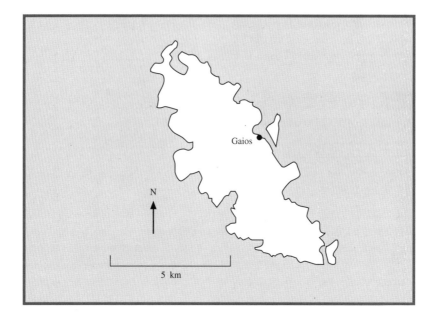

T his well-wooded and fertile island is one of the smallest of the 'Seven Islands' in the Ionian Sea, and passes almost without mention by medieval historians. Its size always made it subordinate to its large neighbour Corfu, and it was never the home of one of the baronies for long enough for it to be given any defensive castle buildings; only a small Venetian fort was built quite late to overlook the harbour at Gaia. The island had no real existence independently of Corfu, sharing its government and clergy, and one of the few times that Paxos is mentioned was in the late 14th C when it was given by the Byzantine Despot of Epiros to an Italian, Adamo di Sant'Ippolito, as an inducement for his help in confronting the invading forces of the Navarrese company. Otherwise it enjoyed a few of the benefits of having a larger protector, but suffered the disadvantages of being very exposed; there could never have been any significant chance of defending the island once any major power decided to attack, and in 1513 the Venetians sold Paxos to a rich Corfiote, possibly hoping that he would build some form of defences for himself. The Paxiotes found his rule so oppressive, however, that many fled to Turkish territory on the mainland. Realising that the island would be an easy prey, the Turks, recovered from their defeat at Lepanto, ransacked it in 1577, and caused long-term damage to what remained of its modest island economy; they were to remain an impediment to long-term security until Venetian domination in the whole area was established.

Predictably, given its turbulent past, the island now has very little to show from its medieval centuries, and the EC basilica outside Gaios is its only surviving early building of note.

Gaios   Γαίος

Remains of EC basilica of Agia Marina.★ Unenclosed.
Leaving Gaios by the seaside road going S, in some 3 km. you will come to an enclosed bay towards the S tip of the island, opposite Meganisi. Within 20 m. of the current shore-line of the bay, in a typical EC location, is the roofless shell of the basilica of Agia Marina.

This was originally a triple-nave basilica, although the proportion now suggested by the walls is misleading, as the S aisle has disappeared and the N aisle has been altered to enlarge the nave on that side. The original W wall is now only partially present and a later one has been built some 4 m. to the E, no doubt to allow use of the building to continue on a reduced scale, but this has given an uncomfortable, truncated proportion to the whole. The original length of the basilica was some 13 m. The fine, rounded apse is still impressive, and it must have originally been a distinguished building; the fact that it was built without flanking apses suggests, with other features, a 7th C date. There may well have been a mosaic floor here, which might have given confirmation of this, but there is now no trace of any such decoration.

The beautiful setting provided by this bay is a fitting context for this striking EC basilica, and fully rewards the short journey from Gaios.

RHODES

Ρόδος

Med: Rodi.
Island group: Dodecanese. (*Nomos*: Dodecanese).

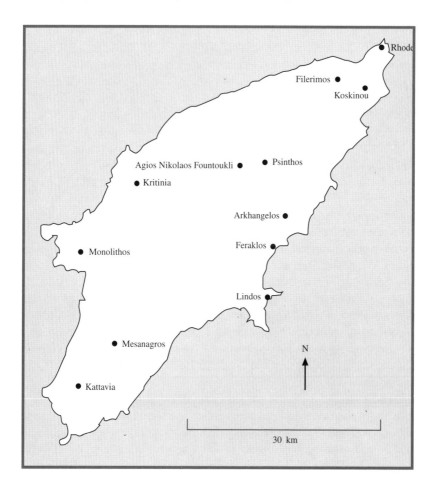

Among the islands of the Aegean, only Crete is larger in extent than Rhodes, but the way that history has left its mark on these two islands is vastly different. For while Crete is identified first with the Minoan civilisation with its impressive excavated sites, then with being the only island occupied by Arab invaders, and later retaining the most widespread and profoundly Byzantine artistic tradition, Rhodes, perhaps more than any other of the Aegean islands, has a modern character that was formed almost exclusively during the later medieval period. While the island as a whole has a known history of almost 2,400 years and still can show survivals from many different ages, it was the presence of the Knights of the Order of St John of Jerusalem, or Hospitallers (see p. xx) that has left the most indelible mark. Becoming established here from 1309 and being finally expelled by the Turks in January 1523, they were here for just 214 years, yet it is impossible to imagine the island, and above all the city of Rhodes, without the overwhelming weight of their legacy. Even the 400 years of subsequent Turkish presence has only left some relatively scattered survivals by comparison with the massive buildings and fortifications that commemorate the tenure of Rhodes by the Hospitallers.

Yet all this has tended to obscure the importance that Rhodes wielded during the Byzantine period, which was due both to its position, its size and its significance to the classical world. The bishops of Rhodes, Kos, Limnos, and Corfu, were the only ones from all the Greek islands to attend the first church council in Nicaea in 325; later, during the EC centuries, the island became the leading ecclesiastical seat for the Cyclades, with its own metropolitan; he appointed eleven suffragans to various other islands, including those as distant as Naxos and even Milos. When the Arab expansion began in the 7th C Rhodes acted as a frontier post for the Byzantine navy, although this did not prevent an Arab general sacking the city, demolishing the bronze statue of the Colossus and having a merchant of Edessa take it home – a load which is said to have needed 900 camels. During the Crusades the island's position again ensured its importance, supplying the Crusaders' force encamped at Antioch in 1097-9, and being visited by various royal crusaders.

The arrival of the Latin emperors in CP in 1204 had much less effect in Rhodes than elsewhere in the Aegean; the island was taken over by a Byzantine family called Gabalas which had strong seafaring traditions, and so did not become subject to the Venetians and their allies in the Aegean. In 1232 the island was absorbed into the exiled Byzantine empire of Nicaea by the reigning emperor John III Vatatzes, but he was continually troubled by the growing power of the Genoese who were in partial occupation by 1248. (As early as 1192 the Byzantine emperor Isaac Angelos had complained to the Genoese that eleven of their number – and he gave their names – had carried out a raid on Rhodes.) However, c.1256 a Byzantine governor of Rhodes was appointed by the emperor Theodore II Laskaris in the person of John Palaiologos, the brother of the future emperor in CP.

After the fall of Acre in 1291 the two orders of the Hospitallers and the Templars had fled to Cyprus and the former had temporarily settled in Limassol while they sought a new and permanent home; the hostility to the Templars, with their general arrest in 1307, may have lent an extra urgency to their search.

Rhodes offered just the kind of base that they needed, and besides attacks by Genoese the islanders had been much decimated by Turkish raids for property and slaves, most recently in 1303. In 1306 a Genoese called Vignolo de' Vignoli, who was established on Rhodes and already claimed to have been given the islands of Kos and Leros by the Byzantine emperor, met the Grand Master of the Hospitallers, Fulques de Villaret, and between them a plan for the invasion and occupation of Rhodes was agreed; Vignoli would be able to retain his castle and estate at Lardos on the E coast of Rhodes as reward for his help. The Genoese presence there created an ambiguous situation, as although they were little wore than piratical adventurers they were Christian rather than infidel, and so should not strictly have been a military objective of the Knights.

However it was managed (and there is still uncertainty as to how aspects of the eventual occupation of the island were handled), from 1306 the process was under way, and by 1309/10 the rule of the Knights Hospitaller had effectively begun. The support of the pope was an important factor, and in September 1307, rather anticipating the reality, he confirmed the Hospitallers in their possession of the island. Although the pope's power was very limited, his authority was to some extent accepted by the local Greeks; the relatively benevolent rule of the Knights must in any case have been preferable to Arab and Turkish slaving raids. One price they paid for their protection was that the appointment of all Greek bishops and benefices in the island was in the hands of the Knights' Grand Master, but the way that this was later changed to allow the Grand Master to chose the Greek metropolitan from a prepared short list of three, which the Latin archbishop then confirmed, indicates how the co-habitation of the Greek and Latin cultures developed peacefully. The principal declared function of the Knights was now to act as a bastion of Christianity against the growing Moslem power of the Turks, and so they were in a state of virtually permanent hostility with the forces a short distance away on the Turkish mainland. For just over two centuries the Hospitallers defied the Turks, suffering prolonged sieges of their heavily defended city in 1480 and 1522; it was to be the price of ending the second of these sieges that they should abandon Rhodes, which they did with great dignity on January 1st 1523. This date closes the final chapter of the island's medieval history.

The organisation of the Hospitallers does from time to time impose itself on the buildings and fortifications that remain in the city, and so should be mentioned briefly here. Besides the 'horizontal' division of classes: knights (*milites*), chaplains *(cappelani)* and squires or sergeants *(servientes armorum)*, there was a 'vertical' division into seven *langues*, or 'tongues': of Auvergne, France, Provence, Italy, England, Germany and Spain, with the last being divided in 1461 into the langues of Aragon and Castile. Each of the langues would, for example, have its own inn *(auberge)* or headquarters building, where the knights could meet, and where they could give hospitality to eminent visitors. Different sections of the fortifications were also allocated as the defensive responsibility of different langues.

The City of Rhodes

I. The Old City.
From here reference can be made to the accompanying plan of the medieval city. Numbers that follow the mention of a building indicate their location on the plan.

Although the city was planned entirely around the use of sea transport (the Colossus of old, as it straddled the harbour mouth, gave legendary emphasis to this), now only a minority of visitors will arrive here by this means. So we will start by approaching the Old City on foot from the direction of the new town and harbour (Mandraki), and past the sequence of large public buildings that resulted from the inter-war Italian colonial rule. The only one of these that is of interest to the medievalist is the massive basilica (dedicated to the Annunciation) that now serves as the metropolis of Rhodes, and lies close to the harbour. Although only built in 1925, it exactly reproduces the scale and plan of the medieval church of St John which occupied the area at the summit of the Street of the Knights in the Old City(**6**), and which was accidentally blown up in 1856. So if you carry a memory of this with you, you can supply it mentally to its original home when you reach the site; only the fountain should be omitted from this exercise, being a modern Italian import that did not exist in the medieval ensemble.

From this direction you enter the Old City by a gate only created in 1924 (although in 'period' style) and called by the Italians the Porta di Libertà, now Pyli Eleutherias, and sometimes just the New Gate. Its function now is largely to cope with the motor traffic, which is directed round the outside of the walls beside the second (or Commercial) harbour. Once inside this gate you enter the unique ensemble of public buildings known collectively as the Collachium (or Collachio, Chastel, or Conventus) – the name given to the citadel area that was the exclusive domain of the Knights – and once inside it their weighty aura begins to descend. Whatever opinions there may be about the taste which produced the modern Grand Master's Palace, most of the other buildings in this matchless ensemble have either been left with only minimal adaptation to modern use, or, after Turkish alterations, restored sympathetically by the Italian or Greek authorities; they can thus speak for themselves with a voice from the great medieval age of Rhodes. Most of the interiors cannot be visited, but their mellowed sandstone facades nevertheless shed a silent and powerful atmosphere.

The first open space you will cross is the Arsenal Square, now rather confused due to the remains of a classical Greek temple to Aphrodite that were discovered in 1922, but just beyond these ruins is the Inn of the Langue of Auvergne (**2,** restored in 1919). One facade of this building looks on to a small square to your right, the Plateia Argyrokastrou, and here you will find an early Byzantine survival that is unique in the city; it is a baptismal font that has been converted to a small fountain. It was brought here from an excavation at the village of Arnitha towards the S of the island, and coins of Justin II found at the site suggest that is of the 6th C; the four crosses carved on it in relief are all different, and show that the so-called 'Maltese' cross was already in use at this period. Also facing on to this Plateia, the 14th C building with an external stairway, known as the Palace of the Armeria(**3**), served as the original Hospital of the order; like many such official buildings of the Knights, it now houses administrative offices. On the N side of this Plateia the simple, single-story four-square building is the only one of the old gun-powder stores to have survived; it can be dated by the escutcheons of the Grand Masters J. de Milly (1454-1461) and J.B. degli Orsini (1467-1476). The display in the Museum of Decorative Arts, also in this complex (usual museum hours) includes a fine collection of Iznik ceramics (often misleadingly called 'Rhodian ware'), but no medieval artefacts.

The broad, cobbled Plateia Megalou Alexandrou that opens out before you as you continue through the gateway in the Inn of Auvergne offers perhaps the richest range of architectural wealth in the city. To the left is the facade of the **Panagia tou Kastrou,**★★ (**4**) now converted to a **Byzantine Museum** (usual museum hours, entry charge); to the right the Street of the Knights leads up towards the Grand Master's Palace; and adjacent to this and with its main facade and entrance opening on to the Plateia, is the New Hospital, now the Archaeological Museum.

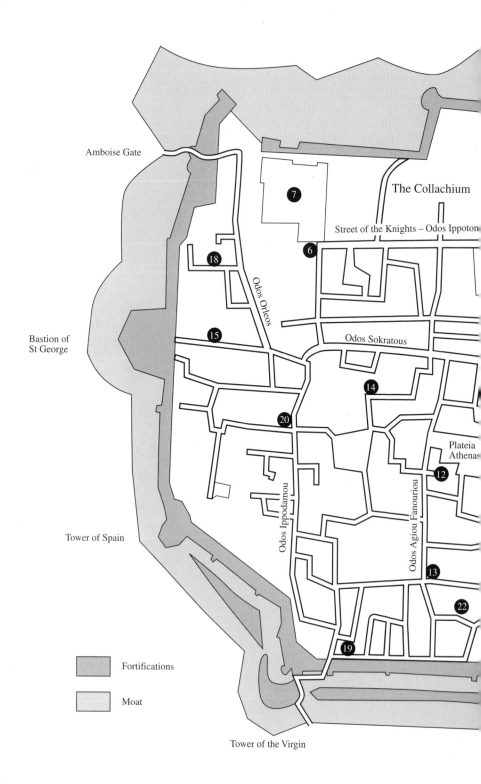

Amboise Gate

The Collachium

Street of the Knights – Odos Ippoton

Odos Orleos

Bastion of
St George

Odos Sokratous

Plateia
Athenas

Tower of Spain

Odos Ippodamou

Odos Agiou Fanouriou

Fortifications

Moat

Tower of the Virgin

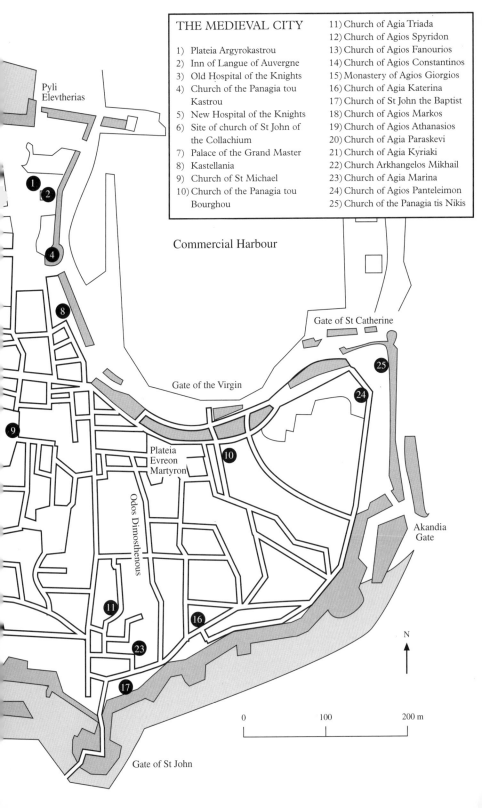

THE MEDIEVAL CITY

1) Plateia Argyrokastrou
2) Inn of Langue of Auvergne
3) Old Hospital of the Knights
4) Church of the Panagia tou Kastrou
5) New Hospital of the Knights
6) Site of church of St John of the Collachium
7) Palace of the Grand Master
8) Kastellania
9) Church of St Michael
10) Church of the Panagia tou Bourghou
11) Church of Agia Triada
12) Church of Agios Spyridon
13) Church of Agios Fanourios
14) Church of Agios Constantinos
15) Monastery of Agios Giorgios
16) Church of Agia Katerina
17) Church of St John the Baptist
18) Church of Agios Markos
19) Church of Agios Athanasios
20) Church of Agia Paraskevi
21) Church of Agia Kyriaki
22) Church Arkhangelos Mikhail
23) Church of Agia Marina
24) Church of Agios Panteleimon
25) Church of the Panagia tis Nikis

Pyli Elevtherias

Commercial Harbour

Gate of St Catherine

Gate of the Virgin

Plateia Evreon Martyron

Odos Dimosthenous

Akandia Gate

N

0   100   200 m

Gate of St John

The Panagia tou Kastrou became the first cathedral of the Knights when they arrived here in 1309, and before they had built the church of St John of the Collachium; a papal bull of 1327 referred to it as the Latin cathedral of Sainte Marie du Chateau. The present building replaced a triple-nave Byzantine basilica which in the 1960's was excavated below the floor of the present building; of the 150 coins which were found then, the location of the majority, which were 11th-12th C, suggested an 11th C foundation. The only part of this church surviving above ground is now part of the N wall; there seems no evidence that there was ever a domed building on this site, and if it was the seat of the metropolitan a domeless basilica would have been predictable. The reconstruction, whenever it took place, must in any case have been very radical, as it is impossible to see any masonry changes which would have been left by a wholesale re-structuring such as this, and in both its overall character and its detail it seems to us to be more consistent with Italian 13th C building practice than anything else; the presence of the Genoese in the century before the arrival of the Knights would seem to provide an explanation for this aspect of its design. The use of the building as a Byzantine Museum is to be commended, and the display is partly of temporary exhibits. On view is a range of icons mainly from the 16th to 18th C, with two further sets of frescoes removed from other churches; one of these is from the 13th C monastery of the Archangel Michael at Thari, and the other is of the 14th C from the church of Agios Zacharias on the nearby island of Khalki. They are not in good condition, but have escaped the fate of over-restoration.

On the other side of the Plateia is the **New Hospital,*** (5) now serving as the Archaeological Museum, and this must be regarded as the foremost single building of the whole city. The Knights never lost sight of their original function as tending the sick and the poor, and this must have been for them, with the Grand Master's Palace, the focus of the life of their Order. The centre of the main facade displays the shield of the Grand Master Anton Fluvian (1421-1437) held between two angels, with a Latin inscription saying that he donated 10,000 gold florins for the building of the hospital, which was begun in July 1440. A second inscription, over a door opening on to the Street of the Knights, records in French that the hospital was completed in 1492; it was therefore only in use in its finished state for some 30 years. In form you will find that it is a simple, two-storey hollow square, with a central courtyard surrounded by broad arcades, reminiscent in some ways of a Western monastic cloister. A closer comparison can however be made with the tradition of the Middle Eastern caravanserai or *khan*, where travellers would be given shelter, and so may hark back to the Palestinian origins of the Order. Large rooms open on to the arcades at both levels, and these would have been used for storage and the various functions of the hospital, but the focal point of the whole building is on the first floor, reached up a broad flight of stone steps. Here the magnificent hall of the main infirmary, some 50 m. long and taking up almost the entire length of the facade, is where the patients would be cared for. Here the long, open space is more reminiscent of the Western medieval tradition of hospitals, still to be seen in France and Italy. The wooden roof could not span a chamber of this width without the row of pillars down the centre which give it the necessary support. The function of the small rooms opening off the main ward is uncertain, but the need for more privacy in this huge chamber can be easily envisaged.

Before looking further at the ward as it is arranged today, it is worth envisaging the daily life that would have gone on here during the few decades that the Knights were using it. In overall charge of the hospital was the Grand Hospitaller who was the leader of the langue of France, and who appointed an infirmarer (usually also from his langue) who served a two-year term. He had to visit all the sick day and night, and it was under his supervision that the physicians tended the sick, as did eight 'brothers', one from each langue of the Order. All patients were visited twice each day, and the physicians gave verbal instructions as to their treatment which was noted down by a scribe accompanying them. The patients for their part had to observe strict rules of behaviour and religious observance, saying their confession and making a will before they were admitted, not playing dice or cards, keeping silence and only reading books that concerned religion. Each bed was curtained, and the patients' food was served on silver plates. The chapel was in the recess in the centre of the E side of the ward, and which forms the faceted bay projecting over the main entrance; here a chaplain celebrated mass each day, and requiem mass in the event of the death of a patient.

Today the visitor just sees a lofty, echoing space with none of the furnishings that would have accompanied the life of the hospital. The main items displayed are sarcophagi or tomb slabs of knights of the Order or other local officials that were rescued from the ruins of the main church of the Order, St John of the Collachium, after its destruction in 1856. You will find them dating from the 14th C escutcheon of the Spanish Grand Master Juan Fernandez de Heredia (1377-1396) to that of an English knight, Thomas Newport, of 1502. The other rooms on the first floor that are open are devoted to the display of classical art, mainly sculpture, that has been found in Rhodes and other islands of the Dodecanese. The only EC exhibit is a 5th C floor mosaic that the Italians (as was their habit) removed from its original site of Agia Anastasia at Arkasa, on the island of Karpathos, and installed in the open air area on the first floor adjacent to the exhibition rooms. It is of interest in having several inscriptions, but it is difficult to see all of it. Other floor mosaics transported and displayed in the Museum are pre-Christian.

Returning to the Plateia Megalou Alexandrou you only have to walk back to the corner of the New Hospital to find yourself looking up what can claim to be the most perfectly preserved medieval street in Europe: the **Street of the Knights (Odos Ippoton)**. While alterations and restorations have occurred, and the identity and function of all of the buildings is not always certain, we nevertheless can experience here a superb sequence of late medieval secular buildings; it runs precisely E to W, and the only significant change that has occurred is that the vista at the upper end of the street, which is now open to the sky, would until 1856 have been closed off by the building of the cathedral of St John of the Collachium.

Opposite the S facade of the New Hospital are, at the bottom of the street, the 'Inns' or auberges of the langues of Italy and of France; on the same side, further up, is the small Gothic church of Agia Triada (restored in 1938 but now again closed for repair), with what was probably the house of the chaplains of the langue of France just beyond it (now the Italian Consulate), and then the Inn of the langue of Provence. Few of the buildings on the S side of the street are identifiable, but just beyond the Hospital is the house of a rich Knight, Diomède de Villaragut. The Inns can in some cases be identified, but the individual knights would mostly live in their own houses within the collachium. This brings us to the modern Italian portico and the site of St John of the Collachium, and it is here that you must imagine the large basilica that has been reproduced beside Mandraki harbour. To the right is the large, open courtyard of the Grand Master's Palace, erected on what was probably the site of the original 7th C Byzantine stronghold.

The **Palace of the Grand Master**** (7) (usual museum hours, entry charge) remains, we feel, the only real disaster perpetrated by the Italians during their extensive endeavours in the Dodecanese between the two World Wars. Parts of it were certainly ruinous when they took it over, and the lithographs by Witdoeck made in 1825 and published by Rottiers (shortly after it had ceased to be used by the Turks as a prison) show considerable dilapidation, but large sections of the ground floor were then still intact; some of the first storey had survived until the beginning of this century, but everything that was left was demolished without official records, including a fine entrance gate bearing the arms of Hélion de Villeneuve (1319-1346) the second Grand Master in Rhodes, and adjoining complex; we only have Rottiers' lithographs, a few random photographs and the plans made by A.Gabriel in the 1920's to tell us what was lost. The new palace was of course intended to house either the King of Italy or the Great Dictator when either came to stay; with due apologies to the late Osbert Lancaster, the Italians seem to have invented a style for their reconstruction that equates with 'Mussolini manorial'. This approach involved the uprooting from Kos of a number of classical and EC mosaic floors and relaying them here in totally unsympathetic and incongruous surroundings. The bizarre result certainly defeats any attempt to envisage the building as it might have been used by the Grand Masters until 1523.

All this being said, the modern custodians of this monstrous Fascist folly have made the best use possible of what they inherited, and you should certainly not miss visiting the fine and extensive display that has been installed on the ground floor of the Palace. The ceramics, sculpture (including three tomb slabs of Hospitaller figures), manuscripts, coins and illustrative material displayed here provide an excellent and imaginative orientation to Rhodes as a medieval centre from the EC centuries to the departure of the Knights in 1523. Great care has been taken with a further exhibition of Byzantine art, with seven MSS displayed, some of them illuminated, a highly interesting range of over thirty icons, the earliest of the 14th C and four of them double-sided and intended to be carried in procession.

Nothing has so far been said about what remains the other outstanding achievement of the Knights on a European scale, and that is the **fortified walls of Rhodes ***** which form a truly massive defensive system that protected them throughout their time on the island. This 4 km. circuit of the city is the result of successive phases of modernisation, from the original 14th C walls of the Knights when they first arrived, through major reconstruction under successive Grand Masters. They left their escutcheons on the areas that they had built or simply where they were prominent, and these can be found at all points, although it is interesting to find that of the some 150 escutcheons that survive almost 50 display the arms of Pierre d'Aubusson (Grand Master 1476-1503); he had been in charge during the great Turkish siege of 1480 and the reconstruction and reinforcement that took place under him has left an indelible mark on the whole city. The resulting complex of battlements, towers, bastions, moats, scarps and counter-scarps was still being added to in 1521, and represents a kind of developing copy-book showing how the Knights could call on the skills of the latest international experts to counter the increasing power and dangers of gunpowder artillery. The construction of these huge defences must have entailed the demolition or absorption of much of the earlier fortifications, built to withstand a much lower level of destructive power. It is possible to visit a section of the walls on Tuesday and Saturday afternoons, but only limited areas are open. The enthusiast for late medieval fortification will find that a careful survey can best be made from the exterior, but there are sectors where observation can only be made at a distance.

The different langues were responsible for the different sectors of the defence; that of the English sustained considerable damage through mining by the Turks during the final siege of 1522, and it is still possible to see the large areas of repair that the Turks had subsequently to make in the outer walls when they took over the Collachium.

The St Nicholas tower, the most prominent element of the defences at the end of the harbour mole, had been re-built by the Grand Master Raymond Zacosta (1461-1467); this was a key area of resistance during the Turkish siege of 1480, but a severe earthquake in 1481 caused it major damage and it was re-built by Pierre d'Aubusson (1476-1503); he also added the lower apron defences all round its base.

II. The Bourg.

The other main group of public buildings is in the Bourg (or City), and is focussed on the area of the old market-place, the Plateia Ippokratous, to the S of the New Hospital. This was the area in which all the Greek inhabitants, and any others who were not members of the Order, lived and carried on their day-to-day existence. Facing the end of Odos Sokratous is one of the which displays what is perhaps the most impressive and harmonious of the exteriors in the city, where a broad flight of steps leads up to a terrace balcony; it is known as the Kastellania (8) and probably had the function of a courthouse. Above the flight of steps is the principal coat of arms in white marble; supported by two *hommes sauvages*, it is that of Emery d'Amboise and bears the date of 1507, making it one of the most recent buildings of the Knights. It now houses a local historical archive and is normally closed, but paintings on its wooded ceiling of personifications and virtues are an indication of much other decorative art that must have been lost.

Further to the S are more public buildings of the Knights, such as that of the so-called Admiralty which looks on to the Plateia Evreon Martyron; this was probably never its correct name as there are the remains of inscribed texts both inside and outside the building which are in Greek as well as Latin, and it has been suggested that it may therefore have been where the Uniate Greek bishop of Rhodes had his dwelling after the Council of Florence of 1439.

The main public buildings and the walls are certainly the most prominent features of medieval interest in the city, but there are still many other lesser buildings and sites that will reward a leisured visit.

Byzantine fortifications. There are only minimal parts of the Byzantine defensive system surviving, but sufficient to plot the extent of the fortifications constructed between the 7th and 13th C; they are concentrated mainly in a sector to the S of the old site of the Cathedral of St John and the Street of the Knights, and clearly show the quite restricted area that the Greeks had fortified. To withstand the initial assault by the well equipped Knights in 1306 these fortifications must have been quite substantial, but it is not now possible to do more than plot the extent of their foundations, using excavated sections as a guide; it was certainly this complex that the Knights were to reinforce first when they arrived in 1309. Most prominent is a short series of defensive towers running E / W in a line just N of Odos Theophiliskou, with one beyond Odos Panaitiou, and part of the wall facing the sea on Plateia Evdimiou, but otherwise remains are confined to areas that have been excavated in recent years. Mostly below ground level, some of these have been excavated and can be seen on Odos Evdimiou and again on Odos Panaitiou, close to Odos Sokratous.

Churches of Rhodes. The sites of a number EC basilicas have been identified (five in the city and over 60 on the whole island), but easily the most prominent and impressive is the **church of St Michael★** (**9**) on Plateia Athenas, at the junction of Odos Platonos and Odos Thoukididou. It is now in its excavated state, and fenced, but can be easily viewed. Although two successive later buildings were erected on its site, the original basilica here can be seen to have been substantial, and its full width can easily be viewed from outside the excavated N aisle. This must have become ruined at some later point, as another smaller church was built on its S aisle in the Middle Byzantine period; then, probably in the 14th C, a third, much larger church was erected on the same area; it is this, with extensive barrel vaulting and some fresco remains in the main apse, that you see today. It has been suggested that this may have been built by the Greeks as their metropolis after the Knights had taken over the church of the Panaghia tou Kastrou; there is certainly no indication of another church of comparable size.

Next in both size and prominence is the later church which the Knights would have called **Notre Dame du Bourg**,★ but which is now designated as Our Lady of the Burgh (Panagia tou Bourgou) (**10**); it takes this name from the part of the town that was separate from the Collachium and where all the inhabitants lived who were not part of the immediate organisation of the Knights. It is also now ruined, and is on the junction of Odos Pindarou where it meets Odos Alhadef as it runs due S up from the wall overlooking the Commercial harbour, and passes straight across the chancel of the church, leaving on the left the triple apses of the E end and on the right the nave and W wall. It is a late 14th / early 15th C building and the ground plan is still intact, allowing a clear idea of its scale; the finely carved decoration of simplified foliage on the capitals between the apses is still in good condition and is well lit by the evening sun.

These two churches can of course be seen at any time, and that of the Panagia tou Kastrou can be entered during museum hours. There are some 15 other churches in the Old City which all deserve a mention here for one or more reasons; there are probably seven that were already built before the arrival of the Knights, otherwise all the rest must represent either an initiative by local Greeks or else a collaboration of a Western patron with Greek builders. Few of them are at all large, the wealth of the Knights being mainly directed elsewhere after they had built the three main churches already mentioned; they are given here with an indication of their principal points of interest in a sequence that relates approximately to their level of appeal. The first four are dateable before the arrival of the Knights, and the rest are later.

Agia Triada** (11), on Plateia Leonidou Rodiou (key at nearest house to W). This is both one of the larger and one of the most interesting of the Rhodian churches in everyday use, both in design and in its internal decoration. Its plan is an asymmetrical cruciform one with a dome over the crossing, and extended to W and S. It may have been originally built on a Greek cross plan, which was a type developed in the Dodecanese, and was possibly the katholikon of a monastery; the exterior masonry is hard to interpret, and a minaret confirms its period of use as a mosque. A foundation date in the 14th C is possible, though officially it is designated as 15th C, in spite of apparently earlier frescoes. Apart from its design and enigmatic building history, there are frescoes here of exceptional interest; one area to the S of the chancel is a simple lunette (perhaps originally part of a tomb) with a fine 14th(?) C Byzantine fresco of three bishops, and in the S arm another of St Onuphrios and St Mary of Egypt. But the unique feature here is an extensive, though damaged, fresco cycle that occupies the upper walls and barrel vault of the W arm, and is devoted to Genesis and Exodus episodes. You can distinguish successive scenes of the Expulsion from Paradise, Noah's family and the animals entering the ark (here given the 'chest' form found in Roman medieval fresco cycles), the Deluge, and the crossing of the Red Sea. There are also some Passion scenes.

It may be that Agia Triada represents, in its enigmatic complexities, the meeting of Western and Greek traditions better than any other of the churches of the city; it certainly repays a leisurely visit.

The small but charming 14th C **church of Agios Spyridon** (**12**), just a short distance away to the SE at the junction of Odos Aristofanous and Odos Thoukididou, is more conventional in appearance; it is a domed Byzantine inscribed-cross design, with a large parekklision to the N. The restored exterior is in excellent condition, but it is kept locked as there are extensive internal excavations in progress which have revealed both graves and a subterranean tomb chamber with a 15th C funerary painting in a style that integrates Western and Byzantine trends; it is to be hoped that it may be made safe for visitors in due course.

Access is not a problem with the 14th C **church of Agios Fanourios** (**13**), at the S end of the street of that name, as it is in daily use. It is dated to 1335, and this is consistent with the plan of a domed inscribed-cross; from the exterior this can now only be seen from the Plateia to the E, as a large modern extension has been attached to the W. There are some interior frescoes of c. 15th / 16th C, and most are damaged and very sooty, but an unusual lunette on the S wall close to the entrance (and behind some seating) portrays the donors holding a model of the church and provides the date of 1335. There is no sign of a minaret, and this modest building exemplifies the smaller type of Greek church, built after the arrival of the Knights, that has probably been in continuous use.

Another church from the period before the arrival of the Knights is **Agios Constantinos** (**14**) (sometimes 'and Helena') beside Odos Menekleous. It is a simple, barrel-vaulted hall-church with no cupola, and must date from the 12th / 13th C. It is now closed and the interior is derelict, but it represents the smaller scale of local Greek church building.

All the remainder named here date from the period after the arrival of the Knights, and for the most part they are not in use and are kept locked. Their general character is modest both in scale and building type; few are domed, and the predominant form is a simple barrel-vaulted chamber, usually slightly pointed at the apex. There is very little use of decorative detail, and this severity is even extended to a sparing use of mouldings. The contrast with the major churches already mentioned must always have been extreme.

This severity is happily not the case with the monastic church of

Agios Giorgios★ (15)on Odos Apollonion, near to the W walls and the Bastion of Agios Giorgios. It has one of the most attractive exteriors in the city, although is not in use and is kept closed. Probably 15th C and quite small, it has a relatively large dome with a richly decorative drum; the 24 niches and four windows round the drum are separated by attractive and restrained decoration that must represent a local Rhodian trend.

Agia Katerina★ (16), close to the walls at the junction of Odos Tlipelmon with Odos Irinis, represents a church type that seems to be unique to Rhodes in that its W exterior displays three identical doors each sited under its own gable. It is dated to the second half of the 14th C and in other ways shares in the relative severity of detail and does not have a cupola. Elsewhere this might have been held to be on an EC site, but this has never been suggested in this case. It is kept closed, which is regrettable, as this church is unusual in retaining a fine standing figure of St Peter in fresco inside.

Adjacent to St John's Gate is the very simple hall **church of St John the Baptist★** (17), actually built into an angle of the walls. It possibly pre-dated the building of the walls here, as the Knights filled it with rubble (removed by the Italians last century) in order to strengthen the tower; it must date from the late 14th / 15th C, and an inscription on the walls here dates their construction to 1457. Normally kept locked, the church itself has no particular decorative value, but there is an interesting external sculpture relief on the tower here, above the arms of Anton Fluvian. It is of St John the Baptist, and represents very well the way that Byzantine and W styles became combined under the aegis of the Knights. The emaciated forms of the saint's limbs and his spiky hair are completely Greek, but the text on the scroll that he holds is in Latin.

For the enthusiast, the location is given here of a further range of churches in the city which all date from the period of the Knights' occupation. Individually they are of less interest than those already mentioned above, being of simple plan and little or no decorative detail, but collectively they provide a clear view of the church building practice of the local population.

Agios Markos (18), down an alley off Odos Orpheos towards NW walls; a small 15th C hall church without narthex, now closed and derelict inside.

Agios Athanasios (19), built against the S walls, close to the gate of that name: a small, severe, early 16th C hall church, closed and unused.

Agia Paraskevi (20), on Odos Ippodamou in the middle of the W sector of the city: quite a small 15th C church but unusual in that it has a relatively large cupola with a plain, faceted drum.

Agia Kyriaki (**21**), very close to Arkhangelos Mikhail and the S walls: difficult to approach as access is through a private yard usually guarded by a fierce dog, this is a 14th /15th C simple hall church; the intact minaret indicates its use as a mosque.

Arkhangelos Mikhail (**22**), on Odos Agiou Fanouriou, close to S walls: a medium sized 14th / 15th C barrel-vaulted hall church; closed and derelict, but the interior can be appraised from outside.

Agia Marina (**23**), at S end of Odos Diosthenous, very close to the walls: a very simple 14th C hall church, modernised and in full use.

Agios Panteleimon (**24**), on Plateia Peisirodou close to the far NE angle of the walls: a simple hall church, with a completely modern interior and in full use. It was built as an oratory in 1480 after the defeat of the Turkish siege in that year, and a grand procession came each year on 27th July from St John of the Collachium to worship here and at Our Lady of Victory, nearby. Interestingly, the statute under which it was initiated ordered that both Greek and Latin rites should be celebrated here.

Panagia tis Nikis (Our Lady of Victory) (**25**), in the angle of the walls formed by St Catherine's Gate, and 50 m. NE of Agios Panteleimon: this is now a ruin, but is known to have been built as a thank offering by the Knights after the siege of 1480; this too was the focus of a procession each 27th July. It was a single-nave hall church with cross-vaults, and the fact that it was the result of patronage by the Knights rather than local Greeks is of interest for its construction.

III. Outside the city: the Rhodes countryside.

Outside the city of Rhodes there is still much of interest, and while the influence of the Knights continues to be very apparent, a number of buildings still survive which represent the aspirations of the local Greek population, some from before their arrival. The entries are arranged with the two most prominent sites of Filerimos and Lindos given first, and the rest then in a sequence corresponding to their position on two itineraries, one keeping largely to the E coast, and the other taking in the main sites of the W coast.

Filerimos   Φιλέριμος

EC baptistry ruins, funerary chapel, restored monastic complex.★★ Enclosed; museum hours and charges.

This has been developed as one of the main tourist objectives outside Rhodes town, and is most easily reached from the road leaving Rhodes town down the NW coast, and turning inland at Trianta; the road passes through Ialyssos and then climbs through pine woods to reach Filerimos after 15 km.

This splendid site has always been attractive to Rhodians; the ancient Greek city of Ialyssos stood here, and you will find the ruins of the 3rd C BC temple of Athena Ialysia occupying the level summit. An EC basilica stood beside it, of which the traces of the baptistry and a cruciform font can still be seen. Immediately to the N is the main church building of Our Lady of Filerimos; during the period of the Knights a famous icon, the 'Madonna di Filerimo' was housed here, and during the sieges of 1480 and 1522 it was taken down into Rhodes so that its protective powers could ensure that Muslim forces would not breach the defences.

What you now see is probably the third Christian construction on the site, as there are minimal traces of a Byzantine church as well. You may find this a strange and rather frustrating building to view, as the Italian restoration of the 1930's was by modern standards over-thorough, and it is hard to be sure about what can now be seen; the lithographs of Rottier's artist, Witdoeck, made in 1825, show a largely roofless ruin. The main feature of the interior today is the highly unusual arrangement of the two chapels, that to the N being for RC worshippers and that to the S for the Orthodox; you reach these through a large entrance area, all carefully vaulted. There is a strong feeling of being in a Western architectural ensemble transplanted to a Greek context, but this may be partly due to the Italian restoration. The tower that they built outside, with its huge Maltese cross in relief, has no pretensions to being anything but modern. The peaceful cloister beyond is attractive, but again over-restored.

Do not miss what is perhaps the most authentic medieval survival here, which is a small underground chapel; this is reached down a pathway on the left immediately beside the entrance gate. There must have been an upper church as well, of which this may have been a funerary chapel. The damaged frescoes include representations of five knights of Rhodes being introduced to Christ by their patronal saints; Witdoeck's copies made in 1825 show that only about one-fifth still survive now from that period. The date of those that are left would seem to be 14th-15th C, but Rottiers wrote that one of the kneeling knights that he saw was named as Hélion de Villeneuve (Grand Master 1319-46), and it is possible that frescoes continued to be added over a considerable period.

This level hill-top site has been important to the history of Rhodes, commanding as it does such a clear view of the coast and town; there was a substantial castle here which fell to the initial assault by the Hospitallers in 1306, but only through its betrayal by a Greek; the Knights certainly maintained the castle here, but it has not survived the many later military engagements that took place on this superb vantage-point. Among other military leaders who valued it was the sultan Suleiman, who in 1522 directed his successful siege of Rhodes from this marvellous eminence.

Lindos   Λίνδος

Lindos was always the secondary centre of the island, and the town has been continuously occupied since the 10th C BC. Its harbour was the only other effective one after Rhodes, and this played a significant part in its medieval history. The Knights recognised its value, and ensured its defence by hiring Western mercenaries after they were in occupation, but they also used the town as a source of both revenue and manpower during their rule. While the town has a number of domestic buildings which must partly date from the age of the Knights, it is the Acropolis, with its looming castellated walls, that is the focus of medieval interest.

Lindos, acropolis.
Ruins of large Byzantine church and Castle of the Hospitallers.* Enclosed. Museum hours (gates closed 14.00) and charges.
The castle here is the most prominent and complete of the seventeen that the Knights built around their island of Rhodes. Approaching the acropolis up the long flight of steps, the first building of which you will be conscious is also one of the latest: the arms of Pierre d'Aubusson (Grand Master 1476-1503) set in relief in the wall of the Commandant's quarters face proudly down the coast towards the nearest Hospitaller castle of Feraklos. He would have been only the last in a sequence of Grand Masters to have adopted this superb natural strong-point; in 1317 there must have already been a castle here as the Grand Master Foulques de Villaret, who had so incensed his fellow Hospitallers that he fled here to escape assassination, was besieged by them here. Once you are inside the extensive area of the acropolis (some 100m. x 80m.) the impact of the contribution made by the Knights becomes less prominent. While the Commandant's quarters are still very much present and are the only building still roofed (although cannot be entered), the extensive fortifications of the acropolis, which are so evident from below and are the touchstone of the Knights' presence, become less visible. The classical Greek remains of the sanctuary of Athena Lindia, with its monumental staircase and temple occupying the S area, and now being restored, are a magnificent reminder of their age and of the importance of the island in the pre-Christian centuries. For

the medievalist, however, it is the massive ruins of the Byzantine church of St John that are chiefly of interest here. The church dates from c.1100 and is superb evidence of the strength of the Byzantine presence in the island. The church was built on an inscribed-cross plan, and the whole of the E end survives, with the deep double-framing of the windows and blind niches on the main apse all providing rich relief. It is of interest that the well-cut ashlar masonry technique of the Byzantines seems to have been adopted by the Knights when they came to build the quarters of the governor of the kastro; certainly there is little discernible difference.

Lindos, Church of the Panagia.*
Normally locked; key at one of the nearest houses.
On the way up to the acropolis, a small deviation to the left at just past half-way will bring you to this modest 12th C church.

It follows the traditional, rather severe, Rhodian type of domed, inscribed-cross plan, with a broad drum supported over the crossing; there are no structural additions, although all the paintings are 17th – 18th C. It nevertheless represents, like Agia Irene, Koskinou, the indigenous Byzantine building tradition before the arrival of the Knights.

Entries on the rest of the sites on the island will now be given on the basis of two itineraries; the first of these follows the road running the length of the S (or SE) coast of the island, and starting from Rhodes town.

Koskinou   Κοσκινού

Church of Agia Irene.*
Normally locked; key kept at nearest house to N.
The small village of Koskinou is some 7 km. from Rhodes town, turning up to the right from the main road where it is signed; the church is on Odos Ag Eirene at the E extremity of the village, looking down towards the sea.

Until recently it would have been isolated from the main village area, which may explain how it has survived without significant restoration; even the whitewash is confined to the entrance facade.

It is a cross-in-square, domed church of 11th/12th C, with a severely simple exterior and of modest size; the quite small cupola is carried on a broad and high octagonal drum. The interior is innocent of paintings, and has no alterations other than the usual iconostasis, but the type is completely typical of Rhodian building before the arrival of the Knights, with the exception of a more prominent drum for the cupola, and it should be seen in the context of such churches as those of the Panagia at Lindos and Kattavia

If you have the time to deviate from the main Rhodes / Lindos road this makes a rewarding stop.

Arkhangelos   Αρχάγγελος

Castle of the Knights. ★ Ungated and unenclosed.

At about two-thirds of the way between Rhodes and Lindos this castle is impossible to miss from the road, overlooking both the eponymous village to the W and the coastline to the E.

The entrance, with hinge-sockets still in the threshold slab, is in the SE sector, and the whole area enclosed by the single enceinte is some 50m. x 20m. While not therefore large, the walls still stand up to about 8m. in places; there is no sign of defensive artillery positions. A modern chapel is now all that is to be seen of internal buildings, but there must have been others during its period of use. Finely cut escutcheons of the Knights are still in place on both E and W exteriors, implying that there was never an outer enceinte. There is documentary evidence of the Grand Master being petitioned in 1399 by local Rhodians that the Knights should build a castle here for their protection when this part of the coast was attacked; they were told at that time that they could take refuge in Feraklos, but in 1457 Arkhangelos is known to have suffered a surprise attack by a Turkish force under Mehmet II, and was partly sacked, so a date in the first half of the 15th C for its construction is indicated. The Knights' escutcheons should not be always regarded as providing secure evidence of building dates, but also should not be ignored; those on the W wall are of the Grand Masters Pedro Zacosta (1461-67) and Giovanni-Battista Orsini (1467-76) with the latter repeated on the E wall. As both date from after the Turkish attack they perhaps should be seen as evidence of re-building with new fortifications, or other improvements.

Its function also seems quite clearly suggested by the documentation: the need for a stronghold in which local Rhodians could take refuge in time of danger. Its situation is not a particularly powerful one for defence, but withstanding a prolonged siege could never have been intended, and its outlook must have made it a useful look-out point; one must suppose a chain of such relatively small forts were used to relay signals between Rhodes, Filerimos and Lindos, and the castle at Feraklos was the nearest such signalling point to Lindos. For a seagoing rather than road-using force, a watch on the sea-routes was always needed. This is a little-frequented but interesting site, which well deserves a visit.

Feraklos   Φεράκλος

Castle of the Knights.★ Ungated and unenclosed.

Turning left off the coast road 9 km. before reaching Lindos from Rhodes town, at the sign to Kharaki, in 4 km. you will easily see the remaining jagged walls of Feraklos crowning the hill to your left; the easiest approach is up a steep track leading to an opening in the E sector of the enceinte.

Although now clearly a result of building by the Hospitallers, there was already a castle here before their arrival, as they had made an attack on a castle here during 1306 as part of their initial conquest of the island. Once inside the walls the size of the area enclosed seems surprisingly large for what is now an isolated part of the coast; the walls enclose a polygon of some 100m. x 100m., which is much more extensive than Arkhangelos, and it is known that through enlargements made here the Knights were able to delay the building of Arkhangelos. In emergencies the population from at least 5 km. around was expected to shelter here from danger. The feeling that the castle here was intended to support a considerable population is further emphasised by the presence of several deep cisterns, some now large enough to support fig-trees growing inside them.

There are no significant changes to the masonry of the construction, implying that the Knights started to re-build from the foundations, and no obvious provision for artillery, but the remains of a major central tower of some 10m. square still surmount a large chamber; this would have been the highest point, from which it might have been possible to see Arkhangelos (not visible from ground level), but it is not sufficiently powerfully built to have served as a keep. The predominant function of the castle here would seem to have been for the defence of the local population, with a second use as an observation post. There are no carved escutcheons visible, and the date of the Knights' re-construction is hard to determine accurately, but there is documentary evidence of servants in the castle here by 1347, and we know that land was held in the area by one of the Knights from 1348; a date in the 1330's-40's for its construction is probably the nearest that we can get, and it may well have been modernised later in the building campaign of Giovanni-Battista Orsini (Grand Master 1467-76).

Feraklos offers stupendous views in all directions, and the site is very little visited, so you can expect to have it to yourself.

Psinthos   Ψίνθος

Moní Agia Trias.★

Coming from Kremasti, turn left off road 2km. beyond Psinthos and in about

1 km. you will find this small, barrel-vaulted rural moni a few metres off the road to your left.

Architecturally this could not be more simple, being a hall with only a single apse projecting to the E to give an external clue as to the building's function, and its diminutive scale (some 4 m. from threshold to iconostasis) making it easy to overlook. It is only the diverse and interesting frescoes, dateable by style to 13th/14th C, that cover the interior that make a visit here a rewarding experience; those on the lower walls are easier to see as being less sooty than those in the barrel-vault depicting the major feasts. The apse retains the Rhodian conventional subjects of a deesis flanked by bishops, and there is another deesis on the S wall, facing three imposing military saints; to the right of the doorway is a donor scene, which is perhaps the most interesting and individual work in the interior. The style of the paintings is unsophisticated but vigorous, and the fact that there is so little left on the island of this period gives them an additional interest.

Agios Nikolaos Fountoukli   Άγιος Νικόλαος Φουντούκλι

Domed Byzantine church.★★ Normally open. (See Pl. 13).
Travelling W from Eleousa, after some 4 km. you will see this gem of Byzantine architecture on the left of the road, looking N down towards the sea.

It is not large, but is a perfect example of its 13th/14th C type, quite unaltered or enlarged; the substantial cupola is supported over a Greek cross plan by a decorative drum in which twelve external niches are separated by small fictive knotted colonettes. Even the small belfry with decorative dishes inset into it has the appearance of being integral to the main design, which is often not the case. Although the church is usually open, the frescoes inside it are its least interesting aspect, being quite late and not in good condition; that to the right of the W doorway showing two donors holding a model of the church is the most unusual, but must be a reproduction of an early original. The building should probably be dated in the later 13th or early 14th C, but shows no evidence at all of any W or Latin influence.

Be sure to allow time for a leisurely stop at this beautiful monument in its matchless setting; the island has nothing more perfect of this type to offer.

The entries below concern the sites on the W coast of Rhodes.

Kritinia   Κρητηνία

Castle of the Knights (Kastello).✷✷ Unsigned; ungated and open.
You will have no trouble locating this substantial and superbly sited castle, built some 150 m. above the sea on the W coast, 52 km. from Rhodes city.

Originally intended to be oriented seawards, some later building appears to have been intended to adjust this aspect of its construction so that it could be defended from the E. Built on a polygonal plan, enclosing an area of some 80 x 80 m., the walls facing E and S are now the most complete, and they may be among the more recent phases of building. The escutcheons on the external walls go some way to confirm this; those on the S wall are those of the Grand Masters Giovanni Battista Orsini (1467-76) and Fabrizio del Carretto (1513-21), and two more in the E wall and tower include that of Pierre d'Aubusson (1476-1503); even allowing for some uncertainty over the precise message conveyed by these, the implication must be that Kritinia was (or became) a focus of the Knights' interest for much of the last 50 years of their presence on the island, and the successive phases of building or reinforcement here are the result.

The interior retains considerable masses of surviving building, including the entire apse of quite a large chapel; this has the French royal arms on a small projection from one of the quoins, and it may well be the last part of the ensemble to be built. The E wall and NE tower are the most complete of the remaining buildings, and it is clear that the visual contact across the sea with Alimnia was an important aspect of its siting; the neighbouring castle of Monolithos 17 km. down the coast to the S is not in view, and so would have needed an intermediate relay point, and there is no surviving signalling-point on the coast to the N. The absence of an outer enceinte implies that withstanding a prolonged siege was never one of the primary intentions when the castle here was built and later enlarged.

A greater knowledge of the origins and use of the castle at Kritinia may one day become available; meanwhile, a visit here is rewarding for a number of reasons, and be sure to allow time to explore its possibilities.

Monolithos   Μονόλιθος

Castle of the Knights.✷ Well signed; ungated and unenclosed.
Following the sign from the main asphalt coast road, you will have no

difficulty locating this castle as it rises sheer out of its own pinnacle of rock.

The area covered by its buildings is not at all extensive (some 30 m. x 30 m.), but its siting must have made it virtually impregnable to attack. Today there are few clues left on which to base a reconstruction; a relatively modern chapel has been built in the central area, presumably replacing an earlier one, and there is only one long chamber left with a barrel-vaulted roof intact, its open end projecting due N. There remains just the spectacular siting for the castle here, which provides the main reason for regarding it as an original creation of the Knights; a superb 180-degrees outlook spreads out before you from the rocky plateau which would have been its central defended area, NW towards Cape Armenistes and SE to Cape Fourni, taking in the small islet of Strongilo. The fact that the castles on Khalki and on Alimnia are not visible, hidden by the headland of Armenistes, with Kritinia also out of sight from here, suggests that its function must have involved a further point of contact for message relay. No clues survive as to its origins or later development, with not even any knights' escutcheons to be seen. It can be surmised that it was first built in the 14th C to exploit the remarkable rocky monolith of its site, but that its limitations of observation began to reduce its usefulness and its functions were taken over by the castle at Kritinia.

The superb location of Monolithos alone makes it well deserving of a leisurely visit, but one is left with a feeling that there must have been reasons for its creation which still await explanation; this may one day be forthcoming, perhaps from documentary evidence.

Kattavia   Κατταβία

Church of the Panagia.*
Normally locked; key in house on N side of the cemetery.
The church is easily found in the centre of the village, located in the less usual surroundings of a cemetery. The village of Kattavia, close to the S tip of the island, can be reached from roads going down either the E side from Lindos or the W side from Kritinia and Monolithos; that on the W is slightly more direct, although the final stretch is on a good dirt road, not asphalt, over the flat and exposed terrain.

This was one of the Rhodian villages that was fortified by the Hospitallers to protect the local population in an otherwise undefended part of the island; by 1477 the 'castello' here was reported to have become dilapidated with age, and it was then re-built, as it was in one of the most fertile parts of the island. The defences must have been subsequently dismantled, as there is now no evidence of them in any form. The medium-sized church, which now serves as a cemetery church, offers a simple but attractive example of Rhodian building, with quite a small cupola over a central cruciform plan, and two bays added later to the W to form a large narthex; it is most probably of 12th C construction. Some frescoes can still be seen inside; they are probably 15th C but are undistinguished and in poor condition. The main body of the church has minimal window provision, with only the S arm having a small opening, and this in any case makes the frescoes hard to see well.

The church and its surroundings are attractively maintained, and a visit to this relatively isolated village leaves a strong impression of the kind of medieval rural life that would have persisted in the Rhodian countryside. Although remote from the Knights in their headquarters, the latter were always anxious to promote the prosperity of local Rhodian communities, and a document of 1339 granting tenure of a vineyard close to Kattavia by the Grand Master indicates their interest in even the more remote localities.

Mesanagros   Μεσαναγρός

Church of Agios Thomas.* Open when visited.
Some 3 km. on road SE of the village, close to the road on the left you will find this small domed, rural moni comparable with that at Psinthos.

The exterior is unexceptional, but the frescoes covering most of the interior, which appear to be 14th C, contain some striking passages. While there are deposits of candle soot in many parts, those in the sanctuary, portraying bishops, are the best preserved; less usual are some striking areas of red and black decorative vinescroll ornament. This remote little church must be representative of many that both pre-existed the arrival of the Knights and continued to be built after 1309, their isolation showing little or no impact from the new W presence.

This makes a worthwhile objective on a return detour if you have visited Kattavia, whether returning by either the E or the W coast.

SAMOS   Σάμος

Island group: E. Sporades. (*Nomos*: Samos.)

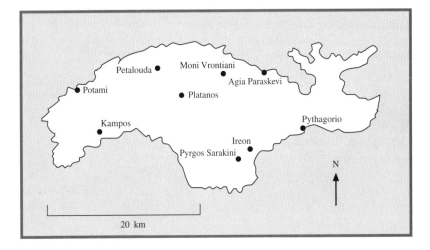

I n spite of its rich vegetation, wooded hillsides and famed wines, the island of Samos had a less colourful history than that of many of the smaller and less well endowed islands of the Aegean. Excavations have revealed a vigorous life on the island from the 4th to 7th C, when Arab raids began; a bishop from Samos was present at the important church council of 787 in Nicaea, and from the 10th C it was part of a theme governed from Smyrna. While covetous eyes must have been cast on it by successive generations of W invaders of the Greek islands, the fact that it lies closest of all to the mainland of Asia Minor (the channel at Pythagorion is under 2 km. wide) meant that it was always too close to Byzantine (and, later, Turkish) influence to allow long-term possession. Its position dominated its history, and, for example, would have been the reason that the Byzantine emperor Nikiforos Focas used it as a base from which to launch his assault on Crete in 960; in the Deed of Partition in 1204 Samos was listed as being allocated to the Latin emperor, but he never occupied it, and from c.1225 it was taken over as part of the Byzantine government based at Nicaea (Iznik). With weakening Byzantine internal power Samos suffered Turkish raids in 1303, 1320 and 1342, but then, with nearby Ikaria, the island was taken over by the Genoese in 1346. After well over a century they had to abandon the island on account of incessant piracy, and they moved much of the population to Chios. This depopulation meant that the island was also one of the earliest to come under permanent Turkish rule, yielding to the Turks by as early as the 1470's – almost a century before Chios was finally occupied in 1566.

The island today has two centres; one is Samos town at the end of a deep bay on the N coast, and the other is the smaller but more lively port of Pythagorio on the S coast. The main centres of EC and medieval interest are closer to the latter, and this has dictated the arrangement of these entries; on the stretch of coast between Ireon and Pythagorio the remains of no less than four EC basilicas can be visited.

Pythagorio (before 1955, called Tigani)   Πυθαγόρειο

1) **Site of EC basilica.**★ Enclosed, but easily seen.

The ancient acropolis of Samos lies on the high ground to the left of the road that leaves the harbour and leads W towards the site of the Temple of Hera and the island's airport; as you leave the town on this road you will see that the area is now occupied by the large modern church of the Metamorphosis, with beyond it a cemetery.

Stopping here and entering the cemetery, you can look down NE from the boundary wall on to the quite extensive site of an excavated Roman villa a few feet below. Within this a modest EC basilica was built, of which the plan can easily be seen, with a narthex adjoining a broad central nave. Fragments of mosaic floor that were excavated in the nave and apse indicate an early 5th C date for the basilica. As might be expected it is possible to find spolia in several areas of the surviving ensemble and the massive threshold, for example, is formed from a large slab of re-used dark marble; this interesting, if unspectacular, survival should not be overlooked.

There are two minor disappointments in the close vicinity: the interesting-looking castle just beyond the acropolis area (the *Frourion tis Logothitis*) in fact dates only from the 1820's, and is an expression of the special status earned by Samiots during the War of Independence. The Moní Agia Spiliani to the NW of Pythagorio (located above the entrance to the tunnel of Eupalinos) which may well have Byzantine origins, now contains nothing of Byzantine or medieval interest, the dank recesses of the cave itself being last re-furbished in 1883; this was probably also when the double-nave chapel at the entrance, which may well have been originally of medieval date, was rebuilt.

2) **EC basilica of Panagitsa, built over Roman baths.**★★
Enclosed; museum hours and small charge.

Just 1 km. beyond the site of the acropolis just described, travelling W towards the airport you will pass another fenced area immediately beside the road on the left.

This is an excavation of an interesting Hellenistic site that must have extended W of the ancient city of Polykrates, and was later the subject of further building by the Romans, who constructed a substantial bath complex here. An EC basilica was built on the N corner of the present site, and the ground plan of its nave and atrium is clear; areas of marble flooring would seem to have been laid over the pre-existing Roman mosaic floor, and you can find classical subjects such as a herm partly surviving under fragments of marble – presumably intentionally obscuring the pagan subject-matter. There were also mosaics installed by the EC builders, although not now visible, and they have been used to date the building to the later 5th C. The baptistry to the SW still displays its recessed marble font, and a number of EC caps and other spolia survive on the site.

3) EC basilica in further excavation adjoining the above, reached from the "Asterias" beach complex.*
Enclosed but can be visited.
Just a few metres to the W, and very close to the sea, three huge piers are the most prominent feature of further extensive classical ruins.
Beside these is the site of quite a substantial basilica (27 m. from apse to threshold), with many fragments of carved marble nearby, deriving from an ambo and the usual enclosures. A heavy layer of gravel covers the floor area, which means that any mosaics remain invisible, but the ensemble is still very impressive.

These two areas of excavation, covering a considerable expanse of the shoreline, form an attractive location which demonstrates clearly the evolving Christian culture that superseded the vigorous life of the Hellenistic and Roman world, and repays a leisurely visit.

Ireon, 7 km. W of Pythagorio: Site of Temple of Hera.
Apse of EC basilica.* Enclosed site; museum hours and charges.
The Temple of Hera is the undoubted classical showpiece of the island, and the huge main temple area with its great altar and one column still intact is truly awesome; this, and the giant kouros found here in the 1980's, now finely displayed in the museum in Samos, must not be missed. Due E of this the apse of an EC basilica still stands; its size seems quite modest by comparison (certainly on a more reduced scale than that of the basilica of Christ Lemniotissa, Kalymnos) and the single

central window is quite small, but without its classical neighbour it would have seemed more impressive. The masonry of the apse is undistinguished, but the effect of the re-used marble columns down the aisles must have been imposing. Although the apse is the only part of the structure still standing, the excavators uncovered the 8.5 square m. floor of a baptistry adjoining the S end of the narthex, and a chapel was located down the N side; fragments of a marble ambo were also found, and the ensemble would clearly have been imposing.

In the storage area to the S of the main site are two fine pieces of marble sculpture which must suggest a more extensive medieval use for the area: one is an 11th/12th C templon member or door lintel, and the other is an impressive but enigmatic marble monolith forming a shallow dish set in a large marble beam. The former suggests a possible later use of the EC basilica, but the visitor will have to decide on the function of the latter.

Pyrgos Sarakini, NW of Ireon. Πύργος Σαρακινή.
Defensive tower, and church of St John Theologos and St George. The tower is locked, the church is open.
Taking the road to Myli out of Ireon, after some 2 km. you will see on the right about 50m. from the road the crenellation of this tower; a broad track leads you to it.

Reaching the tower, you will find that it forms the S side of a very small plateia, with the adjoining E side occupied by the facade of a double-nave church. The tower, at 15m. wide and 6m. deep, is not large, but quite massively built, although it differs from the majority of island towers by having a broad doorway at ground level; although being protected by a short section of machicolation this could not have been as strong defensive a provision as other towers such as those on Samothraki, where the entrance is some 5m. above ground level. Although shut, it is possible to see that the interior had no masonry vaulting, and there would have probably been three wooden floors with internal stairways. The existence of this tower must be due to the Genoese interest in providing protection both for their own personnel and for local Samiots and their stores against attack from pirates and, possibly, Turkish raiders, whose first visit had been in 1303. Given the Genoese connection, a date not long after their arrival in 1346 is most probable.

The double-nave church, of which the S nave is dedicated to St John Theologos and the N to St George, is very reminiscent of those on e.g. Naxos, with the two naves of slightly unequal size, and probably not quite contemporary; the orientation of both to NE/SW may be due to the adjoining tower. The exterior is notable for the huge buttresses which support the S nave and the apse of the N church, and contribute to the fortified character of the ensemble. Like that at Platanos, the S nave and apse are somewhat larger, but here the presumption would be that the Genoese, not Greeks, were the patrons; the interior is very simple, with the barrel-vaulted chambers, innocent of any decoration, linked by a single archway. Given the virtual certainty that the Genoese built the tower, and that the church followed soon after, a date not long after 1346 when the W presence in the island began, is most probable.

This is an attractive site with an unusual combination of interests, and is quite easily reached.

Agia Paraskevi, 6 km. W of Samos town.
EC baptistry font.★Unenclosed.
Taking the road running W along the coast beside the Kolpos Vatheos, immediately after an EKO petrol station turn right off the road down a narrow winding concrete track; in about 300 m. you will come to the small modern church of Agia Paraskevi, with a free-standing campanile.

Just beside this are the remains of an EC cruciform font constructed from marble and brick; it must originally have been housed in a baptistry, and so is further evidence of the rapid expansion of this kind of building in the 5th C. Although now fragmented it must be allowed to speak for the larger ensemble of which it must once (as the very similar survival near Trypiti on Milos) have been part, and no doubt excavation would reveal more of its original context. The sea is here only some 30 m. away, and although only a modest survival the setting is worth the small detour.

Samos can offer a number of small, domed Byzantine churches of the 13th to 15th C, often still in use; most have no interior frescoes, or if they do, except for Petalouda they are later, but their architecture represents a strong local rural tradition. Three are mentioned here as being easy to visit.

Kampos   Κάμπος

This new village is on the road running along the N coast of the island, but if, while travelling W along.it, you take a steep left turn up a narrow road approx. 1 km. before you reach Kampos you will find these two churches. (A sign indication that this is the 'old village', Palaiokhora, has recently disappeared, but may be replaced.)

1) Church of Agia Matrona.* Normally open.

In about 1 km. you will find this church quite close to the narrow road running through the old village. It is built on an almost central triconch plan of modest size (from threshold to templon is some 7 m.) with just the W end slightly extended, and the N and S exedras generously rounded. The prominent cupola is carried on a broad drum with blind windows; the lower windows were formerly larger, although now reduced in size, the ensemble suggesting a building date not later than the 13th C. Inside there are extensive frescoes, with attractive Genesis scenes, but must all date from the 17th C or later.

The lateness of the decoration should not deter the visitor from making this short detour, as the church itself is of undoubted interest, being clearly a product of a prosperous phase in the history of Samos of which we know from historical sources, but of which there is little surviving architectural evidence in the form of Byzantine building.

2) Church of Agia Pelagia.* Normally open.

This is only some 100m. below Agia Matrona, reached down a short track leading down off the same narrow road through the old village beside a new house.

It is very similar in scale and type to the neighbouring church, being again built on a central, triconch plan with the W end slightly extended; the dome here is on an octagonal drum. The windows are unaltered, but the character is of a slightly later age than of Agia Matrona, and it is probably $14^{th}/15^{th}$ C. The interior is innocent of all fresco decoration. The outlook over the lush vegetation towards the coast is quite spectacular.

Church of Taxiarchis Mikhail.* Open when visited.

2 km. S of the convent of Megali Panagia, in open country E of the road between Myli and Koumaradei, you can look down on this church; a sign points down a steep, winding dirt track, and it can be reached in 10 minutes easy walk.

The domed, triconch design has received only a modern tiled shelter against its W wall, and in all other ways remains substantially unaltered; its interior has no decoration, and it is probably a product of the relatively prosperous period of the later 13th-14th C.

All three of these churches indicate the relatively prosperous country existence that would have been enjoyed on Samos during the period of the Nicene empire and later, with local builders able to develop a provincial style with its own distinction and individual character.

Moní Vrontiani   Μονή Βροντιανή

Monastery founded 1476.*
In use; usual monastic visiting hours.
Just before reaching Kampos the road along the N coast has a left fork signed to Vourliotes; leaving this village on the right, the road reaches the monastery in about 5 km. after travelling up through well-tended country.

It must be said that there is very little of artistic interest here, as the present buildings date from 1566 and were heavily restored in 1960, but the monastery does offer an opportunity to experience a substantial and completely traditional monastic complex, much as can be seen on Athos. After entering through a typically massive entrance porch, you will see that the katholikon occupies the central space, with arcaded quarters on three sides. Although now in decline, the scale of the ensemble is another interesting indication of the tolerance of the occupying Turkish power in the 15th-16th C.

Petalouda, reached from Ydroussa   Πεταλούδα

Church of the Koimisis (13th C).** Open. Completely unsigned.
This exceptional and remote little church can only be reached on foot or by 4 x 4 vehicle. Starting from the NE corner of the church plateia in Ydroussa take the steep track (initially concreted, soon just stony), which winds across the wooded hillside. After some 25 minutes' walking the track divides, the main spur curving up to the right; take the left fork, which goes downhill to the rocky bed of a stream, and where a steel water pipe goes temporarily underground. In about five minutes you will reach on your left a new concrete terminal for electric power lines (these you may have already seen from the track); take the path branching down to the left here and in a minute you will come to the delightful, secretive glade in which the church stands.

The outlook down towards the coast here is outstanding, and you may find the domeless and heavily-buttressed exterior, showing no windows except a tiny slit in the apse, is very reminiscent of many such rural churches in W Crete. The interior here is of the simplest possible form, where the barrel-vaulted chamber displays frescoes which cover most of the interior. These represent, where the original layer survives, the earliest wall-paintings on Samos, and contain elements of great interest. In the apse and bema the scenes of the Virgin and fine bishop saints are complemented on the N side by the unusual episode of the dialogue between St Peter of Alexandria and the youthful Christ in a torn robe. ("Who has torn your robe?" "It is the foolish and abominable Arius".) Water damage has obliterated much of the three roundels down the barrel-vault of the nave, but of great interest are the two rows of prophets, each holding a text, that run the length of the vault; those to the E turn towards the altar, and at mid-way the others turn to the W. This would suggest that the lost fresco on the W wall was of the Last Judgement, foretold by their texts. Some of these on the S side contain the earliest and best preserved paintings in the church, and are the basis of a date in the early 13th C, or even the late 12th C, there being no inscription. The standing figures down the lower walls dominate the small interior (only 7 m. in total length); particularly impressive are those of Constantine and Helena, although later re-painting has reduced the impact of a number of the others.

Allow a clear half-day for visiting this unique small church in its beautiful setting, as the island has no other painting of this period and interest to offer.

Potami   Ποτάμι

Church of the Transfiguration.** Open.
Approaching the village of Potami from Karlovassi on the N coast, a large sign indicates an "Ancient Chapel" to the left of the seaside road.

The first structure you will see is the ruin of a small church or chapel; an apse still survives, with part of a W wall which suggests an overall length of some 10 m. This could be a pre-7th C building that suffered from Arab attack (the sea here is very close), or one of the 10th C that succumbed to pirate raids and was abandoned; there is not sufficient left for any certainty.

The real interest of this site is the church that you reach some 100 m. further down the path from the coastal roadway; it stands beside the track as a tall, domed cross-in-square, and various adjoining fragments suggest that it may have been the catholicon of a monastery. Entering it you will be struck by the four fine marble columns that support the cupola, surmounted by well-cut 5th C caps; these are clearly re-used spolia from an earlier building, but the height of the columns makes it unlikely that they derive from the small ruined church 100 m. away, and they must have been brought here from another EC building. There are no frescoes, but further carving is visible at the top of the masonry templon, and more may be concealed by plaster below. The lateral chapels have tall, narrow niches in the thickness of the wall, with only the main apse showing as faceted on the exterior.

The proportions here may well have been dictated by the height of the columns, but in any case it is a building of considerable sophistication which it is unlikely was constructed by local masons. While an 11th C date is possible on some grounds, there might be more solid historical reasons for suggesting that it was a product of the mid-13th C, when the Byzantine rulers in Nicaea were in control of the island and had access to metropolitan building skills.

A visit to this tranquil site is certain to be rewarding.

Platanos   Πλάτανος

Church of the Koimisis Theotokou.★★. Locked; key kept at house immediately opposite the W door.

The large village of Platanos is one of the highest in the island, and the outlook over the whole of the W of Samos is truly staggering; looking across to the summit of Vigla at over 1400 m., you can see down to the right both the N coastline and the Turkish mainland, and on the left the S coast with the island of Fourni beyond.

This church, located in the centre of the village, cannot be missed and is of considerable interest. Originally built on a double-nave plan with separate doors to each of the naves, a large later narthex was added which has a single porch and entrance. It is clear that from the start the S nave was intended to be "primary" and larger, and the N "subsidiary"; the E exterior shows that of the two faceted apses the masonry is uniform but that on S side is larger, and it is this nave which carries a cupola, while the N is smaller and domeless. The masonry is undistinguished and the decoration of the interior is late and rather disappointing, but there is one feature of great interest: set in the floor under the cupola of the S nave is a plaque carved in worn relief with the double-headed imperial eagle. The inference of this is strongly that it must be a product of the Byzantine dynasty based at Nicaea during the Latin empire, between c.1225 and 1261, or up to c.1300, when Samos remained one of the islands kept under Greek control; it is unlikely to have been initiated after the first Turkish attack of 1303. The smaller nave would have been for the indigenous RC population, in this case predominantly Genoese, and the ensemble reflects the intention of the Byzantines to provide for the Italian minority on the island. In this way it suggests a more substantial and carefully planned version of the smaller double-nave church to the S at Pyrgos Sarakini, and provides an interesting comparison with the considerable number of double-nave churches built under Venetian rule on Naxos and elsewhere.

Your climb up to Platanos will be rewarded both by the outstanding 180° views and by this (in its way) uniquely interesting church.

SAMOTHRAKI   Σαμοθράκη

Med: Sanctus Mandrachi, Samandrachi.
Island area: N Aegean. (*Nomos*: Evros).

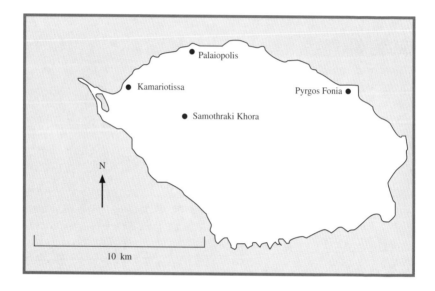

T his mountainous but quite fertile island is mentioned in several
    medieval sources from the 6th C, and judging by an inscription
    which commemorated the restoration of baths here by the
emperor Justinian, must have known some prosperity; later it was
famous for its goats and its honey. The location of the island was not as
advantageous as that of Limnos, being well to the N of the 'Channel of
Romanía' (Dardanelles), and so when, in the *Partitio Romaniae* of 1204
it was allocated to the Latin emperor Baldwin, it did not later fall into
Venetian hands. Recovered for the Byzantines by Michael VIII in 1261,
the island became involved in both the civil war of 1341-47, being
seized, with Limnos and Lesbos, by John V Palaiologos, and later in the
Genoese dukedoms of the N Aegean.

It is the latter which have left by far the most prominent mark on the
island's buildings, although lasting only from c.1430 to 1456. It is indeed
only through inscriptions on some of those buildings (see below) that we
know as much as we do about the presence and personalities of the
Genoese dynasty of the Giustiniani who were involved here. Quite when
Palamede Gattilusio arrived here is not known, but he had begun

building his *kastro* at Khora by 1431, and was dispossessed by the victorious sultan Mehmet II in 1456. The same year, however, as part of the crusade launched by pope Callixtus III to recover CP, a cardinal Lodovico Trevisan had arrived in the Aegean with a small fleet, and was able to re-take Samothraki (with Limnos and Thasos), installing garrisons on all three islands. To have the banner of Saint Peter flying from three island castles all so close to his newly conquered city of CP was a provocation that Mehmet could not bear for long, and in 1459 Samothraki was re-taken by the Turks, who were to remain (except for a Venetian hiatus of 1466-79) until 1912.

All the major medieval sites surviving on Samothraki originated during the 25 years or so of Genoese occupation; an alphabetical sequence has been adopted, as providing the easiest form of reference.

Kamariotissa   Καμαριωτισσά

The large modern church of the 'Panagia Kamariotissa' was renovated in 1985, and it was probably then that traces of the previous EC basilica that last century were said to exist on the site disappeared.

Church of Agios Andreas.* Usually open.
This is in open country approximately 3 km. SW of Kamariotissa, and is easiest to reach by walking parallel with the beach to beyond the spit with wind turbines; it is sited some 100 m. from the sea.
You find in this isolated spot a small, barrel-vaulted single-chamber church of the simplest kind; it is probably of 14th C origin, and a plaque reports its renovation in 1871, but it displays on its W facade the only EC fragments to be seen in the vicinity of this town. Although heavily whitewashed, there are four pieces of a marble templon set into the stone work that are probably of 5th C date. While the locality is of the kind favoured by EC builders for a basilica, there is no evidence that the spolia originated here, and the fragments may have originally been part of the furnishings of the main church in Kamariotissa. The only interest inside the church is its masonry iconostasis.

Khora / Samothraki

Kastro.★★ Unenclosed. (See Pl. 27).
Sited unmistakeably on an outcrop of rock as you approach Khora from the N.

Like most of the khoras of medieval foundation, this is built well inland and out of sight of the sea. The first part of the Kastro that you reach is the base of a Byzantine tower some 5 m. high surviving from an 11th/12th C fortification; built against a rock face, there is now no entrance or other aperture and it appears filled with earth. Its triple courses of thin bricks make it indubitably of Byzantine origin, however, and it must have formed part of a structure that the Genoese were later to extend.

Just beyond this tower to the N a flight of steps leads up to some modern concrete offices; although a highly insensitive disfigurement, this modern intervention does allow us to see at eye level a well-preserved marble plaque that was originally located over what must have been the main entrance to the Genoese extension, and tells us much about its origins. Its six compartments contain two Greek inscriptions flanking a single-headed eagle (an emblem used by the Genoese family of Doria), the Gattilusi escutcheon with the BBBB emblem, a double-headed eagle probably representing the Byzantine imperial family (although this was also adopted by the Giustiniani) and a Byzantine Palaiologue monogram. (For the significance of these arms, see p. 194). The two inscriptions record in grandiloquent terms that the "great, noble and patriotic Palamede Gattilusio built this tower from its foundations"...... The Gattilusi, although Genoese, were unusually well integrated into Greek life, marrying into the Byzantine imperial family, speaking Greek and living in the islands and a mainland base at Ainos through alliances with the Greeks in CP. It is of interest that Palamede Gattilusio should have had this inscription carved in Greek, as it must indicate that (to those of his local subjects who could read) he wished to point out how his actions were for their protection, as "the fortress will strike fear into his enemies." A 19th C German epigrapher recorded a date of 1433 on this inscription, so it would seem that this tower, next to the Byzantine defences, was Palamede's second contribution to the defences of the Khora. When the scholar, collector and merchant Cyriacus of Ancona visited the kastro in October 1444 he called it "the new inland town", and wrote interestingly in his account that John Laskaris (whose name must imply that he was a Greek) was governor there on behalf of Palamede Gattilusi, who lived mostly at Ainos; the castle must then have just been built, but was thus entrusted to a Greek governor. (On Thasos this position had been given to a member of the Grimaldi family.)

The main area enclosed by the surviving remains of the kastro can be entered further round, and you find there a polygonal area some 60 m. x 20 m. The kastro occupies the natural rocky outcrop and adapts to the shape of its higher points; craggy fallen remains now leave little idea of the original layout, but a tower further to the W carries another marble plaque with the single-headed eagle, the Gattilusi arms, the Palaiologue monogram and a short Latin inscription round the border stating that "Palamede Paleol[ogus] Gatilu[sius] lord of Aenos built this tower on 26th March 1433", a further date in Greek being unfortunately illegible. This suggests that the tower here was built a year before the much larger plaque was placed on the tower that you will have just passed. Beyond this almost the only survival is a cistern with its plaster lining still intact.

In spite of its incomplete state this is one of the most historically interesting sites connected with the Gattilusi, and should form part of any itinerary.

The large main church of the Khora was rebuilt in 1875 and can now offer nothing of medieval interest; its showpiece is a large modern reliquary which contains the skulls of the Five Martyrs of Thrace, who met their deaths in 1835, and are depicted in national costume in an icon of that period.

Palaiopoli   Παλαιόπολι

Parts of four medieval towers.* (See Pl. 33).

There are two separately fenced sites here; the main classical 'Sanctuary of the Great Gods' is the prime tourist attraction (open 9.00-15.00, closed Mondays, entry charge).

The visitor arrives initially at the highly interesting and impressive classical excavation. The Museum is reached first (separate entry charge), and is naturally mainly devoted to the classical finds of the site, but there are some silver and copper Byzantine coins, a number of fragments of Byzantine pottery and some minor Byzantine bronze artefacts, a balance and some weights. A relief fragment of classical sculpture of dancing girls, displayed here, was seen by Cyriacus of Ancona on one of the Gattilusi towers when he came here in 1444 (see below).

The great majority of the massive excavated ruins that cover the slopes either side of a deep gulley at the main site here are classical (7th C BC to 1st C AD), with only one survival from the medieval period at the outer NW sector; this appears to be the base of a square tower built partly of classical marble spolia and rising now to some 2.5 m. Archaeologists could not identify it, and it is still sometimes given the title of the *Ruinenviereck*, or 'the rectangular ruin'; given the presence nearby of three other medieval towers it seems more than likely that this is the base of a fourth, which was either unfinished and abandoned as being inappropriately located, or later dismantled.

For medievalists the chief interest is NE from the main site at a separate fenced area, where three further towers survive to varying extent. They can easily be seen from the road running beside the sea below, but can best be visited from the level of the Sanctuary by following an easy goat-track through ilex oaks for about 1 km. beyond the Sanctuary site; the gate here should be unlocked. The towers are grouped with two close together, linked by a low wall, and with a third some 30 m. away downhill towards the sea; of the three one is probably 90% still present, one some 9 m. away 30% and the third 20%, and will be referred to here as A, B and C. It is possible that C was the earliest, and was then superseded by A and B; A is the largest with a base measuring 10m. x 12 m., and the other two 6m. x 7m. A dilapidated low wall links A and B, but seems never to have been taken to any height, and one may speculate on its function. None of the towers have entrances at ground level, and must have been entered via a ladder through an opening some 5 m. up (although the ground may have fallen away somewhat); a cistern with plaster lining is close to A, but does not seem to have been defended. The interiors are now empty, and each story must have had wooden flooring and linking stairs or fixed ladders.

They are always referred to as the Gattilusi towers, and we know from the account of Cyriacus of Ancona of 1444, mentioned above, that Palamede Gattilusio was indeed the builder of this *turris*; the traveller remarked that he found a number of inscriptions in the tower with both Greek and Latin writing, and it is known that the Genoese lord "loved greatly to hear learned discussions". You may see how the builders have indeed made use of classical carved marble spolia at several places, but the point of greatest structural interest here relates to the corbels for machicolation (or *machicoulisses*) at the summit of A; while the small corbelled projecting vent on the SE side was probably a latrine, the corbels running round all four sides of the summit are still in place but now have nothing to support. It seems possible that there may have been wooden machicolation as was usual in N Europe, but which the Crusaders had begun to make of stone. Which ever was the case here the model is likely to have been the new fortifications at Pera, where the Genoese had recently renewed the walls of their quarter on the other side of the Golden Horn from CP; nothing now survives of these, however, so the visitor with binoculars may wish to speculate on the evidence here, and at the Pyrgos Fonia (see below).

At the foot of the steep hillside below the towers the ground plan of what must have been a Byzantine church can be seen; this may have been the original location of a church dedicated to Agia Paraskeve that was later replaced by the building beside the road some 300 m. to the W. There is still a major annual commemoration of this saint on 26th July, which neither the historical importance of the saint nor the scale of the present church fully explains.

What was the function of these towers? They could not have sheltered any substantial numbers, but were still constructed to withstand a minor assault, and (as always) the entrance door is several metres above ground level; the usual explanation of a base providing warning of attack from pirates or other hostile forces seems again to be the most probable one. The Kastro at Khora is directly S of here, and is out of sight behind the high ridge that separates the two fortifications, but a minor outpost on the ridge could have relayed a sun or smoke signal; alternatively, a messenger despatched on foot could reach Khora in under 90 minutes, which is today's walking time.

Be sure to allow an extra hour or so for extending your visit of the Sanctuary to include these impressive towers.

Pyrgos Fonia   Πύργος Φωνιά

Genoese tower. Unenclosed.
Reached from the coast road some 11 km. E of Palaiopoli; stop at the small bridge and follow the stream through old plane trees for some 200 m.

Built mainly of sea-worn local stone to a square ground-plan, the tower faces NE towards the sea, only 30 m. away. It is still some 13 m. high, and may have lost about a metre at its summit; again, there is no escutcheon or inscription, but the assumption must be that it is another survival of the Gattilusi presence on the island. Several points of interest emerge here. As in tower A at Palaiopoli one of its features is the presence of corbelling close to the summit of the NE and SE faces; unlike there, however, there is a continuous recess in the stonework some 2.5 m. from the top which could have accommodated the woodwork for a machicolation, and on the SE face some timber is still embedded horizontally in this channel (see the entry on the Palaiopoli towers, above). Again, the entry is some 3.5 m. above ground level, but here a piece of curved marble spolia has been re-used to form a lintel. A further difference here concerns the internal structure; although it cannot be entered, the stonework has fallen away at two points to reveal how quite high up the builders incorporated quite sophisticated internal brick spiral staircases. Even from outside, the interior masonry, combining ashlar and triple courses of brick, can be seen to be relatively elaborate.

The isolation of this tower is hard to explain. There would have been at least one more needed close to the headland of Kariotes for a visual signal to be relayed back to the towers at Palaiopoli; perhaps its remains still await discovery. The enthusiast for medieval fortifications will find plenty of interest in these survivals from the Gattilusi period.

SANTORINI now often called: THIRA Σαντορίνη or: Θήρα

Med: Santa Erini, Sant' Herini.
Island group: Cyclades (S). (*Nomos:* Cyclades).

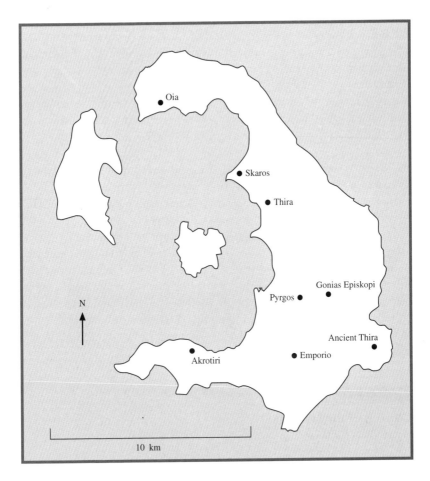

T rue to the usual priorities of their time, none of the medieval historians or writers who mention this island comment on what is to the modern eye its most memorably grand and impressive feature: its volcanic origins which gave it its unique harbour, formed when its crater blew out in prehistoric times, and now circled by towering cliffs full of richly coloured minerals. Numerous eruptions of the volcano have been recorded, with those in 727 and 1457 being notable (the former caused, it was alleged, by divine displeasure at the recent iconoclast edicts of the emperor), and the most recent in 1956.

While Thira is its classical name, for most of the medieval period it was called after a late 3rd C saint named Irene who was exiled here under Diocletian, and who died on the island in 304. Like many of the islands that were not mentioned in the *Partitio Romaniae* of 1204, it was taken over and held from 1207 by an Italian family, in this case the Barozzi, originally from Bologna, as a fief of the Duke of Naxos; one of the four suffragan bishops appointed by the Latin archbishop of Naxos was allocated to Santorini. The Barozzi remained as lords of Santorini until driven out in 1276 when so many islands were recovered for the Byzantines; in the treaty of 1303 between the Greek emperor and the Venetians, which ended the seven years' war with the emperor Andronikos II, the Barozzi were able to recover their lordship of Santorini, but then held it as suzerains of Venice, not of the Duchy of Naxos.

When Nicolo Sanudo succeeded to the dukedom in Naxos he cast covetous eyes on the relatively rich island of the Barozzi, and after extracting an oath of allegiance, in 1335 actually occupied the island himself. The next year he awarded the fortress on Akrotiri to the Gozzadini, but retained overall lordship. It continued to be acknowledged as belonging to Venice in the 1419 treaty between the Venetians and the sultan, as well as in that of 1446. Only in 1566, with much of the Archipelago, did Santorini come under final Turkish occupation, but somehow the Bolognese family of the Gozzadini continued to be able to live on here into the 17th C, perhaps being too unimportant to be ejected. There continues to be a substantial RC element in the population into modern times.

Gonias Episkopi
Γώνιας Επισκόπη

Church of the Panagia★★.
Open daily 9.00-17.00.
Well signed and easily found near the centre of the island, and below the mountain of Profitis Elias.

Dating from before the Fourth Crusade and all the subsequent political activity, this 11th C Byzantine church is undoubtedly the most interesting, complete and authentic of the medieval survivals on the island.

An inscription beside a portrait over the S door of the narthex, recorded in the 18th C, announced that (like the monastery of St John on Patmos) this was a foundation of the emperor Alexios I Komnenos

(1081-1118); while not proven, this could indeed be true. The name implies that it was the seat of a bishop, and the location of the island may mean that the imperial interest in the foundation was linked to political intentions. Its plan is unusual, and this is partly explained by the 12th C building replacing an EC basilica; this would have had a six-bay nave, and it is probable that the two columns which now support the vault in the bema were originally from the ten columns down the nave of the EC building. The 12th C builders retained the earlier apse and synthronon, with the two lateral chapels; while the naos was given some of the characteristics of a conventional domed, inscribed-cross design, the W sector was widened by the addition of two lateral barrel-vaulted chambers; this width is retained in the narthex, which thus has five bays, although only two openings into the naos.

Besides the survivals from the EC basilica, numerous items of classical spolia have been re-used inside as well as outside, and both the W columns supporting the dome actually rest on pagan marble altars. You will find considerable areas of the original 12th C fresco scheme still in place. The unconventional interior layout will have called for an unusual distribution of the normal scenes; most complete are those in the SW bay of the naos, where the scenes of the Anastasis and (on the S wall) of the Koimisis contain some the best preserved areas in the church, with noticeably fine painting in the apostles' heads, and an early version of the Virgin Blachernitissa with a striking image of the youthful Christ. A lively figure of Salome forms part of the scene of the Feast of Herod, occupying part of the tunnel vault leading to the S bay, and the long sleeves of her dress may represent a typical dancer's costume of the period; this is part of a small group of scenes concerning the Forerunner. Among miracle scenes in the comparable vault on the N side are quite detailed representations of the Healing of the blind man and of the Centurion's son. The frescoes in the bema are more conventional, with half-length figures of bishops in the arch soffits. Very few island churches except some of those on Crete and Naxos can offer frescoes of comparable condition and quality.

But the most striking and genuinely unique feature here is the marble templon with its coloured patterning. Although a later wooden iconostasis now surmounts it, the brilliantly inventive designs cut into its marble stand out in startling relief. This has been achieved by cutting away from the white marble surface, allowing the pattern to stand out in white against the chiselled-out recessed areas which have been filled with a black and red compound derived from the two colours of volcanic rock on the island; these have been ground up and set in a strongly adhesive medium that might be resinous in origin. There may have been other examples of this technique on the island, or elsewhere, but the highly individual result would now seem to be unique to this church.

Allow time for a leisurely visit here; the layout of the building tends to conceal areas of interesting fresco or antique sculpture from too rapid a viewing.

Ancient Thira.
Extensive ruins enclosing chapel and ruins of 6th C church★★.
Fenced and gated; open daily 9.0-14.00, except Monday.
Signed up a steep, hairpinned road, some 5 km. from Kamari.

The extensive ancient site, occupying some 800 m. of the mountain S of Kamari, is primarily of classical interest, with the main development taking place in the last two centuries BC, under the Ptolemies. However, like so many sites, its continued occupation into the Christian era led to adaptation and new and identifiably Christian structures, besides being enclosed by a wall in the Byzantine period. The only complete building here is the first one that you will see on entering the excavation; on the site of a small EC basilica of the 4th/5th C, dedicated to the Archangel Michael, a double-nave chapel of Agios Stefanos has been built. Among spolia used in its construction are three thick columns dividing the two naves and moulded sections round both apse arches; absence of any decorative detail, combined with this re-use of old material makes it hard to date, but two tomb covers in the N wall have inscriptions which suggest an 8th / 9th C date.

Continuing SE along the main axis of Thira you will pass the immensely impressive remains of the S Agora and Stoa Basilike; due W of this up a turning beyond the Stoa, and close to the Sanctuary of Egyptian Deities, is the only other Byzantine survival so far recovered. It is the plan with some low walls still intact, of a small, single-apse church, probably of the 6th C and perhaps originally domed. It is possible that other church buildings will eventually be identified, as this was clearly a substantial and flourishing community for much of the medieval period.

Emporio   Εμπόριο

Classical temple converted into church of Agios Nikolaos Marmarinos ★.
Can easily be seen beside the road on the left, on entering the village from the NW. Locked, key in nearest house.

So little was done to this tiny 3rd C BC Temple of Thea Basilica when it became a church that it could be said not to be medieval at all, and is really still a classical building although dedicated to "the marble St Nicholas". The windowless cell of grey marble, 5m. square, is entered by a door in the SE wall, and a slight bulge in the NE wall is the only sign of an apse. Its ceiling is formed from massive marble beams and a small shrine faces the doorway opposite the door in the SE wall, but the interior wall and ceiling surfaces are still of the original marble.

It deserves a visit as being one of the very rare examples of a classical building remaining virtually unaltered when taken over for Christian use.

Four Kastra*.

Santorini was said in the 14th C to have four kastra, and it is probably the remains of these that we can still visit today as four medieval fortified sites, all spaced at intervals on high ground round or near the rim of the ancient volcano; they share sufficient characteristics in common to be most easily discussed in a single entry, although spread right across the island. All four are unenclosed and can easily be visited. Starting from the N they are:

1) **Oia**: the siting of this kastro high on the headland gives it an astounding outlook from due N continuing round to the SE, right across the crater and its islands; both Pyrgos and Skaros are visible, and nothing could enter the crater from the N without being seen from here. There is little more now than a modest fortified emplacement, but there are signs that outworks could well have been more extensive.

2) **Skaros (Imerovigli)**: on the headland just N of Thira, this now has the most diminished remains of the four kastra; it may have been the least strategically important of the chain, as the outlook is only S and W across the crater, which is already covered by the others.

3) **Pyrgos**: this appears to have been the largest, and may well have been adopted as the chief dwelling of the ruling family of the island. Winding alleys bring you to a small plateia and from this the medieval entrance gateway leads into the area that would have formed the kastro. Numerous churches still remain, and although none still have original interiors the ensemble conveys strongly the character of a family stronghold.

4) **Akrotiri**: the extent of the kastro here, entered from the W by a restored entrance tunnel, can still be clearly seen. The hill-top is crowned by two recent buildings, but the pathway of mortared lava up to it passes

semi-ruined barrel-vaulted chambers and a cistern with its plaster lining still in good condition. To the E is the nave of a substantial barrel-vaulted church with a fine limestone floor; the E end has collapsed but the fluted marble columns and other classical spolia suggest that this was a building of some grandeur. The presence of this quite sophisticated building must be due to the Bolognese family of Gozzadini, who were installed here from 1336, and who still managed to live on in this kastro in some style into the 17th C, perhaps too insignificant to be banished by the Turks. The outlook N and S from here was clearly originally intended to guard the S approach into the crater, and Skaros is visible, but higher ground to the W some 200 m. away means that it was not the highest point in the locality.

All four of these kastra share a number of characteristics; all are built in the same technique of rough undressed lava held in mortar; their scale is comparable, and although that at Pyrgos was almost certainly the largest, and so is the most probable home of the ruling family, they could never have been intended to shelter large numbers of the population; that at Akrotiri has perhaps most of its original forms left, and was probably the last to be abandoned by its Italian inmates. The homogeneity of type and building system argues for their being initially the product of a single planned campaign, and there seems good reason to regard them as being the product of the presence of the Barozzi family, lords of the island in the 14th C. When Nicolo Sanudo occupied the island in 1335 the Gozzadini remained in the castle at Akrotiri, so at that point it is probable that the system was already built. Their modest size and defences mean that none would have remained long impregnable from a sustained siege, and their siting strongly suggests that their primary function must have been to provide a lookout system to warn of approaching danger, with the capacity to pass on information to other kastra in the system. For this, the castles at Oia and Akrotiri must have been the most important, being able to watch the main access points to the crater/harbour.

A minor Italian family associated with Santorini for many years in the 16th C was the D'Argenta, who claimed in 1577 that there were then five castles on the island, of which they owned one; this suggests that a fifth may have been present which had views of the E coast (unguarded by the four above); if this was the case it has not survived, but could have been in or near the site of Ancient Thera, with its sweeping panorama E towards Anafi and N towards Monolithos.

SERIFOS

Σέριφος

Med: Serfento, Serfeno.
Island group: Cyclades (W). (*Nomos*: Cyclades).

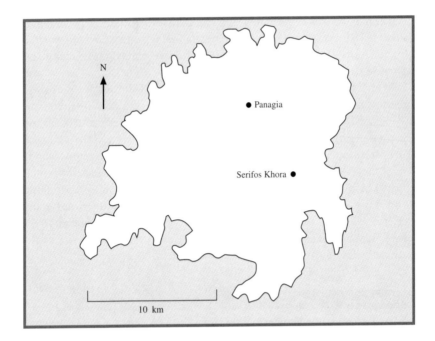

One of the smaller of the Cyclades, and lying to the W of the main grouping, the rocky inland terrain of Serifos, and its more isolated location, meant that it was not as desireable as some of the islands to the E; its only wealth was in the form of minerals, with iron ore being mined here into recent times. Not mentioned by medieval historians, and omitted from the lists of islands in the Partition of 1204, Serifos was not included among the eleven islands of the original duchy of Naxos, and it was left to Andrea and Jeremia Ghisi, another Venetian family, to acquire control of it, helped by fellow Venetians, Domenico Michiel and Pietro Giustiniani. During these years the Latin bishop on Serifos was appointed as a suffragan by the archbishop of Athens.

The Veronese admiral Licario, acting for the Byzantine emperor, attacked and captured Serifos and Sifnos in 1276, and they returned to Greek rule for 20 years until the counter-attack of the years following 1296. In the 1303 treaty between Venice and the Byzantines, Serifos was among the five islands acknowledged as belonging to the Serene Republic, by whom they were then directly governed. Under this regime a new family, the Bragadini, appeared on the island, to be largely supplanted later in the 14th C by the first Venetian to operate the iron mines commercially, Ermolao Minotto. The comparative wealth that this generated made Serifos a target for more raids, and in 1393 a determined robbery of leading islanders was attempted by a Venetian called Adoldo, helped by Cretan mercenaries; when they would not tell him where their money was concealed he had them hurled from the castle on to the rocks below.

In the 1419 treaty between the Venetians and the sultan, Serifos is specified as belonging to Venice, but c.1420 Buondelmonti found no evidence of the material well-being of 30-40 years earlier, with all the islanders living in constant fear of attack and dispossession by pirates or Turks. The extent to which Venice could protect any of the many islands which then owed the Republic direct allegiance is dubious, and although from 1494 the entire archipelago was nominally under her direct control, it was still the task of the leading local families to organise any defence. The last decades of degenerating Western rule ended in 1537, when Serifos became one of the many islands that fell to the Turks before the attacks of Khaireddin Barbarossa.

Khora. Kastro

Ruins of Venetian castle.* Unenclosed.
You can reach the summit of Khora by a choice of routes through the maze of steep alleys; provided you are climbing you will reach it from one of two access points.

The summit, which was the original acropolis of the island, was at one time completely occupied by the medieval castle, but there is now very little of its fabric left; just below the summit houses crowd in and the area that would have been enclosed by the castle now has three churches within it, with a fourth on the highest point, and only some traces of defensive walling with attractive quoins can still be seen. The building must have been in place from early in the Venetian occupation of the 13th C, but must have been altered over the years. It is possible to speculate on the point at which the Venetian Adoldo threw down the islanders who would not reveal where their money was kept. The climb here is worth it for the orientation and outlook, but sadly has little material of the medieval period to offer.

Panagia   Παναγία

Church of the Koimisis (formerly Xilos Panagia).★★
Locked; key held in the shop across the street to the NE.
The church is easily seen from the road above this village in its peaceful and quite fertile valley, and cannot be missed as you reach the small plateia at the end of the village street.

This modestly sized but perfect little building represents a relatively rare survival in the islands: a 10th C domed, inscribed cross church that has not suffered any significant alteration. It has three apses, a high cross vault and the cupola is carried on piers, while a further point of interest is provided by two fine marble columns still standing outside the W door; these must indicate that there was at one time a porch here. (This suggests that the later addition of a narthex, so frequently found, may have been developed as an enclosed substitute for an open porch). When a wooden iconostasis was installed here (probably in the 17th C) the finely carved marble templon was dismantled, and substantial parts of it can still be seen stacked and neglected outside the N wall.

Inside there are still quite extensive remains of frescoes, although no complete scenes; where fully visible they appear to date from the 12th C. The most complete and best preserved are in the diaconicon (light switch on the right behind the door), where three standing female saints occupy the N side of the vault. There is a synthronon in the main apse and more frescoes of the usual bishops, who here approach the small marble throne from either side; this suggests that the church here may at one time have been the home of the island's Orthodox bishop. See also the wall tomb in the S aisle with good frescoes of Abraham and Lazarus, but unfortunately no inscription still visible. Finally, note the carved marble slab acting as a loosely placed step into the bema; is this another part of the old templon?

Be sure to take your time here, as (outside Naxos) the Cyclades now offer very few churches with so little alteration.

If you have reached Panagia, the **Moní Taxiarkhon** (Μονί Ταξιάρχων) – (usual monastic hours) some 3 km. beyond has an attractive site, and its tree-shaded courtyard repays the short further distance. It has been said to have a foundation date of c.1500, but there is now nothing to be seen which is earlier than the plaque of the two-headed eagle in the floor of the katholikon which is dated 1690. The katholikon was restored in 1719 and 1973-83, and its Russian brass candlesticks and Egyptian silver lamp indicate international patronage of an earlier age.

SIFNOS

Σίφνος

Med: Sifano, Sifanto, Siffono, Serphanto, Serpho.
Island Group: Cyclades. (*Nomos*: Cyclades.)

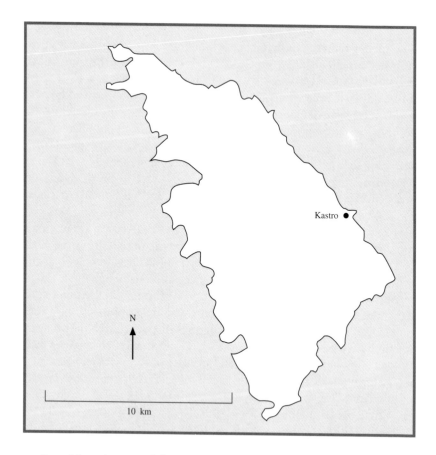

Although one of the closest islands to the central group of the Cyclades, Sifnos is not mentioned by any of the medieval historians of the Aegean area, and was omitted from the lists of islands in the famous Deed of Partition of 1204. Like other islands of the Cyclades, it was in fact by the personal efforts of Marco Sanudo and, (as he would have been the first to point out) at his expense, that Sifnos was first to come under W rule as one of the Duchy of the Archipelago. It was also in company with other islands of the Cyclades that in 1262 it was recovered by the new Greek emperor just re-installed in CP.

But the inherent weakness of the Byzantine power had begun to be felt, and a few years after 1300 Sifnos was the target of an annexation by a member of the Hospitaller order, called Januli (or John) da Corogna. Although Pitton de Tournefort, who was on the island c.1700, thought that he was told by the Sifniotes that Januli came from Bologna, it is far more probable that they told him his family came from La Coruña, in Spain, as the Frenchman goes on to say that he saw an octagonal column near the kastro gate with "MCCCLXV MI SLCE, Yandoly de Coronia" cut in it in "Gothic characters". He goes on to say that "we saw at the House of the Vicar of the Latin church the document by which Otuly de Corogna settled an Estate in 1462, for the benefit of the Church in the Castle", which gives his account some conviction. Januli left the Order of the Hospitallers and announced, to the anger both of the Sanudi who still regarded Sifnos as a property of the Dukes, and of the Grimani who were their vassals, that he was now lord of the island.

In spite of a relatively small power-base, the Corogna dynasty managed to survive in defiant isolation on Sifnos; when the Florentine priest Buondelmonti was here in c.1420 he remarked that the Corogna possessed a strong tower in a fine garden, but that there was a great preponderance of women in the population, and although they understood no Latin "would not relinquish the Catholic faith". In 1434 the Corogna asserted in a document that they were still there and proud "esse liberum dominium insule Siphani", but not long after this Januli gave his daughter Maria in marriage to Angelo Gozzadini, one of a family from Bologna. Lordship of the island was then transferred to the Gozzadini, who were to remain Lords of Sifnos and Kythnos until 1617; they became very Hellenised over the years, living, it was said, alla greca and without even the benefit of Latin clergy. The inhabitants were then reported to be happy and well-disposed, with many of the women living to be over 100.

Kastro.*** Ungated and permanently open.
The medieval history of the island has left it with an undoubted medieval showpiece: the unique survival of the Kastro. It must have been one of the Corogna lords who dictated the main forms of this fascinating survival. Although there is no doubt that it was initially planned and built as a well-defended centre of population, the term 'kastro' does not seem to be a completely appropriate term for it, as the same term is applied to structures with a far more military character that abound in the Cyclades. As one of the earliest, if not the first, of such concepts, it has a significant place in the history of urban development in the Aegean. The comparable kastro on Kimolos may well have inspired it, as traditionally founded by families from Sifnos, and the kastro on

Astypalia founded in the 15th C, must also owe something to Sifnos. There is now very much less evidence surviving from some of the later kastra such as those on Antiparos and Milos, but its much less military character is more reminiscent of the kastra on Astypalaia and Kimolos.

What you will find yourself entering is a complex of lanes and small houses, operating at various levels, and in plan forming an extended oval along the ridge of the cliff-top, and looking across the straits to the islet of Polyaigos; one could imagine a population of perhaps 2000 souls living a rather crowded existence here. There are a number of small churches, although all of later foundation, and the main one of the Panagia is dated 1635. The quality of existence that its inhabitants still maintain must be relatively authentic, with all vehicles successfully excluded and even building materials carried only on donkeys. The site has clearly been populated from early times and there are at least three large, if damaged, Roman sarcophagi in the narrow streets. The small **Museum** is well worth a visit, and among its mainly classical Greek and Roman collection there is a display of over 80 Byzantine coins, including twelve gold hyperpera.

The only area that appears still largely untouched is at the NW end of the complex, where the walls survive of what must have been the palace of Januli da Corogna; the local stone blocks are set off by some white marble quoins, and the scale of building is different from anything else within the walls. From earlier this century there is a report that this building (sometimes referred to rather grandly as a "chancery") carried a Latin inscription with the date of 1374 and mentioning the da Corogna family, but there is no trace of this now. Immediately opposite this is a derelict church which, although locked, can be seen to be of W design, with pointed interior vaulting and arches.

Allow time for a leisurely visit to this largely unique survival.

SIKINOS Σίκινος

Island group: Cyclades (SW). (*Nomos*: Cyclades).

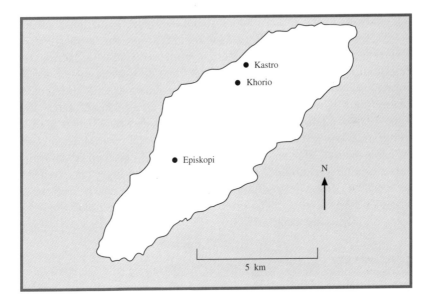

This little, rocky island only enters historical knowledge with the coming of the Fourth Crusade in 1204, although even then it is not mentioned in the subsequent *Partitio Romaniae*; however, by 1207 it had been swept into the new Duchy of Naxos of Marco Sanudo. It has some fertile areas which, combined with no very effective defences, made it quite an easy and attractive prey to the Veronese admiral Licario who recovered it for the Byzantine emperor in 1276. Its position towards the outer fringe of the Cyclades subsequently left it vulnerable to attack from pirates, and by the 15th C it had been abandoned. With much of the Archipelago it came fully under Turkish control in 1566.

The only road runs up from the harbour at Alopronia some 3 km. to the main focus of the population located in two villages which face each other across a saddle of land some 400 m. apart. The NW one of these is called Khorio, and although it has in the past been the more dominant, it is now less populous and exhibits more symptoms of decline. Even so, it has five churches, of which two are double-nave and may have medieval origins, although overlaid by later modernisation.

The other village is (rather misleadingly) called Kastro. There are traces of defensive building surviving, but these are now so insignificant that anyone seeking a fortified castle here will be disappointed. The village now houses the main services and is generally more active, and the name of Kastro may possibly derive from the fortified **monastery of the Zoödokhos Pigi*** which dominates the village to the SE. You can reach it by following a track rising through the village, sometimes named as the Odos Zoödokhos Pigi. The outlook from the monastery is spectacular, with the sea visible on both sides looking across to Folegandros to the SW and Ios to NW. The door in its high walls is normally kept locked, but it is opened each evening about 6 p.m. by the one nun now left, who lives in the village. The area enclosed (externally some 40 m. x 40 m.) is largely filled by the domed, whitewashed church within this rather forbidding enceinte; it is well maintained and is probably 16th C, but has nothing very special to offer in its interior. Some of the surrounding monastic buildings, however, may well be medieval; the simple forms of the trapeza, for example, will be authentic, although it has recently been given a concrete floor and had windows opened in the outer wall to the SE.

Episkopi   Επισκοπή

Church converted from classical building**.
Unsigned and open. (See Pl. 14).
From Khora take a stony mule-track (unsigned) that leaves the sea to your right as you follow it due W for about 1¹/₂ hours or 8 km.; the landscape is magnificent, with terraces dropping steeply to the sea some 200 m. below.

Eventually you will be rewarded with the sight of this uniquely attractive, if enigmatic, building. Now a church dedicated to the Koimisis Theotokou it is easily the most interesting sight on the island. Its almost cube-shaped outline is distinguished initially only by an apse, the top of a cupola and the empty arches of its small belfry, and to arrive at this fascinating edifice in its remote setting, with just a superbly empty mountainous surround, provides a delighted shock.

Its origins have been much debated, but the most convincing explanation is that we are looking at what was originally some form of classical tomb-temple (or *heroön*) that was converted to a church by the addition of an apse and cupola. It must have initially been a pagan building, but cannot have been of conventional temple form, and a date of 2nd / 3rd C AD is likely for this late classical building type. Its conversion to Christian use probably took place at some time from the 7th to 9th C, but before or after this is still possible. In the 1880's

Theodore Bent was told that it had been a temple of Pythian Apollo, and that within living memory the monks had taken refuge from attack by pirates behind the 'battlements' that fence in the roof; he was even shown the remains of a kitchen remaining up there.

Before entering it, we can confirm the classical elements such as the continuous dog-tooth ornament round the top of the original enclosing wall (extended upwards by the further dry stone walling) and the pair of columns with Doric caps either side of the door. The appearance of the W wall (8 m. wide) suggests that it may have been inserted between the N and S walls (12 m.), filling in what had been an open arcade supported by these columns; the orientation is very precisely E / W. Inside, its unstable condition has made it necessary to support the narthex, apse and two bays with scaffolding, but even so the internal space is easily read. A very high, narrow narthex is roofed by huge slabs of stone, which must survive from the original classical structure in which they would have been the roof of the portico, and the naos has the shallowest of bays to N and S – only one m. deep; the cupola is supported over this square space. There is no surviving decoration. Outside again, the small barrel-vaulted chamber to the NW has fresco remains inside that may be 15th C, and there are fragments of other monastic buildings, now destroyed. A deep cistern survives in front of the W door.

Allow time for a leisurely visit to this unique and beautifully sited building, and feel free to speculate on its past. Most of the questions it asks the viewer still await a secure answer.

SKIATHOS   Σκίαθος

Med: Schiatus.
Island group: N Sporades. (*Nomos*: Magnesia).

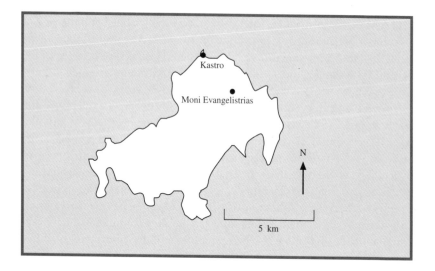

T his small, mountainous and wooded island is the closest of the
N Sporades to the coast of Thessaly and the Pelion peninsula.
It only enters medieval history after the Fourth Crusade of
1204, when, with most of the other Aegean islands, its name does not
appear in the Deed of Partition, but it became the object of the private
enterprise of the brothers Andrea and Geremia Ghisi. They had already
laid claim to Tinos and Mykonos, and then extended their territory to
include not just Skiathos but Skopelos and Skyros as well; when
Geremia Ghisi died in 1251 he had passed most of his life as the first
self-styled Lord of Skiathos. The campaign of the Veronese admiral
Licario on behalf of the Byzantine emperor in 1276 brought both
Skiathos and Skyros back into Greek hands; it was to remain under
Byzantine control for almost two centuries until, in 1454, the inhabitants
decided that they preferred the protection of Venice to that of the
Genoese or the Turks; accordingly, from 1455 the Venetian Senate began
sending a noble to govern each of the N Sporades islands of Skyros,
Skiathos and Skopelos as rector.

The islands continued to be ruled in this way until the campaigns of
Khaireddin Barbarossa in 1537 and 1538. In the second of these he laid

siege to the three island strongholds; in the case of Skiathos some of the islanders, who had retreated to the Kastro at the N tip of the island (see below), decided that their best course was to capitulate. Their Venetian rector, Memmo, who was organising the defence of the stronghold, and had received a wound early in the action, was treacherously killed by one of the Greeks he was trying to defend, and then ropes were let down to haul the Turks up into the Kastro. The sense of honour that ran through the violent nature of Barbarossa left him so incensed at such an act of treachery that he had the individual who had committed the murder beheaded, but still carried off all the inhabitants into slavery, leaving the island completely uninhabited. It was only in the next century that the population began to drift back, and then it was entirely domiciled for safety within the medieval kastro, which would remain the focus of the island's population into the 19th C.

The result of long periods of depopulation has meant that the principal entity surviving from the medieval period is the Kastro, but the comparatively late useage here has overlaid much of the authentic medieval origins that would have been here.

Kastro.***
Ruined fortified walls enclosing three churches and nine chapels, with eight more chapels outside the walls. The whole locality is open and ungated, and individual buildings usually unlocked.

This evocative and daringly sited group of buildings at the N tip of the island represents its principal medieval showpiece; it can either be approached by sea, landing at the beach below the Kastro and walking up, or by land; if you decide on the former, you will be able to visualise the conditions under which Barbarossa's attack was launched in 1538, but if the latter, allow time for at least the last 2 km. to be covered on foot.

The complex of buildings here is the oldest inhabited area of the island and in the medieval period was known as Palaiokastro, implying a yet earlier presence. In several ways it brings to mind the Palaiokhora settlements that survive on Kythera or Aigina. The fortified walling is still partly present although fragmentary, and (if arriving by land) you enter the rocky enclosed area at its highest point through the original defensive gateway; it may well have been in this vicinity that Geremia Ghisi had lived out his many years as lord of the island. Until the liberation of the island from the Turkokratia in 1829 this was its main town and the focus of the population; it was then abandoned and has only since been receiving attention in relatively recent times.

The buildings within this enclosure consist now mainly of three churches and nine chapels in varying stages of restoration; some have had modern decorative ceramic pieces inserted on their exterior walls. The principal survival among them is the simple, medium-sized hall church known as the Church of Christ; its foundation may date from not long before the attack of 1538, although the extensive frescoes on its walls are 18th C. The gilded iconostasis is also 18th C, and only the Passion cycle, partly still to be seen on the S wall, may perpetuate an earlier scheme. None of the other churches have as much to offer in decorative interest, although a leisurely survey of the area is essential to gain an idea of the layout of what is in effect still a medieval village. There is just one small and enigmatic building built on a square plan and roofed with a fine brick cupola which invites speculative examination. On the map of the site displayed in the Church of Christ it is said to be a mosque; this may have been its function during the Turkokratia, but it is just possible that it was adapted to this function from a previous Christian use. In any case this is the only dome to be found within the Kastro complex, even if it does lack a drum.

The attraction and interest of the Kastro means that it deserves a leisurely visit, offering as it does a range of features rarely found united in one locality: its extraordinary siting, perched on the cliff above the tiny bay; its status as a medieval stronghold that was abandoned almost two centuries ago, and so has not suffered from modern depredations; the fact that its layout must be entirely unaltered, and so faithfully maintains a medieval village concept; and the proportion of church buildings to secular housing which is also striking, but must be regarded as typical; all these conspire to make a visit here a rewarding and memorable experience, for which at least half a day should be allowed.

Moní Evangelistrias   Μονή Ευαγγελίστριας

Monastery, in use.*
(Open 8.00-12.00 and 16.00-20.00).
Beside the road 4 km. due N of Skiathos; easily seen.

The construction of this monastery dedicated to The Annunciation (the last of several on the island that is still in use), now in a good state of preservation, is said to have taken place between 1794 and 1806; while this may well be true of the surrounding monastic buildings such as the trapeza, the appearance of the katholikon makes it very likely that it ante-dates them, and could well be of late 15th / 16th C date. Its construction is in general not what would be expected of quite a remotely sited building in the last years of the Turkokratia, being of some sophistication and high quality workmanship. The exterior now has no rendering, and a cross formed in the brickwork of the E wall suggests that this was always the case. The scale of the octagonal drum and dome is impressive, and a small blind semi-dome emphasises the outer narthex. Inside, there is again no rendering except in the apse, where the frescoes are 18th C; at any period it would have been standard practice for frescoes to cover the whole interior, and it must be assumed that this was not an exception, but that all the rest are now destroyed. Again, the date of the apse frescoes suggests that a late 18th C rebuilding of the monastic ensemble took place at which stage this earlier church building was integrated into the scheme and received its apse paintings. The high quality of the building technique here is again very evident in the careful brickwork exposed inside the lateral semi-domes.

The impressive katholikon here in its peaceful setting (the only monastery still functioning on the island) makes this a rewarding and interesting objective.

SKOPELOS

Σκόπελος

Med: Scopulus.
Island group: N. Sporades. (*Nomos:* Magnesia.)

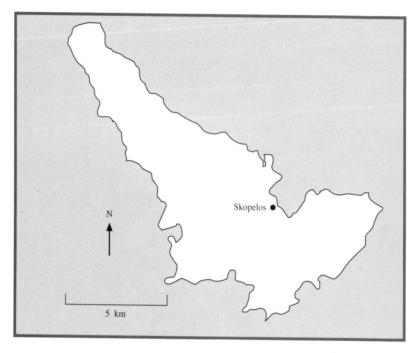

Skopelos was not mentioned among the islands listed in the Partition Treaty of 1204, and so was left open to the two members of the Venetian Ghisi family, Andrea and Geremia, already Lords of Tinos and Mykonos, to take it over in a spirit of private enterprise. In the treaty of 1403 the Turks acknowledged that Skopelos, with Skiathos and Skyros, were all held by Venice, although this might not have been strictly true. Later in the century the islanders held out in some areas against the Veronese adventurer Licario, who had embarked on a recovery (on behalf of the Greek emperor) of several of the Greek islands probably in 1276, but he knew that Skopelos lacked water supplies, and his blockade of it was successful; the Ghisi were sent back in chains to CP. Nevertheless it was not to be until 1540 that the island was finally occupied by the Ottoman power.

For a medievalist this is in some ways a rather frustrating island, although the rewards are potentially quite substantial. The medieval survivals are centred on the S end of the island; Glossa, in the N, although a fine site, now retains nothing of the medieval or Venetian survivals earlier reported there. The major part of the island, between Glossa and Skopelos town, offers a number of later churches among well-watered olive and fruit groves, but otherwise the enthusiast must dwell on the fine position of Glossa itself and the superb pine-clad landscape of the coast road. Skopelos town does however retain a greater number of Byzantine churches than almost any other of the smaller islands, but of the numerous monasteries on the island, the only two to contain buildings that date to before the 17th C are difficult to visit: one (Moní Episkopí) is privately owned and the other (Moní Taxiarchon) is so remote that a guide is adviseable. Nevertheless, the fact that the buildings of Skopelos remain so relatively unexplored even in recent years means that you may well discover more than is given here.

Skopelos town   Χώρα Σκόπελου

1) Kastro. * Unenclosed.

The summit of the kastro built here by the Ghisi family in a dominant position overlooking the harbour from the W has now been partly taken over by a taverna and some small houses; the enceinte is still partially preserved, and this, with a clear indication of the rocky outcrop on which it was sited, gives a clue to its general scale, which must always have been quite modest. The Ghisi were a proud family, but did not regard this island as one of their main strongholds, and their kastro seems not to have been extensive or well supplied; certainly the lack of an internal water supply in the siege of c.1276 was crucial.

Much better preserved are a group of churches focussed in the area immediately to the E and S below the kastro; they are all whitewashed and in good repair, are roofed in the local grey-green schist (an absence of brick suggests that no clay was available on the island). Although now lacking interior frescoes and with only later icons (though some of these are of quite high quality), they present an unusually complete and attractive sequence of small to medium sized Byzantine island churches which have not received the recognition that they deserve; collectively, they would earn a ** entry. The official archaeological reports do not usually offer a date at all; they may in general be later than they seem, but this is still an undecided area. All are locked when not in use, but the key is in each case kept in a nearby house, so just ask around; most are open daily as a matter of course.

2) Church of the Panagitsa tou Pyrgou.★

This domed church has one of the more spectacular settings overlooking the harbour, and although it may have been enlarged on more than one occasion (the narthex is certainly later), its core building on a domed, inscribed cross plan is probably 14th / 15th C. The dedication *tou pyrgou* (of the tower) suggests that there was once a lighthouse on this small headland.

3) Agios Antonios.★

This has the distinction of being almost certainly the oldest church in Skopelos, as well as the most prominent, and the most spectacularly sited, occupying a rocky platform below the kastro and overlooking the harbour. However, it has the least architectural interest of the group given here, being of the simplest hall form, and with no internal decoration.

4) Agios Athanasios tou Kastrou.★

The only church within the walls of the old kastro, this is one of the simplest in design, being a modest in scale and single-nave in plan; in spite of its size, its location within the kastro suggests some early importance, and it is thought to have been the original metropolis of Skopelos before the bishop moved down to the Moní Episkopi (see below).

5) Agios Giorgios Kyratsos.★

An imposing dome with a tall, blind-arcaded drum marks out this church; it is one of the more substantial of this group, and although the icons in its iconostasis are 16th to 18th C in date, the building itself appears to be 14th C.

6) Church of Christ.★

This is the largest of the churches here, and is in effect a domed basilica, with a short, three-bay nave lined by six columns; its status as perhaps the most central and frequented of the group is suggested by an impressive roofed arcade, with bench seating, extending along the exterior of the S wall. There is also a gallery entered from street level as well as quite a late parekklision and belfry. The periods involved in its building are difficult to establish, but may run from the 15th to 19th C.

7) Church of the Evangelismos tou Theotokou (Annunciation).★

Another superbly sited church looking out over the harbour; its plan of a domed, inscribed cross is probably 15th C, and the icons on its carved wooden iconostasis are 16th to 17th C.

8) Church of the Koimisis.*
One of the larger of the group, with a cupola supported on a tall, octagonal drum, this is said to be a 17th C foundation, but could well be somewhat earlier.

9) Church of the Zoödokhos Pigi (Life-giving Fountain).*
This small, single-chamber domeless church is probably 15th C, and has two good 18th C icons, one being of the subject of its dedication.

The broad and rocky headland opposite Khora and the harbour, and rising steeply to form the E arm of the bay, is the home of several convents and monasteries; they are linked by quite reasonable dirt roads, and with one exception can all be visited. Like others to the S and W of Khora they are 17th and 18th C foundations and offer the same architectural experience – a picturesque setting for a conventional series of post-medieval monastic buildings; some, such as the **Moní Agia Barbara** (with an external inscription giving its foundation date of 1697) are quite fortress-like. The exception here is the **Moní Taxiarkhos**, which is said to enclose some earlier building, but this is now disused and closed; its inaccessibility is such (a guide is advised as it is sited away from the road system on the exposed E side of the Paloukhi headland) that it is not covered here.

The **Moní Episkopi,** ** however, is a different matter. This is beside the road on the right as you are leaving the town going E; it is identifiable from the exterior by the marble supports of a balcony that project from the wall high above the road.

The problem here is that the building (which is attached to a private house) has been privately owned since 1830; the present owner may allow you inside to view, but arrangements have to be made in advance. The site may well have been occupied by a classical temple, and was later replaced by a three-aisled EC basilica, which judging by a surviving cap was probably 5th / 6th C. The courtyard is now occupied by a simple, medium-sized, domeless 17th C hall-church, but built into the interior N wall a long marble inscription records that in 1078 a complete re-building occurred and its function changed to that of a monastery. Its name suggests that it either then served, or later became, a bishop's residence, and the outer wall of the E side of the complex may be connected with this. The present church occupies the site of the N aisle of the EC basilica, which must have been of considerable size; its construction incorporated various pieces of 11th C Byzantine architectural sculpture from the second church, but it is free of any interior painting and any recent restoration has been undertaken with great sensitivity to the interest of the site.

If you are able to negotiate a visit here you can be sure of an interesting and (in its way) unique experience.

SKYROS Σκύρος

Med: Schiro.
Island group: N Sporades. (*Nomos*: Euboea).

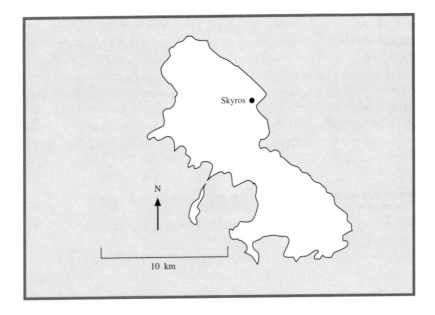

lthough frequently linked with Skiathos and Skopelos, the attractive and fertile island of Skyros lies some 65 km. from them to the SE, and at various times its history was separated from theirs; (in modern times it is governed from Euboea rather than from Magnesia). Not mentioned by Byzantine historians, Skyros enters medieval history when it is the only island of the N Sporades named in the Deed of Partition of 1204 as belonging, with the two other islands of Limnos to the N and Tinos to the S, to the new Latin emperor in CP. As in a number of other cases, the paper ownership of an island did not necessarily convey title, and after Marco Sanudo had established himself in the Duchy of Naxos by 1207, the Venetian brothers Andrea and Geremia Ghisi extended their own princedom beyond the islands of Mykonos and Tinos which they had already occupied (the latter also nominally belonging to the Latin emperor) to the Sporadic islands of Skyros, Skiathos and Skopelos.

In the sea-born campaign of 1276 of the Veronese leader Licario, who was acting for the new Byzantine emperor in CP, Skyros was brought back under Greek control. This had ceased before 1403, as in the treaty of that year betweeen Venice and the Turks Skyros, with Skopelos and Skiathos, was acknowledged to be held by Venice, but after 1453 the islanders here and in Skiathos and Skopelos were all desperate for a force that would give them some protection from the plague of pirates, and a Venetian admiral who had just occupied Aigina came N and was welcomed as their protector. Their only stipulations were that their traditional privileges would be preserved and that they could retain their own bishop; these wishes were granted, and from 1455 a Venetian noble served as rector on each of the three islands. At that time there were four castles on Skyros, but already (it was said) three of them were in ruins, so it was in the remaining one that still overlooks the Khora that the Venetian rectors became established; later, two were in residence and remained there, sent from Euboea, and governed the island until finally driven out by the Turks after Barbarossa's raid in 1538.

Skyros town / Khora

Kastro and ruins of Church of St George ('Episkopi').**
Open and unrestricted.

The kastro itself crowns the rocky summit very visibly above the town to the N, and cannot be missed. It can be reached on foot by negotiating the maze of steep alleys and stepped passageways up to the topmost part of the town. By car you reach it by taking the road downhill and looping left round the head of a small valley before climbing again; this approach, while less authentic, does allow you to get a far better view of the whole site from several angles.

The kastro enceinte encircles the whole of the summit of the rock on which it is built; in the S and SE sectors it is possible to see how the 13th C stonework has been laid on a few courses of earlier Hellenistic rectangular blocks. The natural strength of the site means that it must always have been the strong point and acropolis of the island. A lion in weathered white marble relief above the outer gateway of the kastro is quite unlike the usual Venetian device seen all over their empire, and may well be a re-used classical piece; as usual this will commemorate the long Venetian presence here from 1453 to 1538. After traversing the courtyard of a small later monastery inside this gateway, a tunnel some 30 m. long leads you directly into the area enclosed by the enceinte of the kastro. This is much more complete than is the case with most of the comparable fortifications in the Sporades, and within it at the S end of the area is a fine double-nave barrel-vaulted store room.

But by far the most interesting building is the ruined 9th C church at the N end of the complex; known by various dedications as St George of the Arab, St George of Skyros or simply as 'Episkopi' – 'the church of the bishop' – there seems no doubt that it was the official seat of the island's bishop, and so that is how we will refer to it. Its date is known from a long inscription on a marble member which must have formed part of the fabric and is still on the site, of which a translation reads: "In the year 895 in the reign of Leo [emperor as Leo VI 886-911] and Alexander [co-emperor 886-912] and in the time of Saba, metropolitan of Athens and of Saba bishop of this place." The church that you see here would originally have had a dome, but probably due to a partial collapse it was renovated perhaps during the Latin period and given the form of a basilica, roofed by barrel-vaulting.

In 1807 a further reconstruction divided the two lateral apses and made them separate entities. So what you will now see is virtually the entire E end of a triple-nave basilica of which the three apses still survive, as well as substantial parts of the N and S walls. Most of the W part has gone, but the three doorways are still visible. The main apse still has the seating of a synthronon as well as the marble columns which divided a tall, triple-arcaded window. The central light has been converted to a single throne, and intriguingly traces of fresco left here show that at one time the apse was plastered and a painting of the Communion of the apostles occupied the space, with (early last century) part of the text of the Eucharist still visible. There is also earlier painting visible in both the other old window niches.

The bishop of Skyros, who would have occupied the throne you see here, had been of unexpected importance, and after the Fourth Crusade had become one of the ten suffragans of the archbishop of Athens; he was the only bishop to be appointed to an island see. The ground level has risen substantially outside all three apses, and this may be the reason for the windows being filled in from below, and a number of marble fragments survive, besides the long inscription.

The kastro of Skyros would always be of interest as the chief medieval survival of the island's defences, but substantial remains of 9th C churches are extremely rarely found, and when there are some surviving fresco fragments as well the site will always be of ** status. The chief points of comparison are with Orkhomenos (Skripou) in Boeotia, of 873, and Gavrolimni (Etolia), but there is nothing quite comparable among any of the islands.

SYMI Σύμη

Med: Simia, Le Simie.
Island group: Dodecanese. (*Nomos*: Dodecanese).

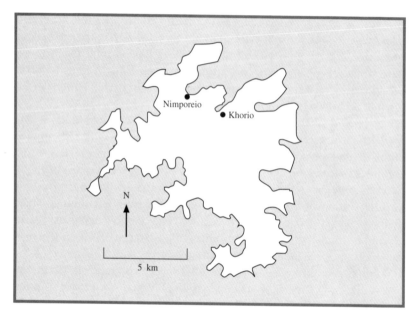

L
ike its neighbour Nisyros, the island of Symi goes unmentioned
by the earlier medieval historians, being passed over by the W
invaders in favour of the larger and richer islands. Again, it is
only the arrival of the Hospitallers on Rhodes that brings it into
documentary sources, as its position nestling under the S shore of the
long Knidos peninsula was too favourable for it to be ignored. It must
have been under their tutelage before the middle of the 14th C, as in
1351 the inhabitants made representations to the Order that they could
not afford to pay the *mortuaria* (a tax comparable to death duties); it is
probable that the Hospitallers were already in control by 1320, as on
Nisyros.

Reliance on the reports of later travellers produces a wide range of
responses to the island and its inhabitants, as, for instance, when a
pilgrim, Anselme Adorno, called here in 1470 he reported that the men
were so violent and bad-tempered that the Turks did not even want them
as slaves, and that in any case they were such good swimmers that even
if they were captured they could make good their escape from the

mainland by swimming the intervening channel. This facility in swimming was extended to diving for sponges, and the capacity to spend unusually long periods underwater was witnessed in the 1680's by Bernard Randolph, who saw a hole in a ship's hull repaired by divers working underwater on the outside of the ship. When canon Pietro Casola visited Symi on his way to Jerusalem in 1494 he was told that the air here was so good that "men live to be 110 or 120 years old". Boschini reported in the 17th C that there was made here "un vino pretioso", which was traded with other islands.

This lack of historical importance before the Knights is reflected in the surviving monuments; the single reported find of EC mosaics can now no longer be seen.

Symi town: Khorio.

Hospitaller castle.★★ Unenclosed.
Reached by foot from Egalio up a winding, stepped track of some 500 steps; a clearer overall view of the site can be had from the road leading S out of the town.

The castle remains are far from complete, but are sufficient to allow an estimate of the importance it eventually assumed for the operations of the Knights of Rhodes. The site must always have been the acropolis of the town, and the castle has a polygonal plan that follows the forms of the rocky summit. The first part of the castle that you will see is some Cyclopean walling adjoining the building of the Knights; here they had an entrance, with machicolation, that is now filled in. (This re-use by the Knights of classical fortifications was quite common, recurring on Alimnia, Khalki and Tilos.) When Christoforo Buondelmonti visited Symi c. 1418 he reported that a well-provisioned castle was there, and it had probably been well established and functioning by the mid 14th C. In 1457 Turkish forces under their young sultan, Mehmet II, attacked the castle here as part of his campaign of intended subjugation of the Aegean, but the defenders threw down large amounts of boiling oil and liquid pitch, of which the island produced a lot, and they had to withdraw after ten days. The Turks had dug tunnels as part of their siege tactics, and those caught in the tunnels were reported to have been boiled alive.

The energetic Grand Master of the Knights, Pierre d'Aubusson (1476-1503), would no doubt have regarded Symi, with Khalki, Alimnia and Tilos as part of his scheme of consolidation of the Rhodian defences, as over the blocked-up entrance is an escutcheon of his arms quartered with those of the Order; however, they bear the date 1507 – four years after his death – and only 15 years before their forced withdrawal from Rhodes, and so indicate the caution that is necessary when using the Knights' escutcheons as accurate evidence of date. This building forms a rounded redoubt and is the largest surviving part of the Knights' castle; two further redoubts face NE and E, with sections of the enceinte that can really only be seen from the road above (some 500 m. away to the SW). A rounded archway leads into a space between two sections of the enceinte, and from here you can climb up some rocks to a tiny plateau on which the decorative floor of a small church is retained, formed from limestone tiles and areas of pebble inlay; this could be 15th / 16th C, and may well be part of Aubusson's building operation. The date at which this small church itself was destroyed is unknown, but the much larger late church of the Panagia tou Kastrou built against the N edge of the enceinte no doubt replaced it; the five handsome escutcheons located proudly as spolia on the the S wall of this church were no doubt taken from the castle of the Knights, and include those of Jacques de Milly and Raimondo Zacosta, who were both successively Grand Masters between 1454 and 1467.

It is not fully clear why the Knights should have chosen to build their castle in precisely this spot; although they were able to re-use the earlier materials still available here, it could never have been large enough to shelter any significant numbers of the local inhabitants, and it is in fact a rather enclosed site with mountains to S, W and E. The only way that it could have formed part of their signalling and defensive system would have been if they could relay signals over the mountains to the S or E; this may have been what they did, as Rottiers in 1825 was shown a tower in the centre of the island with spaces for three fires, and was told by a local inhabitant that the signals were made from there which involved lighting three fires, either singly or in combination, to indicate the extent of Turkish shipping that had been sighted. While this was related some three centuries after the Knights had left, it does provide an explanation for the castle's function, which would otherwise be inexplicable, being out of sight of all land except the Turkish headland of Knidos to the N, while the nearer one of Dorakis (some 10 km. away) is invisible. Shipping traversing the channel to the N could be observed, but to pass this information on needed a further link to the S. Its purpose may also have involved propaganda to demonstrate the zeal of the Knights in showing the Christian symbol so close to Turkey that the castle here continued to receive their attention.

Allow plenty of time for a visit to the Castle here, as both the building itself and the superb outlook repay leisurely study.

Nimporeio village.
Floor mosaics of EC basilica, and burial / refuge chambers(?).** Both sites open.

Starting from below the headland NW of Egalio crowned by the church of the Evangilsmos, follow the path round the shore of the bay for some 4 km. (starting as a good dirt track, it becomes a goat track and the last 200 m. is on pebbles beside the sea). Nimporeio has five small white churches, four concrete jetties and about seven houses; follow a stony track which leads inland between the second and third jetties, and then some steep steps lead you to where three of the churches are built immediately adjacent to each other, some 20 m. above the sea and 80 m. from the shoreline.

The EC basilica was on this site, and along the exterior of the N wall of the N church is a protected area where the surviving floor mosaics of the basilica can be seen. The area is some 20 m. x 3 m., and it forms a colourful and engaging composition, contained within a decorative floral border, that includes a camel driver leading a camel and a stag being chased by a hound. The mosaics would have originally been found in the N aisle of the EC basilica, and have been dated to the second half of the 6th C; considerable losses have occurred within the living memory of local inhabitants, but the surviving areas are still exhibit a lively charm.

'Burial / refuge chambers' (?). About 60 m. to the S of this spot, and uphill, you will find a strange, vaulted structure, now almost entirely underground, and consisting chiefly of ten chambers (each about 3 m. x 4. m.) opening off a central broad hall-way; the ensemble seems to have been built in one phase, and uses barrel-vaulting in local stone throughout. There is no lighting or window openings and entry is now through the roof of an end chamber. They could have been built any time after the 5th / 6th C (it is unlikely that they are classical in origin) and of the various guesses that have been made as to their function that of burial chambers seems one of the more probable; other suggestions include a shelter against pirate raids, a school for icon painters during iconoclasm (!) or as a caravanserai for travellers or pilgrims. Lack of any comparable structure means that we shall probably never know, but one thing is evident: currently nobody knows.

The two items here make this a uniquely rewarding objective for a half-day excursion from Egalio, and you may be able to arrive at a personal explanation of the function of the second of them. It is helpful to bring a torch.

THASOS

Θάσος

Island region: N Aegean. (*Nomos*: Kavala).

The extent of the EC remains on Thasos suggests that it enjoyed some importance into the 6th C; it is so near to the coast of N Greece that during the medieval period, as now, it was administered from the mainland city of Christoupolis (modern Kavala), and its importance returned in the 13th C. It was too remote from the Cyclades to have come under Venetian control, and the Byzantines used its port as a naval base in their operations against the Latin invaders. They could not resist the Genoese, however, and from 1307-1313 a nephew of Benedetto Zaccaria called Tedisio was in control. The Byzantines then recovered it, and in the early 15th C its bishopric was raised to the status of archbishop, but at some point before 1434 it was again in the hands of descendants of Francesco Gattilusio, who appointed an Oberto Grimaldi as a local governor (see below); at this point the Gattilusi held six islands in the N Aegean.

It succumbed to Ottoman rule in 1455, but in 1456 a papal fleet gathered by pope Callixtus III for a crusade to recover CP from the infidel, and sailing under the command of a cardinal Lodovico Trevisan, captured Thasos and placed the island under papal rule. Re-taken for the sultan by the admiral Zaganos in 1459, Mehmet generously gave part of the island (as well as Limnos and Samothraki) to the dispossessed Byzantine despot of the Morea, Dimitrios Palaiologos. It was finally under full Turkish control by 1470, but was to experience a more varied history in the post-medieval centuries than most of the Aegean islands.

The surviving remains on Thasos reflect the periods of its prosperity quite well. As there is no clear route to tour the island, entries are given below in a purely alphabetical sequence.

Alyki   Αλυκή

Ruins of two EC basilicas.★★ Unenclosed.
From the road along the SE coast only the excavated pre-Christian sanctuary is visible, but from just beyond this a foot-path leads up to the basilicas on the small headland overlooking the bay.

The two basilicas lie parallel and only a metre apart, with considerable remains of both still to be seen; no dedication is known. As with other early churches in the region, the E/W orientation appears to have been less important to the builders than the location, if constricted by features of the site; here the apses face due SE, and neither basilica could have occupied this position if the orientation had been more precise.

The first that you will reach (Basilica A) is the smaller (18 m. from apse to entrance), and the development of the apse and bema is of some interest; there was a space beneath the altar, and this, with a pronounced extension of the templon into the nave, indicates that the apse was the site of an important grave visited by pilgrims. Excavated graves outside the W end all confirm the sanctity of the area and its cult status.

The second (Basilica B) is larger, measuring 24 m. from apse to nave threshold, and can be assumed to have been built later to accommodate increasing numbers visiting the grave in A. Even more has survived here, with post slots for the templon, the base of an ambo just off centre in the nave, with lead holding pegs still showing, some re-erected columns and there are even some faded fresco remains in the NW corner of the presbytery. You can also see how the bottom member of a screen on the N side of the bema has jagged remains of what must have been a marble screen of pierced lattice work; all this suggests that the interior here was of considerable grandeur, and it is surprising that no record survives of the personality who was the centre of this attention. A small chapel has also been excavated to the S of B. The dating of these two basilicas has been fixed fairly conclusively at the early 5th C for basilica A and late 5th for basilica B.

Progressing along the low cliff just 60 m. further on from B, the face of the quarry from which the marble for these buildings was cut falls away down to the sea; its quality is very crystalline, and although superficially it may resemble Proconnesian marble, this factor means that it can be broken very easily and prevents it being carved with any great refinement.

This is a dramatic coastal site in the impressive tradition of the EC basilicas of the Aegean, and compares with Agios Stefanos, Kos, and Agia Foteine, Karpathos for interest and setting.

Some 5 km. due W of Alyki is the newly established **Convent of the Archangel Michael** in a dramatic position on the S coast. Although of 12th C foundation, and in a very attractive cliff-top setting, there are now no survivals to be seen of its medieval origins. The katholikon retains some earlier masonry but in general this must be regarded as a recent creation.

Kastro

Village, with site of castle and carved inscriptions.**
Unenclosed. (See Pl. 28).
On the N outskirts of Limena a dirt road is signed NE to Kastro, which you reach after 10.5 km., winding up through wild and magnificent country.

It will provide the best idea of the setting here if, after reaching this remote village, you traverse the disordered jumble of old houses that constitute Kastro to reach the small late church of Profitis Elias on the further edge of the village and overlooking a steep valley. This is built on the site of the original stronghold erected here in the 15th C by another Genoese, Oberto Grimaldi, who acted as a captain for the Gattilusi. The low wall that still surrounds it is all that is left of the enceinte, and the remains of a tower still rise to a few metres to the E.

On returning to the village, you will find that the church, renovated in 1804, has embedded in its SE exterior corner two carved inscriptions that must have been taken from the original kastro – probably in 1804. The lower one, mounted upside down, is in good condition (except for generous whitewash) and the most interesting. The three escutcheons it shows are those of the Gattilusi flanked by the Grimaldi; the Gattilusi presence in the N Aegean is well known from their lordship of Lesbos and Samothraki, and their prominent buildings there, but the Grimaldi, originally a Genoese family and now comfortably established as princes of Monaco (where their escutcheon now adorns the car number-plates), are less well known in the area. Although the family name appears often in archives, the only other visual evidence of their presence in the Aegean is a later plaque in the floor of the RC cathedral of the Virgin within the kastro on Naxos. Here the inscription, in Latin and Greek as on Samothraki, runs: IN CHRISTI NOMINE FACTUM EST MCCCCCXXXIIII DIE PRIMA APRILLIS and then what must be Oberto Grimaldi in Greek, with his age of 42. As 1534 is surely an error, this most probably means that the castle on which the plaque was placed was completed in 1434. Oberto Grimaldi had been made a captain by the Gattilusi and put in charge of the island, and this village would have been his stronghold. A second, damaged, Greek inscription installed higher up the wall refers to the kastro being built "from its foundations". This evidence of the protection that the Italian lords of the Aegean wished to be seen to be giving to their subject islanders seems to be little known.

While the physical survivals here may not be extensive, their interest and the unmodernised nature of their surroundings in these wild mountains have made it a ★★ site.

Thasos / Limena   Θάσος Λιμένα

1) Acropolis and Kastro★★. (See Pl. 16).
The shortest route to the medieval Kastro is to take the steep paved footpath signed to the Ancient Theatre (but to include one of the basilicas as well, see below). After reaching the theatre, leave it on your left and continue as far again up a foot track to the acropolis.

The medieval builders have here left some substantial, though now incomplete, remains; by this route you will reach the Kastro not by its original entrance but through a dismantled section of wall at its N extremity. Two towers look down W over the town and coast, and across to Kavala. On the E edge of the area the ruins of a small chapel survive, the apse still retaining fragments of painted fresco plaster, and broken columns suggest that there was quite a rich interior here. The most impressive part of the complex is beyond this area, however, where much of the original gateway and guard-room survives on the S boundary of the Kastro. Here huge panels of ancient marble have been re-used as part of the Genoese fortification, and below the gateway on the exterior the builders installed a rather charming 4th C BC relief of a funeral feast scene.

The whole ensemble here is an interesting example of the re-use of a classical strong point by the medieval Gattilusi lords, and contrasts with their towers on Samothraki in that the latter were erected on a selected high point apart from the major classical fortifications of the nearby Sanctuary, while here the ancient walls were in a position that could be easily adapted.

2) Remains of five EC basilicas in and near Limena.*

The extent and prosperity of the town in the EC centuries is indicated by the number of surviving basilicas that have been discovered here; they have all been dated to the 5th/6th C and while the original dedication of none of them is known, all can be visited as indicated.

The most prominent of them lies unenclosed in its own plateia in Limena two streets back from the harbour frontage, and constitutes the main open space in the heart of the town. Only the E end is now visible, with the W two-thirds having been paved over, but what is to be seen indicates a basilica of considerable size, and it must have been the largest now known here. A number of columns remain, with two re-erected, and there is an area of floor mosaic visible in the NE corner, but it would seem to be for an adjacent chamber rather than the basilica itself.

The second within the town itself is known as the **Agora Basilica**, as it lies within the precincts of the ancient Agora (fenced, usual opening hours, no charge). It is sited adjacent to the S end of the 4th C BC stoa, and it may have been this feature which dictated a N/S orientation: the main features now are the apse and the S end of the W aisle, and the W wall of the stoa must have formed the basis of the E wall of the basilica. As at Alyki this departure from normal orientation can be explained by the presence of local features, which must have been given greater importance than the creation of conventional directions. More unusual, though, is the presence of a pronounced crossing, still very evident in the ground plan; (this would have been even more easily seen if the Bulgarians had not demolished standing parts in 1941.) A Roman mosaic was found here, and re-use of local spolia would be expected, and can be seen, for example, in the marble steps into the bema, where bronze pivot sockets for ancient doors still remain.

The third EC basilica occupied the headland known as *Bryokastro* (or *Ebraiokastro*) to the E of the harbour, and is reached by following a completely unsigned footpath that leads up from the most Easterly area of the ancient excavations and takes you up behind the modern boat-yard; the site is fenced, but can be entered, and a small modern church of **Agioi Apostoloi** occupies its centre apse. This was originally a temple site, and the triple-aisle basilica, 20 m. from apse to threshold, was the second building here; it was only discovered in 1959 when foundations were being dug for the modern church. There are considerable spolia with two columns re-erected; eight graves were excavated, and some can still be seen outside the apse and inside the N aisle, and there was a small circular baptistry at the N end of the narthex. In several respects this is comparable with the larger complex at Alyki; it can easily be included in a visit to the Ancient Theatre and the Acropolis, as the footpath continues up the hillside past this headland.

The fourth and fifth basilicas are on the same excavated site due W some 3 km. along the coast road from Limena, and some 50 m. N of the road, with parts only some 5 m. from the sea; the site is fenced but can be entered, though not from the beach. Nearest to the road is the earliest, Greek area of excavation, and then two spans of a Roman brick colonnade form the most prominent feature of later building, where a hypocaust to the NW suggests the presence of baths. The plans of the two basilicas are at right angles, with the smaller one lying parallel to the coast and oriented SE/NW. This has had its S aisle truncated, where the larger one now abuts on to it; the length of apse to threshold here is 14 m., and there were extensions outside the narthex. The presumption must be that quite a small 5th C basilica was built first, but with growing numbers became too small; the larger one was then built, and it would appear that the main apse of the first may have been converted into a baptistry, with stone seating round the walls. In both cases the orientation may have been dictated by the Roman bath buildings. This is perhaps the most interesting of the basilica sites in Limena in that its development can be followed quite readily; although harder to locate than the others, it repays the diligent searcher.

Limenaria — Λιμενάρια

Between Skala Marion and Maries, and easily visited from Limenaria:
Monastery of the Panagia / Koimisis Theotokou. ★ Closed 1.00-4.30.

This lies in open country to the W of the road between these two villages, and roughly mid-way between them, 800 m. up a dirt track winding through olive groves.

All the monastic buildings here are modern, but the katholikon could be later 15th C, with the customary pitched roof and schist tiling. It has two features of interest: an internal fountain in the N wall, and an unusually complete and homogeneous fresco scheme in a well-preserved state. The latter is probably 17th C, but could well be re-painting over an earlier layer, and the subject of the Zoödokhos Pigi is adapted successfully to the niche with the fountain; particularly impressive are images of five monastic saints on the N wall and an exceptionally large and expressive Koimisis. The katholikon is unusual in having only one window, and that quite a small one in the S wall; this may suggest later changes during the Turkokratia, as the frescoes are the most accomplished and complete on the island, and better fenestration might have been expected for them to be seen without artificial light.

The frescoes make this a rewarding objective for a visit, and the monastery is readily found in attractive country.

Theologos   Θεολόγος

Churches of Agios Dimitrios and Agia Paraskeve.*

This village in the wide Dipotamos valley was the medieval capital of the island, and although there are now no visible remains of a kastro, it is probable that there would have been some kind of defensive position on the hills to one side or the other. The two churches here are both 15th/16th C, and both built with the local characteristics of sloping timber roofs tiled with schist, and neither has a dome; both are on the S/E side of the village street, and their keys are available in nearby houses.

Agios Dimitrios is the most interesting and remains the largest and most prominent with a spacious external portico that must, in the absence of a plateia, have provided the focus of much of the social life of the village. There are no frescoes except in the apse (the Virgin Platytera), but there is an unusually decorative 18th C iconostasis and a glazed wall case contains a number of books and icons, at least one of which might be of 16th C date; this is the most engaging internal feature.

Agia Paraskeve is smaller, but has some 18th C frescoes, with an unusually impressive group of martyrs depicted in full length along the S wall.

THIRA: see **SANTORINI**.

TILOS   Τήλος

Med: Piscopia.
Island group: Dodecanese. (*Nomos*: Dodecanese).

The mountainous but quite
fertile island of Tilos lies mid-
way between Khalki and
Nisyros, and these three
islands form a straight line that
ends at the Armenistis
headland on the W coast of
Rhodes. Although retaining
substantial buildings from
antiquity, Tilos did not figure
in medieval history until the
arrival of the Hospitallers on

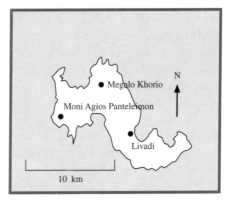

Rhodes early in the 14th C; it was then its location in this island chain
that gave the island a new importance, linking Rhodes with Kos in a
communication and signalling system of the Hospitallers. Although their
physical investment in Tilos was not large, the island was clearly
important to them, as Mehmet II in 1479 tried for eight days to capture
the castle here, before having to withdraw with relatively heavy losses;
the Turks must have placed a high value on the elimination of this post,
which would have been vital in warning of the forces approaching to
initiate the siege of Rhodes the next year. The Grand Master, Pierre
d'Aubusson, was so impressed by the bravery of the islanders that he
awarded them a large quantity of corn. The island would have passed
into Turkish hands with the final expulsion of the Hospitallers from
Rhodes in January 1523.

Megalo Khorio   Μέγαλο Χόριο

Kastro: ruins of Hospitaller castle.★★ Unenclosed.
*The castle, easily seen crowning the hill above the village to the N, can be
reached in about 40 minutes of scrambling climb; there are no tracks for most
of the way.*

This inland village, the principal one on the island, is quite rich in pre-
Christian survivals, and the main church of Arkhangelos Mikhail (re-

built in recent times) is unusual in that it occupies the site of a classical temple; a very well-preserved 5th C BC wall forms the N end of the narthex and the retaining wall of the church enclosure. These quite extensive classical remains continue on the mountain top above the village, where there was a substantial fortress in pre-Christian centuries. The fine classical gate-way (probably 5th C BC) still survives here, although slightly altered by the medieval builders.

The area enclosed at the summit is a polygon of some 40 m. x 50 m., and the reason for the choice of this site as a defensive position must surely be the very extensive opportunities for all round observation, and relay of information to other islands. To the NW is Nisyros, with the village of Nikaia clearly visible; to the SE Khalki and Alimnia can just be seen, while the Turkish headland of Knidos occupies part of the horizon to the NE. It would seem that the superb potential for observation of this site was indeed its main value for the Knights of Rhodes. It should be mentioned, too, that Tilos offers one more example of the Hospitallers building on to existing classical foundations and walls, as they did also on Symi, Khalki and Alimnia.

Now, most of the defences must have been dismantled, and there are no Knights' escutcheons displayed. There must have been much more substantial fortifications than are now surviving for the highly trained soldiers of Mehmet II to have been repelled in their assault and siege in 1479. The remains of a number of buildings and several cisterns can still be seen, and these would have been vital to the defenders when they were besieged here for eight days; the Knights and soldiers who would have formed the garrison were assisted by local inhabitants, although there is no record of any precise numbers.

The only intact building on the summit is the small barrel-vaulted chapel dedicated (like the village church below) to the Archangel Michael, which offers two points of interest: it incorporates some block walling of the classical building previously here, and this probably accounts for its orientation due NE / SW. Of greater interest to the medievalist are the quite extensive fresco remains in the apse and on one transverse vault of the roof, which are certainly Byzantine, and appear to date from the 15th C. The best preserved and most interesting are in the apse, where under a damaged figure of the Pantocrator, a small image of a naked, nimbed youth stands in a small aedicule, beside St Peter of Alexandria and St Spiridon. This iconography is probably one form of that of a dialogue in which the 4th C bishop of Alexandria asks the young Christ who has destroyed his clothing, to which Christ replies that it is the heretic, the abominable Arius; this subject became popular in the late Byzantine period. A fragment of a Transfiguration scene is probably from the 14th C. Given its siting, the ensemble here is of considerable interest, and demonstrates how a fortified position such as this served (as in other islands) both for the protection of local inhabitants, as well as housing a garrison of the Knights. A final point can be made about a name previously used of this kastro; it has been called Episkopi, and (rather than implying the presence of a bishop) it probably refers to the capacity to see "both ways" (*bis-skopi*) (i.e. N and S) from the summit.

For the climb up here you will be rewarded by a range of interesting and thought-provoking features, some of substantial interest, and all in a spectacular setting.

Moni Agios Panteleimon.★★ (See Pl. 15). Normally locked. In season a minibus leaves Megalo Khorio for the monastery each Sunday morning; at other times the key is held by the butcher in his shop in the village.
From Megalo Khorio take the surfaced road N to Agios Antonios and then, turning left, follow a winding dirt road (unsigned) running W and S along the cliff slopes, always within sight of the sea; the distance is some 9 km.

This small, fortified rural monastery, now unoccupied, was built on a terrace in a broad, rocky, shrub-clad ravine on the W side of the island, high above the sea. A huge, spreading plane tree marks the entrance, and the miracle-working spring that was the reason for the foundation provides abundant water to a trough lower down. The small monastery has mostly later buildings, and is protected by an unusual tower at the gateway which was presumably to help in the sighting of, and protection from, pirates. The foundation is said to have taken place in 1470, and the only part of the small complex which may date from this time is the small, domed katholikon; here there is a restored 15th C portrait of the ktitor, a monk named Jonas. It would be unusual for a monastery to be founded so dangerously close to the sea, and visible from it, at any time after the 15th C, so the 1470 date is probably correct.

Even if you are unable to achieve entry, this makes a rewarding goal for a superbly scenic walk; the patronal saint's feast is celebrated 25th-27th July, when it will certainly be open.

Between Livadi and Megalo Khorio.
Ruins of small kastro above the road.★ Unsigned and unenclosed.
Easily seen to the W of the road on the far side of a small valley, some 4 km. from Megalo Khorio; a brief scramble gets you there.

Now very ruined, this must have served as a small neighbourhood stronghold and refuge for the protection of local farmers and their families. (One is reminded of the description by Buondelmonti when he visited Leros c.1418, where all the local inhabitants were said to retreat inside the castle walls each night for safety.) The area enclosed on this desolate hill-top is some 40 m. x 40 m., and the one building that still has a roof is a small, barrel-vaulted chapel in which shadowy remains of later Byzantine frescoes still occupy the N wall. The fact that even the extensive quantities of building stone from the many fallen buildings that must have been here are still on the site, and not re-used in more recent times for local building, reflects the remoteness of the location. This makes a very worthwhile detour that offers a vivid reflection of the later medieval conditions of life on the island.

THIRA: see **SANTORINI**.

TINOS Τῆνος

Island group: Cyclades (N). (*Nomos*: Cyclades).

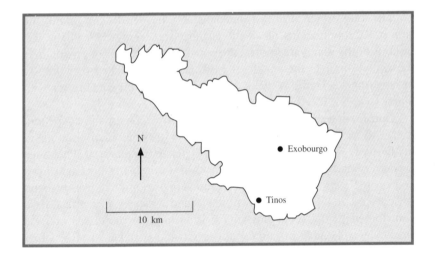

Tinos, on the N fringe of the Cyclades, was well placed on some of the major navigational routes, and in spite of not having a deep harbour was both quite prosperous and well populated during the medieval period. It is not mentioned by any of the medieval historians, being first named in the Deed of Partition of 1204. The case of Tinos provides an interesting example of the realities of possession after the Fourth Crusade; in the *Partitio Terrarum* the island is explicitly named as one of the eight that were assigned to the Latin emperor, yet we find in 1207 the islands of Tinos and Mykonos were occupied by the Venetians Andrea and Geremia Ghisi as vassals of the emperor. They were later to add Skyros, Skopelos and Skiathos to their possessions, making them the most powerful of the Venetian families after the Sanudi, Lords of Naxos. In 1390 Tinos and Mykonos were inherited by Venice, and the islanders were so anxious for the firm yet benevolent oversight of the Republic that they begged the Venetians to rule them, and so after a public auction they were administered (with the island of Delos) by a citizen of Venice who paid rent to the Republic for them. Rectors were appointed for two-year periods, and in 1413 it was Giovanni Querini who, having filled this position, bought the uninhabited island of Astypalia and incurred the wrath of the Venetian Senate by populating it with families from Tinos and Mykonos (see page 28). In the peace agreed with the Turks in 1540 Tinos, with Crete, Cyprus and some of the Ionian islands were all that was left to the W powers, but in the end this was the only major island of the Aegean to remain in Venetian hands right down to 1715 – the longest held of all their possessions.

The long presence of the Venetians here has left it with one of the largest RC populations of all the islands, and from 1328 all the RC bishops of the island are known; the papal inscription still surviving over the church door in the plateia of Mykonos makes it clear that the RC bishop Angelus Venier is being appointed in 1677 on equal terms with Tinos.

Considering the length of time that it enjoyed Christian occupation, it has to be admitted that the island is somewhat disappointing to medievalists – and even, indeed, to Venetian enthusiasts. The huge modern church of the Panagia Evangelistria dominates the main town and port (Khora), and the influx of funds that its miracle-working icon (discovered in 1822) brings to the island twice a year must have contributed to the rebuilding in modern times of the entire housing stock; you will search in vain for any significant Venetian survivals other than Exobourgo, and from the Byzantine period there is unhappily not even a record. A small number of post-Byzantine icons have been assembled in the small museum close to the Evangelistria, providing the only artistic link with the medieval period.

The convent of **Kekhrovouni** (some 4 km. N of Khora and open 9.00-13.00 and 14.30-18.00) may well have been a 12th C foundation, as claimed, but everything now visible there dates from much later; several churches and chapels can be seen within its walls, but its growth has clearly been piecemeal since the 18th C.

Exobourgo   Εξοβούργο

Venetian kastro.★★ Unenclosed.

The mountain of Xobourgo ("outside the town") is some 15 km. due N of Khora, and it may be indicative that the kastro itself, the only survival of Venetian presence, is unsigned. Passing Moni Kekhrovouni, follow signs to Mesi, after which turn left and the kastro will be in view; alternatively, the kastro can be visited from the village of Xinara, but with slightly further to walk.

The neo-classical Church of the Sacred Heart (re-named in 1895, it was formerly Agia Sophia) is the large later RC church at the foot of the mountain that you cannot escape seeing, and perpetuates the Jesuit presence on the island. The mountain which is, after Tsikinias to the E, the highest on the island, had three centres of population in medieval times: the Borgo (town) which was unfortified, the Exobourgo whose inhabitants lived "outside the town", and the Kastro. Now only the latter survives to any identifiable degree. The kastro must have its origins in the 13th C arrival of the Ghisi, and it may be that the ruined, four-square building on the left of the road as you approach the foot of the mountain is the surviving part of what would have been quite a grand entrance from an early stage of its existence; certainly the vaulting that is left is quite elaborate, and suggests an intention to impress.

Entry must always have been from the NE, as the whole S and W sector is sheer. An outer enceinte still partly survives, and it is through this that the ascent is now made; the whole area enclosed is quite substantial, and must be equivalent to approximately 100 m. x 100 m. if it was level. The apron-shaped area between the enceinte and the main surviving buildings was reportedly large enough to provide shelter for a substantial part of the island's population when this was needed. Advancing up the slope it is hard to identify the various surviving fragments of building, but one of the largest consists of a wall section with a blind arcade; this has the correct orientation for a chapel, but could have been a secular hall. Below this, to the NE is the largest structure still standing and still partly roofed, of which the plaster lining suggests that it was the main cistern. The Turks dismantled the castle after 1715, but considerable remains still survive, with extensive outer walling and massive projecting buttresses descending to the E almost down to level ground. No fortifications adapted for cannon survived the Turkish destruction, and by this date they could be expected to be quite extensive.

A pre-18th C drawing shows the mountain with its defences and buildings still intact; although the lower zone seems quite extensive, the general appearance of the fortifications seems relatively unmodernised for that date, and the impression here is that by 1715 the kastro had long ceased to be of material or strategic significance to the Venetians. When compared with the 16th/17th C fortifications of Crete and the immense contemporary Venetian fortress of Palamidi, above Navplion in the Peloponnese, which they built at vast expense in 1711-14, this has the air of being an unmodernised backwater. This view is confirmed by Pitton de Tournefort who was here c.1700, and wrote that the garrison consisted of fourteen badly-dressed soldiers, of whom seven were

French ex-convicts, although there were 40 bronze cannons and three iron. One should feel some sympathy for the Venetian commander on Tinos, Balbi, who, faced with the might of the Turkish forces, quickly surrendered Exobourgo; eventually returning to Venice he was tried and imprisoned for this act, but surveying the scene of his last stand the modern viewer might judge that the Republic could have been more whole-hearted in its support of this small colony, and less severe in its censure of Balbi.

ZAKYNTHOS   Ζάκυνθος

Med | Italian: Zante.
Island group: Ionian / Eptanisous. (*Nomos*: Zakynthos).

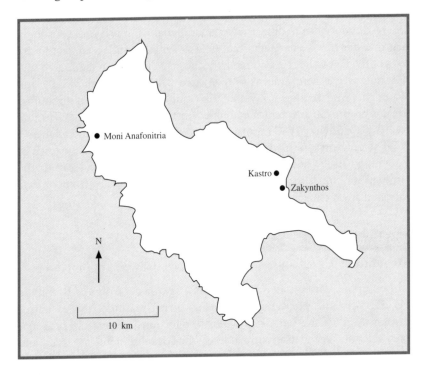

With the other Ionian islands, the proximity of Italy meant that the medieval history of Zakynthos was often more affected by incursions from the W than by Byzantine rule from the E. In the early Byzantine period the island was linked administratively with Achaia, but in 467 the first of several W invaders arrived in the person of the Vandal king, Gaiseric, who pillaged the island and transported hundreds of the inhabitants. Attempted Arab invasions in the 9th C were defeated, but in 1099 Zakynthos was plundered by Pisan forces, although being retained by the Byzantines. They lost the island in 1185, when the admiral of the Norman king William II of Sicily, Margaritone of Brindisi, occupied Kefallonia, Leukas and Zakynthos and gave himself the title 'Lord of the Ionian Islands'. He died in 1194, and he was succeeded by his son-in-law Matteo Orsini; this dynasty survived until 1339 as 'Dukes of Zante', when it was succeeded by the Tocco family.

In the Deed of Partition of 1204 the island was listed as being allocated to Venice, but the Venetian Senate was always having to assert its suzerainty over the independently-minded ruling dynasties here, and in 1357 when the Tocco rule began the Senate insisted that a Venetian noble would come and live on the island as rector; again, in 1389, it appears that Carlo Tocco had tried to claim that his family was Genoese, and so did not have to obey the Venetian Senate, but was told brusquely that this was not the case, and that he was Venetian and so subject to the laws of the Republic. Turkish control, never so effective in the Ionian sea, did not arrive here until 1479, and in 1483 was replaced by the Venetians, who arranged to retain Zakynthos by payment of an annual tribute of 500 ducats, and it remained in their hands for free after the treaty of Carlovitz (1699) transferred possession of the island to them.

The epicentre of the devastating earthquake of 1953 was the town of Zakynthos itself, and almost all of its buildings were destroyed; the contents of the Museum have been formed principally from objects salvaged from churches ruined in this disaster.

Zakynthos town

Museum.** Usual hours and charges; open daily except Mondays.

Although the Museum here houses only a few pieces from the Byzantine period, with the great majority being post-Byzantine, the extensive display (one of the largest provincial collections of post-classical art) provides an opportunity to follow the development in style and iconography of one of the larger and more prosperous of the Ionian islands; their location as the closest of the Greek islands to Italy had far-reaching effects both politically as well as artistically. From the middle-Byzantine period are some fragments of decorative architectural sculpture, which hint at the kind of losses that occurred in 1953; a fresco painted in a wall-niche is said to be of 12th C date and to come from the Kastro, and represents the Greek presence there prior to the coming of the W powers.

Otherwise the collection is virtually entirely post-Byzantine; over 100 icons and many other items all show the characteristic tendency to merge a Western and specifically Venetian style and iconography with the local inherited Byzantine tradition. The whole of the interior of the church of St Andrew from Valimes has been reconstructed, and although of 17th C date the main forms of Palaiologue style remain very evident, and this ensemble which includes a long cycle of NT scenes retains its Greek origins to a substantial extent; the whole of the W wall is occupied by the Byzantine form of the Last Judgement, with a coil of fire descending from Christ's throne down to hell. More Venetian in subject-matter is the large iconostasis of St Demetrius Kolla of 1690, where the three largest icons, forming the doors into the sanctuary, are all of popes, including Sylvester "archbishop of Rome"; the artists, however, Gerasimos Kouloumpis and Giorgios Gryparis, were local Ionian artists. In other ways too the Byzantine elements were supplanted by W forms; where the decoration on the front cover of a Greek liturgical book would have displayed the descent of Christ into Hades (the Orthodox Easter scene, and known as the Anastasis) those here display the Resurrection instead – the Western subject for Easter.

The collection here offers a highly interesting insight into the confluence of two strong artistic traditions, and given the huge losses that occurred in the 1953 earthquake we are fortunate that so much fine material has survived.

Kastro.★★ Enclosed and gated. Open daily except Mondays.
Take the broad winding Odos Philikon, signed to Bokhales, that climbs steeply W out of the town; after 1 km. take left turn (again signed to Bokhales) and you will reach the Kastro.

The origins of the huge castle here must go back to before the arrival of the Orsini in the 13th C, as some fragmentary evidence of Greek presence before this date has been found. This must have been largely overlaid by the fortifications put up by the Orsini and Tocchi, and (after 1483) the Venetians. Even so, what you will see here dates from several later periods of building, as an earthquake in 1515 is thought to have obliterated much of the kastro that may have existed prior to this date. The 1953 earthquake seems to have done little damage here.

The approach is dominated by the huge entrance where the Lion of St Mark is carved near the massive entrance gate. The three shields below it will be those of the Venetian families of the Calergi, Barbaro and Avogaro. Three successive gateways lead the visitor through three enceintes on the W sector, with the third of them bearing another lion and two more shields with the initials MT and FP below them; the latter may be those of Francesco Priuli. The interior space of some 150 m. x 300 m. is now quite wooded, but with many buildings partially surviving; the population of the town and its surrounding country could readily have been contained here for a period. The predominant period of the buildings here seems to be 16th C, but there is one structure occupying the highest point at the S end of the enclosure, and this could be 15th C or earlier, and so survive from the first building here. A medium-sized church in the centre of the enclosure, dedicated to St John the Baptist, has completely Venetian detail of the 15th / 16th C and appears to have always housed the Roman rite. Besides the outer gateway, the only major fortification is the SE bastion, where there are cannon still in position, and this is certainly 16th C. An interesting feature is the quite sophisticated chanelling which must have been installed to conserve the rainwater falling on this extensive area.

Like much else on Zakynthos, the local origins of the kastro here have now been thoroughly overlaid by the later Italian presence, but the result is still highly impressive and the colonial past of the island can be read in its massive fortifications.

Moní Anafonitria. Μονή Αναφωνήτρια.*
Enclosed and gated; open at usual monastic hours.
In one of the most Westerly locations on the island, though not on the coast, the monastery, with its substantial defensive tower incorporated into its entrance, is easily seen quite close to the road.

The monastery is said to have been founded in 1429 in the year before Carlo II Tocco began his reign. It became the leading ecclesiastical centre of Zakynthos, incurring such obligations as contributing to the salary of the only schoolmaster in the island. The layout is typically Greek, with the monastic buildings forming a hollow square in which the katholikon is located. The earthquake damage has been relatively slight here; an attractive external arcade has suffered, but the main structure of the katholikon is undamaged. Its design (given the prestige of its founder) is a surprisingly simple triple-aisled, domeless basilica, with few decorative features; the three apses offer no brick patterns or other ornament. Inside, the six nave caps are of the simplest kind, and all the W part of the nave is white, although this was unlikely to have always been the case, and in and near the bema you will find some damaged remains of frescoes which could well be 15th C; those in the apse itself are now too smoky to be read.

The monastery here has been fortunate in the associations it has maintained; besides those of its founder, a 16th C abbot, Dionysios, was held in such esteem by the Venetians, who had then assumed control, that the monastery was made over to him and he was canonised in 1622. Although not artistically impressive, the monastery exemplifies the leading part that could be played in the changing history of an island that had existed for so long as a dependent colony.

GLOSSARY.

Ambo. A raised platform usually located in the middle of the nave of an EC church; in its developed form it had steps leading up from both E and W, and although it had the functions of a pulpit it was also the focus of some ceremonial actions.

Apse. The large recess at the E end of a church; it is rounded on the interior, but its exterior can be either rounded or faceted.

Arcosol. A tomb formed from a horizontal niche over which an arch has been carved.

Bartizan. A projecting turret, usually on the corner of a fortified building.

Bema. The area of a Byzantine church adjoining the apse, and corresponding most closely to the chancel or presbytery of a W church or cathedral.

Belfry. Used here to indicate an external masonry framework built on to a church, often over the doorway, in which bells could be suspended; this is distinct from a *campanile*, which is free-standing. The use of bells was not always allowed during the Turkokratia, and these can often be later additions to the churches where they are found.

Cabling. A term that describes the convex 'filling' applied to the vertical, concave fluting of a column; it was usually only used in the lower part of the column.

Campanile. Bell-tower that is free-standing, and built separately from the church or katholikon that it serves (cf. *Belfry*).

Chrysobull. Literally 'gold seal', but applied to the document to which the seal is attached, and its contents; it was issued by the Byzantine emperor.

Conch. A 'shell-shaped' concave semi-dome that surmounts a rounded apse.

Corbel. A stone or brick projection from a wall, usually intended to support an element of roofing in either stone or wood.

Cufic. External wall ornament formed by tiles or bricks; thought to derive from the Arabic city of Kufa.

Cloisonné. A building technique in which cut blocks of stone are separated ('enclosed') by ceramic tiles set on edge.

Despot. Title created in the 12th C for the holder of the highest political rank after the emperor and co-emperor.

Diaconicon. The chamber 'pertaining to the deacon' that is usually located on the S side of the main apse of a Byzantine church, and is used for storing liturgical books, vestments, etc.

Dodecaorton. The collective name for the 12 major feasts of the Greek church; although not completely stabilised before the 11th C, their representation in art (as opposed to purely liturgical useage) is normally found to be: Annunciation, Nativity, Visitation *or* Presentation in the temple, Baptism, Transfiguration, Raising of Lazarus, Entry into Jerusalem, Crucifixion, Anastasis, Ascension, Pentecost and Koimisis.

Doux. A military title, best equated with 'general'.

Elkomenos. An uncommon episode of the Passion that depicts Christ being brought, or 'dragged' to Calvary.

Enceinte. Fortified perimeter wall of a castle or fort.

Epigonation. Part of the liturgical vestments of a bishop; it takes the form of a square of stiffened embroidered cloth, and it hangs by one corner from his girdle. There is no W equivalent.

Epimanikia or **manikia.** A pair of richly decorated cuffs worn by a bishop during celebration of the liturgy; there is no W equivalent.

Epitafios. A large piece of textile, usually silk, on which the image of the dead Christ is embroidered; it is used once a year in the procession for the Burial of Christ on Holy Saturday, and is usually of exceptional richness.

Epitrakhilion. Corresponds to the W stole, worn round the neck by priests and bishops, and often richly embroidered.

Exonarthex. An additional or outer *narthex*; if present, it would be the first part of a Byzantine church that was entered, and is always adjacent to the (inner) *narthex*.

Flabellum. A fan used by the clergy in the Greek liturgy, usually of metal and decorated with images of angels.

Fresco. Strictly, this term should only be used of wall painting where the pigment was applied while the plaster was still wet (Italian *fresco* as opposed to *secco*, dry); here the term is used loosely of all wall painting.

Frourion. In contrast to *Kastro*, this is used here to indicate a fortified building with a purely military function, often smaller, and corresponding to a fort or fortress.

Iconostasis. A screen that separates the sanctuary from the *naos* of a Byzantine church; those usually found now are of carved and gilded wood, and support a number of icons. It developed from the marble *templon*, and a transitional form is of masonry, on which images were painted in fresco; the decorated wooden iconostasis became almost universal in the post-Byzantine period.

Kastro. Used here to correspond with either 'castle' or 'citadel', and could fulfil a purely protective function for non-combatants (cf. *Frourion.)*

Katholikon. The principal church of a Greek Orthodox monastery.

Koimisis. The 'falling asleep' of the Virgin, referred to as the 'Assumption' in the W; it is one of the *Dodecaorton*.

Ktitor. The founder (and often the first owner) of a Greek church or religious institution.

Machicolation. The part of a fortified building forming a gallery projecting round the top of a wall or tower; it could be of wood, but was more frequently built of stone.

Manikia. *See* **Epimanakia**.

Naos. The central floor area in a Byzantine church.

Narthex. An area of a Byzantine church equivalent to a porch, but usually running the full width of the W end of the building.

Opus sectile. A technique for creating designs with inlaid marble or other mineral that is cut to geometrical or figurative shapes.

Pallium. Used here to refer to the stole worn by a W bishop.

Parekklision. Chapel adjoining a Byzantine church or *katholikon*.

Phialostomia. Small ceramic cups or tubes with crimped edges that are set into the exterior masonry of Byzantine churches; they are popular on Chios.

Prothesis. Chamber to the N of the main apse of a Byzantine church used for preparing the eucharistic gifts; it is of greater sanctity than the *diaconicon*, and had its own programme of decoration. In smaller churches it could be reduced to a niche.

Protospatharios. One of the more elevated titles of the many dignitaries in the Byzantine court and imperial hierachy; a sub-division existed between bearded and eunuch holders of the office.

Sigillion. Literally a seal, usually of lead, attached to a document issued by a bishop or high official; the term is applied also to the contents of the document.

Spolia. A term used to denote isolated fragments, usually marble and often carved, deriving from earlier buildings.

Squinch. Architectural term used of the concave form spanning the corner of square bay, and usually used to support a cupola.

Synthronon. Masonry seating, often of several superimposed tiers, located round the interior of the apse of an EC or Byzantine church.
A bishop's throne could be located in the middle of the upper row.

Talus. A sloping or 'splayed out' wall built to strengthen the exterior defences of a castle or other fortified building.

Templon. Screen of marble or masonry across the apse of a Byzantine church; it developed into the *iconostasis*, q.v.

Theme. An administrative area of the Byzantine empire.

Trapeza. The refectory of a Byzantine monastery or convent.

Triconch. A building form incorporating three apsidal *conches*, usually adjacent and with two opposite each other.

Turkokratia. The historic period denoting Turkish rule over formerly Byzantine territory.

Virgin, icongraphic types. Although not always used consistently, the following are all mentioned here: 1) Eleousa: "the compassionate" (kissing the infant christ, who is often held in both hands. 2) Nikopoia: "the victory maker" (usually bust length and frontal, the Virgin holds before her a medalliomn with an image of the youthful Christ). 3) Platytera: "wider than the heavens" (usually in the conch of the apse, the frontal figure has her arms spread widely to eith side). 4) Zoödokhos Pigi, the "life-giving fountain", an image in which water flowing from a fountain, with the Virgin above it, heals the infirm and sick gathered around it.

SOME OF THE MAIN DYNASTIES AND RULERS IN THE GREEK ISLANDS.

Given below are the names of most of the principal rulers, (dukes, lords, counts, governors, etc.) and dynasties involved in the medieval history of the Greek Islands; this is intended to be used only as a convenient reference tool, and considerable simplification has been necessary. Thus, while for the Venetian Doges and some of the Byzantine emperors dates are recorded to the nearest day, and are undisputed, in many other cases no such certainty exists; not only are the records fragmentary, but the realities of title and possession were often not only disputed at the time, but can still be uncertain and open to discussion today.

The principal sources used to compile these tables have been: A.Gabriel, *Cité de Rhodes*; V.Grumel, *Traité d'Etudes byzantines, I: La Chronologie;* W.Miller, *Essays in the Latin Orient*, and: *The Latins in the Levant*; K.Setton, *The Catalan Domination of Athens*; and: *The Papacy and the Levant (1204-1571)*, vols. I & II; and B.J.Slot, *Archipelagus Turbatus. Les Cyclades entre Colonisation Latine et Occupation Ottomane.*

BYZANTINE EMPERORS IN CONSTANTINOPLE FROM 1081 TO 1204:

The Komnene Dynasty:
Alexios I Komnenos 1081-1118
John II Komnenos 1118-1143
Manuel I Komnenos 1143-1180
Alexios II Komnenos 1180-1183
Andronikos I Komnenos 1183-1185
Dynasty of the Angeloi:
Isaac II Angelos 1185-1195
Alexios III Angelos 1195-1203
Akexios IV Angelos 1203-1204

LATIN EMPERORS IN CONSTANTINOPLE FROM 1204 TO 1261:

Baldwin I of Hainaut, Count of Flanders 1204-1205
Henry d'Angre of Hainaut (his brother) 1206-1216
Peter of Courtenay (his brother-in-law) 1217
Yolande (his widow, sister of Henry d'Angre) 1217-1219
John Colonna, cardinal of Sta. Prassede (regent) 1220
Robert of Courtenay (son of Yolande) 1221-1228
Narjot of Toucy (baron, 'caesar' and regent) 1228-1231
John of Brienne (king of Jerusalem) 1231-1237
Anseau of Cayeux (regent) 1237-1238
Narjot of Toucy (again, as regent) 1238-1240
Baldwin II of Courtenay (son of Yolande) 1228-1231 and 1237-1261

BYZANTINE EMPERORS IN NICAEA FROM 1204 TO 1261:
Theodore I Laskaris 1204-1222
John III Dukas Vatatzes 1222-1254
Theodore II Laskaris 1254-1258
John IV Doukas 1258-1261
Michael VIII Palaiologos 1259-1261

BYZANTINE EMPERORS IN CONSTANTINOPLE FROM 1261 TO 1453:
Michael VIII Palaiologos 1261-1282
Andronikos II Palaiologos 1282-1328
Andronikos III Palaiologos 1328-1341
John V Kantakouzenos 1355-1376
Andronikos IV Palaiologos 1376-1379
John V 1341-1391
Manuel II Palaiologos 1391-1425
John VIII Palaiologos 1425-1448
Constantine XI Palaiologos Dragases 1449-1453

DOGES OF VENICE FROM 1204 TO 1453:
Enrico Dandolo 1192-1205
Pietro Ziana 1205-1229
Jacopo Tiepolo 1229-1249
Marino Morosini 1249-1253
Ranieri Zeno 1253-1268
Lorenzo Tiepolo 1268-1275
Jacopo Contarini 1275-1280
Giovanni Dandolo 1280-1289
Pietro Gradenigo 1289-1311
Marino Zorzi 1311-1312
Giovanni Soranzo 1312-1328
Francesco Dandolo 1329-1339
Bartolomeo Gradenigo 1339-1342
Andrea Dandolo 1343-1354
Marino Falier 1354-1355
Giovanni Gradenigo 1355-1356
Giovanni Dolfin 1356-1361
Lorenzo Celsi 1361-1365
Marco Corner 1365-1368
Andrea Contarini 1368-1382
Antonio Venier 1382-1400
Michele Steno 1400-1413
Tommaso Mocenigo 1414-1423
Francesco Foscari 1423-1457

EARLIER OTTOMAN SULTANS:
Othman 1307-1326
Orkhan 1326-1362

Murat I 1362-1389
Bayezit I 1389-1402
Mehmet I 1402-1421
Murat II 1421-1451
Mehmet II ("the Conqueror") 1451-1481
Bayezit II 1481-1512

GRAND MASTERS OF THE KNIGHTS OF RHODES, 1305-1523.
Foulques de Villaret (Langue of Provence) 1305-1319
Hélion de Villeneuve (Langue of Provence) 1319-1346
Dieudonné de Gozon (Langue of Provence) 1346-1353
Pierre de Corneillan (Langue of Provence) 1353-1355
Roger de Pins (Langue of Provence) 1355-1365
Raymond de Bérenger (Langue of Provence) 1365-1374
Robert de Juilly (Langue of France) 1374-1377
Juan Fernández de Heredia (Langue of Spain) 1377-1396
Philibert de Naillac (Langue of France) 1396-1421
Anton Fluvian (Langue of Spain) 1421-1437
Jean de Lastic (Langue of Auvergne) 1437-1454
Jacques de Milly (Langue of Auvergne) 1454-1461
Raimondo Zacosta (Langue of Spain) 1461-1467
Giovanni-Battista Orsini (Langue of Italy) 1467-1476
Pierre d'Aubusson (Langue of Auvergne) 1476-1503
Emery d'Amboise (Langue of France) 1503-1512
Guy de Blanchfort (Langue of Auvergne) 1512-1513
Fabrizio del Carretto (Langue of Italy) 1513-1521
Philippe Villiers de l'Isle-Adam (Langue of France) elected 1521, left Rhodes
    when the Knights were expelled in January 1523; d.1534 in Malta.

DUKES OF NAXOS ('OF THE ARCHIPELAGO'):
1: The Sanudo dynasty:
Marco I (nephew of Doge Enrico Dandolo) 1207-1227
Angelo 1227-1262
Marco II 1262-1303
Guglielmo 1303-1323
Nicolo I (grandson of Marco II) 1323-1341
Giovanni (brother of Nicolo I) 1341-1361
Fiorenza Sanudo (Duchess, daughter of
Giovanni Sanudo) 1361-1371
Nicolo II dalle Carceri son of Fiorenza and Giovanni dalle Carceri 1371-1383
2: The Crispo dynasty:
Francesco I 1383-1397
Giacomo I 1397-1418
Giovanni II (brother of Giacomo I) 1418-1437
Giacomo II 1437-1447
Giovanni-Giacomo (as infant) 1447-1453
Guglielmo II (uncle of the former, and regent) 1453-1463
Francesco II (nephew of Guglielmo) 1463

Giacomo III (under the regency of the widow of Guglielmo II) 1463-1480
Giovanni III 1480-1494
Francesco III (illegitimate son) 1494-1510 (Venetian governors 1511-1517)
Giovanni IV from 1517
Two other members of the Crispo family remained as dukes until the conquest
by the Turkish sultan Selim II in 1566; he then created as titular duke the
Portuguese Jew, Joseph Nasi, who died in 1579.

LORDS OF ANDROS:
Marino Dandolo 1207-1233
Felisa (widow of Marino Dandolo) 1233-1244
Jacopo Querini (as 2nd husband of Felisa) 1244- ?
Maria Sanudo 1371-1384
Pietro Zeno 1384-1427
Andrea Zeno 1427-1437
Crusino I Sommaripa (son of Maria Sanudo) 1440-1462 (also Lord of Paros
    and Antiparos)
Giovanni Sommaripa (his grandson) 1466-1468
Crusino II Sommaripa 1468-c.1500

CATALAN LORDS OF AIGINA:
(Prior to 1317: Boniface of Verona (1296-1317) married the daughter of Otto
    of Cicon, governing Karystos and Aigina.)
Marulla (Maria) of Verona (d.1326) and
Don Alfonso Fadrique 1317-1338
Pedro I Fadrique 1338-c.1350
John I Fadrique c.1350?-c.1355?
James Fadrique 1355?-1359
Boniface Fadrique 1359-1375?
Pedro II Fadrique 1376-1380
Don Luis Fadrique 1380-1382
John II Fadrique 1382-1394?
Alioto I 1394?-1418
Alioto II de Caopena 1418-1440
Antonello de Caopena 1440-1451 On his death the island was inherited
    by Venice.

PALATINE COUNTS OF KEFALLONIA AND ZAKYNTHOS, DUKES OF LEUKAS:
Margaritone of Brindisi, admiral of Sicily and 'Lord of the Ionian Islands'
    1185-1194
Matteo Orsini (his son-in-law) 1194-1238
Riccardo Orsini 1284-1291
Giovanni Orsini 1303-1317
Niccolo Orsini 1317-1323
Giovanni Orsini 1323-1335
Nikiforos Orsini (under his mother's regency) 1335-1339
Leonardo I Tocco (son of Guglielmo Tocco, governor of Corfu,

d.1335) 1357-1381
Carlo I Tocco 1381-1399
Leonardo II Tocco (brother of Carlo I) 1399-c.1414
Carlo II Tocco 1430-1448
Leonardo III Tocco 1448-1479
Antonio Tocco 1481-1483

LORDS OF LIMNOS:
Paolo Navigajoso ('Grand Duke') c.1260
Jacopo Gattilusio, Lord of Lesbos 1414-1419
Nicolo Gattilusio 1449-1456
John Navarre, papal nuncio; governor 1461-1465

LORDS OF LESBOS:
Francesco I Gattilusio 1355-1384 (married Maria Palaiologina)
Francesco II Gattilusio 1384-1402/4
Jacopo Gattilusio 1403/4-1428
Dorino Gattilusio 1428-1455
Domenico Gattilusio c.1445-1458
Niccolo Gattilusio 1458-1462

LORDS OF SAMOTHRAKI:
Palamede Gattilusio c.1431
Dorino II Gattilusio 1455-1456

LORDS OF SKIATHOS, SKOPELOS AND SKYROS:
Geremia Ghisi (brother of Andrea, Lord of Tinos and Mykonos) c.1207 -1251
Filippo Ghisi (of Skopelos only) d. by 1284

LORDS OF TINOS AND MYKONOS:
Andrea Ghisi 1207-after 1259
Bartolomeo I Ghisi fl. 1290
Bartolommeo II Ghisi (his grandson) 1311-1341
Giorgio II Ghisi (and triarch of Euboea) 1341-c.1352
Giorgio III Ghisi d. 1390
Thereafter Venetian governors from 1406: in Mykonos until 1537, and in
    Tinos until 1715.

LORDS OF THASOS:
Dorino I c.1434 [Oberto Grimaldi, governor 1434]
Francesco III Gattilusio 1444-c.1449

Some suggestions for further reading.

The bibliography of writings on medieval Greece and its buildings is enormous, so this book list has had to be highly selective; titles have been limited to the two headings given, to what a non-specialist reader could be expected to have access, to publications in English, and to books on Greece where the islands are given coverage. Normally the earliest edition is cited, but in a number of cases reprints, revisions or new editions of the title have been issued, and the reader is advised to use these.

Historical background.

Philip P. Argenti: *The Occupation of Chios by the Genoese, 1346-1566.* 3 vols. Cambridge 1958. A definitive study based on contemporary documents.

The Cambridge Medieval History, Vol. IV, Part I: Byzantium and its Neighbours. Cambridge 1966. (Ed. J.M.Hussey). Although concerned with many other areas of the empire, this still remains an essential compendium.

Anthony Luttrell: *The Hospitaller State on Rhodes and its Western Provinces, 1306-1462.* Aldershot (Ashgate) 1999. Some of these collected articles give detailed insights on medieval life on Rhodes.

D.M.Metcalf: *Coinage of the Crusades and the Latin East in the Ashmolean Museum Oxford.* London 1995. For numismatists this is the most accessible study, and contains detailed historical information on the Greek Archipelago.

William Miller: *Essays on the Latin Orient.* Cambridge 1921. Several of this assemblage of articles concern the history of the Aegean and Ionian islands.

William Miller: *The Latins in the Levant. A History of Frankish Greece.* London 1908 (repr. 1964). This general study contains several chapters devoted to the history of the Greek islands during western occupation.

Donald Nicol: *Byzantium and Venice. A study in diplomatic and cultural relations.* Cambridge 1988. Concerns elements of Greek island political life.

The Oxford Dictionary of Byzantium. 3 vols. Oxford 1991. (Ed. A.P.Kazhdan). Contains entries on a few of the Greek islands.

K.M.Setton: *The Papacy and the Levant (1204-1571).* 4 vols. Philadelphia 1976-84. In Vols. I and II the author discusses papal dealings with some of the Greek islands.

J.P.A. van der Vin: *Travellers to Greece and Constantinople. Ancient Monuments and Old Traditions in Medieval Travellers' Tales.* 2 vols. The Hague 1980. An excellent collection and discussion of travellers' texts, with mention of a number of the islands.

Architecture and art.

Manolis Chatzidakis (Ed.): *Byzantine Art in Greece: Naxos*. Athens 1989. A well-illustrated study of the Byzantine wallpaintings on Naxos.

Paul Hetherington: *Byzantine and Medieval Greece; Churches, Castles and Art*. London (John Murray) 1991. Covers the islands of Euboea (Evia) and Leukas, as joined to the mainland, with the same emphasis as in this book.

Paul Hetherington: *The 'Painter's Manual' of Dionysius of Fourna. English Translation & Commentary*. London 1974 (repr. 1981.) Reference to this post Byzantine text will often elucidate the iconography of island church frescoes.

Pauline Johnstone: *Greek Island Embroidery*. London (Tiranti) 1961. Although the subject is not covered in the text, this study is the only accessible one for enthusiasts of this aspect of Greek island life.

Konstantin Kalokyris: *The Byzantine Wall Paintings of Crete*. New York 1973. One of the most convenient general studies in English on Cretan monumental painting.

Beata Kitsiki Panagopoulos: *Cistercian and Mendicant Monasteries in Medieval Greece*. Chicago 1979. Among the buildings discussed here are some found in Crete.

Elias Kollias: *The City of Rhodes and the Palace of the Grand Master*. Athens 1988. A well-illustrated survey of the government and visual aspects of medieval Rhodes.

A. Komines (Ed.): *Patmos, Treasures of the Monastery*. Athens 1988. A well-illustrated study of the monastery buildings and their contents.

Richard Krautheimer: *Early Christian and Byzantine Architecture*. Pelican History of Art, Harmondsworth, 2nd ed. 1975. This is a general study, but reference is made to individual buildings on the Greek islands.

Lila Marangou: *Amorgos. Monastery of the Panayia Khozoviotissa*. 3rd ed. Athens 1996. An excellent and well-illustrated handbook of this uniquely spectacular building.

Doula Mouriki: *The Mosaics of the Nea Moni on Chios*. 2 vols. Athens 1985. A specialised study of the most important surviving Byzantine mosaics in the Greek islands.

Ioanna Papantoniou: *Greek Regional Costumes*. Nauplion (Peloponnesian Folklore Foundation) 1996. Several islands are included in this well-illustrated study; many of the costumes are held in the Museum at Nauplion.

Arnold C. Smith: *The Architecture of Chios; subsidiary buildings, implements and crafts*. London (Tiranti) 1962. Although concerned with largely post-medieval material, this book gives a unique insight into the visual elements of everyday Chiote life.

INDEX OF PEOPLE

(The names of saints are not included).

Villaret, Foulques de, Grand Master, 228, 267
Villeneuve, Hélion de, Grand Master, 259, 266

Wace, A.J.B., historian, 32, 230
Watteau, Antoine, artist, 174
William II, king, xxii, 148, 337
William II Villehardouin, prince, 213
Witdoeck, P.J., artist, 266

Zaccharia, Benedetto, 34, 323
Zaccharia, Martino, 34, 35
Zaccharia, Tedisio, 323
Zacosta, Raymond, Grand Master, 260, 269, 320
Zaganos, admiral, 323
Zeno, Marco, son of Pietro, 24
Zeno, Pietro, lord, 24
Zoe, empress, 39